THE PACESETTER
The Untold Story of Carl G. Fisher

Jerry M. Fisher

Best wishes, Jerry Fisher

LOST ≋ Fort
COAST Bragg,
PRESS California

The Pacesetter: The Untold Story of Carl G. Fisher
Copyright © 1998 by Jerry M. Fisher

Lost Coast Press, 155 Cypress Street, Fort Bragg, CA 95437
(707) 964-9520 • fax: 707-964-7531
e-mail: lostcoast@cypresshouse.com

Library of Congress Cataloging-in-Publication Data

Fisher, Jerry M., 1940-
    The pacesetter : the untold story of Carl G. Fisher / by Jerry M. Fisher.
      p. cm.
    Includes index and bibliography.
    ISBN 1-882897-21-8
    1. Fisher, Carl G. (Carl Graham), 1874-1939.   2. Automobile industry and trade—United States—Biography.   3. Real estate developers—United States—Biography.   I. Title
CT275.F559F53   1998
333.73'15'092--dc21
   [B]   97-51403
                                            CIP

Acknowledgment is made to the following publishers for the excerpts contained in this book:

From *Billion Dollar Sandbar* by Polly Redford Copyright © 1970 by Polly Redford. Reprinted by permission of McIntosh and Otis, Inc. From *The Fabulous Hoosier* by Jane Watts Fisher Copyright © 1947 by Robert McBride Co. Copyright renewed 1974 by Crown Publishers, Inc. Reprinted by permission of Crown Publishers, Inc.

Cover design by Theresa Whitehill, Colored Horse Studios, Elk, CA

Book production by Cypress House, Fort Bragg, CA 95437

Printed in the USA

3   5   7   9   8   6   4   2

First Edition

This book is dedicated to my sons

Graham & Andrew

Acknowledgments

M ANY INDIVIDUALS contributed their time and efforts to the writing of this book. Each gave in their own unique and special way. Needless to say, I am extremely grateful.

Those who helped in research are Dawn Hugh of the Historical Association of Southern Florida; Sam Boldrick, Archivist of the Florida Room at the Miami Dade Public Library; Sister Mary Rachel Schulte, Sisters of St. Francis; Jim Hoggatt of Indianapolis Motor Speedway; Marybelle Burch and Pam Wasmer reference librarians, Indiana State Library; Kelley Griffith, Library Director of Marian College; Karen Rade, Director of Montauk Library; Mark Patrick, Curator of Detroit Public Library, National Automotive History Collection; Janice Nessel, manager of Montauk Manor; Suzanne Gosman, President of Board of Trustees of Montauk Library.

Assisting in Fisher ancestry are Sue Buckner, Marty Davis, Martha Sturges, Louise Diver, and Helen Muir, in memory of Bill Muir, Carl's attorney.

Assisting in photos are Arva Parks, Miami's leading historian (Parks), the State of Florida Photographic Archives (SPA), The Pete Chase Family (Chase), Lester Pancoast (L.P.), Fisher Island Photographic Archives (FIA), Historical Association of Southern Florida (HASF), Myrna and Seth Bramson collection (SB), James D. Fox, Curator and Assistant Head, Special Collections Library, University of Michigan (UM), Lisa May, Vermont Records Center, Union Carbide (UC), Sandra Fitzgerald, *Indianapolis Star/News* (ISN), Spencer Riggs (SR), Suzanne Gosman of the Montauk Library (ML), Ron

McQueeney of Indianapolis Motor Speedway (IMS), and Patricia Lowe, librarian of Will Rogers Memorial (WRM).

A special thank you goes to the following individuals for their invaluable advice and helpful suggestions: John Martin Smith, author, leading historian, President of National Automotive and Trucks Museum of the United States; Donald Davidson, recognized historian of the Indianapolis Motor Speedway; Howard Kleinberg, noted columnist, author, and historian on Miami; Lois H. Muniente, for her help in preparing and editing the manuscript; and in memory of W. Earl Givens, author, historian and Director for the State of Nevada on the Lincoln Highway Association.

To many of my friends who continued to give their supporting help and encouragement along the way are: Cecile Roth, Joan Lycke, Elizabeth Job, Robert and Ellen Akin, Bill Akin, Laura S. Ditmer, Ph.D., Kenneth Lloyd Billingsley, Walter Williams, John Clark, Dr. Tom Kerrian and Carl Norberg.

Finally, no book could have been written without Carl G. Fisher himself; Carl's wives, Jane and Margaret Fisher; my grandfather, Amos Fisher; and my mother, Dora Fisher, who all in their own way contributed a wealth of information.

Preface

A BOOK of this nature deserves an explanation to the reader on how and why it was written.

My grandfather, Amos Fisher, lived with my parents shortly before his death. It was during this time my grand-father gave the Fisher family album which contained numer-ous photos and newspaper clippings to my mother for safe keeping. It was through this album, along with the stories it invoked, I learned about Carl Graham Fisher.

As I grew up hearing the exploits of Carl G. Fisher, it became apparent few knew of his name. Likewise, the Ameri-can nation has never identified or recognized the man who had so radically changed it.

Maybe that was Fisher's own fault for not pushing him-self. Nothing prevented him from founding the "Fisher Speedway" or "Fisher Beach" or "Fisher Highway." But that was not his style even when others wanted him to do so. For Fisher, the project was always more important than his par-ticular role in it. Perhaps awareness of his own faults was what held him back. Worldly honor was without meaning to Carl. Working, building and dreaming were his only val-ues.

The legacy of that dreaming lives on everyday. The city Fisher carved from a jungle still stands, having weathered many hurricanes. Montauk, New York and Fisher Island en-dured, prospered and are now fashionable places to live. The Indianapolis 500 remains the world's premier racing event, a gold mine for its home city and state. The Lincoln and Dixie highways, awesome accomplishments for their time or any time, helped liberate the nation from regionalism and paved the way for our Interstate Highways.

A year before Fisher's death (1939) the *Saturday Evening Post*, on April 9, 1938, lamented that *Who's Who* still did not know him, still true after 60 years and more remarkable when one considers the squads of lesser lights granted inclusion in works of biography. Fisher's employee, publicity man, Steve Hannagan, for example, earned a slot in *Current Biography*.

The Pacesetter was written for others to discover and know about a man whose accomplishments changed American lives forever.

Jerry M. Fisher

Contents

Engaged to one woman, Carl quietly marries another — a teenager sets up housekeeping. The teenager soon finds herself hostess to the prominent businessmen of Indianapolis, as Carl's friends indulge his preference to entertain, rather than be entertained. She must also maintain several homes at once.

Disturbed by America's lack of good, hard-surfaced roads, Carl announces his idea for a road from New York to San Francisco to be financed by private business rather than government. Automakers are enthusiastic, the public is enthusiastic, but the most influential man of all — Henry Ford — refuses to participate.

Sponsored by an Indianapolis auto club, Carl and 70 others drive from Indianapolis to San Francisco, raising interest in a road across America. Everywhere they are met by crowds eager to further the cause. Communities even improve their section of the route for the tour.

Although Carl hoped to put off announcement of a specific route until $10,000,000 had been raised, the new Lincoln Highway Association decides to announce the route at a Governors Conference. Publicity results in checks pouring in from all over America, but it becomes clear that the $10,000,000 goal would not be reached.

The Lincoln Highway Association finally recognizes that only the government could fulfill their goal of a coast-to-coast road that would be continually maintained. Carl's desire to build the road free of politics has to be sacrificed to reality. The association laments the loss of the name to route numbers, but marks the original route as a memorial.

Having sold Prest-O-Lite, Carl and Jane go to Miami for the winter. Seeing an unfinished bridge and signs of development in what was to become Miami Beach, Carl's curiosity leads him to become involved in what was then mainly mangrove swamp but what he thought could become a wonderful winter playground.

The history of the peninsula reveals a history of failures. Even the native Indians had never established a permanent settlement there. Attempts to grow coconuts had failed. John Collins from Pennsylvania had come to try to recoup money he lost in the coconut venture. He wanted to grow avocados, then ran out of money before he finished his bridge.

Carl lends money to Collins to finish the bridge and receives two hundred acres of land. When the bridge is completed, development starts in earnest. Another developer, J. N. Lummus, has sold lots but needs more capital. Carl lends Lummus money also, and acquires more land.

People in both Miami and Indianapolis consider Carl "crazy" for trying to develop a mangrove swamp. Clearing the mangroves and dredging sand from Biscayne Bay slowly begin to transform the landscape. Carl builds a miniature railroad to carry materials.

In December 1913 lots in Carl's development go on sale. Carl announces plans for city water and sewers. All kinds of sports facilities, from golf to polo, will be built. Carl and Jane go to Europe for the races in 1914 and narrowly escape World War I.

Jane and Carl move into their new home on Miami Beach. Carl sponsors a regatta to attract tourists and prospective residents. Collins Bridge becomes congested and a new causeway is planned. Carl's new Lincoln Hotel opens as does the Roman Pools.

Carl advocates the importance of an air force in war and serves on the National Advisory Committee on Aeronautics. Speedway races are canceled in 1917 and 1918. Carl brings international polo to the Beach and builds the Flamingo Hotel.

Hearing that the President-Elect is planning a Florida vacation, Carl invites him to the Beach. When all signs indicate Harding will not accept, Harding comes to Florida and stays at the Flamingo, reaping Carl a harvest of publicity for Miami Beach.

Carl is thrilled about the news that he is to become a father. Before the birth in November, Carl's father dies. Less than a month after he is born, Carl Jr. dies. Carl and Jane are grief-stricken. He returns to Miami Beach; she follows him shortly after, but they are beginning to grow apart.

Carl has made friends with a new priest at Miami Beach and has difficulty with some of his business associates at Montauk. In Miami Beach he spearheads an effort to rid the resort of Capone, meeting him stare-for-stare in the courtroom.

The stock market crash and reduced returns from Miami Beach put Carl into severe financial straits. For a few years, the summer season at Montauk flourishes, but in 1932 the corporation goes into receivership. Carl and wife Margaret begin to quarrel. Carl does what he can to assist his relatives during the hard times, but his largess is much reduced.

Bankrupt, Carl loses his homes and his yachts and lives on a much-reduced income. He sells off valuable personal property and moves to a small home in Miami Beach. He and Margaret separate. A few old friends remain. Galloway leaves. Carl's illness progresses steadily until his death on July 15, 1939.

Childhood portrait of Carl Graham Fisher. (HASF)

The Pacesetter

Chapter 1

An Enterprising Young Man

Twelve-year-old Carl Graham Fisher squinted intently at the writing on the blackboard and then looked around the classroom at his fellow sixth-graders who were dutifully studying. He glanced at his teacher, who was working at her desk. Then slowly, deliberately, he closed his book, gathered his belongings, and rose from his seat. Carl walked out the door of the red school house and closed it quietly behind him. It was 1886 and there were no laws in Indiana to compel "the stupidest boy in school,"[1] as he was then regarded, to return. It would be another eleven years before the state required compulsory education of children between eight and fourteen.[2] Carl knew his mother would object to his ending his formal education, but as the oldest of three boys, he had a winning argument: the family needed any money he could make, and he wasn't making any in school. His job in a grocery store would be a welcome addition to the family income, and school hours would no longer interfere.

Carl's lack of success in school was the result of poor vision. Born January 12, 1874, with a case of severe astigmatism, Carl was half-blind. Early poverty and the limited technology of the time prevented his condition from being diagnosed and corrected until he was thirty-one. His poor vision made any writing on the blackboard nothing but an undecipherable jumble of characters, severely limiting his learning. But he had no way of knowing how poor his vision

1

really was, and it did not hamper the physical activities at which he excelled.

Running backward was his specialty. He practiced diligently and even challenged other students to races, which he usually won running backward while they ran forward.

Thirty years later, in his 40's, Carl could still beat his friends this way.[3] Games and sports, from swimming to ice skating and roller skating, seemed to come naturally to him, but the schools of the 1880's had little use for athletics and still less for his boundless imagination and energy. He used his physical prowess to promote the grocery store where he worked, displaying banners that advertised the store when he sledded down a steep hill in Lebanon, Ohio.[4]

Carl was determined to support his family. Ida, his mother, had left Carl's father and moved to Indianapolis with her three young sons. She took in boarders to support them. Albert Fisher, born in 1847, seemed to have a promising future practicing law when he married Ida Graham, described as "a firm-minded, steady-eyed woman"[5] by Carl's first wife, Jane, and a " hard, strong, stubborn, determined' woman"[6] in Polly Redford's *Billion-Dollar Sandbar*. Albert had been admitted to the Indiana Bar in 1871 and had been "A belligerent county prosecutor."[7] Unfortunately, Albert practiced not only law, but also the art of lifting the bottle. His alcoholism plunged the family into poverty. Carl, their firstborn, was born in Greensburg, Indiana, a town in Decatur County, southeast of Indianapolis.

Ida, a native of Martinsville, Ohio, had lived in Indianapolis with her parents before her marriage. She moved back to Indianapolis when she despaired of her husband's ability to support their family. The small family led a meager existence, but never went hungry or turned to crime. Ida instilled in them early that they must take responsibility for their actions. There was no question that Carl and his brothers loved their mother. Throughout Ida's life, Carl always provided homes for her and showed concern for her welfare.

His father's numerous departures and alcoholism prevented them from ever having a close relationship. Carl supported his father financially until his death. The pain and shame of his father's absence would remain with Carl throughout his life and he never gave up hope of reuniting his parents. Carl, whose honesty in business dealings was commented upon by his associates, may have gained that attribute from his father. Carl, when he was fifty-nine, wrote to a prospective client: "My father was a lawyer, and he always told me that if I would stick to doing what I thought was right, I would never get in very serious trouble."[8]

Albert Fisher shared few of the industrious traits of his forebears. A hundred years before, his grandfather Philip Fisher, had come to America with high hopes about the freedoms and opportunities of the New World. Philip had left Berlin in 1770 and settled in Pennsylvania before moving on to Pendleton County, Virginia. His only son, Jacob, "Rode on horseback to the wilds of Ohio to 'Spy out the land' and ascertain the feasibility of establishing a home for himself"[9] when he was in his early twenties. On March 3, 1800, Jacob bought 200 acres of land in Concord township, put in a crop, and returned to Virginia for his wife, the former Barbara Kyle.

Both Jacob and his wife survived encounters with Indians in the War of 1812. Jacob went to war and became a member of a government surveying squad which was confronted by a band of Indians at a river crossing. Terrified, they tossed their instruments into the water and fled. At home, Barbara and other women from the area spent their nights in a fortified block house on the Cochran farm west of Roxabel "in order to insure protection from possible forays by the red men."[10] The women spent their days at their own homes, but Barbara found that the Indians did not limit their forays to darkness. Six Indians appeared in her yard, but luckily presented no danger. They drank at the well and then returned to the forest.[11]

Jacob and Barbara survived the War of 1812 and the perils of the frontier and lived full, productive lives. Jacob was an early developer of real estate in Indiana.[12] When he died in 1866 at the age of 92 (Barbara died at 78), Jacob left five daughters, four sons, and numerous grandchildren.

Carl Fisher seemed to have inherited the initiative of his grandfather, rather than the inertia of his father. For the young, ambitious boy, the grocery store job was just a temporary one; new opportunities soon beckoned. It was the age of rail, and some forty railway lines crisscrossed Indiana. The narrow gauge Illinois line passed through Indianapolis, and Carl became a "news butcher," hawking candy, peanuts, books, and magazines and even shining shoes. This experience, Carl later maintained, developed his salesmanship. He had developed his own surefire sales method. "... to good friends he'd tell about the apron he'd invented to help him out when business got slow. It looked like an ordinary news butcher's apron — the kind with pockets in front to hold change — but it could be raised to reveal a large, lurid picture of a naked woman beneath. When his regular sales pitch fell flat, Carl would pick out a likely looking drummer and raise his apron. Taking advantage of his victim's surprise and the guffaw that followed, he would sell the man a cigar and maybe a Laura Jean Libbey novel if he could make it sound sexy."[13]

When the passengers finally discarded their newspapers and dozed off, Carl munched on peanuts, his favorite snack, and settled down to read. Carl read at night to the rhythm of the swaying railroad cars as they continued their journey during the night. The more he read, the more his imagination grew. Reading opened the door to another world where his daily dreams could run wild. J. Krishnamurti's book *Think on These Things* seems to apply to Carl although written nearly 80 years later.[14] Carl's favorite stories were biographies of men who provided Carl with male role models that he lacked at home. From his reading, he acquired two heroes: Abraham Lincoln and Napoleon, whose pictures were to hang above his bed throughout his life. The Civil War had ended only twenty years before; there were still many veterans with tales of the horrors of war. Abraham Lincoln was a natural hero — he had lived in Indiana and was a national martyr. The military exploits of Napoleon also fascinated Carl. Napoleon's courageous daring, defiance of danger, and determination stirred Carl's imagination. Here was a man of action, not content to spend his life in the sanctuary of his library. And whatever the merits of his conquests, Napoleon Bonaparte was above all a man in charge, a leader, not a follower. The traits of one hero balanced those of the other: action, adventure, and daring on one hand, and civic conscience, sacrifice, and public spirit on the other. But it was Lincoln whose name Carl chose for some of his projects — not his own or Napoleon's.

The man whose philosophy Carl came to admire was a contemporary — Robert Ingersoll (1833-1899), known as "the great agnostic." A lawyer, like Carl's father, Ingersoll was the son of a stern Presbyterian minister. After Charles Darwin's *Origin of Species* was published in 1859, Ingersoll became a popular public lecturer, explaining agnosticism to all who would listen. His experience in court had made him a skilled debater. The titles of Ingersoll's lectures were provocative: "Some Mistakes of Moses" and "Why I Am an Agnostic." Ingersoll had other interests as well. He also lectured on Shakespeare, Robert Burns, Abraham Lincoln, Thomas Paine, and Voltaire.

Ingersoll's appeal was expressed in a brochure of the Ingersoll League: "Ingersoll's immortal writings enable you to live ruggedly, comfortably, sanely. Look at the world from his viewpoint, adopt his attitude and you will find yourself equipped to deal with all life's emergencies, major and minor. So infectious is his gay, humorous viewpoint that you will adopt it before you have read a hundred pages of his singing, buoyant, fighting prose! His attitude is so sensible, so rewarding — so certain of *victory!*"[15]

Ingersoll could cite his own success: he was a well-known attorney; had served as a Colonel in the Civil War; and was Attorney General of Illinois from 1867-1869. His national reputation as an orator was made in 1876 when he gave the nominating speech for James G. Blaine at the Republican convention in Cincinnati. When Blaine lost the nomination, he campaigned for Rutherford B. Hayes. His personal life was apparently impeccable. "His most bitter enemies could never deny that he led the most exemplary of lives, that he was upright, courageous, charitable and generous to excess, patriotic, a loyal friend, and a faithful and tender father and husband."[16] He had married a fellow free-thinker, Eva Amelia Parker, in 1861, and they had two daughters. When Ingersoll died on July 21, 1899, the July 22nd issue of the *Chicago Tribune* said of him: "Splendidly endowed as he was he could have won great distinction in the field of politics had he so chosen. But he was determined to enlighten the world concerning the 'Mistakes of Moses.' That threw him out of the race."[17]

Ingersoll's appeal for Carl and his other followers came not from his attacks on religion, but from his positive approach to living a happy life. The iconoclast explained his philosophy clearly and succinctly: "I have a creed for this, the only world of which I know anything: (1) Happiness is the only good. (2) The way to be happy is to make others so. (3) The place to be happy is here. (4) The time to be happy is now."[18]

Carl's enthusiasm for Ingersoll and his philosophy was shown in his success in selling Ingersoll's books, which were collections of Ingersoll's lectures. He sold so many that he won a national prize. Even in later years when he had become a millionaire and acquired a vast library of his own, its centerpiece was a collection of Ingersoll's works, bound in maroon linen stamped in gold.[19] Like his mentor, Carl placed little stock in organized religion. His conversation was laced with "goddams" and "by Jesus" and "Christ on a bicycle!" In his correspondence he was more discreet, using dashes for profanity, even "hell" and "damn." Any anti-religious animus he had seemed to have a quaint respect for religious propriety.

Ingersoll's creed of seeking happiness here and now became Carl's philosophy. His exuberance for life led him to take financial and physical risks that more cautious men would have never considered. Ida's clothesline became a tightrope for Carl's hijinks; once he built a pair of stilts so tall that they had to be mounted from a second-story window.[20]

Carl's education did not cease, although its formal phase was over. When he gave up his job on the train, he went to work in a bookstore, where he had access to volumes of history, biography, adventure, and fiction. He could read to his heart's content, a habit that he continued throughout his life. Later, when money was of no concern, Carl ordered multiples of books for his friends, once purchasing 3,000 copies of one book.[21] His interests were eclectic: one list of 41 books he requested included H. G. Wells' *The Outline of History;* Allen Tate's *Jefferson Davis;* Lillian Eichler's *The New Book of Etiquette;* Andre Tridon's *Psychoanalysis and Love;* and Neltje Blanchan's *Bird Neighbors.*[22] Carl often left his guests downstairs to be entertained by his wife while he retreated upstairs to read.

Another job, working in a bank, gave him some first-hand knowledge of the financial world.

Carl's poor vision did not seem to curtail his desire to play as hard as he worked. During Indiana's steamy summers he swam in the White River and various "old swimming holes" that his friend James Whitcomb Riley made part of Indiana lore. He was an accomplished swimmer and diver and savored the water all of his life, eventually living in Florida in the winter and Long Island in the summer so that he could enjoy water sports the year-round. He was known as one of the best ice skaters in Indianapolis and was a whiz on roller skates as well. After he took up canoeing, he won a challenging race sponsored by the Indianapolis Canoe Club.[23]

The high-wheeled bicycles that had become the latest mania in Europe and America started Carl on his successful career in business. Like his brothers Earl and Robert (Rolla), Carl was a gifted mechanic. The three were always dismantling things, discovering how they worked, and putting them back together again. The high-wheeled bicycles of the time were powered by direct drive, with pedals affixed to the front wheel just as they are on a tricycle. The principle was simple: the larger the wheel, the faster the speed, hence the name "high wheels." Here was a mechanical device with great speed that Carl could tinker with and race. With his leg muscles well developed from his love for running backward, Carl found the bicycle an ideal vehicle.

Early bicycle days. Carl Fisher in front. (HASF)

Bicycles were becoming big business, and Carl saw a way to make money while enjoying himself. Ida had taught him the value of saving money, and he had saved $600 — no small sum in those days when a large box of Cracker Jack's cost a nickel and a ham-and-cheese sandwich a dime.[24] Only seventeen, he was ready to start his own business while back at the school house, students were busy dividing fractions and memorizing the annual rainfall of Brazil. The Fisher brothers opened a bicycle repair shop on Pennsylvania Street. Early pneumatic tires were notoriously unreliable, and even at twenty-five cents a patch there was no shortage of customers. But the shop did not limit Carl's fun. Leaving his brothers in charge, he went on barnstorming tours, stunt driving and racing with the "Speed Kings," Barney Oldfield, Tom Cooper, and "Plugger Bill" Martin. They played carnivals in Ohio, Illinois, and Indiana, with Oldfield the star of the show.

Oldfield, from Wauseon, Ohio, later became a legend for his auto-racing feats. He was the first person to reach the then-astonishing speed of 60 miles per hour, and the first to turn a 100-mile-per-hour lap in a demonstration car (slightly larger engine), on a one-mile dirt track at the Indiana State Fairgrounds a few days before the Indy 500 in 1916. Oldfield never forgot his humble beginnings on the two-wheelers. After decades of racing fame, he still recalled the early days of bicycle racing and his being the bottom man in a triple pileup on the Newby Oval.[25]

It took work and practice for Carl to win a berth on the racing team. The team manager set stringent qualifications. "He was told that they could not use him unless he learned to fall off a bicycle at 30 miles an hour without hurting himself, whereupon he got a friend to teach him wrestling and also practiced jumping and falling off a bicycle," wrote Charles Edgar Nash in his book *The Magic of Miami Beach*. "The next year when he applied again and demonstrated his ability, he was taken in as a member of a racing team."[26] Always willing to experiment, Carl built his own equipment, trying out different types of bearings and gear ratios. At the Newby Oval, Carl tried rigging an engine to a bike, an experiment that could have ended in disaster.

In Indianapolis, Carl joined the Zig-Zag Cycling Club and the Flat Tire Club, whose names reflected the early bicycles' inherent faults. With the seat over the front wheel and a small rear wheel, the high wheels were unstable vehicles. Although a "safety" bicycle with chain and sprockets was entering the market, it was the high wheelers that Carl initially rode and raced. His bicycle sported a five-foot wheel, as big as they came, and his numerous crashes gave him a new nickname — "Crip" (for "cripple") — for all the injuries that he incurred.[27]

Among the two bicycle enthusiasts who were members of the clubs, Carl met two men — A. C. Newby and James Allison — who later became key business associates. Newby had founded the Zig-Zag Cycling Club. The three shared modest backgrounds. Newby had earned $1.50 per week at his first job at the Dickson Trade Palace. In 1890 he founded the

Indianapolis Stamping Company, which made parts for chain-driven bicycles with triangular frames and equal-sized wheels, the design that became the standard for the next 100 years. Newby also started the National Motor Vehicle Company and was one of the founders of Butler University.

Like Carl, Allison had little formal education and had little respect for what he did have. "...the only thing I got out of my eight years in school that has been of any value to me was learning to read, write, and cipher," wrote Allison when he was 53. "I did not learn to speak English in school but by conversing with educated people and reading good books."[28] Allison became a major industrialist. Although he was naturally cautious while Carl was impetuous, the two became fast friends and business partners. "Fisher was the partner with vision and a host of new ideas, while Allison was the detail man who carried out the innovations. They made a perfect pair,"[29] Nash commented.

The bicycle clubs organized trips along the White River and developed the area's first bicycle paths. Carl persuaded Newby, the only member with spare cash, to finance a wooden race track for bicycles. The Newby Oval, a one-quarter mile

The Zig Zag Cycling Club in Indianapolis. Carl Fisher third from right front row with small cap looking away from camera. (SB)

board track with a grandstand seating 15,000 spectators, became the scene of six-day bicycle races that were popular with bicyclists and spectators alike.[30] The days of the bicycle fad were soon to be over, however. Only a year after the Newby Oval was completed in 1898, interest in bicycle racing had declined so drastically that Newby began to consider dismantling the track.[31] His Zig-Zag Cycling Club lasted only six years, a major reason being the location of its clubhouse — next door to a burlesque theater which attracted so many club members that the respectable ones resigned.[32]

But while the fad lasted, the proceeds from Carl's bicycle shop and from exhibitions provided a comfortable living for the Fisher family. Carl had not been content with being the proprietor of a bicycle repair shop; although still just a teenager, he knew that the real money to be made was in the manufacture and sale of bicycles and he took some risky steps to expand his business.

Chapter 2

A Businessman at Seventeen

Carl had demonstrated his talent in salesmanship when he worked on the railroad. "Fisher was a master salesman," recalled an old friend. "You couldn't be with him more than half a minute without feeling that life was a pretty damn exciting proposition."[1] Carl was now to test that talent in the big leagues.

Although still a minor and possessed of little in the way of financial assets, Carl did not hesitate to take the train to Columbus, Ohio, and ask for an appointment with George C. Erland, one of the nation's top bicycle manufacturers.

Not only did Erland grant the brash young man an appointment, he was so impressed by his accomplishments and manner that he gave the young Hoosier a dealership and 120 bicycles on consignment.[2] Carl never forgot this act of confidence. When he developed Montauk Point on Long Island years later, he sent the deed to the first house that he built there to Erland, writing him: "I owe you everything I have in this world." Erland, then in his 80's, declined the offer, saying, "You don't owe me anything, Carl."[3]

Carl housed the bicycles in his new showroom on Pennsylvania Street. With one successful business deal completed, Carl set his heart on even higher stakes. The Pope-Toledo bicycle, he was convinced, was the paragon of bicycles. Traveling to Toledo as he had to Columbus, he was disappointed to find that Colonel Pope was not as accommodating as George

Erland. For five days he waited to secure an appointment, and finally his patience prevailed: Colonel Pope would see him.

Carl's proposition was a daring one for a young man of 19 with limited assets. He asked Pope to sell him 250 Pope Toledo bicycles at cost, indicating that he planned to give away fifty of the bicycles. If successful, this promotion would not only bring Carl business, it would bring welcome publicity to the Pope-Toledo name. To lend support to his proposal, Carl furnished Colonel Pope with three references, one of whom was his banker.

The '99 GRANDE
$30.00

Dunlop, M. & W., Kokomo or Hartford tires, Christy, Wheeler or Sager saddle—everything the best on the market. A six month's guarantee with each bicycle. Positively the only all tool steel bearing machine sold in the city for less than $40. There are more than 2000 Grande riders in Indianapolis. We refer to any of them for an opinion of the Grande.

C. G. Fisher & Co.,

112 N. Pennsylvania Street.

(I.S.L.)

Colonel Pope considered the proposition for two days. But Carl was successful; he went home with a contract in his pocket. Putting up the bicycle shop as collateral, he obtained a $500 loan and immediately began to plan a series of promotional stunts to ensure the success of his proposal.[4] Advertising, he believed, should have the impact of news, and he planned to make news.

Indianapolis was a thriving manufacturing city in the 1890's. In the 1880's, a 5,000-square-mile gas field had been discovered northeast of Indianapolis. Manufacturers flocked to the state. A total of $300,000,000 had been invested in factories in the state by 1893.[5] "... in the late 1880's and the 1890's: Indiana's golden age was at hand,"[6] wrote Indiana historian John Bartlow Martin. The United States Census recorded Indianapolis's explosive growth. In 1880, the population of the city was 75,056; ten years later, it had mushroomed to 105,436. By 1900, there were 169,164 residents, more than double the population twenty years before. The city continued to grow: the 1910 Census count was 218,497.

Martin called Indianapolis "the best place"[7] to be in the 1890's and 1900's.

Here were the fine restaurants, the celebrated bars; here were the brawl and bustle of commerce and industry; here were the magnificent buildings constructed with little regard to cost; here ready to hand were the inventors' marvels; here were fashionable ladies and gentlemen, some of them famous everywhere, riding around the Circle in handsome carriages; here were literature, music, and art, and here sin beckoned from a narrow doorway; here, in short, was a farm boy's new and shining dream world.[8]

One of the less savory aspects of Indianapolis was noted in the 1890 Census: there were almost as many brothels in Indianapolis as in New York.[9]

In the growing, bustling city in which Carl Fisher endeavored to make his mark and his fortune, he knew he had to do some extraordinary things to get his customers' attention and their business. One day, people on the second floor of homes and businesses suddenly saw a head wearing a floppy hat go by their windows. They rushed to see what was going on and saw Fisher, riding on a bicycle some twenty feet high, jostling through the horses, buggies, and street cars as he made his way down the street. Besides all of the attention the giant bike garnered, it also engendered the Fisher bicycle, the only enterprise of Carl Fisher that bore his name. Building and riding the bike made him aware of an inherent deficiency, and he and his brothers redesigned the mechanism. The Fisher bicycle was the result.[10]

Carl had more tricks in store. The early lessons on Ida's clothesline were only training for a more stunning performance. According to his wife Jane, he strung a tightrope between the roofs of two buildings on Washington Street, strapped on a padded suit, and rode across on a bicycle. Ropes attached to the handlebars were held by men on the opposite roof.[11] When the snow came, he built a racing cutter out of bicycle tubing and drove it down Capitol Avenue. The light cutter easily outpaced all others.[12]

All of these antics made Fisher a local legend and folk hero. However, some thought of him as a showoff. The Indianapolis police, guardians of public safety, were not amused with Carl's tricks and on more than one occasion issued warrants for the arrest of this public menace. On one occasion, Carl advertised in the newspapers his plan to throw a Pope-Toledo bicycle from the top of the city's tallest building, with a new bicycle offered to whoever brought the frame back to his bicycle shop. The police announced that if he tried this stunt, he would be arrested on the spot. Undaunted, Carl announced the date and time. The chief of police was furious. Bank robbers and purse snatchers could wait. Bagging Carl Fisher was priority number one.

At 9 a.m. on the appointed day, ten policemen surrounded the building, blocking access from all sides. Crowds jammed the streets to see what would happen, wondering whether Fisher would be able to get to the building. The police seemed to have finally achieved a victory.

Young Carl Fisher Portrait. (HASF)

But promptly at 12 noon, as advertised, a bicycle suddenly came crashing down to the pavement. Cheers rang out as the crowd scrambled to claim the bicycle. The startled policemen bolted up the fire escape and the stairs, but Carl had prudently planned his escape down a back staircase. Carl always managed to stay one step ahead of the police: on the previous night he had slept on the roof with the bicycle at his side.

Unable to find their prey, the thoroughly embarrassed police, armed with a search warrant, raided the bicycle shop. All they found was a conspicuous sign reading: "You can come to see me in the police station. I just gave myself up."[13] That time, the charges were dismissed. Publicly, the police chased him, but privately, many were his friends. Even though his successful antics made them look incompetent, they felt lucky that he had not chosen a life of crime. Once Carl paid double the fine that was levied — to cover the next offense.

Before long, it was apparent that the antics of "Crazy Carl Fisher," as he was known, were more of an asset to Indianapolis than a dangerous liability. And a good thing, too — Carl was on a roll.

He gained national publicity for Colonel Pope when he hired his friend, George L. Bumbaugh from Springfield, Illinois, a country-boy daredevil who designed and made the balloons he jumped from at country fairs. Bumbaugh's advertising slogan was: "My exhibitions satisfy — now booking for next season." Half of the $500 mortgage on the bicycle shop was paid to Bumbaugh for one thousand small balloons; the rest paid for full-page advertisements in newspapers throughout the state. Each of the balloons carried a tag with Carl's name and a number. One hundred of them were lucky numbers good for a free bike at Carl's shop.[14]

The stunt created widespread excitement. Some Hoosiers were so eager to get a free bike that they loaded rounds into their shotguns and shot at the balloons as though they were hunting geese. People from all over the state streamed into the bicycle shop to claim their bicycles. To obtain maximum publicity, Carl had arranged a full civic presentation featuring brass bands with the Mayor of Indianapolis officiating. George Erland and Colonel Pope might have had some skepticism about Fisher's ability to carry out his promises, but now it was clear that he was not only a showman, but also a shrewd businessman.

The bicycle shop flourished. Buying a bicycle from Carl became the thing to do. Years later, on December 20, 1938, Carl wrote Barney Oldfield that "If all the people who told me that they had bought a bicycle from me had done so, I would have sold more bicycles than were manufactured in those days."[15]

Carl's booming business enabled Ida to stop taking in boarders. In his success, Carl didn't overlook his father; he began sending money to Albert, still hoping to reunite his parents.

For all of Carl's reputation as a crazy, publicity-seeking show-off, there was a different personality behind the antics. Those who met Carl were surprised to discover that he was really shy, unaffected, and even uncomfortable when the conversation centered on him. His mother once told her daughter-in-law: "Carl was always too absorbed in the thing he was doing to realize it was he who was doing it."[16] Steve Hannagan, a publicity man whom Carl later hired to publicize some of his promotions, was often disappointed and upset with Carl's refusal to take the spotlight.[17] Joe Copps, who was head of the publicity bureau of Miami Beach and associated with Carl for many years, remarked: "He always wanted to put on a show, but he insisted on remaining in the background himself. He was hard to photograph and hard to interview. He wanted actions to speak for themselves."[18]

Like all fads, the bicycle craze finally reached its peak. Even with the colorful stunts, being a bicycle magnate was not enough for Carl; like Napoleon, he was always planning his next campaign. The horseless carriage had been invented, and Carl was ready to mount the running board. The joy and fun with bicycles had only been the dress rehearsal for the real love of his life, the internal-combustion engine.

Chapter 3

Love Affair with the Automobile

Carl Fisher loved speed and he loved racing — and the automobile offered more of both. In 1898, he became one of the first men in Indianapolis to own an automobile when he imported a two-and-a-half horsepower French De Dion Bouton motor tricycle. It cost him $650.[1] Shortly after, he purchased a Mobile steam wagon.

Realizing that there was no contest between the bicycle and the auto, by 1900 he had converted the bicycle shop into an auto dealership, one of the first dealerships — if not the first — in the country. When there was no longer sufficient room in the bicycle shop, Carl went looking for a place to expand. He chose two blocks of expensive residential real estate at 400 North Capitol Boulevard and established "Automobile Row." While some Indianapolis residents like Booth Tarkington lamented the loss of trees to make way for commercial property, Carl was sure that he had made the right move. He carried Oldsmobiles for R. E. Olds, the first American to mass-produce cars, but he also sold Reos, Packards, Stoddard-Daytons, and other brands. "He sold so many makes of cars that his garage resembled a motor show,"[2] commented historian John Bartlow Martin.

Carl put his promotional skills to work to ensure the financial success of the new venture. With the full cooperation of the police, he announced that he would push a vehicle off an Indianapolis building and then drive it away. When the car landed, the crowd was amazed to see that it bounced and tottered back and forth, but it landed upright. While Carl came down from the roof, his brother Rolla cranked up the car, and Carl drove through the town to wild cheers. As usual, he had carefully planned the stunt, practicing with models and deflating the tires to eliminate excessive bounce.[3] Showroom contests brought in more customers. One contest offered a free set of tires to the person who correctly guessed

the number of live bees in a glass container.[4] Carl again found balloons attracted prospective customers — but instead of purchasing hundreds of small balloons from George Bumbaugh, he paid $4,800 for one huge, scarlet-red balloon and offered rides to prospective buyers.[5] Humorist Will Rogers was later to poke fun at Carl's balloon promotions, claiming that Carl had attached a grand piano to a balloon and sent it aloft with a woman playing the piano. She supposedly landed in a hog pen near Lafayette. Rogers said that Carl was publicizing a harmonica franchise and sold two harmonicas with the stunt.[6]

Carl's success was as much the result of hard work as of his promotional stunts. Eighteen-hour days were the rule with Carl. "He had to be doing something all the time,[7] according to inventor and racer Gar Wood. "I have a new hen coming off,"[8] Carl would say whenever he had a new idea. Some were intimidated by his brusque manner and seemingly-endless energy. Carl walked around smoking cigars (disdaining cigarettes as "pimp sticks") or chewing tobacco, cursing openly whenever his mood dictated. "He really was a good-hearted man, despite what other people thought," remarked Emma Webb, one of his secretaries. "He could be very abrupt. He wanted things done yesterday if he told you about them today. If something wasn't done right, he got very angry."[9] Carl's secretaries were usually very fond of him, at least two of them having been his mistresses both before and during his marriages.

Carl did demand much of his employees, but never anything he would not do himself He valued their opinions and actively solicited their ideas with a suggestion box. Employees whose suggestions he used were given a five or ten-dollar-a-month raise.[10]

Carl took the time to get to know his workers. "It always pays well in any sort of business to know all your employees, from the truck drivers up," Fisher said years later, "and to stick by them in any sort of trouble."[11] He never hesitated to hire anyone who was more intelligent than he was, either. "I have a great many men working for me," he noted, "whom I consider have more brain power than I."[12]

The automobile business made Carl rich, but he was not interested in money for money's sake or for social pretensions. He usually ate lunch at Horace "Pop" Haynes' restaurant at 114 N. Pennsylvania Street. Carl loved Pop's steak and potatoes, which he sometimes ordered three times a day.[13] There he sat and talked for hours with his racing friends, including Barney Oldfield, Gar Wood, Eddie Rickenbacker, and General Robert Tyndall, a future mayor of Indianapolis.

It was at Pop's that he met William Galloway, a black waiter who was to become not only his employee, but also a lifelong friend and confidant. Galloway was an intelligent man whose demeanor and manners impressed Carl. When Carl discovered that Haynes was paying him only six dollars a week, he offered him a job taking care of his home for ten

The BEST PLACE to STOP

WHEN IN

INDIANAPOLIS

Never Closed

Fisher's Garage

330 NORTH ILLINOIS STREET

Three Squares North of Claypool Hotel

(I.S.L)

dollars a week.[14] (By comparison, the average wage for a teacher in 1900 was only seven dollars a week.)[15] Galloway could not refuse such a generous offer and immediately went to work for Carl.

Carl and Galloway soon became friends, having a mutual respect and admiration for each other at a time when racial prejudice and segregation were ubiquitous. Carl judged a man not by his earthly suit, but by his actions. Carl had empathy for less-fortunate individuals. Many people were uncomfortable when they saw the genuine respect with which Carl treated Galloway during times when prejudice prevailed.

Carl had no patience for white supremacist practices or being in the company of self-important, aloof people. Carl's first wife, Jane gave an illustration of this: "Once when we were traveling through Georgia, the conductor asked Galloway to leave us and go to the Jim Crow section of the train. Carl argued with the conductor. 'I'll bet any money you like,' he said furiously, 'that if you will take off your shoes and Galloway takes off his, he'll have the cleanest feet.' Carl won. Galloway stayed with us."[16]

The prospering automobile business hadn't taken away Carl's zest for racing. He was as eager to race autos as he had been to race bicycles and purchased a one-cylinder Winton with a top speed of 60 miles an hour.[17] In 1901 he left his staff in charge, and with Barney Oldfield, Webb Jay, and Al Webb toured the Midwest, billed as "The Big Racing Four." Some of the fans remembered them from their bicycle-racing days. A flat fee of $500 was charged for each performance, but they did not charge at all if the promoter didn't clear $500. For $10, fans were offered a ride in a race car. In a single season, Carl cleared $20,000, which he invested in his business.[18]

In those early days of the automobile, the four would often race against horses as well as against the clock. Usually the horse led the way when the race began, but Carl would gain on it and win at the finish line. By staging the longer races first, Carl made each succeeding race more exciting by closer and closer finishes.[19]

In 1902, Carl and Barney Oldfield began a series of racing exhibitions in the Mid-West with Louis Chevrolet, Tom Cooper, Walter Winchester, and Earl Kiser. Conditions had changed, however — automobiles were being produced at a rate of 200 a week. They were no longer a novelty. Even with sizable crowds, dividing profits among six people did not result in sufficient money to keep Carl on the summer circuit.

Carl continued to race, however, even earning the title of a "driver of national reputation"[20] from *The Columbian* magazine. In March of 1903, Carl challenged Conrad Mueller, a Cadillac dealer, to a race to Columbus, Indiana, for a $500 prize. Carl drove a Winton, his brother Earl an Oldsmobile, and W. A. Carr a Cadillac. During the race, Earl became stuck in the mud. Carl stopped to help him, while the Cadillac surged ahead, only to bog down also. Once the Cadillac was freed from the mud, its bearings gave out, and the car arrived in Columbus towed by horses. The triumphant Fisher, already in Columbus, was ready to head back. "Get a horse!" he yelled.[21]

Carl's limited vision may have contributed to his daring bravado. There were no speed limits, and Carl observed none. Once his Stoddard-Dayton went sailing over a ditch which he apparently had not seen, but his terrified passenger (his friend William Herschell) had. Turning to him, Carl calmly said, "Bill, we made it, didn't we?"[22]

It was inevitable that tragedy would strike during the races. The Fisher brothers built two cars, the Twin Mohawks, and entered a race in Zanesville, Ohio. During the race, one of them plowed through a fence, mowed down a group of spectators, smashed into buildings and wound up in a poultry exhibit. The locals were outraged. Fisher could not answer the question of the number of people who died because, as he would reply to those who asked, "They were dying for the next two years."[23] Another track accident severely injured Fisher's colleague Earl Kiser,

At the same time the English newspapers described a road race on May 25, 1903 from Paris to Madrid and called it the "Race to Death." Drivers and spectators were killed partly through bad organization, and partly through the foolishness of spectators.[24]

These tragedies had a great effect on Carl; more and more, he began to think about limiting racing to tracks which could be designed to make safety a primary consideration.

In 1904, Carl ordered a new race car from the Premier Company in Indianapolis, emphasizing that he wanted power and endurance from the vehicle. He planned to race it in William Vanderbilt's International Road Race on Long Island in the fall, "heralded as the first major competitive event of its kind in the country."[25] But when the entry form for the race arrived, Carl discovered that his new car exceeded the 2,200 pound limit by more than 300 pounds. Cutting 256 half-dollar-sized holes in the frame and 28 three-quarter-inch holes in the rear axle, in addition to removing half of the 12 lugs on each wheel, did not lower its weight sufficiently.[26]

The five-mile Diamond Cup race in Chicago on October 1 also had a weight limit. Carl entered it and won. Even though he drove a stripped-down Premier Comet rather than his new race car, he set a new world's record of 2:02 minutes for the first two miles.[27]

Carl did attend the Vanderbilt race later that month, hoping that someone might sell him a car already entered. None were available, and Carl had to be content to watch a French Panhard win the race, averaging 52.2 miles per hour.[28]

In 1905, Carl finally got his chance to race the specially-made Premier in a five-mile handicap race on November 4 at the Indiana Fairgrounds Track. Carl had wanted to enter the 100-mile event, but once his competitor saw the Premier in a practice run, they refused to race against it. Carl won the five-mile race, averaging 59.21 miles per hour, after giving a 78-second head start to a Premier and 58 seconds to two Nationals.[29]

Carl had managed to race successfully even though his vision had been progressively worsening. He had sought help, even in Europe. The solution, ironically, was found right in Indianapolis. One day he ran into Bill Holtz, a local policeman who was wearing a bandage over his eye because of an injury suffered in a fight. When Carl told Holtz about his own vision problem and expressed his concern about finding no help anywhere, Holtz advised him to consult his eye doctor. Carl took the advice and was fitted with his first pair of glasses at the age of 31.[30] The horn-rimmed spectacles became a Fisher trademark along with the floppy hats he wore to cover his balding head.

The improvement in his vision brought back memories of his being called "stupid" when the real problem was that he couldn't read what was on the blackboard. Whenever Carl learned about anyone — especially children — who had poor vision, he would send them to specialists at his expense. He did the same for those with foot problems. "Health, he said, was the most important need for a child; education had secondary value."[31]

Carl's vastly-improved vision enabled him to take up tennis, baseball, and polo. Although he began to play tennis relatively late, his friend Fred Wellman said, "He plays a remarkably fast and consistent game, holding his own in the stiffest competition."[32]

Golf, which was too slow for him, did not become a favorite. The size of the ball, along with the distance, evidently was a problem. "If I hit a good ball, I can't see the goddam thing," he explained, "and if I hit a bad one, I sure as hell don't want to see it."[33]

Chapter 4

Prest-O-Lite Leads to Fortune

Carl's automobile business was prospering, providing him with an income far beyond what he and his family needed or wanted to spend. Even so, he was always open to new business opportunities, particularly if they involved automobiles. One bonanza seemed to come from out of the blue.

Most of the cars that Carl sold were open vehicles, suitable to drive only in the daytime during fair weather. There were some kerosene and carbide lamps available, but they were unreliable and had little lighting capacity for a motorcar.

While leaving for lunch one day in 1904, Carl noticed an elderly man loading up a contrivance that had been left in the shop for several days. It was a small metal cylinder about a foot long, with a three-foot length of copper tubing with a forked tip attached to a valve at one end. The cylinder contained compressed acetylene gas which was then used for lighting buoys and lighthouses.[1]

The old man was Percy C. Avery, who had purchased the French patent for the invention. When Avery lit the device, Carl could see that its brightness was far superior to anything then available. Avery told Carl the gas was explosive if not handled carefully. The automobile manufacturers whom he had already approached had turned the invention down for just that reason.[2] Avery had exhausted his finances in trying to develop a safe method of compressing the gas. Carl

26

told Avery to return the next day so that he could demonstrate the light for Jim Allison.

Allison, too, thought the invention had possibilities, but he was concerned about its safety. He decided to test the cylinder to determine whether or not it could withstand a strong impact. Allison went to the West Washington Street bridge over the White River and heaved the cylinder on the rocks below, assuming that if the tank could withstand this test, it would be safe on automobiles. The canister did not explode, and Allison reported the good news to Carl.[3]

Carl and Jim sold stock to raise the capital for a half-interest in Avery's patent, and the three became partners in the Concentrated Acetylene Company, naming the product "Prest-O-Lite" for its instant flame. The company was incorporated that same year. Their first factory was set up in a frame shed on Pennsylvania and 28th Streets where Avery and one assistant, Jack Noble, constituted the entire staff, with Noble filling the tanks from a hand pump.[4]

The 1904 Packard was the first car to feature the new headlamps.[5] Sales escalated as automobiles became more popular, but the explosive danger that Avery warned about was all too real.

Fires, explosions, and a "phenomenal"[6] growth in business caused frequent moves. There were frequent explosions while work continued on increasing the safety of the new lights. The factory at 211 East South Street was located near a sauerkraut plant. When the factory exploded, the force of the explosion blew up the sauerkraut plant. Wet, smelly kraut was sprayed all over a nearby hospital. Multiple lawsuits resulted, and the City Council forbade charging the tanks within the city limits. The construction of a new factory resulted in more tragedy. Concrete froze during the cold weather and collapsed, killing seventeen of Fisher's workmen.[7] The factory was rebuilt.

Over time, fifteen other Prest-O-Lite factories across the country exploded, leading to a tide of new lawsuits. Carl's wife Jane wrote: "Carl and Jim evolved a code to keep these tragedies secret. When the Bayonne, New Jersey, plant blew up, a wire was sent: 'Bayonne gone at ten-thirty.' When the entire plant exploded in Omaha the message was: 'Omaha left at four-thirty.'"[8] Carl spent up to 200 nights a year on the road, selling, negotiating, and testifying in court against lawsuits resulting from the many factory explosions. Fortunately, technology eventually brought an end to most of the danger. The tanks were lined with asbestos.[9]

Jim Allison was in charge of production. Their longtime friend Lem Trotter noted, "Fisher was the dreamer but Allison had the most brilliant mind of any man I ever knew. He was the industrialist."[10] Allison later commented on his and Carl's philosophy on dealing with others who questioned their judgment. "Neither my partner nor myself ever antagonized a man who told us we didn't have a damned bit of sense, or didn't know what we were talking about. We always upheld the employees' ideas and theories — even though we didn't believe in them. We would then call them all together and let them argue the question through to the satisfaction of everyone, and would not permit them 'bite-back.'"[11] Neither Carl nor Allison had much formal education and neither

Cartoon captures public's sentiment against Prest-O-Lite factories.

(I.M.S.)

thought very much of its value. "I presume of the high priced employees or those drawing over common wages, educated through schools would not exceed three in one hundred. The manager of our company for a great many years — doing a *business* of six million dollars annually — was formerly a piccolo player with Ringling Brothers circus,"[12] Carl said of Prest-O-Lite.

In 1906 Avery withdrew from the firm, which changed its name to the Prest-O-Lite Storage Battery Company. The bright headlights had no competition, and demand was so strong that they kept building factories to try to keep up with the orders.

Carl and Allison's profits came from more than the sale of lights. Customers needed their cylinders refilled practi-

cally as soon as they ran out of gas. To accommodate them, Fisher and Allison started a special-delivery service that could deliver overnight. Jim Allison later explained the efficiency of the service. "In the evening at eleven-thirty we would go to the post office and pick up the orders that were mailed to us as late as four o'clock in the afternoon from such cities as St. Louis, Terre Haute, Cincinnati, Dayton and other places within two hundred miles, and fill orders that night. For some time the customers couldn't understand when they mailed an order in the late afternoon how their goods could be on their steps the next morning."[13]

Carl found another use for the lights. In 1905, he promoted a race to set a record for a 24-hour race at the Indiana Fairgrounds, offering to set up banks of Prest-O-Lites around the course. With the lights installed, the race began on November 16. W. F. Clemens and Charles Merz broke the previous record of 1,015 miles at 1 p. m. the following day and set a new 24-hour record of 1,094 miles.[14]

Within six years after it was started, the company was worth six million dollars. This was no small accomplishment when in 1910, a postage stamp and a pound of coffee cost five cents.[15] Carl was thought to have the "golden touch" and naturally attracted a series of parasites, sycophants, and conmen. Jane Fisher told the story of a man from Dayton, Ohio, who managed to talk his way into an audience with Carl by hailing the merits of a miracle fuel he called "Zolene." To demonstrate, he dropped some white cubes into boiling water, then added a "secret" *additive* from a small bottle. After the brew cooled, it was poured into the empty gas tank of an automobile. To Carl's astonishment, the car started, and he drove it around.

When Carl returned, he proclaimed the fuel the biggest discovery since the telephone, far surpassing Prest-O-Lite. Even the normally-calm Allison was unable to contain his excitement. But there were doubters, including marine engineer John Levi, who had designed the *Eph 1*, Carl's yacht.

The inventor claimed Zolene would work with salt water so Carl promptly had a barrel of it shipped from New Jersey.

The Zolene did work with salt water, and the news spread. Now there literally could be oceans of fuel. A local editorial proclaimed that Zolene was a discovery beneficial to mankind, second only to radium.

Carl and Jim Allison paid $30,000 for the rights to the "secret" and even set up an experimental plant without running any preliminary tests. Unfortunately, the white cubes turned out to be gasoline residue, as John Levi had suspected, and the secret additive nothing but pure gasoline, which gave the water solution enough power to run the car.[16]

After that, whenever Carl became excited over some new project and friends warned him to be cautious, they would take him aside, sit him down, and say, "Skip, [short for Skipper, reflecting Carl's love of boating], remember Zolene?"[17] In his initial enthusiasm, Carl had even named one of his boats the *Zolene*.

Sometimes Carl missed out on opportunities that did result in great success. He was intrigued with the idea of an "iceless icebox," and had bought one of the first made for Blossom Heath. Even though Carl thought it would "revolutionize housekeeping,"[18] his interest in Zolene at the time kept him from being one of the first manufacturers of the refrigerator.

The captains of industry, meanwhile, had their eye on Prest-O-Lite. For several years, Union Carbide had sent invention scout Matthew "Bud" Carney to make offers for the company. Every time, Carl and Allison turned them down. The corporation wanted the nation-wide distribution system and the modern plant which Fisher and Allison had built to replace the one which had collapsed. Carl called it a "sunshine factory" because it featured huge banks of windows, in contrast to the usual dark factories then in existence. He wanted ample light for his employees.[19] Finally in 1913, nine years after they had started the company with a $2,000 investment, Union Carbide made them an offer they couldn't refuse: $9,000,000,[20] a staggering sum for the time. The complete transfer of ownership was not completed until June 1917 because of the agreed buyout financial terms.

32

Prest-O-Lite soon outgrew the small factory at 28ᵗʰ and Pennsylvania in Indianapolis. An explosion in the factory caused Fisher and Allison to relocate. In 1912 they built this modern factory on the outskirts of Indianapolis in Speedway, Indiana. (I.S.L)

Their decision to sell Prest-O-Lite was a wise one from an automotive viewpoint. The days of gas headlamps were numbered. The storage battery came into wide use and began to power the new electric self-starter, pioneered by Cadillac and made standard equipment by General Motors in 1912. Electric headlights were used by the entire industry by 1914. Prest-O-Lite bought the Pumpelly Battery Company that year and began to manufacture batteries.[21] Union Carbide wanted Prest-O-Lite for other reasons. The cylinder market was expanding because welding and medical gases were being used in businesses and hospitals. The cylinders could be refilled and sold for the growing market. In addition, new spin-off uses of the gases were being discovered, which further increased sales.

James Allison reinvested his share in Allison Engineering, an experimental firm that would make the bearings for Charles Lindbergh's *Spirit of Saint Louis* and develop the famous Allison airplane engine. In 1929 General Motors purchased the company but retained the name Allison.[22]

With his share of the nine million, Carl could afford to take it easy the rest of his life, but that was not his way. And, as usual, he had been playing as hard as he worked.

His interest in balloons was not limited to using them for his promotions. He had flown enough to earn one of the

Carl Fisher and George Bumbaugh flew a Stoddard-Dayton over Indianapolis as an advertising gimmick. (SR)

nation's first licenses for balloon pilots. Humorist Will Rogers said of his friend: "Carl Fisher holds license No. 17 for balloon pilots in America. I didn't know you could pilot one; I thought the wind did that."[23]

One of Carl's rides lasted 49 hours and took him over the mountains of Tennessee, where he found that the sport, in addition to its inherent perils, also entailed some unnatural hazards. "We heard gun reports from below," Carl wrote. "For four hours this shooting continued all along the route. No sooner had we faded too far in the distance to be the target for one then another spied us and took a turn. I believe they were persons who had no idea that human lives were being endangered. They probably thought it was a stray balloon that had drifted away from a circus."[24]

Carl wasted no time in letting out the ballast and getting out of the area as soon as he could. Because the balloon was such a large target, he and his traveling companion George Bumbaugh were fortunate that the marksmen had such poor aim.

On another occasion he arranged for Bumbaugh's 40,000 cubic-foot *Columbia* to race a car. Because no one could predict wind direction, four cars had to be used. With the right wind, it turned out to be no contest. The balloon beat the car to the village of Miami, some 65 miles north. By the time the car arrived, Bumbaugh and Carl had dismantled the balloon and had taken it to the express office in Miami to ship it back to Indianapolis.[25]

Carl's most famous aerial caper drew thousands of spectators. When the Stoddard-Dayton Company came out with a new model in the fall of 1908, Fisher ordered from Bumbaugh a balloon emblazoned with "Stoddard-Dayton." Carl announced that he would use the balloon to fly a new white Stoddard-Dayton over Indianapolis, and when they landed, he would drive the car away.

On the afternoon of October 30, five thousand people, according to the *Indianapolis Star,* were at the Indianapolis Gas Company plant near Northwestern Avenue and Fall Creek to watch the preparation and the ascent. Worried that they would not be able to clear the plant and its large gas tank, Bumbaugh had to ask for volunteers from the crowd to pick up the automobile and balloon and carry this load of about 3,200 pounds across the shallow part of Fall Creek to the northern bank and hold it down until Carl and Bumbaugh had made their final preparations.

The huge balloon, with Carl and Bumbaugh sitting in the seats of the Stoddard-Dayton, ascended about 4:30 p. m for a flight that lasted until 6:10 p.m., when it descended near Smithport. The *Star* described the scene.

> Five thousand unbelieving people watched the start at the plant of the Indianapolis Gas Company near Northwestern Avenue and Fall Creek, and saw the automobile securely hitched to the balloon to take the place of the customary balloon basket. Fisher and Bumbaugh seated themselves in the automobile, gave the word and away they went, smashing all precedents in the way of aerial navigation....
>
> Cheers from the thousands and hats waved in the air marked the start of the flight as the monster balloon rose slowly and with an even upward movement the automobile was lifted off the ground. A bag of sand was dumped and then another as the machine rose in the air. Fisher, leaning out over the front of the car, waved to the crowd below as the balloon went higher and swept off to the southeast.
>
> The automobile used in the flight was stripped of all the superfluous weight. There were two seats in which the passengers sat as though they were riding atop the smoothest pavement. In order to make the machine lighter the tires were inflated with gas the same as was used in the balloon. The lamps and steps were taken off and the machine was roped on to the bag in the place intended by the builder of the balloon for the basket. During the time taken up by the preparations for the flight more than 100 cameras held by persons in the crowd were snapped several times.[26]

The *Star* noted that Frank L. Moore, vice-president of the Fisher Automobile Company, followed the balloon in one of the company's cars, using long-distance telephone calls to inform the company's office of the progress of the flight, which was uneventful. The *Star* quoted Carl:

The trip was without incident. The only trouble was the lack of air currents. About 100 feet above the ground there was a breeze blowing at about six miles an hour. But after getting above that level the air was perfectly quiet.

We stood directly above the point where she landed for fully twenty-five minutes. We hunted for currents high in the air but there was none stirring. In landing we came down close enough to the ground to drop a drag rope, and several of the men in the crowd that had gathered caught the rope and pulled us easily to the ground. Dr. Frank Hotchins was the first to catch the rope.

... the automobile came to rest upon the ground without the slightest jar.[27]

Carl estimated that several hundred people, in about 250 cars and two to three hundred bicycles and motorcycles, followed the flight and were at the landing.

Some on the ground saw lights on the balloon and thought that it carried lamps. Carl said that actually it was only the reflection of the sun on the polished auto. "We were in the air so high that the sun shone upon us much longer than it did upon the ground beneath us."[28]

After landing, Carl drove the Stoddard-Dayton into Indianapolis, arriving about 7 p.m. the newspaper reported. But there was something they didn't know. "I was as scared as anyone else — but for different reasons," Carl explained. "Actually I had taken the heavy motor out of the car before we went up. When the balloon landed a couple of miles away, my brother was there to meet us with an identical car. it was simple, yet no one ever seemed to figure it out."[29]

It was his most spectacular stunt to date and received national publicity, including hundreds of illustrations. Carl milked it for all it was worth, running advertisements that said: "Stoddard-Dayton was the first car to fly over Indianapolis. It should be your first car."

Carl's name was now recognized not only in Indianapolis, but throughout the state and the nation as well. Customers flocked to his showrooms to buy his cars.

The aerial escapade had more personal ramifications as well. As he sailed over the city, surveying the crowds, one young lady watched intently. "That day the great white automobile rode through the sky was the day I first saw Carl,"[30] wrote Jane Watts, who was shortly to become his first wife.

Chapter 5

Speedway Is Born

Yᴇᴀʀs ᴏF sᴇʟʟɪɴɢ and racing cars had taught Carl Fisher an undeniable fact — the quality of American cars was generally poor and there was little indication that it was getting any better. Tire problems and overheated engines were taken for granted as part of driving. Even new cars right out of his showroom had little reliability.

With a friend, Carl had tried out a new model by driving it on a trip to Greenfield, twenty miles from Indianapolis. On the way back, the car broke down not once, but several times, and the two had to keep tearing posts out of roadside fences so that they could hoist the car up and wire it back together. "There ought to be a track to test these cars out before the public gets 'em,"[1] Carl said.

His driving experience had also heightened his concern for the importance of safety features. He could not forget the race in Zanesville, Ohio, when his brakes failed as he was rounding a curve. The car plowed through a fence and into the grandstand, killing and injuring fourteen spectators. Carl's conviction that American automobiles must be improved set him on a one-man crusade to improve their quality — and the Indianapolis Speedway was designed to do just that. Traveling to Midwestern tracks had demonstrated to Carl that racing improved bicycles and automobiles, like horse racing, improved the breed.

In the rigors of racing, some American cars, frequently modified for racing, had proved themselves. Carl himself had set what the *Chicago Tribune* hailed as a new world record for two miles in 2:02 minutes and two seconds when he won the five-mile Diamond Cup Race on the Harlem track in Chicago on October 1, 1904, driving a stripped — down premier comet.[2] But in endurance races, European automobiles defeated the American cars every time.

Eight days after his Chicago victory, Carl attended the Vanderbilt Cup race on Long Island, where a French Panhard won a 284-mile race at an average speed of 52.2 miles per hour. The Panhard's ability to withstand what was then considered a breakneck speed for such a long distance deeply impressed him. After talking with the European drivers at the Vanderbilt Cup competition, Carl was convinced that European superiority was the result of competition among factory-sponsored teams. Winning grueling races proved to the public the quality of the manufacturers' cars and spurred sales.[3] He was eager to see for himself the European system and got his chance in July, 1905, when he accompanied an

Carl Fisher in one of his Mohawk cars. (HASF)

American team to Europe as a reserve driver for the James Gordon Bennett Cup races.

Carl drove the 85.35 mile Circuit de l'Auvergne course before the race was run. He told his friends later that "The course was the most hazardous ever selected for any race. It twisted its way through the most mountainous part of France. In many places the roadway was so narrow it was impossible for one car to pass another. Several of the turns were protected only by low stone walls, on the other side of which were chasms many hundreds of feet deep."[4]

The European drivers had been driving the track daily for months, not only giving them the advantage of familiarizing themselves with the route, but proving the sturdiness of their automobiles.

It was no surprise that German, English, Italian, and French cars defeated the Americans. The only American car to finish, finished in last place; the other American entries had dropped out because of mechanical problems. Dismayed, Carl said that the European cars could "go uphill faster than the American cars can come down!"[5] Recalling the experience in May of 1937, he wrote Ray C. Thompson, sports editor of the *Indianapolis News*, that

> ...we had two very fast cars, but there was no place in America to test them over a continuous drive of more than two miles, and in order to test them even the two miles in Toledo, we had to hire special guards and do the work at daylight; and even this testing was stopped because the cars made so much noise on the boulevard. So, we went to Europe with cars that were very fast but with no place to test them at high speed for a continuous run of 100 miles or so... As a result, the French beat the tar out of us; in fact, we didn't have either car finish, and I could see that it was a lack of being able to test the cars over a continuous speed run; and I made up my mind then to build a speedway where cars could be run 1,000 miles in a test, if necessary.[6]

While in Europe, Carl inspected European auto plants and visited the huge bowl-shaped concrete speedway at Brooklands in England. His travels left no question in his mind that European cars were superior to their American counterparts not only in durability and performance, but in comfort and handling as well.

He was also introduced to a new form of travel — the hot air balloon. Before he returned home, he made several ascensions.

Once back in America, Carl was eager to convince auto manufacturers that a testing track was imperative to improving American automobiles. Indiana was a logical place for such a track. From the beginning of the automobile age, Indianans had shown a strong interest in building cars. In 1894, Charles Black of Indianapolis built a car for himself. In the same year, Elwood Haynes of Kokomo had the Apperson brothers' machine shop build him a vehicle with the chassis on a buggy bed and a one-cylinder engine attached to the wheels. Haynes, a field representative for the Indiana Gas and Oil Company, wanted faster transportation for his job.[7] Haynes and the Appersons later produced cars together and then went their separate ways in automobile manufacturing. Cars were being built all over the state, from Auburn to South Bend to Connersville.

Over a hundred different makes were manufactured in Indiana in the early days of the automobile. Only sixteen lasted more than 15 years: American, Apperson, Auburn, Cole, Davis, Duesenberg, Elcar, Empire, Haynes, Lexington, Marmon, Maxwell, McFarlan, Studebaker, Stutz, and Waverley Electric.[8]

As part of his campaign for the track, Fisher began a concerted effort to warn American automakers that their industry was in danger of losing their business to the European carmakers. He told them that European companies "can take over the entire American market any time they decide to export cars in sufficient quantity to meet the demand."

If you don't start building cars the public can buy with confidence, you won't even be able to give 'em away. The only way to gain the public's confidence quickly is to prove the dependability of your products on the race track. You'll learn ten times as much racing against each other as you will from listening to the complaints of your customers.

Road racing is doomed. The farmers will fight you every inch
of the way if you try to test your cars on the open highway.
What this country needs is a big new race track designed for
automobiles instead of horses.[9]

Some listeners took his advice to heart. Within weeks,
some industry representatives and young Indianapolis sportsmen formed the Indianapolis Automobile Racing Association
(IARA).[10]

On November 4, 1905, the IARA sponsored a 100-mile
race at the Indiana Fairgrounds. W.F. Clemens won in 1 hour,
53 minutes, and 21.8 seconds, five minutes faster than the
international record. Of the nine cars entered, only the two
Nationals actually finished the race; Clemens' car was Arthur
Newby's personal National.[11]

Carl then urged the IARA to challenge the 24-hour distance record of 1,015 miles. To light the track at night, he
had Prest-O-Lite lamps placed about every 25 feet around
the course. On November 16, a cold frosty Thursday afternoon, the attempt began at 2:45 p. m. At 1 p.m. the next day,
the old record was broken. A new record of 1,094 miles had
been set at the end of the 24 hours.[12]

These successes gained Carl support for his racetrack
from Tom Taggert, three-time mayor of Indianapolis. He proposed that the track be built at French Lick Springs, where
he and his associates were building a new spa and hotel.
Unfortunately, the area did not provide sufficient land for
the racetrack.[13]

In another attempt to gain support for his project, Carl
wrote to the editor of *Motor Age* magazine, who had encouraged responses to the suggestion of building a large track:

The American manufacturers annually spend thousands of
dollars in building high speed racing cars to compete with
French cars and without possible chance of winning, and I
think this is largely due to the fact that American drivers do
not have a chance to thoroughly test their cars continuously
at high speed for weak spots in construction, or to become
entirely familiar with and have their car under perfect control
at very high speeds.

There is no question in my mind that it takes weeks and

months of practice handling a car at 75, 80 and 90 miles an hour to be able to properly gauge distances, numerous road conditions and the response of the car to such conditions. It has been my experience that quite a number of racing cars, when tested over the best roads we had in this country, seemed to have wonderful speed. There was no accurate way to time them for any distance, and the best anybody could do was to guess at what the cars were doing.

It seems to me a 5-mile track, properly laid out, without fences to endanger drivers, with proper grandstands, supply stores for gasoline and oil, and other accommodations would net for one meet such as the Vanderbilt Cup race a sufficient amount to pay half of the entire cost of the track.[14]

No new prospects for the track developed, however. Meanwhile, Carl had taken up a new interest — putting automobile engines into speedboats. By the summer of 1906, there were about 40 speedboats built by the members of the Indiana Motor Club in the White River near the edge of Indianapolis. Carl raced his boat, the *Eph IV,* using a six-cylinder, 70-horsepower engine, and won every race at a September regatta at Ottawa Beach, Michigan. He became so enthusiastic about speedboat racing that eventually he wanted to build a water speedway at Riverside Park with a natural amphitheater on the bluff above the west bank of the river. "I'll make enough money out of the first regatta to pay for it, then make enough money to enlarge every park in Indianapolis,"[15] he told local journalist William Herschell. But Mayor Charles A. Bookwalter, an old friend, opposed it, fearing it would commercialize the park. Nothing came of it.

Carl's interest in an auto racing track remained high, even though no one had come forth to build it. The financial panic of 1907 had caused many businesses to cut back or fold, although Prest-O-Lite and the Fisher Automobile Company dealership remained prosperous. Over lunch at "Pop" Haynes' restaurant on North Pennsylvania Street, Carl and his friends frequently discussed the track. On a dinner napkin there he drew for them his design for a three-mile track, a design which became the prototype for the Indianapolis Speedway. His idea that the track would be banked on the curves to allow for greater speed was a first for American racing. Carl had seen a banked speedway in England, where English sportsman Hugh Fortesque Locke-King had built Brooklands, a two-and-three-quarter-mile high-speed track in Surrey. Some of its banking was so steep "that men could not climb it on foot."[16]

Finally, Fisher was challenged to do more than just talk about and promote such a track. On an autumn day in 1908, on the drive back from a business trip to Dayton, Ohio, Carl and Lem Trotter, his real estate broker and advisor, had been forced to stop three times to refill the radiator and repair a tire. Trotter chided Carl about the many times Carl had insisted that a racetrack was badly needed to eliminate such problems. Trotter even had in mind a location for the track: the old Pressley farm, about five miles northwest of Indianapolis.

The next day, the two went to inspect the site. The farm had been divided up into four 80-acre tracts. The Ben Hur Traction Line and the Big Four Railroad ran along the property. Carl was impressed; he instructed Trotter to get the options on the property while he arranged the financing.

By December 12, Trotter had obtained an "ironclad option" for the property at a total price of $72,000. Fisher and Jim Allison invited three mutual friends to join them in the expensive venture: Arthur Newby of the National Motor Vehicle Company; Frank H. Wheeler of the Wheeler-Schebler Carburetor Company; and Stoughton Fletcher, a prominent Indianapolis banker whose grandfather had founded the Fletcher National Bank. Allison and Fisher put up $50,000 apiece.[17]

But before the articles of corporation were filed, Fletcher had to withdraw; his bank thought that such an investment was not good for its "conservative reputation."[18] The "old society" of Indianapolis looked down upon race car drivers just as they looked down on jockeys. Some residents believed that Indianapolis industrialists and bankers even discouraged Henry Ford from moving to Indianapolis. One who knew Allison and Fisher said that they were just "poor boys with big ideas, and other people wouldn't put up a dime to help 'em."[19]

After Fletcher's departure, Fisher and Allison took over his shares, resulting in their holding a 60 percent controlling interest in the "Indianapolis Motor Speedway Company" when the articles of corporation were filed on February 9, 1909. It was capitalized at $250,000. Fisher was president; Newby, first vice-president; Wheeler, second vice-president; and Allison, secretary-treasurer.[20] July 4, 1909, was chosen as the opening date of the track with the American Automobile Association, a contest board, as the sanctioning body.

The cost of the huge project had a great influence on the partners' decisions. At their meetings at "Pop" Haynes' restaurant, the founders decided that brick and concrete were too expensive and accepted instead Carl's suggestion of a mix of crushed stone and asphaltum on a clay base. The course would be in the form of a three-mile rectangle, with a twisting two-mile infield course for other events.[21]

With so much money invested, the group wanted to try to raise money even before the track opened. Carl suggested a balloon race that would draw thousands of spectators. To this end, he formed the Aero Club of Indiana to encourage interest and to bring the national balloon races to Indianapolis. Carl was the group's first president. He also enlisted the help of Robert H. Sturm, secretary of the Indiana Motorcycle Club, in hopes that the Federation of American Motorcyclists would hold their national championships at the Speedway.

Although actual construction of the Speedway was not scheduled to begin until March 15, the program was in place by March 1. The balloon race would take place on June 5; there would be automobile races on the July 4th weekend; motorcycle championships were scheduled for August 13 and 14; and there would be more auto races during the Labor Day weekend.[22]

The auto racing plans were soon dashed. P. T. Andrews, a New York engineer who was the superintendent of construction, told them that it was impossible to finish the race track by July 4: a creek running across the southwest corner required two bridges over the fifty-foot wide track, and the bridges might not be completed in time even for the motorcycle championships.[23] The founders quickly changed plans, rescheduling the first auto races for the weekend after the motorcycle championships and the second races for early October.

Andrews had another suggestion. He told them that the planned three-mile track would be very close to the boundaries and that a two-and-a-half mile track would leave room for additional grandstands in future years. The founders were in agreement.[24] Carl had some good news. The projected cost was $220,000, less than they had expected. Only $184,000 in cash was needed.[25]

Andrews went to work with a crew of 450 men, 300 mules, 150 road scrapers, four six-ton rollers and three 10-ton rollers.[26] By late April, the only construction problem that had arisen resulted from the heavy rains that had impeded the building of the bridges.

To promote interest in the speedway, Carl hired Ernest A. Moross, a well-known press agent and promoter, as "Director of Contests."[27] Moross soon had the Indianapolis newspapers publishing stories that aroused the public's interest in the new track. He invited the Indianapolis press to a tour on May 1, when they were driven around the track in three of Carl's touring cars. Heavy planks were in place where the bridges would be. More publicity resulted when Lewis Strang, a member of the Buick racing team that Moross had invited, predicted that world records would be set on the new track. As the only American driver who had raced on England's new Brooklands race track, Strang had strong credibility.

Carl had high hopes that the publicity and the novelty of balloon racing would bring in 20,000 paid admissions for the balloon race on June 5. He also hoped to participate himself but first had to meet the qualifications for an international balloon license. He managed to complete the last of the ten required ascents, including one night flight, on June 1.[28]

The thousands of people who came to view the races were far more than the founders expected — as many as 75,000 by some estimates. Unfortunately, the hoped-for 20,000 paid admissions did not materialize. Since there were no fences, most spectators parked along the outlying roads and viewed the spectacle for free. Only 3,500 paid admission.[29] The traffic jam even prevented Governor Thomas R. Marshall from participating in the preliminary ceremonies. He had to walk the last mile and arrived an hour late.

Because the wind had died down by the end of the balloon race, no new distance records were set, but the *St. Louis III* improved the endurance record by two hours, staying aloft for 45 hours and 50 minutes. Carl's balloon finished fourth, but he had a memorable trip. As his balloon ascended, Carl unfurled six American flags and threw red roses to the crowd while a military band played "*The Star-Spangled Banner.*"[30]

Carl and George Bumbaugh, his co-pilot, thought they were prepared for anything on their long flight. But when night fell and they anchored the balloon to a tree with a drag rope, they saw lights approaching. When they shouted down, the lights disappeared only to reappear shortly afterwards. Shouting again was followed by the lights' disappearance. After three instances of the lights appearing and disappearing, the men readied their revolvers. "We're surrounded by moonshiners," Carl said.

Several tense minutes followed; then Carl began to laugh. "If we're not the damnedest couple of fools," he said. "Those aren't moonshiners' lanterns down there — they're will-o'-the wisps!"[31] He had figured out that the source of the elusive lights was the marsh gases below.

They did find themselves the target of rifle fire the next day as they flew over the hills of Kentucky and Tennessee. Fortunately, neither they nor the other balloonists who had also been targeted were harmed.

By July 1, the grandstands and 41 other structures were practically complete. Carl even had a small chapel built near the track for the racers and their families. Services were held on race mornings, and on file there were the names and addresses of all the racers and their next-of-kin. But the race-track was behind schedule. Concerned that the entire summer's programs would have to be canceled if progress wasn't made quickly, Carl ordered Andrews to start working around the clock, using light from open-flame burners attached to the gas lines that were already installed in the infield. He offered Prest-O-Lite tanks to be used in clusters where the light would not be sufficient.

The 24-hour work schedule began, with Carl spending eighteen to twenty hours a day at the track. It was on one of those July nights that Carl and his future wife Jane Watts witnessed a tragedy that caused Carl to act against racial injustice. Jane described the incident.

> One night as we watched, one of the Negro workmen fell into a vat of boiling tar. Carl ordered the screaming man lifted into our car and drove him, while the flesh literally dropped from his bones, to a hospital to which Carl and Jim [Allison] were generous contributors. An intern met us at the door with a stretcher. When he saw the color of the man's skin, he jerked back the stretcher. "We don't treat niggers at this hospital," he said. I was afraid for Carl in that moment — he was so angry. He asked the intern softly, carefully, if he would please treat the agonized workman. But the intern was indifferent. "Take him to the City Hospital — they treat niggers there," he said. We retraced our way five miles to the city institution and on the way the screaming mercifully stopped. The man was dead.
>
> That was the first time I heard Carl really curse. The words seemed to pour from his soul. Somehow, it sounded right and just that he could swear at such a time. I knew he was making a promise.
>
> This tragedy opened Carl's eyes to the agony behind racial problems. He took a personal revenge on the hospital that turned away a dying man. Not only did he withdraw his support of the institution, but he persuaded Jim to do the same. He said, "I'll put that goddam place out of business." And he did — within two years the hospital closed its doors.
>
> It was about then that Carl began giving to Negro institutions. He made contributions to aid their schooling, housing, hospitalization and YMCA.[32]

Regardless of the tragedy, work had to continue. The first use of the track was to be for the motorcycle races on August 14, 1909. When some of the cyclists arrived a week early, planning to practice before the races, the track was still not completed. The crushed stone surface was not to their liking either; they thought it dangerous. Carl assured them it would be finished in time for some practice when a final coat of oil was rolled onto the surface to make it safer. But the five railroad cars of oil that he needed were somehow misdirected. Furious, Carl demanded that a special shipment be sent. Some cyclists wanted the races canceled and others suggested it be transferred to the Indiana fairgrounds. Only Fisher's assurances that they could practice on the morning of the races and that they would have a good chance of setting new records kept the event alive.[33]

Fearing that spectators would not come because of the talk of the track's not being finished, Moross urged Carl to get a prominent racer to try to set a record on the track the day before the race. Californian Ed Lingenfelder, the champion of the West, agreed to try and covered 25 miles in 25 minutes.[34]

Then another delay — rain forced postponement of the Friday races to Saturday, and Saturday's to Monday.

About 3,500 spectators attended on Saturday, but the opening amateur races were slow; the cyclists were cautious on the sharp turns. Spectators began to leave. Before the professional races were slated to start, Carl argued with race officials who wanted to cancel the remainder of the program because they felt the track was dangerous. Only Ed Lingenfelder and Jake De Rosier were willing to participate in the ten-mile race. De Rosier's tire blew out, and only Lingenfelder finished. Only four of the 46 entrants participated in the amateur title race; the 25-mile professional race was canceled because there were no entrants. The officials announced that the Monday events were also canceled.[35]

Fortunately, practice for the first auto races was scheduled for the following week, and successes there gained favorable publicity. Several drivers averaged over 70 miles per hour; Barney Oldfield set a record of 76.27 miles per hour.[36] But the constant pressure of the heavy cars pounded the oil into the crushed stone, and ruts and chuckholes began to appear. Sharp pieces of stone were cast into the air, threatening the cars and drivers behind them.

Concerned about the track condition for the next day's races, Carl closed the track at 3 p. m. so that the holes could be patched and another layer of oil could be applied to keep down the dust. Even though the work continued through the night, oil was still being applied when the gates opened at 9 a.m.[37]

August 19, 1909 opening day of the three-day automobile races, proved to be a direct contrast to that of the motorcycle races. Before noon, 15,000 had paid admission. The overflow crowd had to view the races from the infield. Carl was jubilant. An Indianapolis newspaper had written that "Only a fool would build a racetrack nearly five miles from downtown." Years later he remarked, "Everyone said I was crazy to put the Speedway five miles out of Indianapolis. It was such a long trip for a horse and buggy. But even then I was looking forward to the time when every family would own a car."[38]

But tragedy quickly ended Carl's elation. By the time the three days of racing were over, one driver, two riding mechanics, and two spectators were dead.

However, records were set on opening day. In the second race, there was a new world's record of 66.93 miles per hour for engines of not more than 300-cubic-inch displacement. Problems arose in the feature race, the 250-mile Prest-O-Lite trophy race at 2 p.m. By the 30th lap, with the leading cars averaging 65 miles per hour, the track was breaking up rapidly. Flying pieces of stone shattered some of the drivers' goggles. A car driven by William Bourque hit a chuckhole, swerved into a ditch, and turned over. Both Bourque and his mechanic were killed.

The condition of the track was such a concern that the officials discussed with Carl whether or not they should cancel the next day's program. Carl was adamant, insisting that 90 percent of the track was still in good condition. He assured them that the rest could be repaired by race time the next day, and the ditches would be covered with heavy planks.[39]

An even bigger crowd of 25,000 attended on Friday. Another record was set; Lewis Strang won the 100-mile race with an average speed of 64.74 miles per hour.[40]

On Saturday, the final day, 35,000 spectators were on hand. Seventeen of the world's most powerful cars had entered the 300-mile Wheeler-Schebler Trophy Race. A $10,000 silver vase made by Tiffany's of New York was to be awarded to the winner. Spectators crowded toward the edges of the track as the race was run; when the police moved them from one spot, they moved to another. Suddenly, one of Charley Merz's front tires blew. His car soared through the air for almost 100 feet, through a group of spectators, and landed upside down in the muddy creek bed. Merz survived, but his mechanic, Claude Kellum, was killed, as were two of the spectators. Several more were injured.[41]

The full extent of the accident was not known to the judges until later; they allowed the race to continue. Then another car hit a chuckhole and crashed into one of the timbers supporting the pedestrian bridge across the track. The officials immediately ended the race with only 235 miles completed by the winner, Lee Lynch. The accidents subdued the crowd; some were drawn to the wrecked cars, but most left quietly.[42]

The newspapers were merciless on Carl Fisher; he felt personally responsible. He decided he would only reopen the speedway if he could find a road material that would ensure safety for men willing to risk their lives. The material would have to withstand the extreme weather changes throughout the year and resist buckling and grooving.

Rumors that the Automobile Association of America would not sanction any more races at the new track prompted an announcement from Carl:

> Our principal desire was to create a Speedway suitable for races that would excel any in this country or on the Continent. Financial success was of secondary importance — and still is. We are ready to spend $100,000 or more, if necessary, to make the Speedway safe for spectators as well as drivers.
>
> The track will be paved and guardrails will be constructed on all of the turns before another race is scheduled. When the job is completed, we definitely will have the world's finest and

safest race course; and I'm sure everyone connected with racing will want to return to Indianapolis at the earliest opportunity.[43]

Carl and the other founders turned to Andrews, their New York engineer, for advice. After spending weeks conducting extensive tests, he advised them that a concrete track would cost $110,000 and last many years, but brick would last longer, provide better traction, and increase speed by another mile or two.[44] Its cost, however, was 50 percent more than concrete. Nine-inch-thick concrete retaining walls extending 33 inches above the track surface would be built along the outer edge of the banked curves to protect spectators.[45]

In Carl's mind, there was no question. Brick it would be. And to try to recoup some of the cost, he suggested more auto racing in December, estimating proceeds of $15,000 to $20,000. The others were concerned about the effect of cold temperatures on the automobiles, drivers, and spectators. Jim Allison's offer was a compromise: invite the manufacturers to race for records, with no prize offered, just for the beneficial effects from the publicity. There would be no admission charge, and the founders would not have to put up any more money. With these provisions, the races were set for December 17 and 18.

Work on the brick surface began in early September. Each of the three million paving bricks, weighing ten pounds apiece, was placed in position by hand and pressed into two inches of sand. The level was checked continuously by inspectors, allowing no more than $3/8$ of an inch variation. Two applications of filler were applied to make the joints flush with the bricks.[46]

The track was finished in 63 days, but the auto manufacturers were not showing the expected interest in the December races. Carl, who had been out of town, rushed back to save the events. He knew big-name drivers and record-breaking performances would encourage the manufacturers to participate. Soon he had Lewis Strang and Walter Christie signed up, and Governor Marshall agreed to attend. For the first ride on the new track Carl chose James J. Jeffries, former heavyweight boxing champion of the world. Newspapers throughout the country published photos of the ride.

Carl had another promotional idea that was known to only a few. He had a brick removed from the starting line of the track. From it a mold was made, and a "gold" brick (actually a mixture of bronze and brass, as used in the manufacture of Wheeler-Schebler carburetors) was made. On December 17, the Governor placed the brick in position, announcing the formal opening of "the world's greatest Speedway." The brick was removed at the end of the day's activities and placed on display in the Speedway's downtown office.[47]

All the promotion and publicity was no match for the weather. The 9° temperature kept attendance down to only 500; many huddled around bonfires until the races were underway. It was so cold that the four motorcyclists made only one trip around the oval.

The auto racers had to bundle up in scarves and mufflers — one driver even had a stocking cap with holes cut in it so that he could see.[48]

The next day the three drivers still participating were prepared: they had stored the needed fuel and oil in heated rooms. The effect was dramatic. Strang achieved a speed of 111.86 miles per hour and set a five-mile record of 91.813 miles per hour. Carl was elated by their achievements. The $700,000 investment made by the Speedway investors, he thought, would be paid off in five years.[49]

The next big racing weekend proved him right. On May 27, 28 and 29, 1910, a total of 42 events, from 5 to 200 miles, were on the program. About 60,000 spectators paid admission, and no major accidents or injuries occurred to mar their enjoyment, except for a broken leg suffered by Herb Lytle.[50]

Carl believed that another way of raising revenue was to feature the new and different, and planned an "Aviation Week" beginning on June 13. Wilbur and Orville Wright, who toured the United States putting on exhibitions, were the featured attraction. Few attended on opening day, but a widely-publicized record-setting flight that day quickly raised attendance.

Walter Brookins flew a Wright biplane to an altitude of 4,384 feet, a world record. The next day there were more than one thousand spectators, and on Wednesday attendance mushroomed to 19,000.[51]

Attendance at the July 4th and Labor Day auto races was a disappointment. Carl began to think of changing the racing schedule to one 1,000-mile race or one 24-hour race. The idea for a 24-hour race was soon discarded. The manufacturers favored it because it would prove the durability of their automobiles, but Carl and his business associates knew that spectators would not be willing to spend 24 hours at the Speedway.[52] They decided on a 500-mile race with $25,000 in prizes, a race that could take place during the daylight hours and last no longer than their previous programs.[53]

In *75 Years of Racing*, Rich Taylor noted the importance of this decision.

> Carl Fisher was a lot better businessman, and a genius of a promoter. In 1910, he made two basic decisions that guaranteed that the Indianapolis Motor Speedway would be the most important race track in the world, and the Indianapolis 500 the most important single race.
>
> First, he made the unprecedented move of holding just one race each year, and that a grueling 500-miler. And then he made sure that he offered the richest purse in racing. In 1912, when he increased the total purse to $50,000 and the first prize to $20,000, the Indianapolis 500 became the highest paying sporting event in the world. His competitors thought he was crazy, but Fisher knew what he was doing.
>
> The huge purse and resulting media attention meant that the 500 took on a life of its own, over and above being one of the races that counted towards the AAA National Championship. Even before World War I, many American drivers and engineers thought of the rest of the AAA season as merely a warm-up for the 500. Others chose to skip the remaining races to concentrate solely on the Indianapolis International Sweepstakes. Among other things, this meant that many teams headquartered in Indianapolis year-round, which increased both the importance of the race and of the Speedway as a test track.

(I.M.S.)

*First trip around the Indianapolis Motor Speedway in May, 1909.
Carl G. Fisher, giving the press a hair-raising ride, is at the wheel
with W.S. Gilmore, managing editor of the* Detroit (Mich.) News, *then
a member of the staff of the* Indianapolis Star, *and other Indianapolis newspaper men who were on hand to see Fisher make the spin.*

Indianapolis immediately attracted the best cars, the best drivers and the newest innovations. Witness Ray Harroun's unusual
Marmon in the inaugural 1911 race. Car builders knew that
their latest technological advances would get the most attention if introduced amidst all the hoopla that surrounded the
500, drivers knew that a reputation could be made overnight
and passenger car manufacturers knew that having their name
painted on the side of the winning car was worth millions in free
publicity. Racing in the Indianapolis 500 International Sweepstakes became not only the pinnacle of a driver's career, but a
legitimate year-round business. And that was good for the drivers and teams, the fledgling American automobile industry, the
paying spectators who now flocked to see the best racing in the
country, and, of course, Carl Fisher and his partners, who made
a tidy profit on their original investment.[54]

To accommodate the huge crowd expected for the first
500, even more grandstands and bleacher sections were built

Carl Fisher's white Stoddard-Dayton. (I.M.S.)

in the spring of 1911. Racing teams were building new cars for the competition, with 46 cars entered. Wealthy Americans imported European cars to drive in the first Indianapolis 500. By mid-May, almost all of the outstanding drivers entered were making practice runs at the Speedway.

The day before the race, Carl planned another publicity-seeking event. Bob Burman was to make an attempt to break Barney Oldfield's speed record for one mile. Five thousand people were there to give Burman an ovation after they witnessed Burman's success in covering a mile in an average speed of 102.127 miles per hour.

A crowd of more than 80,000 poured into the Speedway on race day. Earlier in the day, the security force had to clear out 200 people who had climbed over the fence and hid under the bleachers and in the trees. Forty of the 46 entrants had qualified for the race by covering a quarter mile on the straightaway at 75 miles per hour. The night before, Carl had led them in a dress rehearsal of what was to become a tradition.

At 10 a.m. on race day, an aerial bomb explosion signaled the entrants to start their engines. To everyone's surprise, the race was started in a manner never before seen. Instead of the standing start which was used in earlier races, Carl led the entrants in a rolling start, driving a white 1911 Stoddard-Dayton serving as the pace car. The entrants were arranged in eight groups of five abreast behind him. At forty miles per hour, staying in formation, they followed Carl for one lap around the track. The start was another thrill for the crowd as Carl had to swerve his pace car off the track into the pit area in front of the roaring, smoking race cars when he crossed the line and the starter's flag fell.

Ironically, the first "500" was won by Ray Harroun, who had announced his retirement the year before after winning the 1910 AAA driving championship. Harroun, who drove for the Marmon factory, decided to participate after Howard Marmon told him he could share the driving with Cyrus Patschke. Important also was the large first-place purse and the prestige of winning this big race.

Harroun was almost disqualified before the race. He had designed a stream line racing car with a single seat. Other drivers had protested because, unlike the other drivers, he did not carry a riding mechanic to inform him of cars coming up from behind, creating a driving hazard, they claimed. Harroun quickly solved the problem; he welded a steel-framed mirror — the first automobile rearview mirror — to the cowling of his auto.[55]

Harroun had a strategy for winning the race, but not by superior speed. He had noticed during practice runs that cars driven higher than an average 75 miles per hour blew out tires and had to spend more time in the pit. Racing at no more than 75 miles per hour, he concluded, could win him the race. Finishing his race in six hours and 42 minutes, he claimed his victory, averaging 74.59 miles per hour.[56]

The success of the first "500" went beyond Carl's and the others' expectations. Carl promptly increased the prize money to $50,000, anticipating even more entrants the next year.[57] Except for temporary interruptions by two World Wars, the Indy 500 continued to be a major sports event. It survived a 1923 attempt by the state legislature to prohibit commercialized sports events on Memorial Day by a governor's veto.

The speedway had mixed success in fulfilling Carl's desire to build a track to test cars. Owner Eddie Rickenbacker in 1946 claimed that "approximately 70 percent of all the mechanical improvements that went into the private automobile were originated on the Indianapolis Speedway, or at least perfected there."[58] Indiana historian Howard H. Peckham disputes this as "pardonable exaggeration.... Early auto companies did use the speedway for testing their cars, on race day and other days, but, as they consolidated and grew bigger, they developed their own proving grounds and laboratories in the 1920s."[59] Pecknam also cites reasons why he thought Michigan, not Indiana, became the center of the automobile industry. "Manufacturing geniuses," as he calls Henry Ford, Walter Chrysler, the Dodge brothers, Billy Durant, and Alvan Macauley, had good business sense in addition to an ability to produce cars. "They understood the importance of a network of local dealers and knew the features in a car that would appeal to families."[60] Of the Indiana automakers, he names only Studebaker as concentrating on a family car, while others, such as Stutz, Duesenberg, Marmon, National and Premier, were more concerned with race cars in their early manufacturing days. "Speed meant little in a family car, since early roads would not permit it, and it was not the only measure of durability. Carl Fisher missed his guess there, but he brought fame to Indianapolis."[61]

Chapter 6

A Surprise Marriage

To the surprise of everyone, especially Gertrude Hassler, his fiancé, Carl Fisher quietly married Jane Watts on October 23, 1909, while the Speedway was being repaved.

Jane Watts was a blonde, pig-tailed 15-year-old school-girl; Carl was a 35-year-old prominent, successful business-man, his fortune estimated by Gertrude to be about $2,000,000 and his annual income at $800,000.[1] Carl had met Jane only that spring, although he had been the object of her idol worship since she saw him on October 30 of the previous year as he flew over Indianapolis in his white Stoddard-Dayton.

Carl was the catch of Indianapolis and unquestionably far more worldly-wise than his young bride, who described herself as a "sheltered 'mother's darling"[2] who had never even ridden in an automobile. "Fisher traveled in a fast crowd," according to Indiana historian John Bartlow Martin. "They drove to Dayton for week-end parties, they raced their cars along dusty country roads. He dressed well, drank well, and often beside him in his runabout sat a pretty girl in a choker collar and hat with sweeping brim."[3] There were always women," Polly Redford wrote in *Billion-Dollar Sandbar,* "whom he chased so cheerfully and so wholeheartedly that they never forgot him."[4] Apparently women found Carl almost irresist-ible. A sister of one of the girls to whom he had been engaged said that "Carl Fisher has the most kissable mouth I have

(IMS)

ever seen in my life."[5] Jane herself wrote of his "dark magnetism" and "strangely beautiful face."[6]

While Carl was still unaware of her existence, Jane Watts had been keeping a scrapbook of newspaper clippings about his exploits. With other members of a girls' club to which she belonged, Jane bicycled through Indianapolis, hoping to see Carl in his big white Stoddard-Dayton. She even hung around his automobile shop and the Columbia Restaurant where he lunched. He was, she thought, a "daring hero and champion."[7] And like her schoolmates, she appreciated the fact that Carl had given uniforms to their baseball team at Shortridge High School.

Unexpectedly, she saw him in person at the Canoe Club, where she had gone with her family to attend her first big party. Her brother Roy was embarrassed by her stopping cold and staring at Carl, and he urged her to move along while

John Philip Sousa's band played "Stars and Stripes Forever" in the background.[8] They did not meet that night, but were introduced shortly afterward by a friend, Harry Buschmann.

The unlikely relationship progressed rapidly. Carl frequently drove Jane to see the progress of the Speedway in his "fabulous white car with the black patent leather upholstery."[9] She wrote that she was "Too shy to notice then all that would later become so familiar: the careless white hat pushed back, buccaneer fashion, over a face perpetually wreathed in a dimpled smile, the broad shoulders in the first yellow polo coat I had ever seen, the fine strong hands — a racer's hands — on the wheel. Altogether I found Carl so dazzling that at first I could not look at him. This was the start of what to me was a fairy story...."[10] Sometimes she sat in the grandstand, watching the work on the track, embroidering guest towels for her hope chest. He had told her shortly after they met that he was going to marry her.

Her stepfather, James Buchanan Watts, was somewhat wary of the April-August relationship. A farm implement salesman, he had long admired Carl's accomplishments but frequently asked Jane: "What does a big man like Carl Fisher see in a kid like you?"[11] Her mother made no objection.

One incident suggested to Jane that there might be another woman in Carl's life. On June 5, the day of the great balloon race at the Speedway, a "young woman I had never seen before dashed down to the balloon and presented Carl with an enormous bouquet of American Beauty roses."[12] Carl scattered the roses to the spectators as the balloon took flight. Although only fifteen, Jane realized "I was not too young, however, to turn cold all over at the sight of this beautiful blonde young woman, as if I had an inkling of the fact that she was shortly to change my point of view about women — and men."[13] The beautiful blonde was Gertrude Hassler.

The summer passed quickly, with the flurry of finishing the Speedway and holding the opening events. Just as quickly, Carl informed Jane that they were to be married. "I've a Prest-O-Lite suit on in Los Angeles," he told her; "If we marry now, you can come on the trip. I'm tired of traveling alone. I've got to cut out this courting business and get back to work."[14] Jane was becoming accustomed to Carl's practical, rather than romantic, attitude. Instead of "honey" or "darling," his pet name for her was "wench," and rather than saying he loved her, he would tell her, "I wouldn't trade you for two skunks."[15]

It was to be a small, private home wedding. "Mr. Fisher ain't much for fuss and feathers, Ma'am,"[16] Galloway had informed Mrs. Watts. But at 6 a.m. on the wedding day, a German street band serenaded Jane under her window in the pouring rain. Wagon loads of flowers, potted plants, and potted trees and a total of three bridal bouquets arrived shortly after.[17]

Only Jane's family, Carl's mother, and Galloway attended the wedding. "Carl looked nervous and was flushed,"[18] Jane noted. Before October 23, Carl had seen Jane only in pigtails and homemade dresses; that day she wore her hair in an upsweep, and her blue wedding dress, trimmed in gold braid, had been made by the leading dressmaker in Indianapolis. Before the minister had finished the ceremony, Carl thrust the wedding ring at her and said, "Here take it! Good God, we must be married by this time!"[19]

The marriage was made public that same day by the *Indianapolis News*. Along with a photograph of the newly married couple, the newspaper printed the following:

> One of the surprises in Indianapolis today was the marriage of Carl G. Fisher and Miss Jane Watts, the daughter of Mr. and Mrs. J. B. Watts of 724 North Capitol Avenue, which was solemnized at noon at the Watts home. The Rev. Neil McPherson, pastor of the Tabernacle Baptist Church, officiated.
>
> Mr. and Mrs. Fisher left at 12:20 o'clock for Chicago and from there will, it is expected, go to California and for a trip through Mexico. The bride is well known in social circles of the city and Fisher has almost an international reputation as an automobilist and aeronaut. Fisher desired to steal a march on his friends by surprising them, and in a measure, he did it.[20]

Once on their honeymoon trip on a Chicago-bound train, Carl ripped off the gold braid, telling Jane, "That's the way I

INDIANAPOLIS NEWS, SATURDAY, OCTOBER 2

Carl G. Fisher Becomes a Benedict

MR. AND MRS. CARL G. FISHER.

One of the surprises in Indianapolis today was the marriage of Carl G. Fisher and Miss Jane Watts, the daughter of Mr. and Mrs. J. B. Watts, of 734 North Capitol avenue, which was solemnized at noon at the Watts home, the Rev. Neil McPherson, pastor of the Tabernacle Presbyterian church, officiating.

Mr. and Mrs. Fisher left at 12:20 o'clock for Chicago, and from there will, it is expected, go to California and for a trip through Mexico. The bride is well known

was a hitch when the marriage clerk informed Mr. Fisher that Miss Watts would have to sign the application for the marriage license.

This did not seem to disconcert Fisher and Moore. They left hurriedly and raced to the home of Miss Watts for her signature and then back again to the clerk's office. The ceremony was scheduled for 11 o'clock, but it was 11:20 before Mr. Fisher and Moore had completed the arrangements. Immediately after the ceremony they went to the union station. The only persons present at the ceremony

(I.S.L.)

like my woman, little wench, unadorned the way God made her."[21] Giving her a copy of the *Ladies' Home Journal,* he went to see a man about a boat, leaving Jane to cry herself to sleep. On her wedding day, it was clear that "There would always be men, business, big money and big deals. They came first."[22]

Carl was back when she awoke, telling her he was sorry, but he had asked boat builder Clement C. Avery to be aboard the train to discuss building them a honeymoon yacht. The yacht was to be ready when they returned from California. Jane described her honeymoon as being "like the last lap of a race. We rushed to California and once in Los Angeles, Carl vanished into the law courts. I always said I spent my honeymoon with his brother Earle.... I had no concept of Carl's industrial genius, nor his financial resources."[23]

Waiting for them on their return were piles of wedding presents. Upon opening one gift, Jane discovered it was actually a gift for Carl from Gertrude Hassler, the enclosed note vowing "eternal passion." Carl's only reaction was, "You shouldn't open things that don't have your name on them, honey."[24]

Carl had to break the news of his marriage to Gertrude, a singer. He asked Gertrude to come to his office, where he called her "dear" and told her he was married. He gave her some money to lighten the blow.[25] Gertrude was not mollified. Estimating his fortune at two million dollars and his annual income as eight hundred thousand dollars, she asked for a settlement of half a million dollars in a breach-of-promise suit that came to trial three years later.[26] Headlines in the *Indianapolis Star* read: "Singer Asks Half-Million: Gertrude W. Hassler, concert singer, charges capitalist with breach of promise." The story was accompanied by a photograph of Gertrude wearing a large hat.

Carl G. Fisher, sportsman, promoter, capitalist, and president of Prest-O-Lite Company was sued in Superior Court, Room 1, yesterday for $500,000 in damages by Gertrude W. Hassler, soloist, who charges breach of promise to marry. In 1900, she says she met Mr. Fisher and that for nine years he paid her constant attention and promised repeatedly to marry her. Mr. Fisher's marriage to another woman was a painful surprise to her the plaintiff says, and she adds that she lost not only her prospects of sharing in the fortune Mr. Fisher has accumulated but her health has been impaired.

The complaint charged that when the plaintiff met Mr. Fisher she was wearing a pair of velvet slippers and that the defendant pleaded for one of them declaring that he not only had fallen in love with the plaintiff, but also with the slippers. The slipper was given to him and he kept it in his room for the entire nine years, the plaintiff says.

During their acquaintance Mr. Fisher is alleged to have called on the plaintiff daily, when she was here and to have written and telegraphed to her daily when she was away on concert tours. When they became acquainted the plaintiff says Mr.

Fisher was a poor man selling automobiles. He would bring prospective customers to her home and she charges introduce her as "his best and only girl" and induce her to sing to them, in that way, she alleges, and assisted him in building up his business.[27]

Gertrude established Carl's romantic promises to her by recounting that he had

promised her a winter home in the South and a summer home in the North. "Then we will build us a castle up in the mountains, and we will have our ponies, our saddle horses, our automobiles, our boats, our dogs and guns, a good piano, and you can sing and I will lie down before the fireplace and listen...and then we will go down into old age, happy and joyful, loving each other until the grave."[28]

Gertrude asked for a share of Prest-O-Lite because

practically every day he asked her advice about the business; and she gave him advice, worked with him, practically wrote all his advertisements for various magazines advertising said business and in fact did as much of the work as defendant did himself; he made her his memory; he would give her a dozen things in one night to remember so that he would not forget them the same day; and said business prospered from the start, and by reason of said business in a few short years, and by reason with the help and advice and labor of this plaintiff with this defendant, said business so increased and prospered.[29]

The jury found some merit in her suit and awarded Gertrude $55,000, but she eventually settled for $25,000. Carl attempted to use the $25,000 as a business expense on his income tax but was unsuccessful.[30] Jane was devastated by the scandal of the trial and accused Carl of not loving her. His assurances that he did placated her, and she was convinced that he was sincere.

The couple's first home was a large first-floor apartment on Capitol Avenue that had been furnished by Galloway while they were on their honeymoon. "Bachelor quarters" was Jane's description of it, as Galloway had furnished it to suit Carl's taste. Carl particularly liked a leather pillow embroidered with the motto: "A woman is only a woman, but a good cigar is a smoke." Their bedroom contained a huge, department-store-size revolving rack for Carl's many suits and overcoats. Above the bed were portraits of Carl's heroes, Abraham Lincoln and Napoleon, and a piece of sandpaper which Carl used to strike matches. A spittoon and a jar of salted peanuts were at bedside. The entire household shared in shelling, roasting, and salting the 100-pound bags of peanuts he brought home so that jars of salted peanuts would be available throughout the house. "Practicability," Carl informed Jane, was what he wanted in a home, and that meant spittoons and hooks to hang things on. He had not forgotten her — a large, glass-fronted player piano was the surprise gift she found there.[31]

In November, Carl planned a trip to Florida on the *Eph*, their newly-completed honeymoon yacht, and Jane learned more about what she called Carl's "lusty and incomprehensible personality."[32] Carl had invited Harry Buschmann, the friend who had introduced them; John H. Levi, the engineer from Seabury Shipyard who had brought the *Eph* from New York; and, of course, Galloway. But Jane was not invited. "There won't be any room for a woman on such a little boat. among so many men,"[33] Carl explained.

Jane had no intention of staying home; she informed Carl that the boat had been purchased for their honeymoon and she intended to be on it. The men's protests that she would be too concerned about clothing and baths and food did not dissuade her. She ordered four identical skirts and twelve identical blouses so that she could change often and look fresh. Because the bathtub was being used as a coal bin, she would have to bathe in cold river water.

Fifteen-year-old Jane proved a match for the men. To test her mettle, she was forced to try a chew of tobacco and bite the head off a fish, and they began to accept her as one of them, a "high-powered, hard-swearing and lovable crew."[34] She excused Carl's initial reluctance to take her along by explaining that "It was simply that Carl was a bachelor almost 40 years old, and was accustomed to being with men."[35]

On Christmas Eve they arrived at the port of New Orleans. Jane and Galloway shopped for a tree, trimmings, and presents, and the other three went off on their own — and didn't return. Jane and Galloway finally retired to their quarters.

When the trio came back the next day, Carl had an explanation for their long absence: the proprietor of a jewelry store where Carl intended to buy Jane a gold bracelet had thought they were hoodlums and called the police. After they were released, the three got into a "football" game, their pigskin a roast pig John Levi had bought for Jane. The police again took them into custody. Jane was skeptical, suspecting alcohol as playing a part in their escapade. Weeping, she told Carl, "I had never expected to marry a drunkard." But even so, the 15-year-old thought "Carl and his friends were wonderful and important personages in my young eyes, and

Carl Fisher with Jane in lap. (HASF)

I could not understand why they wanted to play like a bunch of noisy little boys."[36]

Jane might have been more upset if she had heard the version of their activities as was recounted by one of the men to Polly Redford, Miami Beach historian. The three, Redford wrote, "went ashore to see where the action was. They found it in one of the pleasure palaces for which New Orleans has long been famous, and did not return until Christmas morning when, still full of holiday spirits, they presented Jane with a roast pig as a peace offering. The point of the story, however... was that when the madam opened her door on Christmas Eve and saw who it was, she cried out, 'Why, hello there, Carl! Gee, it's great to see you!'"[37]

A more serious situation presented itself soon afterward. According to Jane, a hurricane beached the yacht in Mobile Bay. Howard Kleinberg, author of *Miami Beach,* a comprehensive history of Miami Beach, disputes Jane's version. "Weather bureau records show no hurricane activity in December 1909. Instead, the Deep South suffered an extreme cold wave in the period between Christmas and New Year's, hardly grist for a hurricane. Levi's version is considerably more understated. He said they ran onto a sandbar, spent the night, Carl and Jane then got off the vessel, and left John to see matters through, including necessary repairs."[38] Carl decided to ship the boat back by train, but the yacht's size rendered that plan impossible. John Levi volunteered to sail it back, and Carl and Jane settled on meeting him in Jacksonville.

Two weeks later they received a telegram: "Arrived safely. Miami pretty little town. Why not meet me here instead of Jacksonville."[39]

Carl and Jane stayed in Miami for a week and were so "enchanted with the jasmine-scented Miami moonlight and the soft warm air"[40] that Carl negotiated to buy two lots on Biscayne Bay for a winter home. He withdrew from the deal when the seller raised the price a thousand dollars overnight.

Back home in Indianapolis, Jane was determined to excel in her role as wife and hostess of one of the city's most prominent citizens. Carl was not satisfied with their rented apartment. He thought it was too small and bought the house to remodel it. Carl wanted large rooms, large furniture, and large fireplaces "big enough for a man to walk into and turn around."[41] Except for the white he preferred as the color of his cars and his hats, he wanted everything painted yellow, like sunshine.[42]

Just as the *Eph* was the first in a series of yachts, the house in Indianapolis was the first of several homes, with the two keeping suitcases always packed, ready to shuttle from one to another. There were seven homes in five years, including a house in St. Joseph, Michigan; a house in Miami; and Blossom Heath, an old homestead on the northwest side of Indianapolis. Carl had a house built for them in Detroit, right on the river, so that he could watch boats being built. They moved out of that house the day after they moved in. The smoke from the passing boats had covered them with soot as they sat on the porch to enjoy the view.[43]

Blossom Heath, their primary home, was a showplace. Its 60-foot living room featured Oriental rugs, a billiard table, and a piano, with a huge fireplace where logs burned all day long. "What use is a fireplace without a fire?"[44] Carl said. The twelve bedrooms allowed for plenty of guests, with the Fishers accommodating friends and family, especially on speedway race days. There was also a spacious glass-enclosed porch. It had a large stone fireplace, along with couches, writing desks, and a Victrola. A button on the porch activated a player piano on the sleeping porch above.

A separate house was built for Carl's mother. Also on the estate were extensive gardens, stables for riding horses and later polo ponies, a greenhouse, and a glass-enclosed tennis court so that they could play in the rain. Carl had a platform built on the sidelines so that his friend, poet John Whitcomb Riley, could watch. There was even a small swimming pool for the dogs and a honeybear.

Carl sent Jane to Grand Rapids to buy furniture for their homes. He gave her an unlimited budget with only one stipulation: everything must be large, "No sissy furniture a man won't dare sit on."[45]

Jane's photo taken July 15, 1915. (I.S.N.)

Blossom Heath was featured in an Indianapolis Sunday newspaper article on February 2, 1913. Betty Blythe wrote, "I think that what pleases me most is its simple dignity. There is absolutely no suggestion of the ornate, no display of highly polished wood, no gingerbread work apparent, as to either house or furnishings." The greenhouse, she noted, "… is one of Mr. Fisher's pet fads, and it serves a utilitarian purpose in addition to supplying the house with beautiful flowers the

71

year round. Hot house delicacies have been appearing on the family table regularly all year."[46] Blythe could find nothing to criticize.

Jim Allison and Frank Wheeler, Carl's Speedway partners, were his neighbors on Cold Spring Road. Unlike Carl, who had renovated and added to existing buildings, Allison built his estate on 64 acres, with greenhouses, five spring-fed lakes, a gardener's cottage, and a building that housed the power plant, coach house, and servants' quarters with a tunnel connecting it to the mansion.[47] In the 1960's, Marian College acquired the three contiguous estates, creating a 114-acre campus.

At Blossom Heath, Jane was very sensitive to her position as the bride of the "bachelor prize"[48] of Indianapolis. Many of the "society" families had viewed Carl as a matrimonial prospect. Jane knew she was not of their rank and was determined to be a hostess above reproach. Still a teenager, she pleased Carl when she learned to ride horseback and studied French and the manners, dress, and houses of women she admired. She promoted Galloway from factotum to butler. Carl really did not understand her concerns as he didn't much like "society" anyway. When early in their marriage she cried over the fact that she had worn a simple dress to an elegant party where the other women wore Paris gowns, he thought that her being prettier than the others was more important than any dress she wore.[49] In his own dress, Carl was very particular. He valued comfort and simplicity above all, wearing well-made sports clothes or business suits with perforated patent leather shoes made to order. His polo coats were imported from England.[50]

Carl was a social maverick. He liked to socialize, but only at his own home. To Carl, parties with their social gossip and banter were a waste of time. The invitations he accepted were mostly business, and his friends understood that he preferred to entertain them. Many people who met Carl found it difficult to believe that his formal education had ended by the sixth-grade. Self-educated, Carl could speak with authority on almost any subject. But at times, his actions would make even his friends wonder. At a relaxed dinner party, he picked up a cut-glass goblet that one of the guests had given them as a wedding present and threw it out the window at a cat fight. He was proud that he hit his target, oblivious to the fact that he had broken the prized goblet.[51]

Jane's knowledge of her husband in those first years of marriage had grown tremendously. She had quickly become aware of his swearing and his spitting and his strong cigars. One day she had tried to get him to reform his swearing by swearing herself all day, shocking Carl, but any reform lasted only one week. Most of all, she knew he lived in, and preferred, a man's world. "He was happiest with his own lustily humorous friends with whom he could organize tennis matches, stage the races in which he ran backwards and the others forward, wrestle and play pranks and behave like a boy. But he loved books and was well read and he liked his literary friends. Booth Tarkington came often, and so did Elbert Hubbard."[52]

She was more naive about Carl and women: "I did not know in those days that such creatures as 'other women' existed. Carl liked everyone; he liked women, and I knew he loved me, but his best and happiest hours were spent with men."[53] Jane would eventually learn that there would be "other women," and the marriage would end. But years after they parted, she wrote, "I divorced. I married again and again. I couldn't stay married to them because life was just too drab. It was too humdrum. You see, living with Carl Fisher was like living in a circus; there was something going on — something exciting going on — every minute of the day. Sometimes it was very good; sometimes it was very bad. Still, it was living. It was excitement, aliveness, that I never found again."[54]

Chapter 7

A Road Across the U.S.A.

Carl's European travels had taught him that not only European cars, but also their roads, were superior to those in America. European roads were mostly hard-surfaced. Carl loved to drive, but as his wife Jane noted, "...there was little pleasure when the motorist spent half his travel time bogged down in mud or changing tires split by the rocks and roots that made traps of every roadway. Such misadventures could send Carl into streaks of cussing...."[1] He began to dream of a hard-surfaced road across the United States that would be marked for travelers and carry traffic in all kinds of weather.

Carl knew well the deplorable condition of his county's — and the rest of the country's — rural roads. One of Carl's touring cars had more than 100,000 miles on its odometer, according to his friend George Denny.[2] One day when he was driving with Denny, they came across a road being repaired. As Denny told it, "...we came across a bad stretch in Henry County. Men and teams were dumping gravel in piles in the center of the road. Fisher stopped his car and remonstrated with the foreman, pointing out to him that he was using twice as much material as was needed and was failing to properly spread the gravel. About all we could get out of the foreman was that was the way the supervisor told him to do it. Apparently his observation as to this particular work was correct, for on our return to Indianapolis that night we bumped into a particularly high pile of gravel and blew out a front tire."[3]

This was an example of the "wasteful economy"[4] the county practiced and Carl and his business friends objected to — the practice of building ordinary rock roads that cost about $3,000 per mile and lasted only three years.

According to the American Road Congress, maintaining heavily-traveled rock roads cost $600 to $1,000 a year per mile.[5] Paved roads cost $10,000 per mile, but lasted 20 years. The first rural concrete road had been paved in 1908 in Wayne County, Michigan, a few miles from Henry Ford's office in Detroit; maintenance costs were only $25 annually. Freighting costs were also substantially cheaper. Moving one ton of freight over a paved road cost only 1 to 8¢ per mile, as opposed to 18 to 35¢ over a rock road.[6]

Carl's own Marion County Indiana roads were little different from roads in the rest of the U.S. Of the 382 miles of "allegedly improved"[7] roads in Marion County, only a few miles were considered in good condition. In 1912, practically all of the paved roads in the entire country were within cities' corporate limits. The more than 2,000,000 miles of rural roads were unmarked and unconnected, used mostly as farm-to-market roads. Some were graded and had been topped with gravel or macadam, but most were unimproved dirt roads.[8]

Cities opposed taxing their inhabitants to build roads for "city dudes to run their gas buggies over."[9] Driving was considered an "idle sport."[10] Only 28 of the 48 state governments had spent any money on road construction or maintenance. There was no federal highway system. Travelers who wanted to go any distance took the trains, which in 1900 recorded 16,038,000,000 passenger miles.[11]

Carl and his business associates had already spent their own money on a mile and a half of the Crawfordsville pike from the Emrichsville bridge to the Speedway, which Denny said was "the best stretch of county road in Marion County."[12] They also maintained other stretches of the road and had spent $30,000 in building a driveway on the Myers Road on the west side of Riverside Park. Carl had even purchased an Indianapolis city license for his car — not required because he lived outside the city — because the funds were used to maintain the city streets.[13]

In 1912, Indianapolis businessmen requested that the Marion County commissioners end the practice of "wasteful economy." When the commissioners ignored the request and vetoed a request for more money for highway maintenance, Carl decided to run for, and was elected, a county commissioner on the Progressive Party ticket. He promised to donate the $2,500 salary plus $2,500 of his own money to be used to build better roads. The *Indianapolis Star* of October 24, 1912, reported that "In addition to the $5,000, the county will get, in the person of Mr. Fisher himself, the services of one of the nation's foremost experts on road construction."[14]

"It is part of Fisher's creed to take the road problem as far as possible out of politics," said Denny. "He maintains that the building of highways requires as much centralization and uniformity as the administration of our school system."

"'What,' Carl asked, 'if every school township were to try to fix its own course on its own system of education? The whole business would be in confusion.'"[15]

Carl's platform, according to the *Star*, was:

Stop wasteful economy.
Make every penny count.
Good roads are cheaper than poor ones.
A little money wisely expended goes further than all the thousands thrown annually into the mud holes.[16]

But Carl's vision of good roads extended far beyond Marion County. To his friend Jim Allison he had first confided his dream of a transcontinental highway. "The automobile industry should be willing to finance a road across the country; think what it would do for the American automobile,"[17] Carl said.

Carl often told a story that illustrated his frustration with the driving conditions of his time:

Three of us drove out nine miles from Indianapolis and being delayed, were overtaken by darkness on the return trip.

To complicate matters, it began to rain pretty hard, and you know automobiles didn't have any tops on them in those days, so we all three got pretty wet.

We guessed our way along as well as we could, until we came to a place where the road forked three ways. It was black as the inside of your pocket. We couldn't see any light from the city, and none of us could remember which of the three roads we had followed in driving out; if, indeed, we had come that way at all.

So we stopped and held a consultation. Presently, by the light of our headlamps, reflected up in the rain, one of us thought he saw a sign on a pole. It was too high up to read and we had no means of throwing a light on it, so there was nothing to be done but climb the pole in the wet and darkness to see if we could make out some road direction on the sign.

We matched to see who should climb. I lost. I was halfway up the pole when I remembered that my matches were inside my overcoat and I couldn't reach them. So down I had to come, dig out the matches, put them in my hat, and climb up again.

Eventually, by hard climbing, I got up to the sign. I scratched a match and before the wind blew it out I read the sign. It said: "Chew Battle-Ax Plug."[18]

This experience, Carl said, helped spur him into a campaign to build the first U.S. transcontinental highway. Almost a decade had passed since that rainy night, but very little road improvement had taken place in the interim. Around the fire at Blossom Heath, Carl gathered his friends in the automotive industry to urge and argue them into supporting his new project. "The automobile won't get anywhere until it has good roads to run on," he told them. "Why can't we build a highway across the continent from New York to San Francisco?"[19]

Carl meant that "we" literally. He had no faith in the political system's ability to accomplish the task. If there was to be such a road, the automobile industry, which had the highest stake in the venture, would have to build it.

From his business offices in the Prest-O-Lite factory, Carl began an intensive letter-writing campaign to obtain support from industry leaders and, most importantly, Henry Ford. Ford's own advertisements two years before had said that

Henry Ford "stands out, independent and alone, clear and strong, as the most dominant factor in the automobile industry of today."[20] In 1912, he was still the dominant factor. Three-fourths of the automobiles being produced were Fords.[21] Carl knew that if Ford were to support the highway, its success would be assured. Even the *Ford Times,* the company magazine, was a strong advocate of good roads.[22]

In a four-page letter to Ford on September 6, 1912, Carl carefully outlined his plans for the construction and financing of the highway:

My dear Sir:

Mr. Allison and the writer have for sometime been working on a plan to build a National Rock Highway from New York City continuous to San Francisco.

We think we have the details of this plan now in such shape that it can be taken up with a few of the larger manufacturers, like yourself, and you will please note that your decision in this matter may either complete the plans or spoil them.

Our idea is to collect $1/3$ of 1% each year for three years, or $1/5$ of 1% each year for five years. This question to be decided by a committee of those interested. This amount to be taken from the gross receipts of all automobile manufacturers and dealers of automobiles and automobile sundries and accessories, and with these receipts, which if all manufacturers enter into this game — as it now appears they will — we will have a fund considerably in excess of $10,000,000.00.

Our plan is to spend this entire amount, or all moneys received, for actual purchase of material for the road, we to do absolutely no construction work of any kind ourselves, but to make contract with the various States and Counties thru which this road will pass whereby they agree to put the material which this fund furnishes on the road as per specifications prepared and given to us by the Government Engineers, without charge to us.

The selection of the route is to be left entirely with the National Committee, to be selected later.

The assessments on signed agreements are to be made payable to a Trust Company hereafter selected, which will furnish bond to our Association for all moneys which they collect. None of the moneys are to be spent until the entire subscription of at least $10,000,000.00 will be guaranteed. If, for any reason, this plan should fall thru the moneys are to be returned to those having made payment with 3% interest on the same.

Mr. Allison and the writer propose to pay the expenses incidental to the proportion of this plan up to a point where it is either a success or a failure.

It is part of the plan that all subscriptions be signed and closed up before January first, 1913 and the work be completed by May first, 1915, so that a corps of 25,000 automobiles can be taken over this road to the opening of the Panama Canal Exposition in San Francisco either in May or June, 1915.

It is a part of our plan that we enlist the cooperation of all automobile owners in the United States to the extent of a membership, which will be of two classes — a $5.00 membership, and a $100.00 membership, for which we issue a National Highway button. It is also a part of our plan to have large 12" window bronze metals cast, one of which will be issued to each dealer who contributes a total of 1% to the fund.

A fund of $10,000,000 will give us $5,000 per mile to spend on the road in material. Since the material and the building of the road represents only from 30 to 50% of the cost of the road we should have no trouble to receive for our $10,000,000 — all cash — a $25,000,000 road.

Practically every manufacturer in Indianapolis has agreed to this plan and our guarantees from this city will run considerable in excess of $300,000.

It has been suggested that we could cooperate with the Lincoln Memorial Fund, which already has $6,000,000 appropriated and which it might be possible for us to secure to assist in the building of this road. However, this is a suggestion that does not entirely meet with the writer's approval. I am of the opinion that the automobile people can build and present to the automobile users of the United States this road without any outside assistance, and can be handled by the large automobile men in the same way they handle their business affairs, and the road will be finished and pushed thru without delay and delivered on time; where if we attempt to mix up with government appropriations or if politics is allowed in any way to creep into the proposition, there will be numerous delays and wrangles and possibly graft.

Our plan of purchasing the material only with our money and delivering it to the State and Counties who sign contract under government inspection, puts us in an ideal position to receive one hundred cents on the dollar for every dollar we spend, and it is a certain thing that there will be so much competition to secure this road that we can make very splendid terms with a great many states.

We will be ready in Indianapolis, next week, to hold a meeting and sign up our subscriptions as stated. We then want to bring the plan to you, for your consideration.

We have had a great many good business men and financiers look into the plan and they cannot find any objection to same.

Kindly let me hear from you by return mail.

Yours very truly,

P.S. For your information I wish to give you the following figures:

Some of the best rock roads in Northern Indiana and Northern Ohio, 9' wide, 12" thick of rock with 2" of screening, cost for materials only $1,750.00.

Labor to complete this road, which consists of rolling, sprinkling and oiling, brings the total cost to $4,100.00. The contractor's profit is usually $800. to $1,000 per mile.

If any one of the three routes contemplated are selected there is now some good road which includes the paved streets thru the cities and good mecadamized [sic] roads in small sections for more than a thousand miles of road which will only need minor attention and oiling.

We believe that the Oil Companies will agree to oil this road for us without charge, and after the plan is once started it will become so enormous that all manufacturers of parts and accessories, etc., will be so sompelled [sic] to come in and contribute their share.

Please let me hear from you and consider this letter entirely confidential as we do not want details to get out until we are ready for our big announcement.

C.G.F.[23]

The "big announcement" of the drive for the "Coast-to-Coast Rock Highway," as Carl called it, was to be made to leading businessmen in Indianapolis. They received a printed invitation: "You are requested to attend a dinner given by Carl G. Fisher and James A. Allison at the German House on Tuesday evening, September 10, 1912. 7 o'clock."[24]

To the gathering Carl made his formal proposal. Telling them that the estimated cost for such a highway was ten million dollars, he said he would seek pledges from automobile manufacturers, jobbers, dealers, producers of automobile accessories, and all of their suppliers. He explained the financing as he did in his letter to Henry Ford.[25] All of the money pledged would be used for the road; Carl and Jim Allison would pay all preliminary expenses themselves. "It can be done," Carl said. "Let's build it before we are too old to enjoy it."[26] This statement became the slogan that was printed on the Coast-to-Coast highway stationery.

The response to the letters and the plans announced at the dinner was overwhelming. More than $300,000.00 was pledged at the dinner.[27] Newspapers and magazines all over the U.S. supported the road in articles and editorials. Slogans became popular: "Good Roads for America," "Tightening the Union," and the lasting "See America First."[28] Frank Seiberling, president of the Goodyear Tire and Rubber Company, pledged $300,000.00 without even conferring with the Board of Directors. The day after receiving this pledge, Carl telegraphed other prospective contributors, telling them about the Goodyear pledge and asking them to speed up their own pledges.[29]

Carl was invited to address the American Automobile Association at their annual meeting in New York. "Someday," wrote A.G. Batchelder, AAA secretary, "there will be erected to you one of the finest pieces of statuary obtainable, signifying that you were the man who deserved credit for giving America its first transcontinental road."

"Dear Batch," Carl replied. "I am not much on statuary — and right now I think it a good time to pull out personally and take away from our possible subscribers the idea that this road plan is mine. If any particular noise is made for any particular person or small clique of persons, this plan is going to suffer."[30]

In thirty days, a million dollars had been pledged. Carl's personal requests for support now went only to people he knew well or others who were familiar with the project. He set up a separate office, where his secretary sent out letters signed "Coast-to-Coast Highway, Temporary Committee, Will

J. Dobyns." Pledges were coming in at the rate of $10,000.00 a day.[31]

But the man whose support he most wanted and needed remained elusive. Henry Ford had been in Europe when the letter was sent; Carl's letter was not acknowledged for nearly two weeks. In the meantime, Carl enlisted a host of prominent friends to try to persuade Ford to join in.

One friend, identified only by his initials, "HOS," knew Ford well enough to address him as "Dear Henry." He wrote Ford that "...I think you will agree that if the automobile manufacturers do not take a step of this kind, good roads in America will be many years in the future as compared to the possible results under some such arrangement as this letter outlines.

"I understand that Carl will be in Detroit sometime this week, and he told me that he would call on you while there.

"I cannot but believe that the plan will impress you favorably."[32]

James Couzens, secretary/treasurer of the Ford Motor Company, replied to Carl on September 18. Couzens said that the response to Carl's letter was "pending our having a Directors' meeting, at which time we will be very glad to take up the matter of the contents of your letter.

"Frankly, however, the writer is not very favorably disposed to the plan, because as long as private interests are willing to build good roads for the general public, the general public will not be very interested in building good roads for itself. I believe in spending money to educate the public to the necessity of building good roads, and let everybody contribute their share in proper taxes. Most people will not work if they can get a living without it, and I believe the same can be said in respect to most any public undertaking that is done by private interests.

"However, I will put the matter up, as stated, to our Board of Directors and as soon as we have had a meeting, which will possibly be some time next month, however, we will let you know the attitude of the Directors."[33]

The tenor of Couzens' letter did not bode well, even though

the Board of Directors had not yet met. On September 24, Carl wrote to President William H. Taft for help.

Sir:

As perhaps you have heard, there is on foot, among many elements of the automobile industry, a plan to build a magnificent national highway, from New York to San Francisco, and present it to the people of the United States.

The plan is to get a fund of ten million dollars by subscription from automobile manufacturers, dealers and private owners, and use this fund for the purpose of road making materials. The material so purchased is to be furnished to the counties through which the road runs, and the counties thus favored must agree to do the work of construction.

The project is but ten days old. Already over one million dollars has been pledged — over $300,000 in Indianapolis alone.

While it is our purpose to build this American "Appian Way" without asking any financial assistance whatever from National or State Governments, we do naturally want the endorsement and cooperation of the United States Government wherever it may be had. The assistance of U.S. engineers in preparing specifications, inspecting construction, etc., will be very important.

One of the most important factors in the automobile industry is Mr. Henry Ford, of the Ford Automobile Company, of Detroit, Michigan. Three-fourths of all automobiles now in use in the United States are Ford cars. Naturally, many manufacturers are waiting to see what Mr. Ford will do. And Mr. Ford is waiting to see what public and governmental interest there is in this project.

The importance of this one splendid highway alone to American agriculture and commerce needs little explanation. But when viewed in its larger aspect as a stimulus of ending highways, both tributary to this one road and elsewhere throughout the country, its importance cannot be overestimated. Good roads agitation had been plentiful. Here is a definite plan to stop agitating and start building.

A letter from you to Mr. Ford, commending this Ocean-to-Ocean Highway and voicing the interest of the United States Government in its success, will, we believe, have great influence with Mr. Ford and inspire him to take the active, leading part in this great project which he is at present considering. We trust you can, in all good conscience, lend your endorsement, and that you will be able to assure Mr. Ford that the

Government of the United States will be glad to aid in the construction of this great national highway in any manner permitted under the law.

We feel confident, of course, that the United States Government will take sufficient interest in this Ocean-to-Ocean Highway as soon as its building is an assured fact.

But just at this time, Mr. Ford's interest in the project is of great importance to its prompt and easy accomplishment, for with Mr. Ford enlisted, we believe the necessary fund can easily be raised in thirty days.

Anything you can consistently say to Mr. Ford to arouse his interest will be of material assistance.

Respectfully yours,[34]

Carl also applied to Vice President Charles Warren Fairbanks, Senator Albert J. Beveridge, Thomas A. Edison, and others to try to obtain Mr. Ford's approval. Vice President Fairbanks sent Carl a copy of his letter to Ford, telling him that if Carl didn't think that it "was strong enough, he would gladly supplement it."[35]

Elbert Hubbard, publisher of the *Fra* and the *Philistine*, was told that "A letter from you to Henry Ford will, I know, carry considerable influence... As you know, Mr. Hubbard, the highways of America are built chiefly of politics, whereas the proper material is crushed rock, or concrete. We believe one magnificent highway of this kind, in actual existence, will stimulate as nothing else could the building of enduring highways everywhere that will not only be a credit to the American people but that will also mean much to American agriculture and American commerce. Will you pitch in and help?"[36]

Hubbard was eager to help. He went to Blossom Heath to see Carl and discuss the highway and was the first prominent writer to support the highway.

Carl began to publish an "Ocean-to-Ocean Highway" bulletin with news of the progress being made. The first edition, dated September 19, boasted of $310,000 in pledges, with the Hoosier Club of Indianapolis subscribing $2,000. Carl's Progressive Party had endorsed the highway and pledged that its candidates would give it "active support." A prominent

Indianapolis minister had based his Sunday sermon on the merits of the highway.[37]

Carl finally decided that a face-to-face meeting with Ford was necessary. He went to Detroit, but when he asked for Mr. Ford at the Ford factory, he was told that Ford was at the State Fair.

According to the Lincoln Highway Association (which notes that this story is apocryphal), "He found the manufacturer in the livestock exhibit, studiously observing the pigs, and while both leaned their arms on the top rail of the pig-pens, dark, magnetic Fisher convinced lank, conservative Ford that the plan was righteous and worthy of support."

"'Come to my office tomorrow and bring your paper, and I will sign up,' the story quotes Ford."[38]

Jubilant, Carl gave a celebratory dinner that night, and went to Ford's office the next day. There, the bubble burst. Ford's secretary told him that Mr. Ford had changed his mind.[39]

The magnate's treatment of Carl was not out of character. That same month, while Ford was on his first visit to Europe, some of his most trusted subordinates had prepared a surprise: a new model, longer and lower than the Model T. Ford's reaction was shocking. According to an eyewitness, "He had his hands in his pockets and he walked around that car three or four times, looking at it very closely. It was a four-door job, and the top was down. Finally he got to the left-hand side of that car that was facing me, and he takes his hands out, gets hold of the door, and bang! He ripped the door right off! God! How the man done it, I don't know.

"He jumped in there, and bang goes the other door. Bang goes the windshield. He jumps over the back seat and starts pounding on the top. He rips the top with the heel of his shoe. He wrecked the car as much as he could."[40]

Needless to say, no one else in the company dared to question Ford's ideas on design. He had, after all, proven already to the world that his ideas had made the Ford Company the most profitable in the U.S. From October 1, 1908, when the Ford Model T was introduced at a price of $950, the price had been reduced regularly because the car remained substantially the same from year to year. By 1914, the Model T price had fallen to $440. By then, its nearest competitor cost almost twice as much. Ford's car sold for cash, and by 1914, there were over 59,000 unfilled orders each month.[41]

Besides the obvious price advantage, the Model T was not as adversely affected by bad roads as were its more expensive, heavier competitors. It was the farmers who lived on the dirt roads who most needed such a car. "The Model T might have been made for the farmer. Where the back roads and swamps of the farm states were the undoing of other cars, they made the Model T. Severely functional in its appearance, the car would lurch through mud, ford streams, and plough through snow, attributes which found the greatest favor on the farm."[42] A Ford advertisement boasted that the body could be removed from the chassis by unloosening six bolts.

Even European car makers paid homage to Ford. A British trade delegate who visited Detroit in 1913 said, "Henry Ford has shown us how to make motor cars better than any other man in the world. We dream of him at night. Had it not been for Henry Ford we would never have begun the making of motor cars in England."[43] The manager of Germany's Benz Company said, "The Ford Plant is the most remarkable in the world; it is the very best in equipment and method."[44]

Finally, on October 25, James Couzens sent Carl the Ford Company's Board of Directors' official reply to his request:

A Meeting of our Directors was held yesterday, and all of your letters and telegrams in connection therewith were presented to the Directors at this meeting, and a resolution was unanimously passed declining to participate in this plan for several reasons: Principal among them being that we do not believe in building roads by private subscription, and secondly we believe it is better to spend our money in making the price of the cars low, as this will have the beneficial effect of putting more cars in use, and the more cars there are in use, the greater demand there will be for the government building Good Roads.

We, therefore, under the circumstances cannot participate in this plan of yours.[45]

Although this was a severe setback, Carl tenaciously continued to try to persuade Ford to support the highway. On November 29, he wrote him again:

My dear Mr. Ford:

The Ocean-to-Ocean Highway plans are going ahead steadily. Not as fast as they would have gone if you had seen fit to come in with us.

I am in hopes that you will yet change your mind and give us a lift. The whole country expects you to do this for the road, and I am sure that some of these days you will be with us.

I wish to call your attention to a very fine article written by Elbert Hubbard in the December issue of the *Fra* magazine. I think this article expresses to you better than I possibly could just what is expected of the largest automobile manufacturer in the world.[46]

The letter did not have the desired effect.

The $10,000,000 goal that Carl had hoped to reach by January 1, 1913, was not achieved. On February 7, 1913, he made yet another attempt to persuade Ford.

My dear Mr. Ford:

You are no doubt aware that we recently secured the cooperation of the Packard Company, with their donation of one percent, which gives us one hundred fifty thousand dollars more for the Ocean-to-Ocean Highway.

Just recently we secured John Willys' subscription, which adds another hundred fifty thousand dollars. In addition to this we have the Hudson Company and we expect the Pope and several others within the next week or two.

I am in hopes, Mr. Ford, that you will decide to come in and help us.

The entire west is very much in earnest, and this road can be built and be worth to the automobile industry, several times what it cost them, but we must have the assistance of all the big factories, such as yours. Everybody in the automobile business expects you to help in your own way when the right time comes.

Yours very truly,

P.S. We now have more than two million dollars subscribed and we are receiving several thousand-dollar subscriptions from individual owners in all parts of the United States. C.G.F.[47]

Whether or not Couzens influenced Ford in the matter or whether it was just Ford's opposition to others' ideas will probably never be known. Couzens' first letter to Carl indicated that he was disinclined to go along with the idea. Anne Jardim, author of *Henry Ford: A Study in Personality and Business Leadership,* said that "...Couzens' influence on Ford seems to have been incalculable. He was by all accounts a hard, driving man and took control of every aspect of the company's business apart from engineering and assembly which were Ford's responsibility."[48]

A few years earlier, in 1908 and 1909 after the Model T had been introduced, Ford had received offers to sell his interest in the company. Couzens said later that Ford "really wanted to sell. He was sick in body and disturbed in mind."[49] Ford's increasing rigidity and refusal to make major changes in the Model T, even though technology was leaving it behind, are well known.

Had Carl been able to deal with Ford's son Edsel, he might have had more success. Edsel, who had just turned 19 in 1912, was not then in a position to be of much assistance even if he wanted to. Although his father's heir apparent and president of the Ford Motor Company while he was still in his twenties, Edsel was subject to his father's authority and often undermined. They disagreed in their philosophy about delegating authority. E. G. Liebold, Ford's confidential secretary, pointed out their differences:

> Edsel felt that people ought to be given certain responsibilities in certain positions and their authority should be designated. Mr. Ford didn't go along with that line of thinking. He often said to me that if he wanted a real job done right that he would always pick the man who didn't know anything about it. The reason was that if he picked a man who didn't know anything about the job, the fellow never got far away from Mr. Ford. Mr. Ford in that way was able to control what was being done... of course, you couldn't get Edsel to agree to that line of thinking. If Edsel wanted a thing done, he would pick a man he thought was capable of doing it.[50]

F.L. Black, a staff member on the *Dearborn Independent,*

the Ford newspaper, noted that Henry was not consistent in allowing Edsel's decisions to stand. Frequently when someone asked Henry about some matter, Henry would reply: "'Well, you talk that over with Edsel, and do whatever he says. I'm going to turn more of these responsibilities over to him. He's got to run this company.' For a time every decision would be discussed with Edsel Ford, and then [Black noted] 'You would find the old man back in harness reversing Edsel's decisions.'"[51]

During an executive luncheon when Edsel had the temerity to suggest the need for modern hydraulic brakes, Henry Ford angrily shouted, "Edsel, you shut up," and stormed out of the noon meeting.

Edsel did have some successes with his father, including persuading him to finally retire the outmoded Model T. Edsel then took charge of the highly successful styling of the Model-A and directed the new model change to the public. When the Lincoln Motor company went into receivership in February, 1922, Edsel persuaded his father to buy the company for eight million dollars.

> While administering the company, Edsel devoted untiring attention to his great love — styling, or design, as it is now called. It was he who brought to the automobile industry the realization that an automobile could be beautiful as well as functional. Working with the leading auto manufacturers of the day, he literally transformed the Lincoln from one of the ugliest cars into the most attractive mass-produced vehicle in the world. More than any other top American auto executive of his day, perhaps of any day, Edsel took a personal interest in styling; his close attention earned rich dividends for the company.
>
> Edsel was the driving force behind the studied elegance of the company's 1936 Lincoln-Zephyr, regarded by many as the first successful streamlined car, the first Mercury (1939 — a mainstream medium priced car enabling Ford to compete solidly in the market with GM and Chrysler) and the pre-World War II Lincoln Continental, Frank Lloyd Wright's choice as the most beautiful car of all time and certainly one of the world's most admired cars.[52]

Edsel did support the Lincoln Highway. In 1920, he was elected a director, and in 1923, 1924, and 1925, he contributed $5,000 per year for Lincoln Highway Association operating expenses.[53] He gave an additional $5,000 in 1923 to help pay for plans for a campground along the highway.[54]

When Carl sent Edsel the following letter on September 5, 1922, he could hope for a favorable response,

> My dear Mr. Ford:
>
> I am interested in a small way in the Fletcher National American National Bank of Indianapolis; and much to my surprise the Ford Company is not a depositor in this Bank.
>
> I am enclosing, herewith, a list of the officers of this Bank, and you will notice that among this list are Mr. Walter C. Marmon, of the Nordyke & Marmon Co., and James A. Allison, of the Allison Engineering Company.
>
> The Fletcher American bank has been of unusual assistance to the automobile companies during the last two years — at a time when a strong bank with plenty of nerve was very vital to the automobile interests of this locality.
>
> I would like, if you can do so, to favor the Fletcher American National Bank with some of your business.[55]

Carl was not disappointed with Edsel's reply.

> Dear Sir,
>
> Since receiving your letter of Sept. 5th we have had a call from a representative of The Fletcher American National Bank of Indianapolis, and have recently arranged to make a deposit with them.
>
> I am very glad that you have called this matter to our attention, and we hope our connection with the bank will be of long duration, and pleasant. With kindest regards,[56]

David L. Lewis, in *Public Image of Henry Ford,* described the father/son relationship of Henry and Edsel Ford.

> Dissimilar in so many ways, Edsel and Henry Ford were particularly unlike in their desire for publicity and in the extent to which each was publicized. Throughout his life Edsel shunned publicity as much as his father sought it, and was no less successful in avoiding the spotlight than his father was in bathing in it. The younger Ford usually turned down requests for biographical data; almost always refused requests for writ-

ten expressions of opinion; granted interviews only for compelling business reasons; even banned the use of the pronoun "I" in company statements in which his name appeared. During interviews, Edsel was pleasant, but said little. "When he spoke," stated the *Detroit News,* "it was not with the picturesque flourish that would make a tale to be told and retold, but with quiet understanding and reserve." Edsel, although president of the world's most-publicized company for a quarter-century, never conducted a business press conference.

The younger Ford remained in the background for several reasons. Perhaps foremost among them was one cited by the noted industrial designer, Walter Dorwin Teague, who worked closely with Edsel during the 1930s: "An unselfconscious modesty that left no need for the kind of compensations publicity has to offer." Edsel also valued privacy. "I don't want to be in the position that Father's in," he told an associate, "to be set upon by autograph hunters and people trying to sell me some idea. Finally, Edsel surely knew that his father resented sharing the limelight with anyone — including his son. Edsel sought anonymity and he achieved it. In 1933, as he stood in front of the Senate Office Building with members of the Senate Banking and Currency Committee, before which he had just testified, he was waved out of camera range by a press photographer: "Bud, would you mind — this is just for big shots." In 1935, to his delight he was able to visit San Diego's California-Pacific Exposition nineteen times without being recognized by newsmen of any other visitors.

In retrospect, Edsel emerges as one of the most tragic figures in American business history. He was more than talented; he was creative. He was more than hard-working; he had an extraordinary sense of responsibility to his company and community. He was an excellent administrator, and he commanded the affection, respect and loyalty of his associates. Unfortunately, his father, far from rejoicing in and making constructive use of these qualities, restricted and nullified them in his unceasing effort to remold his son into a rough, hard-hitting executive. Clara Ford watched fearfully as the tension mounted between father and son, and, unable to change Henry's course, sensed that it ultmately would become unbearable for both. Edsel, for his part, although often frustrated and sometimes heartsick over the harsh treatment he received from the elder Ford, had too much filial loyalty to fight back. "Father built this business," he would say when in disagreement with a parental decision, "and if that's the way Father wants it, that's the way it's going to be." But the gulf between the two men and the years of persecution took their toll, eventually wearing down not only Edsel's body, but his spirit as well.

Thwarted and opposed for years by his father and Harry Bennett (Ford's personnel director), Edsel underwent an operation for stomach ulcers in January, 1942. Although able to resume his duties after a short rest, he merely shook his head and replied, "The war won't wait." Wan and haggard, and further weakened by an attack of undulant fever contracted from unpasteurized milk from his father's cows, Edsel managed to carry on his work until mid-April, 1943. Almost to the end, his father refused to believe him in danger: if Edsel would only change his diet and mode of life to that which his father had found best, if he would stop worrying and listening to men of the wrong type, he would soon get well. Nonetheless, at age forty-nine, Edsel died, not only of stomach cancer and undulant fever, but of a broken heart as well. Edsel's death dealt Henry Ford the severest blow of his life, a blow from which he never recovered.[57]

Edsel's mother Clara did not speak to her husband for weeks after Edsel's death, and Edsel's wife Eleanor never forgave the old man. On April 7, 1947, the auto pioneer Henry Ford died in Dearborn, Michigan, at the age of 84.

While Henry Ford lacked interest, the rest of America was eager to support the highway project. Teddy Roosevelt, a long-time friend of Carl's, had been elected President but took the time to wire Carl his congratulations on being elected County Commissioner. Carl's telegraph of thanks urged the new President to support the highway.[58] Newspapers and magazines requested articles; Paul R. Martin was added to the staff to write them. Some automobile buyers ordered autos on condition that the Coast-to-Coast Highway be completed. U.S. Representative William P. Borland introduced a bill in Congress "to resume jurisdiction over the old National Road Congress had abandoned eighty years before, and complete it to the Pacific Ocean."[59]

The Hudson Motor Company subscribed $100,000 in February of 1913. In Salt Lake City, automobile businesses promised to raise $1,500,000 for the road if Colorado agreed to do the same. A bill for a million-dollar bond issue was introduced in the Colorado legislature to achieve the goal. Terre Haute businessmen subscribed $5,750.[60]

In March, without any soliciting, a welcome offer came from the cement industry. A.Y. Gowen, president of the Lehigh Portland Cement Company, wrote that the cement industry was willing to contribute a minimum of 1,500,000 barrels of cement and perhaps twice that much. The industry had formed a committee to study the matter.[61]

The Western states, sparse in population and vast in area, were eagerly attempting to promote the road, with cities vying to get the highway routed through their area. Chambers of Commerce, public officials, and civic organizations eagerly sought information. Los Angeles sent telegrams, well aware that a transcontinental highway would bring tourism. "Competition between various sections for the route of the highway was stirring action as nothing else ever had done,"[62] according to the Lincoln Highway Association. Delegations from various states were coming in. Utah and Wyoming promised "all necessary improvement would be done without expense to outside interests"[63] if the highway went through their states.

More support came from the auto industry. Henry B. Joy, president of the Packard Company, wrote: "If a transcontinental highway can be furthered by means of the Ocean-to-Ocean Highway organization, the good roads improvement which will result within the next ten years can hardly be conceived of in advance. Such highway improvement would benefit almost every person in the United States."[64] His Board of Directors endorsed the project unanimously.

Although Indianapolis had been an active automotive city from the beginning of the industry, the center was rapidly shifting to Detroit. Consequently, on April 14, 1913, Carl called a meeting in Mr. Joy's office in Detroit to formally organize. The all-day meeting resulted in decisions to incorporate the organization, to name Mr. Joy as president, to write a prospectus, to set headquarters in Detroit, and to include "Lincoln" in its name.

Joy, whose father had known and supported Lincoln, was behind the use of "Lincoln" in the organization's name. In December of 1912 he had written to Carl, criticizing Congress's plans to memorialize Abraham Lincoln by using the $1,600,000 in the Lincoln Memorial Fund for a monument, and suggesting that the Fisher committee protest to Congress. Mr. Joy's reasoning was that Lincoln had devoted his life to public service, and roads that would serve the public would be the "finest memorial."[65]

The following January, Congressman Borland suggested to Carl that his plan for a coast-to-coast highway would have more patriotic appeal if a name such as Lincoln were used in its title or routing.[66] Carl favored "Lincoln Memorial Highway," but the name was owned by the Lincoln Memorial Road Association, organized by Leslie T. McCleary. The group had been promoting a Lincoln Memorial Road from Gettysburg to Washington. When Congress voted to use the memorial fund for a monument instead, the association realized that their plan was futile.

Carl wrote McCleary:

It might be a good thing for us to change the name from Ocean-to-Ocean Highway to Lincoln Memorial Road. Kindly advise me if you have the name incorporated and if it would suit your plans to turn it over to us in order that we might continue it.[67]

The McCleary group willingly relinquished their claim to the name, as Carl had expected, but he did not expect McCleary's politically-motivated attempt to persuade him to name the highway the "Jefferson Memorial Highway." In a letter to Carl on April 11, 1913, one of the reasons McCleary gave for naming the road in honor of Jefferson rather than Lincoln was: "As Lincoln is the patron saint of the Republican party, so Jefferson is the founder of the Democratic party which for the next four years at least (God Help Us) will be in control of the National Government, and no Democratic statesman could go home to his constituents with any hope or expectation of ever returning to Washington in an official capacity if he failed to secure this signal honor to the father of the Democratic party."[68] Carl's past experience with politicians had taught him to be wary of their role in road building. The association retained the name of Lincoln and used it in the prospectus prepared by Mr. Pardington.

If leadership can be measured by the quality of man one attracts to his cause, Carl's steadfast followers attested to his ability to enlist some of the most capable and influential men of his time in his cause. Arthur Pardington, a Michigan native, had served as Superintendent of the Methodist Hospital in Brooklyn, New York, after studying medicine and pharmacy at New York University. He left that position to become a district manager with the New York Telephone Company. Finally he went to work for the Long Island Motor Parkway Association, which was building a road through Long Island to Montauk point. Pardington had been an active advocate of good roads since the time that many were no more than cinder paths. He had been instrumental in the creation of the Long Island Motor Highway. Carl had met him when Pardington refereed the Vanderbilt races. Shortly after Carl announced his plans for a coast-to-coast highway, Pardington wrote to him:

> I always like to hear of you starting something big, because you never start anything you can't finish. If you find a place where I can help out, call on me.[69]

Henry Joy's financial and organizational talents had been proven in his position as head of the Packard Company. His influence in Detroit was unquestioned. Even though he had supported the highway soon after it was announced and agreed to be the first president of the Lincoln Highway Association, he recognized the perils that lay ahead. In a letter to Pardington when they were preparing the prospectus, he wrote:

> Personally, I am inclined to the opinion that the enterprise has strewn in front of it almost insurmountable difficulties. Yet on account of so much work already having been put into the matter I feel that everything possible should be done to push it.[70]

Soon after Mr. Joy took over operations in Detroit, he was encouraged by a letter from Mr. Gowen of the cement industry, indicating that they would contribute cement on the same basis as the automobile industry: one third of one percent of their annual gross sales for three years, amounting to 2,350,000 barrels of cement or $3,000,000 worth.[71]

An audit completed by Marwick, Mitchell, Peat and Company revealed that there were actual guaranteed subscriptions of $2,316,040; other indefinite subscriptions estimated by Carl to amount to $366,700; and 56 subscriptions of one third of one percent of gross business, estimated to be about $4,000,000.[72]

After the group met again and agreed to file their articles of incorporation with the Secretary of State, Mr. Joy set off on a three-week trip to investigate possible routes, and Carl returned to Indianapolis. F.T. Grennell, city editor of the *Detroit Free Press,* was hired as part-time publicity man. None of the millions of dollars pledged would be collected until the $10 million goal was reached. Their sole operating funds consisted of a $1,000 check from Carl and a similar amount from Mr. Gowen.[73]

Chapter 8

The Hoosier Trail Blazers

J ULY 1, 1913: While the newly-incorporated Lincoln Highway Association was meeting in Detroit under President Joy, Vice President Fisher was embarking on the Hoosier Tour, a cross-country tour from Indianapolis to San Francisco. Although Carl was a director of the Hoosier Motor Club and the prime force behind the Coast-to-Coast Highway, he initially had reservations about the choice the club had made for its annual tour. Over today's modern, direct highways, it is a 2,300 mile trip; then, it was closer to 2,500 miles. The lengthy route was over unimproved county "section line" roads. The drivers would be challenged by mountains and deserts. In addition, Carl was concerned that many good roads enthusiasts would assume that the route taken was to be the eventual route of the Lincoln Highway, even though he had always taken care to emphasize that the actual route would not be chosen until after careful consideration of all the facts.[1]

But he soon began to realize that the tour could act as a stimulus for the campaign of the Lincoln Highway Association. When the Indianapolis Automobile Manufacturers' Association joined the Hoosier Motor Club as sponsors of the tour, Carl's enthusiasm for the venture began to grow. To his friends in the auto industry, he said, "By getting up a caravan of cars and driving clear across the United States, we can show the country how much it needs a transcontinental highway, and we can show that such a road can be built."[2]

The tour was not a joy ride. Automobile trips across the country had been infrequent because of the unmarked and unimproved roads. Adventurous souls, however, had managed to overcome the obstacles.

In 1898, J.M. Murdoch of Johnstown, Pennsylvania, accompanied by his family, traveled from Los Angeles to New York City in 32 days. By 1913 he had made five more transcontinental trips.[3]

Dr. Horatio Jackson from Burlington, Vermont, had made the first trip from San Francisco to New York in 1903 in a two-cylinder Winton, accompanied by mechanic Sewell K. Croker and Bud, a stray bulldog they had picked up near Caldwell, Idaho. As they crossed the western plains Dr. Jackson noted that poor Bud's eyes were reddened from the dust. He fashioned Bud a pair of goggles, and after that Bud refused to start the day's drive without the goggles. One day they met a farmer driving a hay wagon who was so startled by the goggle-wearing dog that he jumped off his wagon and hid underneath it. Dr. Jackson maintained that when Bud saw a rock or hole in the road, he would bark in warning and brace himself. Their trip took 63 days, three weeks of which were spent waiting for parts.[4]

Auto manufacturers early on recognized the publicity inherent in such trips, and they became sponsors, "partly to test factory development in actual service, partly for the resultant advertising."[5]

The Packard Motor Company sponsored a San Francisco-to-New York trip in 1902, with Tom Fetch, the driver, and a mechanic and a photographer. Colonel Sidney D. Waldon of Packard wanted photographs of mountains and canyons. This 51-day trip was the first of the annual Packard-sponsored transcontinental trips.[6]

Packard president Henry Joy had made many test trips himself. On his first trip west, Joy asked the Packard distributor in Omaha to direct him to the road west.

"'There isn't any,' was the answer.

"'Then how do I go?' asked Mr. Joy.

"'Follow me and I'll show you.'

"They drove westward until they came to a wire fence.

"'Just take down the fence and drive on. When you come to the next fence, take that down and go on again.'

"'A little farther,' said Mr. Joy, 'and there were no fences, no fields, nothing but two ruts across the prairie.'

"But some distance farther there were plenty of ruts, deep, grass-grown ones, marked by rotted bits of broken wagons, rusted tires, and occasional relics of a grimmer sort, mementos of the thousands who have struggle westward on the Overland Route in 1849 and '50, breaking trail for the railroad, pioneering the highway of today."[7]

In 1908, two to three months was considered "good time" for a coast-to-coast trip by a non-professional driver.[8]

The Hoosier Tour was headed by experienced transcontinental drivers. Two of them, W.D. Edenburn and John Guy Monihan, had led forty motorists in ten Premier cars from Atlantic City to Venice, California in 1911.[9]

Tour members were selected by Mr. White and Mr. Edenburn, chairman and vice-chairman, who knew that a successful tour would have a great effect on touring in general and on "advancing the interests of the participating manufacturers."[10] Even the guests were chosen with those ideas in mind. There were representatives from the telegraph companies, a photographer, and an observer from the Royal Automobile Club of England. Reporters from the Hearst syndicate, *Indianapolis Star, Indianapolis News,* and the *Chicago Tribune* went along, as well as a field representative from the American Automobile Association.

More than 70 men were initially chosen, each one a "selected specimen from a physical standpoint."[11] All of them had to pass a physical examination before they were accepted since at one point the altitude in Berthoud Pass in Colorado was 11,315 feet above sea level and the ruggedness of the route required much physical exertion.[12] The drivers were selected factory drivers, including Ray Harroun and other Speedway racers. They were prepared for whatever might befall them.

Every automobile manufacturer in Indiana had entered at least one car, for a total of 17 touring cars: a Marmon, two

Marions, a Pilot "60," two Haynes, two Americans, a McFarland, two Appersons, two Hendersons, an Empire, a Pathfinder "40," and two Premiers. Carl drove a Premier even though he manufactured Empires. A Premier truck carried tires supplied by G. and J. Tire Company, and a Brown truck was loaded with camp equipment, spare parts, and other supplies.[13]

White and Edenburn, experienced with the difficulties they would face on the road, insisted that every car carry specified equipment and even suggested where they should be packed:

1 pick or 1 mattock
1 pair of tackle blocks
600 feet of ¾" rope
1 barn lantern, hung on the rear tire carrier, to be lighted if the car's regular lights failed, so the following driver would see it and keep in line.
1 steel stake 3' long, 1½" wide at top, tapered to point for use as an anchor to pull car out of sand or mud.
12 mudhooks
1 full set of chains
1 sledge
Chocolate bars in cans, beans, canned goods, stowed under rear seat.

West of Salt Lake City each car also carried:
4 African water bags, kept filled at all times.
1 4x6 tent, envelope type, made especially for the tour.
This tent was intended to be tied to the top and the wheels of the car. It could be raised from inside and was provided with ground cloth and mosquito-bar ventilating windows.
Camp equipment sufficient to shelter and feed the entire tour was carried on one of the trucks; the provisions in the cars were for emergency use only.[14]

The equipment was used by almost every car somewhere on the tour.[15] There were creeks and gullies to cross without benefit of bridges. Cattlemen's wire fences had to be cut and duly repaired.

One amateur suggestion was rejected, but its author, Elmer Apperson, didn't give up easily. Apperson wanted them to take two 100-yard rolls of canvas to be used alternately on sand. He even sent the canvas to Salt Lake City, each roll weighing 750 pounds; nobody picked it up.[16]

Unless weather or road difficulties prevented, the schedule set the goal of a settlement or recognized stopping place every night. W.S. Gilbreath, secretary of the Hoosier Motor Club, had conducted an extensive publicity blitz for the tour.[17] Everyone seemed to know that they were coming. When the Trail-Blazers (as they called themselves), dressed in khaki suits and high boots, left Indianapolis at 2 p.m. on July 1, the citizens of Indianapolis lined the streets to cheer them on.[18]

The club had been receiving up to 100 telegrams a day; it was as though everyone west of Indianapolis wanted to be on the tour's route. Delegations had been sent to Indianapolis to make their case. The mayor of Price, Utah, came to Indianapolis for this purpose, but was told it was impossible because there were no roads east through Price Canyon. The mayor replied, "We'll build one, then,"[19] and proceeded to do so. When the road was not completed just before the tour was to arrive, the mayor declared a legal holiday and asked all the able-bodied men in the town to help. The tour made it through, as Gilbreath said, "...without a broken axle, a broken part of any kind, or even a puncture. It was rough but we got through."[20]

When the Trail-Blazers left Indianapolis, the tour had already sparked $500,000 in road improvements, including new bridges, filling, grading, and paving. Nevada spent $25,000 to improve the road from Utah to California. Colorado rebuilt sixty miles across Berthoud Pass. More than 30 new concrete bridges were constructed along the entire route, some of which had already been planned but whose construction was speeded up for the tour.[21]

Even on the first 50 miles to Brazil, Indiana, it was evident that the road had been improved. From there on, Carl said later, "...practically every mile of the road had been scraped, dragged, graded or otherwise improved"[22] for the tour. But they still had to remove large rocks, cut down high centers, and fill in ruts as they progressed.

The leaders had set a goal of 150 miles a day, but it was not the roads or the weather that often made this goal difficult to accomplish. It seemed as though every community on the route wanted to recognize and salute them: lunches, dinners, roadside entertainment, road meetings and banquets awaited them. "Every night there was a banquet, a supper or some other celebration, with more speechmaking, and as the local newspaper reporters and the newsmen in the party vied in sending out stories about each meeting, the tour evoked tremendous publicity and interest."[23] In one of the photographs that was taken at a desert camp, Carl later discovered he had had an unwelcome companion: a rattlesnake could be seen slinking away.[24]

In some places, gasoline had been hauled up to 70 miles and offered to the tour for free. Bishop, California, had a complete camp in the mountains all prepared. There a local bank president cooked for them, and leading citizens of the town were the waiters. More than 1,200 automobiles escorted them into Oakland, California.[25]

The rigors of the road and the constant public appearances exhausted the tour members. When he had the time and opportunity, Carl sent back reports to the Lincoln Highway Association. Carl was also keeping a diary, but its entries were terse: "Left Denver 9:30 a.m., arrived Hot Sulphur Springs 11:30 p. m. 105.2 miles."[26] In crossing Berthoud Pass, they went "up grades so steep some of the cars had to turn around in the narrow road and back up the worst stretches because the gasoline tanks were lower than the carburetors."[27]

At a banquet in Price, Utah, where Utah Governor Spry spoke in favor of the Lincoln Highway, only half of the tour members attended; the rest were so exhausted they had gone to bed.[28]

The reports Carl was sending back to Detroit gave great encouragement to the Lincoln Highway movement. For example, the second stop of the tour was Springfield, Illinois, where Governor Dunne told him that the state had allocated $1,200,000, in addition to a similar amount allocated by several counties, for highway improvement.[29] The state was also setting up a highway commission.

Governor Hodges of Kansas accompanied the tour for three days, giving speeches advocating better roads. Colorado Governor E.M. Ammons also joined them for three days and told Carl he planned the highway across his state to be 46 feet wide with a four-foot rock shoulder, and a two-foot, six-inch rock wall around dangerous turns, with six per cent grades. "If we can allow him $1,000 per mile in material we will get a $7,000,000 road across Colorado,"[30] Carl wrote.

Not everything in the West was so hospitable. At Grand Junction, the group's sleep was disrupted by an invasion of bedbugs. Carl was forced to retreat to the roof of a nearby chicken coop in order to get some rest. In the morning, one of the tour members awoke and, thinking he had seen a bedbug on the wall, seized a chair and smashed what was actually a mandolin. Whenever Grand Junction was mentioned in Carl's presence from then on, he always referred to it as the place "where I do believe they have the biggest bedbugs in the whole world."[31]

Even worse, after they left Salt Lake City, a sudden mountain storm thundered through an arroyo after half of the cars had crossed. The rush of water forced them to break out the shovels and the tackle, with lines run from cars that had managed to cross to those still laboring their way.[32]

At Ely, Nevada, they were met by Governor Oldie, who not only accompanied them most of the way across the state, but also promised Carl that "he would call a special session of the legislature, if need be, to act on any proposals the Lincoln Highway Association might put before it."[33]

When they reached Ely, part of the tour went to San Francisco, the others to Los Angeles. One group went to Reno, Lake Tahoe and on to Placerville, Sacramento, Stockton and Oakland/San Francisco. The remaining group went to Tonopah, Goldfield and through Bishop to Los Angeles. Having crossed the Sierras into California and nearing their destination, Carl looked forward to a special celebration. He had telephoned Jane from Kansas City and told her to "throw

In 1915, the LHA made a film of the Lincoln Highway. Here the film crew takes a break. (U.M.L.)

some things in a bag and catch the midnight train."[34] She awaited him in a lodge at Lake Tahoe. Awaiting them and other tour members was a special dinner; they had caught mountain trout in Colorado and shipped it in ice to the Tahoe tavern. For a few days the group refreshed themselves, swimming in the ice-cold water and sitting around a campfire at night, singing song after song, their favorite one the song that Carl and Jane had often sung together early in their courtship, "In My Merry Oldsmobile."[35]

The tour members resumed the trip across California. In Sacramento, Carl met with Governor Hiram Johnson and later wrote to the Lincoln Highway Association that "It will not be necessary for us to build a foot of road in California as they have sufficient funds and a sufficient amount can be diverted from their main highways to this cross-continental road."[36]

On August 3, the 34th day of the tour, they reunited in San Francisco. "What a welcome we were given in the city by the Golden Gate!" Jane wrote. "We paraded on Market Street which blazed with flags and lined with thousands of cheering San Franciscans. President Taft coined the phrase: 'San Francisco knows how!' and San Franciscans did know how to warm the hearts of the dusty Hoosiers who had beaten a trail between Indiana and California."[37]

Although tired and weary, tour members had to listen in the broiling sun to more speeches. Captain Gilbreath sought for some shade before he was to address the crowds. But a photographer spotted Gilbreath, who wore a red silk handkerchief around his head, khaki trousers, and an open-throated shirt. He was carrying a rake handle to which he had attached pennants he had gathered on the tour. Just as Gilbreath was about to give his speech, the photographer caught the pose that was to become famous. Gilbreath jumped up and struck his hands in the air, one holding the pennants. When Carl saw the photo, he exclaimed, "That's the spirit of the Highway!"[38] The photo, known as "The Spirit of Lincoln Highway," was printed throughout the U.S. and according to the Lincoln Highway Association, "perhaps expresses better than anything else the dream created by Mr. Fisher and the realization carried out by Messers. Joy, Gunn, Seilberling and others ."[39]Lincoln Highway Association President Henry Joy later had a lifesize bronze statue made, based on Gilbreath's pose.

The trip was over. Every vehicle had completed the tour. There had been no casualties. They had never been more than 24 hours behind schedule.[40] America had seen that transcontinental touring was feasible.

They returned to Indianapolis by train.[41]

Chapter 9

Most Direct Route

Carl had returned from the Hoosier Tour full of enthusiasm: public response had been overwhelming and newspapers throughout the country had fueled interest in the Lincoln Highway. But almost a year had passed since he first announced his plan to raise ten million dollars, and only $4,200,000 had been pledged.[1] In an attempt to raise more funds, the executive committee had reprinted a report on the Lincoln Highway project and sent it to all makers of automobiles and accessories and their suppliers, but substantial contributions had not materialized.[2]

Carl was ready to try a new approach, one that had originated with Kansas Governor Hodges, who had suggested that Carl present his case for the highway at the Conference of Governors, scheduled to be held in August at Colorado Springs. The association could try to obtain immediate financing for improvement of the roads from the governors. Carl told the association: "All the governors from each state along the road will be glad to be at Colorado Springs, and if we could make our plans complete by that time we can close up the west solid to the continent and have at last three or four million dollars spent next year on the Lincoln Highway.

"If the directors could meet at Colorado Springs August 22, it would clinch all matters now partially closed. These governors want to get busy at once."[3]

Carl had planned to raise the ten million dollars first and then select the route. But to gain support from the governors, he convinced the directors to select the route immediately and try to solicit support for improving the section of the Lincoln Highway that would pass through the Western states. They would also be able to obtain input concerning the route before it was announced to the general public.[4]

No matter which route they selected, they expected criticism. While on the Hoosier tour, Carl had written to the directors: "The rivalry that exists between the different sections of the states through which the road is proposed, is going to be quite a factor to straighten out, but I believe it can be done."[5] The directors were clear in their intent. "...they were agreed that only the shortest, best and most direct route was worthy to be the great memorial they planned and they had not only personal knowledge and experience, but a great mass of collected data on which to base their decision."[6]

Arthur R. Pardington, secretary of the association, was already receiving so many requests from Western communities who wanted to be on the route or to know what the route would be that he had to resort to a form letter to answer all of the requests:

> The route of the Lincoln Highway must, when finally adopted, be governed by the following factors: the directness of the route between New York and San Francisco; second, points of scenic and historic interest and centers of population between these points which can be most advantageously and economically incorporated; third, the character and the amount of support afforded this Association by the local communities which will receive the direct and immediate benefit of the establishment of this great memorial to Abraham Lincoln.[7]

The Lincoln Highway would not be a new road, as such. Instead, it would be based on existing roads that would be improved. There would be no tolls, so that it would be free for all travelers to enjoy. President Joy had already acquired much personal knowledge of routes west as he had lived and mined in southwestern Utah for years and had frequently traveled the Western deserts. While Carl was on the Hoosier tour, Joy

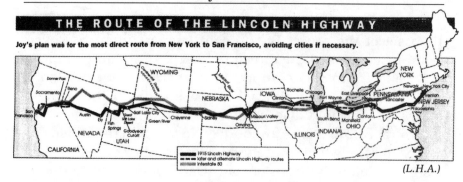

THE ROUTE OF THE LINCOLN HIGHWAY

Joy's plan was for the most direct route from New York to San Francisco, avoiding cities if necessary.

(L.H.A.)

had been exploring a northerly route. Joy had one major concern for the routing: directness.[8]

Fortunately, the association already had in hand a suggested route with a well-reasoned explanation for its choice. Even before the Lincoln Highway Association was formed, Roy D. Chapin of the Hudson Motor Car Company had asked for such a route from Colonel Sidney D. Waldon, an engineer and member of the National Association of Auto Manufacturers who had traveled extensively in the West. Chapin was chairman of the Good Roads Committee of the National Association of Auto Manufacturers and had become a member of the executive committee of the Lincoln Highway Association.

Colonel Waldon's reasoning was so persuasive that the association adopted his basic route. It would be difficult for opponents to fault his argument. Waldon wrote:

> The selection of a route to bear the name Lincoln Memorial Highway requires more careful selection than appears on the surface. It is easy to say that the route should be through the southwestern states to provide touring conditions all the year round. The trouble is that when conditions are right for touring in the level country of Arizona, the mountains to the east and west of it are snowbound.
>
> If a route is considered still farther south, then the worst possible conditions are encountered in the windshifted sand around Yuma, together with the fact that the route becomes a winter route only, inasmuch as the heat is so intense during the summer. When the northern tier of states thaw out, the great volume of touring west begins. In April conditions were actually better for touring east of Detroit than they were for touring across Arizona.

If apparently we must wait until the mountain passes of Arizona and California dry out, we will have waited longer than is necessary for the level plains of Nebraska and Wyoming to get into excellent touring condition. By this time, all the east will also be in shape for cross-country work. In fact, it will be ready before the Sierras permit the passage of automobiles. We can, therefore, practically eliminate any route that doesn't furnish the most direct line from New York to San Francisco.

The route through the center of Colorado, of course, offers wonderful scenic beauties. This, however, introduces difficulties not experienced on the route through Wyoming.

This fact has been recognized by practically every transcontinental motorist since 1903.

The northern route, the original Emigrant Trail, is not nearly so well known as what I may call the central route and, besides, it does not lead to a destination that would be as popular as San Francisco would be.

All things considered, I believe the Lincoln Memorial Highway should run from New York to San Francisco; that it should touch Chicago.

There are no two questions in my mind about the Omaha-Cheyenne-Salt Lake City route being the shortest and offering the least possible trouble to the tourist. All parts of the line will be in condition for travel at about the same time and there is obviously no use in selecting a route where, as in our Arizona experience last April, we made three quarters of the way and then were blocked when almost in sight of the coast.[9]

Twenty years later, Colonel Waldon admitted that when he wrote the letter, the Lincoln Highway "...looked to me like a wild dream to spend $30,000,000 on a concrete highway connecting the Atlantic and the Pacific. Nevertheless, the route interested me."[10]

The troublesome part of the route was the desert. With Henry Joy, Col. Waldon decided on the Pony Express route, south of Salt Lake. Of the three passes through the Rocky Mountains, they chose South Pass. "Our idea," Col. Waldon said, "was to get a continuous route traversable through the largest portion of the year at the least cost. On that basis we selected the route."[11] Before making their final selection, the association leaders studied information on various routes, compiling mileage, number of cities, and percentage of the U.S. population that would be served. Nature was the most important factor.[12]

The directors estimated that it would take twenty years to attain their goal of a continuous route, at that time there being only 650 miles of the entire route paved with macadam or stone.[13] The association had to improve the entire route and obtain connections between sections. "What we really had in mind," Joy said, "was not to build a road but to procure the building of many roads, by educating the people. Beyond question we did bring about what is known as the Good Roads movement in America. We knew that a real road across the country would have to come; our problem was to get steam behind the idea."[14]

In August of 1913, confident that they had chosen the best route available, President Joy had a map prepared, with a red line outlining the proposed Lincoln Highway. This was the map that he, Carl, and Arthur R. Pardington, the other vice president of the Lincoln Highway Association, took to Colorado Springs to show to the Conference of Governors, announcing the chosen route for the first time on August 26, 1913.[15]

In a speech entitled, "Appeal to Patriots," the three formally addressed the governors, explaining their reasoning for this particular route. "The force behind the decision will be only the wisdom of it, which it is hoped will give the selection of route the force, because it is believed that the route of the 'Lincoln Way,' wisely chosen, will have behind it the patriotic force of the whole people."[16] Joy pointed out that no progress could be made if there was continual discussion on the merits of various routes. "That there should be a Lincoln Highway across this country is the important thing; that it should be the most practicable route for the purposes involved is the proper thing."[17]

The three received an enthusiastic response from the governors — except for Colorado Governor Ammons and Governor Hodges of Kansas. The Hoosier Tour had passed through both states, but the Lincoln Highway would not. The host governor's appeal swayed the directors; they agreed to a detour from the Lincoln Highway to Denver. Later the association realized this concession had been a mistake.

With the governors' support assured, Carl, Joy, and Pardington wasted no time in writing the formal announcement to the public. A public pronouncement would garner much-needed publicity and prevent attempts to divert the route. On the train on the way home, they agreed on a formal, dignified, yet newsworthy proclamation and immediately set about to compose it.

Joy was the chief writer, assisted by Pardington, with Carl occasionally commenting on the contents.[18] On September 10, 1913, they wrote:

> WHEREAS: The purpose of this Association is: to IMMEDIATELY PROMOTE AND PROCURE THE ESTABLISHMENT OF A CONTINUOUS IMPROVED HIGHWAY FROM THE ATLANTIC TO THE PACIFIC, OPEN TO LAWFUL TRAFFIC OF ALL DESCRIPTIONS, WITHOUT TOLL CHARGES AND TO BE OF CONCRETE WHEREVER PRACTICABLE. THIS HIGHWAY IS TO BE KNOWN, IN MEMORY OF ABRAHAM LINCOLN, AS "THE LINCOLN HIGHWAY..."

Joy, Fisher, and Pardington arranged for the printing and mailing of the Proclamation before the rest of the executive committee were even consulted. From the inception of the Lincoln Highway Association, action was the watchword. The executive committee later ratified it unanimously.

President Joy often said to Mr. Pardington and those who succeeded him as secretary: "Is that the way it should be done?" The answer was "Yes," and Mr. Joy would reply: "Well, why ask me? Why don't you go on and do it?"[20]

At all levels of the organization, individuals were allowed to make decisions and act on them without conference with their superiors, promoting a high degree of morale and responsibility. The leaders were all men with important positions and limited time: Carl, head of Presto-O-Lite; Joy, President of the Packard Corporation; Seiberling, President of the United States Rubber Company; and J. Newton Gunn, Vice President of U. S. Rubber and President of the U.S. Tire Company.

Thousands of copies of the Proclamation were printed and released for publication on September 14, along with a news story and the address to the Conference of Governors. These were also sent to automobile dealers, manufacturers, chambers of commerce, road enthusiasts, and others who they thought would display the documents and further publicize them.[21] The mailing resulted in immediate publicity nationwide. Checks began pouring in from enthusiastic supporters from Florida to Vancouver. Veterans who had served under Lincoln; farmers — even those who did not own autos but wanted improved roads; ministers; bankers; lawyers; motorists; President Woodrow Wilson; automobile clubs — all wanted to help. Automobile dealers wanted copies to post in their windows. Governors encouraged their constituents to lend support.[22]

Carl, Joy, Pardington and other leaders of the association were invited to address Congressional committees, conferences, the American Automobile Association, and many others — more invitations than they could accept. This did not mean that they were always met with enthusiasm. There were still many farmers and others who felt that improved roads would only benefit automobile owners. Many thought it would only increase their tax burdens. Lincoln Highway workers were often heckled. To overcome this resistance, the speakers catered to each audience, explaining to merchants how the highway would improve business and to manufacturers the advantages it would bring them in distribution, sales and delivery.[23]

The response encouraged the association to call for a national day of dedication to the memory of Lincoln. They requested that states on the route declare October 31 a legal holiday and ask citizens to participate, and that the clergy focus their November 2 sermons on Lincoln.[24] Rev. Frank G. Brainard of Salt Lake City didn't wait. On October 19, he preached enthusiastically from his pulpit: "It (Lincoln) is a name to conjure with. It calls to the heroic. It enrolls a mighty panorama of fields and woodlands: of humble cabins and triumphant farm homes and cattle on a thousand hills: burrowing mines and smoking factories: winding brooks, commerce-laden rivers and horizon-lost oceans. And because it binds together all these wonders and sweeps forward till it touches the end of the earth and the beginning of the sea it is to be named the Lincoln Highway."[25]

Statements from the sermons were issued in news releases to the nation's press. His Eminence, Cardinal John Gibbons, a conservative who seldom commented on civic affairs, wrote: "I am greatly pleased to know that success in the undertaking is assured, as I believe that such a highway will be a most fitting and useful monument to the memory of Lincoln."[26] His statement was sent to all Roman Catholic publications as well as the secular press.

Dedication Day was a resounding success. Parades and celebrations were held in all the major cities on the designated route. J. M. Studebaker spoke at the South Bend festivities. Indiana farmers combined it with Halloween and set jack-o-lanterns on fence posts for miles along the route. "It looked like a continuous bonfire and celebration,"[27] Carl said.

Other government dignitaries advocated the highway to their constituents. Governor Frank B. Willis of Ohio, at another Lincoln Highway celebration, told Ohio farmers that failure to improve roads would result in a waste of $4,700,000 annually.[28] The governor's speech was distributed to newspapers throughout the country.

Free publicity for the proposed highway was there for the asking. Mr. Pardington persuaded forty magazines and trade journals (including the *Harvard Lampoon*) to provide free advertising space for a year. Professional advertising copywriters wrote the copy at no cost.[29]

In all of the publicity, the directors tried to keep themselves in the background. When some newspaper articles identified Henry Joy as President of the Packard Company, Joy ordered it stopped. Said Joy, "...it may create prejudice against the work of the association in the minds of those who may feel that I have created it for the purpose of exploiting Henry B. Joy..."[30]

Publicity and verbal support were all that the association could ask for, but financially they were still struggling. Most of the fund-raising work was left to the officers in Detroit. Carl was busy with Prest-O-Lite and a new project in Florida, and Joy with the Packard Company. It was Secretary Pardington who began to work on subscriptions to fulfill the $10 million goal and to try to enroll prominent men as sponsors. He solicited subscriptions from 3,000 millionaires, but with little response. World War I, which began the following July, was to cut down substantial contributions for several years. To raise money for operating expenses, Pardington began the sale of membership certificates, sold at a minimum of $5 through car dealers and good roads enthusiasts. Certificate #1 went to President Woodrow Wilson. Certificate #2 was purchased by Mary Clark Thompson of Camden, Maine, for $1,000 with the provision that she receive no publicity. Abraham Lincoln's son Robert had Certificate #3.[31]

The certificates did not solve the problem of operating expenses. Small-town buyers of $5 certificates wanted their money spent on work in their own area; Mr. Pardington complied by having it deposited in their area banks until it was needed for construction, but none of this money was then available for operating expenses. The minimum of $5 was not sufficient even to cover costs.[32] Books of membership certificates were sent to the car dealers and road enthusiasts, their sale dependent solely on the cooperation of the recipients. At a time when hotel rooms rented for one dollar (one dollar fifty with private bath), raising the minimum membership fee would price it out of the budget of many and limit membership.

In the fall of 1913, the association had only $6,000 for operating expenses: $1,000 each from Carl, Joy, Seiberling, Gowen, and the Hudson and Packard Motor Car Companies.[33] The costs of printing and mailing 150,000 copies of the Proclamation and "Appeal to Patriots" had put the association in debt for $16,000. The directors voted to borrow $19,000 on the endorsement of all directors, although Joy had offered to personally guarantee it.[34] Ironically, by the end of 1913, the association had received contributions from people in 45 states and seven foreign countries, but with little improvement in their financial situation.

In debt and with no evidence in sight of any substantial contributions, the directors decided to hire two men: H. C. Ostermann to solicit wealthy individuals and H. J. Larsen to travel the proposed route to arouse interest and sell certificates. Although both men began intensive campaigns to fulfill the plan, it quickly became obvious that even their efforts would not be sufficient. A few months after they hired them, the association found that they could no longer afford the services of Ostermann and Larsen; they were asked to continue their work without compensation, and both agreed.

President Joy consulted with Secretary Pardington, who suggested that a new category called "founders" be established, with a goal of 100 individuals giving $1,000 each or 1,000 giving $100 each to finance educational work for the next year and a half. He thought that by that time, business conditions would improve sufficiently to warrant a campaign for larger contributions.[35] By the beginning of 1914, the association was $21,700 in debt. The Packard Company contributed $7,000, and President Joy asked Carl and five other directors, including himself, to underwrite the remainder, which they agreed to do then, as well as in the future.[36]

Carl, whose business connections and winning personality enabled him to obtain contributions easily, was disappointed in the lagging finances of the association. When he sent in a check from a founder he had obtained, he wrote: "It is perfectly easy to get assistance for the Lincoln Highway Association, if your directors only go after it. I think you are too easy with them. You should first give them a good dinner and then a good cussing whenever you want money. I will dig up another founder within a few days which will fulfill my obligation, after which I will quite probably do nothing, unless you commence to yell."[37]

By the 1915 annual meeting, the directors had managed to enlist James Allison, Arthur Newby, Harvey S. Firestone, William Randolph Hearst, the Universal Portland Cement

Company, T. Coleman DuPont, The Paige-Detroit Company, and E. A. Deeds as founders. Mr. Gowan had obtained $500 annually for three years from three cement companies and $300 annually for three years from another. Carl, Joy, Seiberling, Gowen, Chapin, and Willys contributed $2,000 each.[38]

With Carl's $10 million goal proving to be more and more elusive, President Joy proposed another idea: build six sample "seedling miles" in Illinois, Iowa, Nebraska, Wyoming, Utah, and Nevada. The proposal was submitted to the directors, Joy telling them, "The educational benefit of a sample mile of Lincoln Highway road in each state would be of inestimable value in promoting our work. The work of the Lincoln Highway Association would then become a tangible, feasible, sensible expenditure of the funds being raised.

"I would rather do this tangible work at present than to exert extraordinary efforts to raise the ten million dollar fund at a time when the maximum effort would yield the minimum return of any time in twenty years"[39]

Carl's plan of raising $10 million to use for donating material for the highway was not formally disavowed at this point, but their new plan of action in effect abandoned it. The directors agreed to devote their efforts to encourage marking of the entire route, encourage local boards to name the route "Lincolnway" in the section under their jurisdiction, and obtain funds to construct the "Seedling Miles."[40]

From July 1, 1913, through the next fourteen months, the Lincoln Highway Association sparked a revolution in building concrete roads and creating a public demand for them. Concrete was mostly unknown as a hard road surface and thought suspect as a suitable material. Five years earlier, the first rural concrete road had been built in Michigan. Drake Hokanson in *The Lincoln Highway: Main Street Across America* described the public's skepticism:

> [It] "drew motorists from miles around who came to drive the road and marvel at its smooth, even surface. They knew it couldn't last. It didn't quickly show signs of wear, but moisture and Michigan winters were sure to be its undoing. How

could this stuff pour like liquid one day, then, a few days later, be rock hard, impervious to pounding wheels, horses' hooves, freezing, and thawing? No doubt many pocket knives came out to scratch at the hard surface, as people shook their heads and looked closely for the first signs of failure."[41]

Good gravel roads had been considered perfectly adequate, even by advocates of better highways. Dirt roads with a split-log drag used after rainstorms were accepted in many states as satisfactory. Politicians and community leaders were opposed to the expense of hard-surfaced roads and the prospect of raising taxes to pay for them.[42]

Henry Joy's seedling miles were astutely designed to show their superiority over the common mud roads of the day. The seedling miles were purposely built on the open highway, a good distance away from cities with improved roads. Local traffic thus went from mud and ruts to a smooth highway unaffected by the weather. The Lincoln Highway Association described the contrast:

A central aim of the Lincoln Highway Association's plan was the paving of roads in Middle America where impassible pools of mud formed after any rainstorm causing one to several days of delay for rural travelers. (U.M.L.)

Farmers saw their teams trotting with the traces slack when they drove over the Seedlings; they saw the same horses, hauling the same wagon, straining to move the same load at a walk over unimproved roads. Urban dwellers saw traffic proceeding over the concrete roadway regardless of wet weather at the same time when they knew, a mile down the road, men and horse were floundering wearily through mud. The natural result was a desire for a better highway.[43]

The citizens were duly impressed. In Indiana, 67 more miles of concrete road were planned and financed within a year after the seedling mile was built.[44] Illinois farmers offered to haul road materials free-of-charge; urban and rural residents contributed money. In Whitestone county, a one-mile concrete road became three miles with the addition of county funds.[45]

The seedling miles were constructed under stringent conditions, at first with a minimum width of ten feet (eventually raised to eighteen feet by 1918). The first mile was built west of De Kalb, Illinois, in October of 1914. The Marquette Company donated 2,000 barrels of cement, and the state supplied the road machinery and engineers. Consul Corkings of De Kalb had raised $2,000 in public subscriptions. Overall, cement companies donated a total of 33,000 barrels worth $40,000 through 1919, when the project ended.[46] By that time the public was convinced of the value of hard-surfaced roads, and the cement companies found it no longer necessary to donate cement as a means of promoting their product.

With only a small paid staff in Detroit and little in the way of operating funds, the association depended on volunteers to serve as links between the association and the states through which the proposed highway passed. In September 1913, the directors appointed ten state consuls, choosing men who had shown interest and taken action in improving highways. County and local consuls were selected on the recommendation of state consuls. There were few politicians or elected officials, but many professional men, bankers, clergymen, and attorneys. These consuls were, to the communities in which they worked, the Lincoln Highway Association. The association gave them full leeway to handle local and immediate matters at their own discretion, which their loyalty and dedication to the good roads movement enabled them to handle effectively and wisely. At their own expense, the consuls traveled and addressed good roads' meeting, sometimes four or five in a single week. At the maximum, consuls numbered 285, some serving the entire fourteen years of the association's active role in the good roads movement.[47] For the essential role which they served, the consuls' only tangible reward was silver and gold medals and certifications in limited numbers in 1917 and 1918.

Volunteers were also the answer to the pressing matter of marking the route to link the various roads together and direct travelers, as well as prevent anyone from diverting it for selfish reasons. This first of four markings consisted of painting red, white and blue bands on poles, tree trunks, rocks or whatever was available. The marking proved to be a great stimulus to traffic. On one California road, traffic increased 1,000 percent within two years of being marked.[48] In 1916, the association wanted a uniform marking and hired a painting crew to go across country, painting 8,000 markers. The cars, paint, and brushes were all donated. Towns, villages and car clubs along the way contributed to the cost.[49]

There were attempts to divert the route, even from the highest office in the land. On June 19, 1914, President Wilson, a great proponent of the Lincoln Highway, wrote to Association President Joy, requesting that the road from Philadelphia to Washington, D.C., and then to the Washington Monument; Fredericksburg, Maryland; and Gettysburg, be marked as part of the highway. Even a Presidential request did not sway the directors. Joy politely declined the request, writing that any change in the route "would insure its failure as a permanent, useful memorial way."[50]

Warren G. Harding, while still a U. S. Senator, requested a route change in Ohio. He was also refused, but became convinced that the association was right after leading a delegation to the association's offices in Detroit. There he was told that even though many of the directors were from Detroit, the highway did not pass through Detroit.[51] Selfish interests were not allowed to influence the route. The only exception the association allowed in deviating from a direct route was to honor Lincoln. The highway passed by the Kentucky town where Lincoln had lived and by Springfield, Illinois, where he practiced law.

Only Utah was intractable — and successful — in refusing to accept the association's choice of route. No good road existed west of Salt Lake City. The association planned a road just south of Great Salt Lake where the desert was the narrowest. When this route reached Ely, Nevada, travel to Los Angeles or San Francisco would be of nearly equal distance.

Henry Joy inspects direction signs along the Lincoln Highway in 1915. (U.M.L)

Utah wanted a longer southern route that would be closer to Los Angeles and would give travelers an opportunity to see more attractive parts of the state and spend more tourist dollars throughout the state. This route, through Wendover, was plagued by spring floods and winds, which could wash away any construction and add considerable cost.[52]

The Lincoln Highway Association gave the state $125,000 to help finance their route and the state reluctantly agreed to a contract. However, on September 17, 1919, the state abruptly stopped work, claiming a lack of funds. They did nothing further to complete it.[53] With federal highway aid then available, Utah submitted a request for federal aid for their route, and received it, despite an association appeal. The state's choice took precedence. The state of Nevada agreed to the Wendover route and at great expense connected both it and the Lincoln Highway route. The association finally had to accept Utah's route as part of the Lincoln Highway, there being no way to complete their chosen route. The dispute held up completion of the Lincoln Highway for years. The association, however, was proven right when the Wendover route proved very expensive, and the construction was repeatedly washed out.[54]

From the beginning of 1916, the association's chronic problem of obtaining operating funds was resolved. Sustaining memberships of $5 or more annually were established, providing substantial income. In addition, these members — never numbering more than 3,000 — faithfully carried out

Traveling through the desolate desert of Nevada, the Lincoln Highway was considered the most direct route. (U.M.L.)

Field secretary Harry Ostermann meets with a sign-posting crew in the middle of Wyoming in 1916. (U.M.L)

useful functions, serving as delegates to county boards, making personal appeals for special causes, and doing whatever consuls assigned them for special events.

After the death of vice president and secretary Arthur R. Pardington in mid-1915, Austin F. Bement, who was the association's successful publicist, was appointed secretary and manager. In this position Bement managed to build a bank balance and reduce operating expenses. He also began the sale of maps, guides, and other material and increased advertising revenue from the guide. The working staff in Detroit was always kept very small. In 1918, for example, there were only Secretary Bement, Field Secretary Ostermann, two stenographers, a bookkeeper-cashier, and a mail girl, at a time when the association was receiving about 1500 pieces of mail per day.[55]

While the association had its operating funds under control, it still had to determine how the Lincoln Highway could be financed and completed.

Chapter 10

Government — The White Knight

THE "WHITE KNIGHT" that finally was to bring the Lincoln High-way to its fruition ironically was the same entity that both Carl and the association had assiduously attempted to avoid. Carl had feared delays and "wrangles" and even possible corruption if the government were involved. Reflecting this view, the association's first official action was to refuse to affiliate with the National Highway Association because it lobbied Congress for federal construction and maintenance of interstate highways.[1]

By 1916 the federal government recognized the necessity of improving roads nationwide and began to undertake this monumental task. Its highway bill of 1916, however, did not please the Lincoln Highway Association, even though it required all states to establish highway departments and provided $75 million over a five-year period in matching funds for highway construction, financing as much as 50 percent of a project. The government set no priorities; a state could spend the money without regard for the importance of, or traffic on, a route. Adjacent states did not have to coordinate their choice of routes; as Drake Hokanson, author of *The Lincoln Highway: Main Street across America*, noted, "...the improved road of one state could end at the state line in a mud hole or at a fence."[2]

Secretary Bement wrote to Secretary of Agriculture Dave F. Houston, whose department was in charge of distributing

123

the $75 million in federal highway funds, asking for "systematic rather than sporadic highway work."[3] Bement also wrote to highway officials in states through which the Lincoln Highway passed, trying to secure money for improving the highway.

Carl was sent the correspondence between Bement and Houston and commented: "Thank God, Mr. Houston sees the light of day in a continuous backbone of good roads instead of the tapeworm variety."[4]

World War I intervened in this first infusion of federal money; the men who would have been building the roads were instead marching off to war. The Lincoln Highway Association lost its president to the war: Henry Joy joined the army as a member of the wartime industrial staff. He was succeeded by Frank Seiberling, an association vice president and director who had been one of the first supporters of the Lincoln Highway, having pledged $300,000 of Goodyear money in 1912. Seiberling had founded Goodyear Tire and Rubber in 1898 on $3,500 in borrowed money, setting up shop in an abandoned factory. In 1918 his company was the largest tire maker in the world. Seiberling was described as an "inventive genius"[5] for his tire-building machine and straight-sided and cord tires. The detachable rim which he perfected had vastly simplified the task of changing a tire.

Although World War I had temporarily delayed road construction, it also strengthened the federal government's role in financing better roads. Association Secretary Austin F. Bement and Roy D. Chapin went to Washington to offer the government the full services of the association during wartime. In 1917 trucks manufactured in Detroit were loaded with munitions and driven on the Lincoln Highway to the Atlantic seaboard for shipment to France. The convoy was piloted by Mr. Ostermann, Field Secretary of the association. Early fall of 1917 had brought the worst snowfall in thirty years across the Midwest and Pennsylvania. Railroad traffic in the area was nearly weather bound and railroad freight was in disarray. Packard Motor Car Company faced the shipping of a large order of trucks. Packard, in conjunction with the Army Quartermaster Corps, made the decision to drive the trucks in convoy to Baltimore for overseas shipment. The trucks were each loaded with up to three tons of Packard service parts and automobile war materials. The first Packard convoy was organized and departed from Detroit the morning of December 14, 1917. Mr. Henry Ostermann, the Lincoln Highway Association's Field Secretary, led the convoy which angled across Ohio and on to the Lincoln Highway across Pennsylvania and on to Baltimore. "At almost the same time, the first truck was rolling into Baltimore ... the government gave the Packard factory notice to prepare 180 more trucks for immediate delivery to Baltimore by overland travel."[6]

Henry Ostermann piloted several additional convoys over the same 542 miles. During the winter months, snow often blocked the road through the Pennsylvania mountains. Schools in Chambersburg and Bemen Falls were closed several times so that the schoolboys could help clear the roads. Roads broke up under the heavy truck traffic, demonstrating the need for improved roads. The Pennsylvania State Council set aside a half million dollars for repairs.[7]

Ostermann was also instrumental in organizing and piloting a 1919 transcontinental Army convoy. Years later Dwight D. Eisenhower, an officer on the army convoy, credited his experiences on this trip and on the German autobahns during and after World War II as the incentives behind the 1954 Interstate Highway Act.[8]

Starting in Washington, D.C., the convoy traveled on the Lincoln Highway from Gettysburg, Pennsylvania, to the Pacific coast in 62 days, garnering national publicity. There were 79 vehicles, 260 enlisted men and 35 officers commanded by Lieutenant Colonel Charles W. McClure, an overseas motor transport officer. The earlier 1917 trips were only about one-fourth the distance; this route was over 3,000 miles long, with the army setting an ambitious schedule of an average speed of 18 miles per hour.[9]

The army prepared carefully. They had their own purposes: to test the performance of their motorized equipment over an extended distance; to show the public their motor-

Widening a New Jersey river bridge creates problems for both trav-elers and bridge crews in the early 1920's. (U.M.L.)

ized military equipment; and to further support the good roads movement, viewing improved highways as a military asset.[10]

The weight of the vehicles — the trucks averaged eight tons with some weighing up to fourteen tons — made heavy demands on the roads. Army engineers rebuilt and reinforced 100 bridges along the route.[11] The heavy trucks literally tore up some of the roads.

The convoy drew crowds everywhere; good roads meet-ings were held at every noontime and evening stop. The pas-sage of many highway bond issues was attributed to the con-voy and its resultant publicity.[12]

The convoy also stimulated motor traffic, proved the eco-nomic value of improved roads, and gathered data on road construction and military matters. The need for stronger road-beds and road surfaces was clear. There was no question that the federal government had a role to play in building highways, especially in sparsely-settled western states.

By the end of 1918, it appeared that the federal government would pass a second federal highway bill for direct improvement of highways, including the Lincoln Highway. Said Mr. Seiberling, who had succeeded Joy as president: "Upon passage of such a bill, the Lincoln Highway Association could feel that its work was accomplished and that it had successfully achieved the ends for which the organization was incorporated."[13] But, the directors wanted to continue for at least two more years, to ensure that the Lincoln Highway could be traversed year-round and could carry transcontinental freight as well as passenger traffic.

A federal aid bill was passed in 1919, providing 600 million dollars for road improvement and twice that in 1920.[14] Traffic was rapidly increasing throughout the U.S.; motor freight transportation was gaining in popularity.

Time was also causing changes of personnel at the association. In 1920, the Goodyear Company was faltering; Frank Seiberling stepped down as president to devote full time to his company. Goodyear survived, but Sieberling was compelled to leave.[15] In 1921, at age 61 he started all over again with Seiberling Tire.

Henry Joy, who said in 1939, "I consider the Lincoln Highway the greatest thing I ever did in my life,"[16] took Seiberling's place but served only six months. In poor health, he had retired from Packard three years before. In his retirement Joy enjoyed traveling on his yacht and concentrating on his new interest — radio.[17] J. Newton Gunn, the Vice President of the United States Rubber Company, was elected president at the next board meeting.

The association suffered a tragedy in June of 1920 when Field Secretary Harry Ostermann was killed in an accident on the Lincoln Highway. Ostermann, married only seven months, was making his twenty-first transcontinental trip, driving the association's new white Packard twin six. While he was trying to pass another car, the Packard slid on wet grass and overturned; he was crushed by the steering wheel of the soft-topped car. Ostermann was only 43. Henry Joy wrote of him, "Yes, he's gone on ahead."[18]

The Lincoln Highway, meanwhile, saw steadily increasing traffic. All kinds of people from the towns, the cities, and the farms were eager to get to the coast or to see the West. James I. Handley, in the *New York Times* of June 16, 1912, had foreseen these "new" tourists:

> Think of the hundreds of Americans who go on taking their vacations in the crowded trains year after year, seemingly in a rut. An investigation would show them that a motor car journey is as cheap or cheaper in many cases. Old habit is a hard fellow to throw off. We might still be living in caves if some fellow hadn't been curious and decided to see if there was not some better kind of a dwelling, with a change of wall paper once in a while.[19]

Unlike the first tourists who were generally well-heeled, many of these had little money left after buying their cars — usually the Ford Model T — and while they had money for gasoline and groceries, they could not afford hotels and often had to repair their own automobiles. Sometimes these "motor hobos" or "gypsies," as they were called, asked permission to camp in a schoolyard or a pasture, often choosing a site near a stream. Often they did not ask, and in their wake they left their camping refuse for someone else to clean up. Viewing the situation in a positive manner because of the dollars these travelers brought to their cities, city officials began setting up municipal campgrounds, frequently at the edges of towns or near water. Some had running water available with bath facilities. The campers were used to rather primitive conditions. Some were lucky enough to own a tent; others owned just a ground cloth or a tarp to place over the car.[20]

Filled with people from different backgrounds but with a common interest in seeing America, these camps provided an ideal place for socializing and sharing road experiences. Some of the tourists couldn't resist embroidering their tales. Frederick Van de Water described this "new sort of creature among the motor gypsies who angled into tourist camps at night:

> A Road Liar is almost any motor camper who possesses the normal human amount of egotism, plus the average automo-

Automobile tourists stop in camp near Omaha in 1923. (U.M.L.)

bile tourist's yearning to be considered a hard-bitten adventurer.... He is immensely sensitive to thrills and practically immune to the truth....Thus, every road he had traveled becomes, in retrospect, an ordeal through which he brought his car safely only by the possession and exercise of abilities such as few men own. By the time he has made camp at night the difficulties of the day have swelled into tasks before which Hercules himself might have quailed....Any audience will do, and if he succeeds in sending a portion thereof to bed terrified at the thought of the morrow, he feels that his heroism has been proved.[21]

The millions of 1916 Federal Road Act dollars the federal government was appropriating for highways caused the association to take on a new focus; the vast amounts of money to be given required no standards for constructing highways. Money would be wasted on roads that would destruct before they were paid for, the same "wasteful economy" Carl had inveighed against in Indianapolis years before. Secretary Bement asked the president and vice president of the U.S. Rubber Company to persuade the company to finance a search for an "ideal standard."[22] U.S. Rubber came through with an offer of $100,000.

Bement sent 4,600 questionnaires to public and private engineers concerned with highway construction. The returns showed that they were in agreement on two specifics: roads with heavy traffic should be hard-surfaced and should have a well-drained subgrade.[23]

The standards developed from the questionnaire results were used to build 7,161.7 linear feet (1 1/3 miles) of four-lane concrete highway in Lake County, Indiana. It became a model of advanced construction methods. The site was chosen to carry maximum traffic to have the "greatest object lesson value"[24] in demonstrating the contrast between existing roads and the ideal construction. This "ideal section" of the Lincoln Highway was 40 feet wide, paved with steel-reinforced concrete ten inches thick, built to withstand over five times the projected traffic.[25] The area featured underground wiring and attractive landscaping. Edsel B. Ford contributed five thousand dollars for a campground, but the campground was never built because open air camping was rapidly going out of favor.

The section was completed in December, 1922, at a cost of $166,655.16, $110,000 of which was paid by U.S. Rubber.[26] The state contributed $33,000 and the county $25,000, the amounts they would have spent for an ordinary 20-foot concrete highway of that length.[27]

The association had achieved its purpose. Engineers read papers to their colleagues about the section, Sunday supplements featured it, and its construction standards were adopted for high-quality construction everywhere.[28]

Federal highway aid meant the end as well as the completion of the Lincoln Highway. At a meeting in May of 1925, the American Association of State Highways and the Bureau of Public Roads voted to mark selected interstate highways, including the Lincoln Highway, by numbering them.[29]

Even the *New York Times*, in an editorial that same year, lamented the change from a Lincoln memorial to a number: "The traveler may shed tears as he drives the Lincoln High-

*A highway sign along the Lincoln
Highway to guide travelers. (U.M.L.)*

way or dream dreams as he speeds over the Jefferson Highway, but how can he get a 'kick' out of 46 or 55 or 33 or 21? The roads of America would still be on paper if the pleas that were made ten years or more ago had been made on behalf of a numerical code."[30]

Henry Joy, who was instrumental in choosing the name "Lincoln," wrote an impassioned letter to association Secretary Gael S. Hoag, the only staff member who served throughout the existence of the Lincoln Highway Association:

The government, so far as been within its power has obliterated the Lincoln Highway from the memory of man, in spite of the fact that the President of the United States gave to the work very many hundreds of dollars worth of publicity to aid in putting this wonderful main arterial highway to the memory of Abraham Lincoln into actual service for the people of America.

My thought is to send to the President, his cabinet, and all members of Congress a copy of the Lincoln Highway Proclamation and along with it a printed sign saying:

"The Lincoln Highway, a memorial to the martyred Lincoln, now known as by the grace of God and the authority of the Government of the United States as Federal Route 1, Federal Route 30, Federal Route 30N, Federal Route 30S, Federal Route 530, Federal Route 40, and Federal Route 50." [31]

When Carl commented that the government "sees the light of day in a continuous background of good roads instead of the tapeworm variety," it was impossible to foresee that these connected roads would lead to the virtual obliteration of the entity of the Lincoln Highway. But the objectives had been met: the connected highway existed, and the federal government guaranteed permanent maintenance.

As early as 1923, the association had considered disbanding because of the Federal Highway Act and the completion of most of its goals. At the end of 1927, the founders could have sat back and said, "Our work is done." Although they decided not to dissolve the organization, the directors formally voted to end all activities, except for permanently marking the Lincoln Highway. There was $66,000 on hand, and Chapin suggested the money be used for this purpose. [32]

Previous markings had deteriorated over time or fallen victim to vandalism. In 1921, the association completed a new marking of the highway, but by the end of 1924, Secretary Hoag reported 1,574 new poles and 2,157 signs were needed. [33] In an article in the *Lincoln Highway Forum,* Hoag noted the vandalism of signs in Noble County, Indiana, and indicated that it was done by boys. He wrote that perhaps replacing markers could be a Boy Scout project, concluding, "What Noble County needs is more Boy Scouts." [34]

E. S. Martin, chief of the editorial board of the Boy Scout organization, read Hoag's comments when they were reprinted in the local newspapers. He wrote to Hoag, volunteering the Boy Scouts, and the two began to make plans. Hoag, Vice

President Bement, and Colonel Waldon designed a seven-foot concrete post, reinforced with four steel bars, bearing the Lincoln Highway insignia and a bronze medallion in front and an arrow with directional information on the side. The medallion featured the head of Lincoln in relief and the words "This Highway Dedicated to Abraham Lincoln."[35] On September 1, 1928, local Boy Scouts along the entire route placed the new concrete markers according to very specific instructions given by Mr. Hoag, who had driven across the country selecting locations.[36]

Carl's dream of a transcontinental highway had come true and stimulated a good roads movement not only in America, but also in foreign countries. In his letter to President Taft in 1912, Carl had written of the highway's "larger aspect as a stimulus of ending highways, both tributary to this one road and elsewhere throughout the country...." As early as 1916, the association's annual report noted that dozens of organizations had been formed to promote such roads. Recognizing the value of tourist dollars, communities were building feeder and community routes to encourage tourist traffic. Other roads were being constructed to compete for the Lincoln Highway traffic and to promote new traffic.[37]

The Lincoln Highway Association had become the authority on highways; national education authorities had recommended their highway guides for classroom use. Thousands were used as textbooks, and thousands of students wrote the association for information. Overall, the association handled $1,250,000 during their years of operation. Only one instance of misappropriation of funds was recorded: a small sum of money taken by a volunteer in a small town.[38]

The association considered all the funds it received as trust funds, and from the inception of the association, President Joy's policies were scrupulously followed. He had outlined those principles in a letter to Pardington the day after the association was formally organized:

> I want to impress upon you, particularly now at the beginning of the work, that there shall be no one employed by this association except strictly on the merits of the service and for

133

value appropriate with the service rendered. There will be no favoritism in connection with the affairs of this Association toward any employe; the outfit must be organized from beginning to end on a basis of efficiency, economy, and straight square dealing always in every way. Every expenditure of money must be on record plain and clear up and above board.

The records of our receipts and disbursements must be kept absolutely plain and clear and open to inspection of any interested party; and disbursements of any character must be made upon the voucher of the party to whom the money is payable. This Association is trustee for any funds which may come to it to be devoted to the work in question, and the application of those funds to the purposes of the Association must be beyond suspicion and will of course, be audited by disinterested auditing firms of repute from time to time.[39]

In accordance with this policy, all moneys, except for working balances, were invested in government securities or deposited in approved banks. A total of $405,000 was received in trust funds as follows:

Carl G. Fisher — $25,000
General Motors Corporation — $100,000
Goodyear Tire and Rubber Company — $75,000
Frank A. Seiberling — $25,000
United States Rubber Company — $130,000
Willys-Overland Company — $50,000[40]

The funds from Goodyear and from Seiberling were given directly to Utah state officials for construction of the highway through that state. Carl's $25,000 contribution earned interest before any of it was spent. The balance that remained was also invested and earned interest for several years.

The small number of bad debts the association incurred consisted of unpaid bills for advertising in the association's publications. One or two enterprising individuals applied to the association for money supposedly owed them. Because the directors did not think these were justifiable claims, they paid them out of their own pockets to resolve the matter, rather than charging the association.[41]

Much of the association's success was due to its unflagging campaign to keep the Lincoln Highway always before the public. It encouraged record-setting transcontinental trips on the highway to demonstrate the condition of the road and to stimulate travel. In 1916, Bobby Hammond traveled from San Francisco to New York in six days, 10 hours and 59 minutes. "It's a real road which will permit a traveler to average 20 miles per hour each hour of the 24, day and night, day in and day out, for practically a week running,"[42]the Lincoln Highway Association could then boast.

Activities such as these received widespread publicity throughout America, not just in cities along the Lincoln Highway Route, for their uniqueness and interest to the general public. Press releases were sent directly to city editors or news editors rather than automobile editors, to ensure that the newspapers would include them in the main sections of the paper, rather than just automotive news.[43] Henry Joy and the rest of the association credited the press with gaining support for the highway by giving thorough coverage to association activities.

The effectiveness of the publicity was reflected in the number of travelers on the Lincoln Highway route. Mr. Bement estimated that about 150 persons traveled across the continent in 1913. D. E. Watkins, secretary of the California State Automobile Association in San Francisco, estimated that motor traffic into that state in 1916 was 25,000 persons. Most of these vehicles, Watkins reported, had reached California via the Lincoln Highway.[44]

The association regarded serving the public as a top priority and furnished travelers with maps, logs, guidebooks, and road information. Henry Joy, according to Drake Hokanson, "felt every dollar spent by the Lincoln Highway Association was spent for education — that money spent on seedling miles, guidebooks, newspaper space really bought an educated public that wanted good roads. Certainly the association had been no road-building organization; the only construction tool it ever owned was a grader it purchased and loaned to a Utah rancher so he could keep the Goodyear cutoff open."[45] As early as October, 1914, it sponsored a folder on the "Lincoln Highway Route, Road Conditions, and Directions," with directions such as "pass in front of saloon building and turn left around shearing pens."[46]

On March 30, 1915, the association published the first of its official guides. The most elaborate was the fifth edition in 1924, consisting of 536 pages and dedicated to Carl as "The Father of the Lincoln Highway." It offered historical information, routes to scenic areas in the west, and material on highway improvement. All of the guidebooks were financed by advertising.

Besides serving the public directly, the association had also initiated important safety practices, including recommending pedestrians walk facing traffic, painting trees and bridgeheads white to make them more visible, eliminating grade crossings where feasible, and placing warning signs at dangerous spots.[47]

Having achieved its goal in less than the twenty years originally projected by the directors, the Lincoln Highway Association attributed its success to Carl Fisher and the faith-

Gael Hoag and the Lincoln Highway Association Packard, symbols of the past, 1926. (U.M.L.)

ful men who followed his lead: "Only the personal magnetism and obvious sincerity of a Carl Fisher...could have obtained more than $4,000,000 in subscriptions to the original transcontinental road plans, or enlisted the whole-hearted support of the shrewd industrial leaders who organized the Lincoln Highway Association.... Everyone gave of his best. This explains how such great efforts could be brought about through the activities of so small an organization."[48]

"If Carl Fisher never left anything to posterity other than these two national highways which he worked so hard to establish [the Lincoln Highway and later the Dixie Highway], his name deserves to live for all time to come. Other people had talked about such things, Fisher acted and then withdrew from the scene,"[49] wrote Charles Edgar Nash, who traced Carl's career in his book, *The Magic of Miami Beach*. Although Carl Fisher's business interests were primarily in Florida after the first few years of the formation of the association, he remained on the board continuously and contributed financially whenever there was need.

Drake Hokanson summed up the significance of Carl's contribution in *The Lincoln Highway: Main Street Across America*:

> The United States would have eventually gotten paved highways even without the example set by the Lincoln Highway. The democratization of the road came with cheaper cars and the working person's desire to own one. The country simply could not go long with millions of cars and dirt roads; the change was inevitable. What the Lincoln Highway Association did was speed up the process; it made the public accept the idea of long roads built not for local convenience but for the benefit of everyone — roads for the nation, not just the county. This was the Fisher idea, a road for the whole nation as an example to all and a path for all — a democratic ideal that lived on in the words of songs, the names of little hotels and streets, a chain of concrete markers, and the restless psyche of America.[50]

Hokanson, who traveled across what remains of the Lincoln Highway in the 1980's estimated that only ten or twelve of the 3,000 markers set by the Boy Scouts in 1928 remain

Portrait of Carl G. Fisher (I.M.S.)

where they were placed. Others have been recovered and moved.[51] He wrote,

> Whether the directors and officers of the Lincoln Highway Association thought the markers would actually keep the highway alive is not known, but their idealism is expressed by even the few that remain.[52]

The Lincoln Highway is all but gone, but if any portion is to be found, it is out in the country; just out of ear range from the bustling sounds of heavy traffic on Interstate 80, which today parallels the old Lincoln Highway.

A new Lincoln Highway Association has been organized today.[53] Its thousands of members are dedicated to preserving what is left of the original paved highway—an historical landmark which changed forever the way motorists experienced an unsettled country.

Chapter 11

Miami Beach —
An Active Retirement

WARM DAYS and cool nights, fragrant flowers, fresh fruit, good fishing — the joys of summer that Carl experienced in Miami in February of 1910 made him eager to return the following year. A new home already awaited them. Carl had purchased it, sight unseen, from an advertisement sent to him in Indianapolis. The house, a "large square white mansion on the edge of Biscayne Bay,"[1] as Jane described it, gave them a view across the bay of what locals called "the Beach," a strip of uninhabited peninsula, mainly composed of jungle-like swamp land, with a beach on the ocean side.

It was only at John Levi's behest that Jane and Carl had come to Miami at all; Miami — an Indian name which means "big water" — had originally been the site of Fort Dallas, a military fort completed in 1838 during the Seminole wars.[2] Indian settlements, however, preceded the fort by hundreds of years. A map by Conti de Ottoman Freducci in 1514-1515 shows a settlement called Chequiche at the location.[3] In the mid-1540's, 13-year-old Hernando d'Escalante Fontaneda was shipwrecked in the area and for 17 years was a captive of the Tequesta Indians until rescued by the army of Pedro Menendez de Aviles. Escalante's memoir, published in the 1570's, called the settlement "Tequesta."[4] Escalante also refers to the Lake of Mayaimi (Lake Okeechobee), "which is called Mayaimi because it is very large."[5] After the United States purchased Florida in 1821, it set up a military outpost in southern Florida to combat hostile Indians. Civil War General William Tecumseh Sherman began his career there.[6] Fort Dallas remained as a military installation until peace with the Seminoles was achieved, In 1849-1850, Second Lieutenant James M. Robinson built two stone houses for barracks for his men, replacing two old log houses.[7] From the time the fort was abandoned on June 10, 1858, until the railroad reached Miami in 1896, "the Miami area was of little consequence in the annals of Florida,"[8] according to Charles Edgar Nash, in his 1930's work, *The Magic of Miami Beach*. It was too inaccessible.

The early settlers lived in the fort buildings until a fire in 1871 burned all but one officer's home and the stone barracks. The barracks were later converted into a home for Mrs. Julia Tuttle, a prominent citizen who had inherited Florida land from her father and had come to live in Miami with her daughter after the death of her husband. Most of the other houses in Miami had been built from lumber salvaged from ship wrecks, the usual practice along the coast.[9]

Julia Tuttle was instrumental in making Miami a winter resort town. The railroad that made it accessible came to Miami as a direct result of her initiative and generosity. In 1891, she wrote to James E. Ingraham, president of Henry B. Plant's South Florida Railroad: "Someday someone will build a railroad to Miami and I will give to the company that does so one-half of my property at Miami for a townsite. Perhaps you will be the man."[10] Plant was not interested. Ingraham eventually left the South Florida Railroad to go to work for Henry Flagler. Flagler, a multi-millionaire and Standard Oil magnate, like Carl had become "intrigued"[11] with Florida's climate, building the Ponce de Leon and Alcazar Hotels in Saint Augustine. Because there was no adequate transportation for building materials, in 1885 he bought the Jacksonville, St. Augustine, and Halifax River Railroad with its 36 miles of narrow gauge tracks and wood-burning locomotives.

Within four years, Flagler converted the railroad to standard gauge, installed heavier rails and bought modern equipment. Travelers were able to go by train from New York to Florida, without the inconvenience of roadbeds of varying width. By February, 1984, Flagler's railroad reached Palm Beach, where Flagler built the Poinciana Hotel. "Palm Beach was essentially a Flagler creation,"[12] Nash wrote. The railroad brought vacationers and farmers and prosperity to Florida. Farmers could easily transport their produce to the north in the winter for premium prices. "Flagler's winter palaces civilized what until then had been a real jungle complete with Indians and crocodiles — one of the first instances where the pleasure industry, rather than farming, mining, or lumbering, did the pioneering,"[13] wrote Polly Redford in *Billion-Dollar Sandbar.*

Mrs. Tuttle visited Flagler, extolling the virtues of the Miami area. She had purchased more land in Miami and planned to build a resort hotel where the Miami River meets Biscayne Bay. "Here she was living in an environment as near perfect as nature could make it. Every visitor raved about the possibilities of the country, but swore at its inaccessibility. Here was the truly tropical spot in the whole continental United States and civilization was passing it by."[14] She even offered him half of her land. Flagler refused outright.

Then it struck — 1894-95 — the winter of the Great Freeze. Citrus orchards were killed overnight. From Palm Beach to Georgia, plants, trees and flowers were killed or blighted. There were no jobs and no business that winter. "Thousands flocked to Flagler..."[15] Mrs. Tuttle wasted no time; there had been no freeze in Miami. Wrapping a bouquet of flowers in moist cotton, (lime blossoms, according to Miami pioneer Mary Barr Munroe),[16] Mrs. Tuttle sent it to Flagler with a message: if he would bring the railroad to Fort Dallas, she and the Brickell family would share their land with him.

Flagler arrived in Fort Dallas to talk with Mrs. Tuttle, traveling by boat and mule cart for the last 70 miles. Flagler wanted to know what crops grew in the area, according to Captain Charles J. Rose, a Civil War veteran who had settled in Florida in 1890. "We came across a watermelon on Giles' place and took it to show Mr. Flagler. He thought it was a pumpkin at first — it was so large, but we cut it and gave him part of it to eat. He was so pleased with it that he took half of it back to St. Augustine to show the people there. After that he promised us a railroad."[17] In a contract dated October 14, 1895, in exchange for extending his railroad to Miami and building a first-class hotel there, Julia Tuttle gave Flagler the land she had promised. Flagler also agreed to subdivide and plat the land and build streets.

Surveying for the railroad extension had begun in June of 1895, and the laying of track in September. With news of the coming railroad, a steady stream of settlers began to pour into Miami. Florida newspapers throughout the state carried advertisements offering jobs with good wages. Soon there were 3,000 people in Miami, living in tents, lean-to's, shacks, even sailboats. Brickell's store sold out of supplies immediately. But Flagler's men did not arrive until March with the news that the railroad track would be completed to Miami within thirty days and construction of the hotel would begin immediately. A cargo of lumber arrived the next day.[18]

A wood-burning locomotive loaded with building materials arrived on April 15, 1896, and the first passenger train, carrying Mr. Flagler and Mr. Ingraham among other railroad officials, on April 22, "... an event which virtually marked the founding of modern Miami."[19]

On July 28, 1896, Fort Dallas was incorporated into the city of Miami by acclamation of the 312 registered voters present. The vote was unanimous.[20] An editorial on that same day indicated that the citizens preferred to name the city "Flagler," but "... the gentleman who had had so much to do with the development of the East Coast would not permit the use of his name for this city...."[21] Flagler's Royal Palm Hotel opened on January 16, 1897. Nash wrote: "The railroad and the genius behind it breathed the very breath of life into the whole Biscayne Bay region. At last it was accessible to the outside world and once here the traveler was assured of every modern comfort in living conditions. Here was fishing and hunting, swimming and yachting to suit the most ardent enthusiast. Here was the grandest climate imaginable at all seasons, with the accent on winter."[22]

By 1910, when Carl and Jane first saw Miami, the city had grown to a population of 10,000, not including those who vacationed there in the winter season. There were churches, a library, a club, and movie theaters "air conditioned" by letting electric fans blow over blocks of ice.[23] The burgeoning population had also brought pollution; Biscayne Bay was no longer pristine. Sewage and trash had sullied the water.

This was the Miami that Carl had chosen as his new winter home; he loved the water, he loved to race speedboats, and he now had the money and leisure time to indulge himself in whatever he wished. Union Carbide was to offer millions for Prest-O-Lite; when their offer was accepted, Carl's share was $5,633,555.44, most of it in Union Carbide stock.[24] This was a staggering amount of money when by comparison in 1910, the average hourly wage for carpenters was 63 cents and the average monthly salary for teachers had risen to $62.23. Indianapolis friends like Howard Marmon and Harry Stutz came to Miami to visit. John Levi was also there. But even though Carl had told Jane that "I'm going to take it easy,"[25] he was only in his late thirties, used to action, and plenty of it. Jane, not yet twenty, was more content with her new home and the social life in Miami. There were luncheons and teas and tennis with the winter residents. She had named their new house "The Shadows" after the patterns made by the Australian pines that lined the driveway. Carl liked the name so much that when they built a new home, it was also called "The Shadows," as were a series of his yachts.

Carl was described as "restless and bored"[26] in 1912. A new project, however, was literally on the horizon. Looking from his house across Biscayne Bay, he could see the jungle-like peninsula. On his way to fishing trips in the Gulf Stream, he could see the Atlantic side, a far different side; a beautiful ocean beach extending for miles, with coconut palms. He also saw a partially-finished wooden bridge from Miami to the peninsula, a two-and-a-half mile distance. "Collins' folly," the residents called it. When Carl asked the reason for the bridge's lack of progress, he heard the story of John Collins and his financial distress. "...the moment Fisher heard that Collins was 74 years old when he started to build the bridge, he pricked up his ears. Such a man must be worth knowing, perhaps he had a bigger idea than any of his critics dreamed of."[27] When he visited his lawyer, Frank Shutts, also from Indiana, Shutts told him: "You know, Carl, you've got plenty of money and you're too young to retire. Why don't you lend that old man some money and let him finish his bridge. It would give you something to do and give you an interest down here."[28]

Carl was leaning on the door of opportunity and when it opened he was ready.

Chapter 12

Of Coconuts and Avocados

I~n~ 1912 the peninsula to which John Collins was building his bridge — the longest wooden bridge in the world, according to the research done by his son-in-law, Thomas Pancoast — was a place where nobody cared to live. "Miami Beach was then, as it had been for centuries, a forlorn mangrove swamp fronted with a beautiful sea beach known as 'The Beach',"[1] Nash wrote.

It was not without its charm, primarily the ocean beach to which ferries made daily trips for Miamians to swim and picnic. Bathing facilities had been built there in 1904 by an enterprising Connecticut schooner captain, Richard M. Smith, who had come to Miami in 1900 and served as Miami's city clerk and the Dade County tax assessor. He built a two-story building on Ocean Beach on the southern end of the peninsula. Smith had also started a ferry service.[2]

In 1908, Avery Smith from Norwich, Connecticut, saw the bathhouse and, in his words, "an opportunity to establish a pleasure resort and transportation proposition."[3] He purchased a lease to the land with the bathhouse. The following year, he and his friend James C. Warr of Wareham, Massachusetts, formed the Biscayne Navigation Company to develop a beach resort and provide transportation to it. They purchased and refurbished two boats, the *Sallie* and the *Lady Lou*, later building two 60-foot double-decker boats. Wharves were built in Miami and at the beach to accommodate the vessels. The original building was redone, and a pier and a boardwalk were built. The whole enterprise was given the name "Fairy Land."[4]

The rest of the peninsula, swampy and jungle-like, was not suitable for settlement. Development, however, did uncover evidence that there had been some Indian habitation years before. There had once been an Indian village there for more than a century, its population varying from 50 to 100, according to the findings of a site evacuation completed in 1936 by Dr. J.H. Steward and D.L. Reichard of the Smithsonian Institution. The Tequesta (also spelled Tekesta or Tegesta) tribe, they said, had lived there intermittently, alternating with the deep woods on the main land for a change of diet and area. The Tequestas were hunters and fishermen and gathered berries and dug roots. There were abundant natural sources of food: oysters, conchs, deer, raccoon, and land and sea turtles.[5] Because the peninsula lacked metal, the Tequestas used bone for their arrows and spear heads. "The size and strength of these bows amazed the Spaniards who came in contact with them later, for chain mail was of little assistance against the long feathered shafts of reed, with barbed tips ..."[6] The Spanish tried to Christianize the Tequestas, but to no avail. When the Spanish ceded Florida to England in 1763, they transported some Indians to Cuba, where many died. A few survivors returned to Florida.[7]

The earliest white man who might have lived on Miami Beach was a ship's carpenter, John Braman, residing there before 1861. Braman was a naturalized American from the Bahamas, listed in the United States Census of 1860.[8] The federal government was responsible for some other nineteenth-century residents. In 1876 the United States government began building Houses of Refuge along the eastern coast for the victims of shipwrecks. The Biscayne House of Refuge was built on the ocean coast of Miami Beach, stocked with provisions, clothing, blankets, and first aid equipment. Nash notes that many victims of shipwrecks along the coast survived. Only "unusually fierce storms"[9] resulted in many deaths. There were even babies born at the House of Refuge, notably to Jack Peacock, keeper of the house, and his wife in 1885 and 1886.[10]

The tropical climate appealed to some who saw it as the key to producing coconuts for the lucrative New York market. Henry B. Lum from Pennsylvania made his first trip to Florida in 1868. He found three coconut trees growing at Braham's Landing and envisioned a coconut grove.[11] It was Lum's project that brought John Collins to Florida. Although Lum did not return for twelve years, he was anticipating the venture. For 35 cents an acre, he bought a large tract of beach land, which would later become the Ocean Beach development. He enlisted the aid of Ezra Osborn and Elnathan T. Field from Middleton, New Jersey, and obtained financing from old friends. Elnathan Field, "bubbling over with enthusiasm,"[12] had met John Collins at a pomological meeting in New Jersey. Field knew that Collins was interested in new ventures in planting, and his report of the coconut enterprise convinced Collins to advance $5,000. Eventually 60 Northerners invested in the project.[13]

Lum, although an experienced nurseryman, mistakenly believed that each coconut planted would produce a tree, and when the tree matured, it would produce one coconut daily. "No matter what price the yield brought in the market as coconuts, copra, or coconut oil it was bound to net a future for the investors. The real beauty of the whole scheme was its ridiculous simplicity,"[14] Nash wrote of Lum's plan. Lum, Osborn, and Field wanted enough land to expand as well as to discourage competition. They purchased from the government most of the lower east coast of Florida, a 65-mile strip, paying 75 cents to $1.25 an acre.[15] From New Jersey they brought 25 men who had worked at New Jersey lifesaving stations. For the venture, the men repaired lifeboats that were purchased from the government. Men, wagons, mules, tents, a small portable house, tools, and 100-days' worth of provisions were transported from New York to Key West, where a schooner took them to Miami Beach. The schooner anchored a mile offshore, since there were no docks, and the mules were "heaved overboard"[16] to swim to shore with the men. Lifeboats carried the supplies. The schooner then left for Trinidad, where coconuts could be obtained cheaply.

The men faced a formidable task. "Virgin jungle crept right down to the beach, a jungle as dense, forbidding and impenetrable as only the tropics can produce. It was impossible to proceed more than a few feet into its depths without hacking a path with a machete."[17] The workers camped in a natural clearing. An old overgrown Indian trail that went north and south was widened and cleared to be used as a road for the mule teams. On a calm sea, 100,000 coconuts were rafted to shore. When it turned rough, the coconuts were dumped overboard and left to drift ashore up and down the coast for several miles. A total of 38,000 were to be planted on Miami Beach.[18] Even though the site was a veritable jungle, the coconuts were to be planted in neat rows. This was a real challenge. "Some of the men climbed tall trees and sighted to a distant marker, while others struggled through the brush below, carrying long bamboo sighting poles topped with tiny flags, and drove marking stakes as directed at 20 foot intervals across a strip about 100 feet wide. When working in the dense growth in the swamps, accurate planting was facilitated by having the men roped together at 20 foot intervals."[19] No time or expense was spared in planting the coconuts. The work was so arduous that the men refused to return the next year; a new crew had to be recruited. The first shipment of coconuts was planted by spring. The remainder were planted at Cape Florida.

The next year, headquarters were moved near the site of the Biscayne House of Refuge. A total of 117,000 coconuts from Nicaragua were planted on the upper reaches of the old Indian trail; now 155,000 coconuts had been planted. The Lums planted 10,000 on their land. By fall, they had finished. About 117,000 coconuts from Cuba had brought the total planting to 334,000; the original plan was a total of 450,000.[20] The expenses of the three years had decimated the group's financial assets. It would still be three or four years before their crop began to produce riches. Charles H. Lum, in anticipation of the success of the project, had built a two-story home with a porch in 1886. He and his family lived there for three years, growing vegetables, fishing and gathering oysters and turtle eggs. After three years, the Lum family moved, viewing the project as an abject failure. Coconuts usually do best when planted along the shore, as these were planted. But they were not taken care of. In the five to seven years it took for them to mature, only ten percent were to become trees. Rabbits and wood rats ate the tender shoots. They were also smothered by vines and mangroves. The actual annual yield was not one a day, but about one a week. Although the coconuts were of good quality, there were never enough at one time to make up a shipment. Because workers had to travel by water, they were also expensive to gather. No money was left to harvest the coconuts. "By 1890 there was no doubt in anyone's mind that the coconut business had been a mistake, though the empty beach, fringed here and there with the remains of useless but decorative trees, looked more like a South Sea island than ever."[21]

John Collins, upset by the loss of his investment, "... aimed to turn his defeat into victory."[22] He had already lost money in a failed gold mine in North Carolina. He made his first trip to Florida in the early 1890's before the railroad had reached Miami. Collins found land north of Lum's plantation that looked promising. Pine and palmetto grew there, and it had its own fresh water table. "Furthermore, the height and luxuriance of the forest around him proved that this black, sandy soil must be unusually deep."[23]

Collins was born on December 29, 1837, in the family home in Moorestown, New Jersey, where his Quaker forebears had farmed for five generations. At an early age, he made his first attempt at business by spending five dollars on a blackberry bush. In 1855, his father gave him a quarter of an acre of land, which he planted half in strawberries, half in blackberries, producing a crop of 1080 quarts of strawberries the first year.[24] Collins was a shrewd businessman. He started the Pleasant Valley nurseries in Moorestown and proceeded to buy farms near towns where he knew real estate values would rise. After the Civil War, he bought a farm in Merchantville, New Jersey, and raised Wilson blackberries, which he sold in Philadelphia and New York. Realizing the potential market for Kiefer pears, he planted a large orchard.[25] Collins was also "keenly receptive of new ideas."[26] Farm machinery was advancing rapidly, and in 1888 he became a dealer in farm machinery, also selling coal, lumber, and builders' and farmers' supplies. He brought in his son Irving and son-in-law Thomas J. Pancoast as partners — Collins was getting old.[27]

But Collins was not ready to give up on Florida. Used to success in agricultural pursuits, Collins "intended to follow his own inclinations through to a finish, provided the land came up to his expectations."[28] He began to bargain for the land owned by Osborn and Field, in 1907 finally succeeding in purchasing Osborn's share and becoming partners with Field, who still had hopes of receiving a return for his investment. Collins was prudent, however; he consulted native farmers and asked for suggestions from private and government plant experts. The final plan was to plant avocados, then an exotic fruit that could command premium prices. Field preferred to grow grapefruit, a proven seller.[29] In 1907 Collins was the sole owner of a five-mile strip of land between the Atlantic Ocean and Biscayne Bay. The area he farmed was a mile long, 700 feet wide, on the high land west of Indian Creek. A tenant who worked the farm lived in a wooden house there while Collins resided in a hotel in Miami.[30]

Clearing the 160 acres that made up the farm was expensive. At first Collins hired blacks to clear the land with plows, axes, machetes, and mattocks, but it was a time-consuming job, costing up to $300 an acre. Contacting some of the businessmen he knew in the North, Collins ordered sixteen-ton, thirty-five horsepower tractors, which he himself designed with knife-bladed wheels. "The knives chopped up the buried scrub palmetto roots that had been giving so much trouble. Special gang-plows brought them to the surface and permitted their quick removal."[31] The savings was substantial, only a $30 cost per acre. The tractors did more work than 50 men.

Collins planted 2,945 avocado trees propagated by George B. Cellon, a local plant expert. He paid $1 per tree.[32] Making the new crop prosper took some doing. The trade winds blew sand on the new plants and the salt of the sea could cause damage. Field, anticipating another failure, had had enough. He sold out to Collins in 1907. Collins became the owner of 1670 acres of oceanfront land, four and one-half miles along the Atlantic side and a mile along Biscayne Bay.[33]

At first, it looked as though Field were right. The first planting was not very successful. Individual burlap windbreaks were tried, but they were expensive and could be used only during initial growth. Then Collins discovered the Australian pine; he planted them as a barricade. They grew quickly and protected the new plants on the Atlantic side of the groves. Elsewhere they were planted in squares. The new plants required daily irrigation, accomplished through an overhead pipe system. This method promoted evaporation and was later replaced by subsoil irrigation.[34]

There was also a transportation problem. Boats taking the harvest to market were running aground on the turtlegrass flats. Collins had grown four acres of Cavendish bananas and other tropical fruit, plus some garden vegetables. Any delay in the hot sun was detrimental to all of his produce. In 1911 Collins told his family and friends in New Jersey his solution: a mile-long canal which would also cut the distance to Miami in half. His friends thought him crazy; his family worried about the expense. They wished to inspect the property in person. Sons Lester, Arthur and Irving, Irving's wife, and his daughter Katherine and son-in-law Thomas Pancoast spent three weeks in Florida.[35]

At the age of 74, Collins was planning to spend thousands of dollars on ventures that could risk his and his family's fortunes. His son Irving organized his brothers Lester and Arthur, Thomas Pancoast and himself as "support and safety valve for the Florida venture."[36] They agreed to invest in the project, contingent upon John Collins building a bridge as well. A bridge that would bring motor traffic would encourage development of a winter resort and raise the value of the property. The family formed the Miami Beach Improvement Company with this end in mind. The only family members willing to move to Miami to oversee the new projects were Thomas and Katherine Pancoast. Pancoast saw a bright future for the new company from the beginning. "He was flabbergasted at the progress that had been made and at the quality of the produce being raised between the rows of young avocado trees ... overnight he became an enthusiast."[37] Eighteen carloads of Red Bliss potatoes had been grown that year. "'Such potatoes!' said Pancoast. 'They were not the kind that were soggy when cooked, they were firm and mealy, fell to pieces under your fork and simply melted in your mouth.'"[38] But it was the avocado orchard that took precedence. Pancoast knew that he was needed more in Miami Beach than in New Jersey. The next year he and his wife moved to Miami Beach, Collins' son Irving having bought out his business interests in New Jersey.

Collins had the bridge route surveyed and applied for a franchise to build the two-and-a-half mile bridge, but there was opposition. The bridge posed a threat to the Biscayne Navigation Company. Their ferry business would suffer if it were built. Collins made use of a suggestion made to him by Charles H. Ward of Miami: drive his car to the dock and demand that it be ferried to the beach. In the presence of a witness, he was refused.[39] On the basis that the beach was useless to him if he could not transport his car back and forth, Collins reapplied for the franchise. This time it was granted.

Work on the canal had already begun. Laying its route through the jungle was impossible; instead, at a point on the bay shore, timber and brush were piled, waiting for a calm day. Then, the bonfire was lit, producing a "tall, dense column of smoke."[40] From the bayshore, the smoke enabled them to align the stakes with some additional smaller fires. The fill from the canal was used for roadbed for the bridge.

Bids were put out for the bridge; J.I. Conklin was appointed engineer in charge. Work began July 22, 1912. Problems quickly materialized. The marine borer, *limnoria lignorum,* would devour submerged wood; it had to be protected. Surrounding the wood pilings with concrete was the answer, but using forms proved too slow. The concrete had to harden before the forms could be used again. Instead, Collins ordered sheet iron measuring two feet by six feet, wide enough to use as forms. The iron was rolled and riveted into cylinders and slipped over the pilings into the water. The workmen could now pour the concrete as fast as they could mix it. The forms did not need to be removed. This solution was expensive. The sheet iron and concrete cost $10,000. The estimated cost of the bridge was only $75,000.[41] When the bridge was halfway across, the contracting company failed. Collins' credit was exhausted, and he had no ready cash. The bridge stood unfinished until Carl Fisher came to the rescue.

Chapter 13

A Bridge to Development

Although John Collins was an Easterner twice Carl Fisher's age, had a farming background, and came from Quaker roots, he and Carl were in many ways alike. Both were successful businessmen willing to take chances, seizing opportunities that others were oblivious to, and making use of new technology and machinery as soon as it became available.

John Collins and Carl first met accidentally when Carl, Jane, and John Levi went exploring in a dinghy and made their way up Indian Creek in the jungle. As Jane recalled: "... when we got close to a sort of clearing, there stood a little man. He was a very short man. He had a white beard — it was a white goatee — and the whitest shirt and the bluest suit that I have ever seen. He wore a bow tie, a polka-dot blue-and-white tie. It impressed me to see a man so immaculately dressed standing amidst all this wild territory."[1] The encounter was brief. Carl asked Collins how to get back to Biscayne Bay, and Collins said, "Turn around and go back the way you came." They did not even know who he was.

In 1912 when Carl decided to help Collins finish the bridge, he lent him $50,000. Collins gave him 200 acres of beach land, one mile long and 1,800 feet wide from the ocean to the bay.[2] In characteristic fashion, when Carl, Collins and Tom Pancoast went to see the land, Carl raced his speedboat up the newly-dug Collins Canal, the surging waves washing against the banks, causing mud and marl to crumble into

154

(Matlack; HASF)

Seated, left to right: Mrs. T.J. Pancoast, John Collins, Arthur Pancoast

the water. Polly Redford cites Tom Pancoast's dismay as he and Collins looked at the damage being caused, but only "… groaned, 'Oh, my God! But we can't tell this nut to slow down!'"[3]

Collins Bridge was finished in May, 1913, costing 33 percent more than the original estimate. It began where Collins Canal reached the bay. The toll bridge had 2,100 pilings and a 24-foot roadbed, 18 feet of it useable.[4] The Thomas Pancoast family were the first to cross the span by automobile on May 22. Builders, contractors, and journalists accompanied them.

The bridge did not reach all the way to the peninsula. It ended at Bull's Island, owned by Carl, and visitors took a foot bridge to the beach. Cars had to be turned around on Bull's Island until a dirt road was built between the island and the beach.

The official grand opening came on June 12, 1913. The mayor of Miami spoke, comparing the bridge to the new railroad that had reached Key West.[5] The parade of automobiles and other vehicles traveled across the beach, turned around on Bull's Island, and headed back. Neither John Collins nor Carl Fisher was there. John Collins was back home in New Jersey,

Carl was back in Indiana, preparing for the Hoosier Tour. Before leaving Miami, he had asked John Levi to stay through the summer, to oversee the development of Carl's property.[6]

Carl had acquired more land early in 1913 from another Miami Beach pioneer, J.N. Lummus. Lummus, his brother J.E. Lummus, and some associates had purchased the land holdings of Henry B. Lum. In his *The Miracle of Miami Beach*, J.N. Lummus writes that they "... decided that the future of Miami Beach did not lie in growing cocoanuts, but would eventually be a real 'Paradise Under the Sun' for the Sun Seekers of the North."[7] Lummus had first come to Miami in 1895 from Bronson, Florida. Two years later he returned to his job as dispatcher for the Atlantic Coast Railroad for seven years, and then was back in Miami "to make my future home."[8] He worked for his brother, who had a commissary contract with the Florida East Coast Railroad, making weekly boat trips to check supplies and collect the money owed. The business was sold in 1908.[9]

The two brothers went into banking, J.N. becoming president of the Southern Bank and Trust Company, and J.E. president of the Bank of Bay Biscayne. John Collins had received loans from both banks when he started to build the bridge: $10,000 from the Southern Bank and Trust Company and $15,000 from the Bank of Key Biscayne.[10] The experience that Lummus gained in the keys is what, Lummus says, "gave me the vision about building a city fronting on the ocean, so in May, 1912, I formed a company with my brother, J.E. Lummus...."[11] The new Ocean Beach Realty Company bought about 500 acres from Lum and Edmund Wilson of Red Bank, New Jersey. In October, they purchased 80 adjoining acres. The cash capital of the new realty company was $50,000, with the rest of their capital borrowed at 8 percent. There were other investors in the company who soon became impatient with the time it would take to make a profit and sold out to the Lummus brothers. J.N. Lummus then resigned his position at the bank and took charge of the beach development.[12] The only way the Lummuses could pay off their debts and recoup their capital was to sell lots, and they wasted no time in doing so. Before Collins filed his first plat in December of 1912, the Ocean Beach Realty Company had sold over $40,000 worth of lots.[13] Their progress was so rapid that the *Miami Metropolis* took note of it on January 10, 1913: "It took faith to undertake the job of making the waste of sand and the mangrove swamp into an attractive and habitable place, but faith marches at the head of progress, and there are now few doubters as to the ultimate outcome."[14] The Lummuses were building a twenty-foot wide rock road from Collins Bridge through the whole Lummus tract. When the road and the bridge were completed, it would be only a seven-mile drive from the center of Miami to the southern end of the Ocean Beach Realty property.[15]

Carl was not oblivious to the progress being made by the Ocean Beach Realty Company at the southern end of the peninsula just south of his property. Progress made by any of the three developers — the Lummuses, Collins, and Carl — would be a benefit to all. Lummus recalled his first business contact with Carl Fisher:

> Early in 1913, Carl G. Fisher came into my office and introduced himself... Fisher said to me: "I see that you are clearing a great deal of land on the peninsula. What are you going to do?" I told him that we were going to build a city fronting on the ocean. He wanted to know the amount of land which we owned and I told him. "Well," said Fisher, "Why don't you do it all at one time?" I told him we had a very good reason and that was the lack of funds. This conversation must have started something, for within six weeks, after my brother and I met Fisher, we had arranged to borrow one hundred and fifty thousand dollars from him at eight percent interest. But we also gave him one hundred and five acres of land off the north end of our property as a bonus for the land. We had paid one hundred and fifty dollars per acre for the land we gave Fisher. This deal, and this alone, started the big development in Miami Beach. It could not have been done otherwise.[16]

Lummus cites the Dade County Book of Records to prove

that it was the Lummus brothers' Ocean Beach Realty Company that started the first subdivision on Miami Beach, filing its plat on July 9, 1912. In comparison, Collins' first plat was filed on December 11, 1912, and Carl's on January 15, 1914.[17]

The money Carl lent to the Ocean Beach Realty Company was immediately put to good use. They purchased three passenger boats, starting a boat service from Miami to Biscayne Bay, charging five cents per passenger. It was a losing proposition for the company, but they made it up with the sale of lots that resulted from the trips. "Everyone coming to Miami wanted to know what was going on across the Bay, as it could be seen from the Miami side that something was being done.... The boat trip was so popular that some of the people rode back and forth all day as it cost only ten cents per hour for the Bay trip,"[18] Lummus wrote. While lots were selling, the pace was still not brisk enough for the company's financial needs. The Ocean Beach Realty Company resorted to public auctions, an idea Lummus said came from E.E. (Doc) Dammers, "who must have been the world's premier auctioneer of lots, because he proved it."[19] All of the development companies were to take advantage of Dammers' ability.

Bidding on the property for sale wasn't the aim of many of those who attended: everyone received a number on their boat trip over, and numbers were drawn periodically for free dishes, sets of china, crockery, glassware, and other items. J.N. Lummus said that his company "bought chinaware by the carload"[20] to give away at the auctions. "We did not get the prices we actually wanted for our lots, but we were satisfied."[21] By June 15, 1913, the Ocean Beach Realty Company had cleared 40 acres, graded them, and built streets. They were also constructing a ten-foot wide boardwalk.[22]

The Miami Beach Improvement Company was also proceeding rapidly. They held a four-day auction on February 19, 1913, selling 104 oceanfront lots at prices from $760 to $3,700.[23] The giveaways at their auction were attractive come-on's: leather goods, clocks, opera glasses, vases, dinner sets, and Oriental rugs. The 3,000 people who attended were assured that sewers, water, electricity, cement sidewalks, and an elevated boardwalk would be built, and buyers would receive free use of the bridge for five years. A total of $66,000 worth of land was sold, fifty percent of it for cash, the rest in monthly installments. "The striking success of this auction dissolved the last shades of doubt as to the future of Miami Beach,"[24] Nash wrote.

Carl, with his business interests in Indianapolis, could not be in Miami year round. But he had, as Howard Kleinberg put it in his book, *Miami Beach:* "a genius for marketing that eclipsed his colleagues in land sales and development of Miami Beach."[25] He planned to plot 77 city blocks, build streets that would be as wide as boulevards, enlarge Bull's Island and dredge a channel to Government Cut.[26]

Chapter 14

"Crazy" Fisher Again

AₗₜₕₒᵤGH JₐₙE FₗₛₕER enjoyed wintering in Miami, she did not share her husband's newfound enthusiasm for developing the peninsula. When he showed her the new property, she was appalled.

> We walked, stepping gingerly and slapping at mosquitoes, skirting the swamp going toward the Beach. An old alligator roared its resentment of our invasion of their age-old jungle. Mosquitos blackened our white clothing. Jungle flies, as large as horse flies, waited for our blood.... The jungle itself was as hot and steamy as a conservatory. What on earth could Carl possibly see in such a place, I wondered crossly as I picked my way through the morass in my white shoes.[1]

When they reached the beach, he used a stick to draw for her the city he planned to build and told her of the house he was planning for them on the oceanfront. "But I looked at that rooted and evil-smelling morass and had nothing to say. There was nothing a devoted wife could say. Other people were to be less considerate."[2] Her sentiments were shared by many in Miami and in Indianapolis. As Polly Redford put it, "... for a long time everyone thought Fisher was crazy to spend millions pumping up new acreage when, on the mainland, hundreds of miles of high land could be bought so cheaply."[3] Back in Indianapolis, when Carl told his friends that he was planning to spend $75,000 for a "winter playland for himself and his friends,"[4] they showed little enthusiasm. At one point

Jim Allison warned him, "'Don't go on with it. It's too big a job for one man.'"[5]

On Carl's side, besides his considerable resources, both financial and personal, were the natural advantages of the peninsula. The Gulf Stream was only two-and-a-half miles off the beach. The warm shallow water gave the beach "an appreciably milder climate than Miami's...."[6] The mean monthly temperature varied only 14.4 degrees, the average being 67.7 degrees in January and 82.1 degrees in August, the coldest and warmest months, respectively.[7] Oceanfront property would bring premium prices; and Biscayne Bay, which he planned to dredge, would be ideal for boat races. The bay's shoreline would be ideal for yacht clubs and vacation homes for yacht owners. Thus, Carl was not deterred by public or private criticism or the expense and obstacles to be faced in building his "winter playland." Originally, his plans were to reclaim 1,000 acres of lowland; this eventually became 2,760 acres.[8]

At first, Carl hired hundreds of black laborers to hack away the palmetto and mangroves. Jane described the difficulty of clearing the jungle:

> The pigmy-high palmetto had slender roots that reached out like tentacles from the thick top root, and these deceitfully delicate-looking roots turned the steel blades of the machetes. The palmettos were almost impossible even for mules to uproot with chains and grappling hooks. I have seen Carl tugging with his hands at a small palmetto, trying to break it free from the sand, cursing until I stopped my ears.
>
> The mangroves, with their canopy of glistening green leaves, were fascinating; but steely roots showered from the tips to fasten the trees to the ground with a network strong as metal mesh. The vice-like roots defied the heaviest axes.[9]

Jane added that clearing one acre by manual labor cost $1,500.

When Carl was back in Indianapolis, his problem with clearing the jungle was solved inadvertently when he mentioned it to Al Webb, one of his friends from barnstorming days. Webb told him that he was designing a plow to clear some land on the West Coast. Carl asked him to make one for his Florida project. The machete plow with triangular blades cost $1,000 to ship to Florida.[10] Carl bought a $5,000 Caterpillar tractor to pull the plow. It was too large to go over Collins Bridge and had to be transported on a barge.

When they tried out the new plow, Al Webb drove the tractor while Carl sat and watched. The palmettos were ripped out "...as if they were ferns. Under the heaving palmettos, the ruptured land fairly boiled.

"Carl was on his feet whooping, 'Look at 'em boil, Al, look at 'em boil!' He ran along besides the tractor like an excited boy, 'Boil, you goddamn roots, boil!'"[11]

Carl took a turn at driving the tractor, continuing to whoop at the ease with which the plow was clearing the land. Ten acres could be cleared in a day. Al Webb also devised a way to get rid of the mangroves. He fastened a steel cable to a tractor and looped it to 100 trees at a time. "Their trunks snapped with a sound like machine-gun fire as the matted mangroves gave."[12]

The marshy land had to be filled with sand dredged from the bay bottom. Carl had some small experience with dredging near The Shadows. To eliminate the nuisance of garbage and trash floating near his dock, he had hired a dredge to make a protective point of land. In addition, he had an interest in the dredging and development of Point View, a new bayfront subdivision near The Shadows.[13]

The major expense for filling in the hundreds of acres on the peninsula was the dredging. The fill would cost nothing, as the bay bottom was owned by the state of Florida, which charged nothing for it. The extent of the project prompted the Lummus' interests and Carl to act together in obtaining a permit from both the state of Florida and the federal government to dredge the bay bottom and fill in the swamp land. They intended to dredge six million cubic yards of bay bottom at a cost of ten cents per cubic yard, a total of $600,000. The Lummus Company was to pay $315,000 and Carl's company $285,000. No one had attempted such a project before; the federal government issued them Federal Permit Number 1 for the work in Florida. The Clark Construction Company of Baltimore, Maryland, was awarded the bid in July, 1913.[14]

That same month, the Lummus brothers arranged for the county commissioners to inspect the developments. Carl, John S. Collins, and J.A. McDonald of the Ocean Beach Realty Company were all there to accompany them on this tour. The object was not just good public relations. The commissioners were offered a deed to land for a road from Collins Bridge along the canal. They agreed that Dade County would pay one-third of the cost of building the road, with Carl and the Lummus company also paying a third each. Work on the road began almost immediately. "It took ten men one week to cut a right-of-way from where Mr. Collins was then having the canal dug to South Beach. I started cutting the right-of-way at South Beach and Fisher met with his cutting at Fourteenth Lane, or midway on the Carney Tract. This was the first road suitable for automobiles built on Miami Beach, and it was completed in 1913,"[15] Lummus wrote.

The dredges were in Miami a week before the permits even arrived. Carl, having to return to Indianapolis to promote the Lincoln Highway, left John Levi in charge. The *Norman H. Davis,* a "colossal steel-hulled dredge"[16] as Edgar Nash referred to it, dredged the fill for the Ocean Beach Realty Company. The dredge had on board its own complete machine and repair shop and its own ice plant. It had a 1,000-horsepower engine, enabling it to throw a twenty-inch stream of the bay bottom a mile through a twenty-inch pipe. It could move 20,000 cubic yards of fill in twenty-four hours. Two smaller dredges, the *Florida* and the *Biscayne,* were filling in Carl's and Collins' land. The two had 250-horsepower engines with a capacity of throwing 6,000 to 8,000 cubic yards a day in a twelve-inch stream. When the fill had to be carried two miles, the two dredges worked in tandem.[17]

What they were dredging from the bay was a mixture of sand, mud, and marl, resembling "sloppy Cream of Wheat,"[18] as Polly Redford described it. The workers referred to it as "soup." Jane wrote that the "fill was like thick soup. We found the men working in mud and slime up to their knees. They wore long boots to guard against the bite of snakes."[19] Sometimes the dredges broke down, or the pipes parted and the fill went the wrong way. Divers had to clear pipes clogged with weeds. "There were times when a ladder of men standing on one another's shoulders were forced under water to hold the bottom man in place so that he could work cleaning the pipe."[20]

Carl first had to fill Bull's Island, where the Collins Bridge ended, so that the road could be built to the beach. Most of the trees were cleared, but, here, as elsewhere in the development, the best trees were deliberately spared. The *Florida* pumped 300,000 cubic yards of sand on Bull's Island in four days' time, creating 32 acres of land.[21] For aesthetic reasons, the island was renamed Belle Isle in 1914.

The "soup" had to drain and thicken before anything could be done with it. For six months it was left undisturbed so that the algae and marine life could dry or rot away and the smell could dissipate.[22] There were accidents. On Bull's Island, two mules fell into the fill and drowned. J. Arthur Pancoast, Thomas's son, attempted to bury them there, but their bodies resurfaced twice. He had to have them ferried to the mainland for burial.[23] Others, Jane said, fell into the fill "trying to escape the blood-sucking insects."[24] One went in upside down and had to be rescued. Some mules were burned when they backed into the smudge pots Carl had set to burn at night to keep away the mosquitoes and sandflies.[25]

Carl had returned in August and took an active part in the development, often working with the men. "He encouraged them, he talked to them. He knew them all,"[26] according to Jane's account. At night he and Jane would take them sandwiches and coffee.

The shoreline had to be reinforced as well, at a cost of ten dollars a running foot. Steam shovels made dikes out of the bay bottom. Pile drivers sank supports for the pilings, to which wooden timbers were attached with steel cables.[27]

Roads were a top priority in the development. They were built as soon as an area of fill was ready for development. Crews would lay out home, street and hotel sites. To facilitate road-building, in September Carl built a mile-long, narrow-gauge, miniature railroad with small freight cars and a steam engine along Collins Canal to carry supplies while he was building Lincoln Road. Each car was capable of carrying one-and-a-half yards of material. The tracks were so light that they could easily be relaid wherever they were needed. He called it the Alton Beach Railroad, as he had named his development Alton Beach. He had decided on this name on a whim, according to Jane's account. One day when they had boarded the train to return to Indianapolis, he looked out the window and saw a freight train with the name "Chicago, Northwestern and Alton Railroad" on one of the cars. He snapped his fingers and exclaimed, "'I've got it! ...I'll call her Alton Beach!'"[28]

Now a "railroad magnate," Carl, as a joke, had railroad passes printed for his "Alton Beach Railroad." He sent them to the presidents of the largest railroads in the country. The passes looked so impressive and realistic that three of the railroads sent him passes in return.[29]

The railroad carried thousands of tons of rock obtained from the banks of a drainage canal that went from Lake Okeechobee to Miami. Carl had a Brown hoisting engine to scoop a load of rock onto barges, which were then towed up the canal. Another hoist put it on a train of dump cars.[30] The other companies loaded and emptied barges by hand, with the rock hauled by mules from a wharf.

The continuous work brought quick results. Soon, those passing by saw quite a sight: "... the bayside gradually began to look as if it were covered by a glittering, hard-packed layer of snow standing five feet above the tide."[31] J.N. Lummus noted that they still faced a considerable task before anyone could build on the new-made land: "After the dredge work was done, we looked over a wide area of sand and muck and thought that after the silt settled, all we would have to do would be to survey our properties, and sell more lots to build the city by the ocean. This was not the case. The filled-in land became dry, and the gentle breezes were no longer zephyrs. The winds actually blew up sandstorms, so we had to plant grass on our man-made ground."[32]

Good soil was needed to establish new grass. Mulch from the Everglades was brought by barge, spread, and graded.[33] All the blades of grass, the flowers, and the trees were planted by hand. Jane remembered: "Hundreds of Negroes, most of them women and children, crawled on their hands and knees over the earth pushing ahead of them baskets of grass from Bermuda."[34] On his new land, J.N. Lummus hired school children on Saturdays. He gave them free rides and paid them ten cents an hour. "The children had fun out of it, and many of them would run over to the ocean for a brief dip and return to plant more grass seed."[35] Thousands of trees and shrubs were also planted, of many different sizes and species. Nash said they "transformed the place overnight into something pretty close to a tropical fairyland."[36] Carl had placed responsibility for the planting in the hands of Fred Hoerger, a young man who had been their assistant gardener at Blossom Heath. He planted bougainvillea, orchid trees, poinciana, hibiscus and thousands of oleander.[37]

Carl's land was finally ready to be put up for sale.

Carl Fisher's Alton Beach Company office was at 331 Lincoln Road in 1922. (Fishbaugh; SPA)

Chapter 15

Sales Begin at Alton Beach

On December 10, 1913, Carl opened the Alton Beach Realty Company, a few weeks before the winter season began on January 1. A full-page advertisement in the *Miami Herald* listed all the improvements that had already been made and the improvements still to come. In a news story, the *Herald* raved about Alton Beach:

> ...Alton Beach today seems a fairy land, and the story of its development during the past twelve months reads like a romance, to which, however, "finis" has by no means been written, for each day sees some new beauty added to it.
>
> ...more than a hundred acres is covered with a velvety carpet of fine grass, homes are in the course of construction, streets and boulevards made, shrubbery and trees planted, a golf course laid out.[1]

The story noted that Carl had already spent $300,000. His ad promised electric lights and telephones in January, 1914, and city water and sewerage by December 1, 1915. There were twelve miles of rock roads already built, an oceanfront walk, and an observation tower. Under construction were a 300-foot ocean pier, a golf course, tennis courts and clubhouse, and 200 acres of house lots. Carl announced that he was planning a hotel and two eight-story office buildings on Lincoln Road. In January, 1915, there would be a winter festival, organized by the Magic Knights of Miami, featuring a regatta in Biscayne Bay, organized and sponsored by Carl.[2]

The city of Miami was growing apace. Its population at the end of 1913 was 18,240, a 44 percent increase in one year.[3] But Carl knew that his buyers were not going to be local residents; he needed events and amenities to create a real "winter playland" for the prospective customers he hoped to attract. To demonstrate his faith in Alton Beach, Carl announced in March of 1914 that he would build a new $65,000 home on the oceanfront at Lincoln Road, with construction starting later that year.[4]

Carl's Alton Beach Realty Company, Lummus' Ocean Beach Company and Collins/Pancoast's Miami Beach Improvement Company were all advertising to promote sales. "However, the main thing lacking," J.N. Lummus wrote, "was the need of more houses. The Lummus Company had auctioned off lots and sold other lots. Fisher and Collins had auctioned off lots and sold more lots, but the mere fact of owning a lot did not mean that the purchasers intended to build a house."[5] The Lummus Company, which was the first to begin sales, advertised on January 22, 1914, that they had sold 178 lots, mostly to Miamians. To encourage building, Lummus offered a free lot on Collins Avenue to the first 25 persons who would build homes on the lots. Lummus specified the type and minimum cost for the houses. His offer was made in full-page ads in the Miami newspapers. Lummus received a total of 73 applicants for his lots, finally giving away more than 30. Lummus notes that he was not requiring expensive homes. He said that they were "really typical beach houses, inexpensive yet modern at that time."[6] In his book *The Miracle of Miami Beach*, copyright in 1944, Lummus maintains that many of those houses still existed, "having passed through hurricanes and the boom days."[7] Lummus had good reason to try every method to sell his lots; in 1914 the Lummus Company owed more than $460,000 at 8 percent interest, $150,000 owed to Carl Fisher.[8]

The promise of electricity that Carl had promised in his ad was not easy to fulfill. The Miami Electric Company refused to run a line across the bay. The three development companies then had to pay the cost of the line. Lummus wrote: "When Collins ran out of cash, he would say: 'I will give you some land.' And I would say to Fisher: 'You will have to take the land. We are short of cash.'"[9] Eventually, Carl had to build his own generating plant.

Collins and Pancoast were attempting to make the beach more desirable by building a bathing pavilion that opened in January of 1914. Carl lent them $8,000 for the improvements. To save money, the bathhouse was built from driftwood. But there was a new attraction; a 50 foot by 150 foot concrete swimming pool so that swimmers could enjoy the water even when the unpredictable ocean turned rough.[10]

Not far from the pavilion, Thomas Pancoast was building a house on Pancoast Lake (formerly called Indian Lake). Before completing the two-story, poured concrete structure, he and his family of wife and three sons lived in a smaller structure which included a two-car garage, kitchen, dining room and living room-bedroom. The three boys had to sleep in tents. Keeping them company were the crocodiles that sunned themselves on the beach and the mosquitos, which son Russell Pancoast said "'were beyond belief.'"[11] Russell recalled how anyone going into the house was immediately sprayed for the sandflies and mosquitoes. Workmen used newspapers under their stockings to prevent mosquito bites and wore mosquito nets over their wide-brimmed hats.[12] The insect problem would not be resolved until all of the fill was completed, eliminating the breeding grounds on the swampy land.

Carl and Jane returned to Indianapolis for the summer of 1914. He was eager to know what was going on in European auto racing, but not to go see for himself. "'... you can't get a decent steak in Europe,'"[13] he told Jane. It was a very hot summer in Indianapolis, but, as usual, Carl had the fireplace blazing while he fanned himself as he sat in front of it. When he suddenly said, "'For two cents I'd go to Europe,'"[14] Jane immediately went to make arrangements without his knowledge. She had them scheduled on the *Imperator*, necessitating their leaving Indianapolis the very next day to board the boat in New York, not giving Carl any time to object.

On the boat, without the frenetic activity he was accustomed to, Carl sulked. One night, smoke came streaming up from the floor. Carl grabbed an axe, and together with other passengers, managed to squelch the flames originating under the floor.[15] Once in France at the Continental Hotel, he went downstairs with racer Johnny Aitken while Jane unpacked. He returned shortly and told her to pack — that there was going to be a war and they had to go home. He managed to make reservations to leave from England the next day. In the morning, they made a trip to LeMans to watch the European race drivers who were going to race at the Speedway. While they were sitting in the grandstand, the loudspeaker announced that the German ultimatum had been issued to Russia.[16]

Knowing that war was imminent, they rushed back to Paris and hurried to make the *Imperator's* return trip to America only to find that it had been canceled. England had declared war on Germany. The next day while Jane rushed around London seeing the sights, Carl used his money and influence to book passage home. He managed to get them on the *Laurentic,* but they had to travel quickly to Liverpool to board the ship. The crowded boat was accompanied by a British cruiser for 150 miles. After that, it went a hundred miles off course to prevent detection by German submarines. Blackout rules were in effect.[17]

Carl, Jane discovered later, had suspected the fire aboard the *Imperator* was caused by sabotage.[18] In her youthful disappointment of having her first trip to Europe spoiled, she cried most of the way home, even blaming Carl for causing the war.[19]

The war would be responsible for temporarily canceling races at the Speedway and for depressing sales in Florida. But that was still to come.

Chapter 16

Home on the Beach

War or no war, Carl had no choice but to promote the selling of Alton Beach. He had already poured hundreds of thousands into the venture, with very little return. Work continued, making more and more lots available, and he needed something that would bring Northerners to Miami. Henry Flagler had brought the railroad to Miami, but little had been done on highway improvement. Carl's new project was the Dixie Highway, a north-south highway from Chicago to Miami. With W.S. Gilbreath of the Hoosier Motor Club, Carl made plans for the new road, mapping routes and lining up participants.

The new road was first announced in Indianapolis. Carl had posed this question to a reporter for the *Indianapolis News:* "How do you think the country would take a proposal to build a great highway from Indianapolis to Miami, Florida?" The reporter wrote: "It was a tremendous thing, a partnership of the north and south in an intersectional enterprise. Fisher said it could be done, and when he said it — well, it could be done."[1]

Carl faced a formidable task. In 1910, the year he had first come to Miami, roads in the South were the "poorest in the entire country."[2]

Deplorable roads were, indeed, one of the South's most visible deficiencies. Overland travel in the southern United States was difficult during most of the year but next to impossible during rainy winter months. Some communities in mountainous areas of the South were completely isolated from the outside world when rain and snow made the roads impassable, even for a mule. A day of rain could turn a rural road into a quagmire for a full week; and thus affected not only local farmers who needed to transport their crops to market but hapless travelers who found themselves stranded in the middle of nowhere, stuck in the mud.[3]

Instead of improving over the years, Southern roads had deteriorated ever since the Civil War, mainly because of politics. Before the Civil War, the federal government had funded post roads, including a dozen in the South by 1823, and spent $7,000,000 by 1838 for a post road from Cumberland, Maryland, to St. Louis, Missouri.[4] After the Civil War, the federal government no longer appropriated federal funds for roads; influential Southern legislators opposed such spending because of higher taxes and fears that the federal government was usurping states' rights and violating the Constitution.[5]

Southern roads were built and maintained at the county level since colonial times. In lieu of paying local taxes, male citizens were required to work on the roads for a day or more every year. Because Southern states were mostly agrarian, the work was done using farm machinery. But according to Howard L. Preston, author of *Dirt Roads to Dixie*, "Most citizens never spent a day doing road work, preferring either to pay the small annual fine or to enlist the assistance of a local politician who had the power to grant a permanent exemption from the requirement."[6] Those that did work had no training; it was not until 1913 that Southern colleges even offered courses in civil engineering and highway construction.[7] State legislatures gave local governments the authority to use convicts "in their jurisdiction"[8] for road work. Preston writes that it was convict labor that completed most road improvements before 1910.[9]

There were efforts to improve Southern roads before Carl conceived the idea of the Dixie Highway. When the federal government instituted the Rural Free Delivery system in 1896,

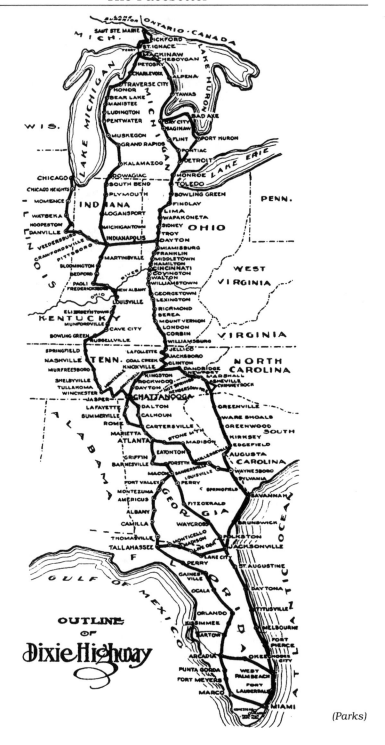

OUTLINE
OF
Dixie Highway

(Parks)

the policy of the Post Office Department influenced farmers to improve their roads. In 1899, the department would not build rural postal routes "where existing roads were altogether unfit for the successful delivery of the mail."[10] Farmers began to improve local roads and join good roads organizations. However, farmers generally opposed bond issues for roads; they did not want to pay for the bond issues even though they would receive the most benefit from improved farm-to-market roads. Bad weather would no longer prevent them from getting their crops to town. Railroad freight rates could go down if the railroads faced competition from improved roads. But the farmers remained opposed to indebtedness. In the 1880's crop surpluses had brought them only low prices; the "crop mortgage system...kept them constantly in debt."[11] Their opposition did not prevail. Bond issues for road improvements were being approved in most Southern states by 1910, except for Kentucky, Arkansas, and South Carolina.[12]

Good roads enthusiasts from other areas were to have a great impact on improving Southern roads. Congress had established a national highway commission in 1892 and the Office of Public Roads Inquiry in the Department of Agriculture in 1893, largely because of the efforts of the League of American Wheelmen, a national bicyclists' organization that sponsored road tours.[13] The Wheelmen seldom sponsored tours south of Pennsylvania because of the poor roads. In 1897, only 2.3% of members were from the South; most members were from the more affluent Northeast where there were more hard-surfaced roads.[14]

One unique method of promoting good roads was the Good Roads Train which toured six Southern states from October 29, 1901, to April 2, 1902. Sponsored by the National Good Roads Organization, the Office of Public Roads Inquiry, and the Southern Railroad Company, the train carried laborers, road-building machinery, and good roads' delegates. Samuel Spenser, president of the Southern Railroad, promoted the tour, seeing more profits for the railroad if rural roads were improved and more goods could be brought to market.[15] At each of the train's 18 stops, an "object lesson" road was built, to demonstrate correct construction methods, show the advantages of well-built roads, and encourage the use of local materials to save money. The founding of fourteen new good roads associations was directly attributed to the tour.[16]

Good roads associations proliferated throughout the South, as well as throughout the rest of the United States. There were 25 in Florida by 1912.[17] The associations lobbied politicians for funds for road improvement and sponsored automobile endurance contests, among other activities. Besides the benefits to farmers, Southerners began to see in good roads a way to improve education, bring enlightenment and end provincialism, as well as increase church attendance and give more equality to women.[18]

But it was the increasing number of automobiles, cheap enough for the middle class to afford, that would bring about the most improvements in roads. Prior to 1910, those traveling to the South went there for their health or were wealthy enough to afford spending the winter in expensive hotels, such as Henry Flagler's hotels in St. Augustine, Ormond Beach, and Palm Beach.[19] Ironically, farmers were often against autos: they frightened their animals, tore up roads, and occasionally damaged their property.[20]

Tourists had begun to travel south, even over the unimproved roads. As early as 1902, automobile racing was held at Ormond and Daytona Beaches, attracting hundreds of people.[21] The American Automobile Association before 1910 began to receive hundreds of requests for information on routes through the South. There was so little information available that it took the association three years to "compile, organize, and publish a detailed routing guide for the region."[22]

In 1910, these new tourists experienced challenging trips. "Traveling into the South meant riding for days over bone-jarring rutted roads, fording streams and rivers, removing fallen trees and broken branches from roadways, getting sunk ankle-deep in mud and sand, and possibly even being stranded for days in some remote wilderness by mechanical difficulty."[23] Motorists who completed such trips received widespread publicity, encouraging others to venture out in their automobiles. Southerners saw in these intrepid new-comers a new source of prosperity; the emphasis began to change from improvement of local roads to the creation of interstate highways.

The September 25, 1913, issue of *Manufacturers Record*, a weekly newspaper, reported on the plans for the Lincoln Highway. The *Record* said: "There is another highway equally as important — indeed, we believe far more important — that demands the energetic co-operation of the business interests of the North and West in conjunction with those in the South.... The highway demanded by the times is one unbroken line from the North and West through the South."[24]

The time was ripe for Carl's Dixie Highway. W. S. Gilbreath was in Atlanta, Georgia, in November, 1914, to attend the fourth annual meeting of the American Road Congress. Gilbreath was trying to obtain approval from the governors of all the states through which the highway — he called it the "Cotton Belt Route" — would pass.[25] A story on the front page of the *Atlanta Constitution* quoted Gilbreath: "It is this lack of a thoroughly connected highway leading through the South which discourages tourists. I think...300,000 auto-mobile tourists would use the road this winter."[26] Estimating that each auto would carry four persons, each person spend-ing about four dollars a day, Gillbreath indicated that the South would gain $6,000,000 per day. His optimism was fu-eled by World War I; tourists who would otherwise have gone to Europe would spend their dollars seeing the United States.

During the next four months, Gilbreath spoke to auto clubs, Rotary Clubs, and associations of business leaders in Georgia, Tennessee, and Kentucky, drumming up support for the highway.

On December 4, 1914, Carl wrote to Indiana governor Samuel Ralston, asking for his help. In support of the road, Governor Ralston wrote to the governors of the states through which the highway would pass, inviting them to a meeting to discuss the highway. Governor Ralston and Tennessee Gov-ernor Tom C. Rye planned the meeting for April 3, 1915, in

Chattanooga, Tennessee, sponsored by the Chattanooga Automobile Club. Carl was there, as well as governors and officials from Indiana, Illinois, Florida, Kentucky, Ohio, Tennessee, and Georgia. About 5,000 Dixie Highway boosters came to promote the inclusion of their towns on the route now being called the Dixie Highway. Already 200 counties from ten states were asking to be included.

Governor Ralston addressed the conference, telling them that the Dixie Highway could be "an advance agent of social intercourse, mutual understanding, and national unity and good will."[27] The other governors promised their support. The *Indianapolis News* reported on the enthusiasm of all those who had come to Chattanooga: "The meeting took on the color of a big carnival. Bands and drum corps were everywhere. Banners told of the virtues of the different communities. There were 'yells' and 'slogans' without number. Every town in every state wished a place in the Dixie Highway Sun."[28]

There was acrimony as well as enthusiasm. Howard Preston wrote that the states and local communities "waged a propaganda war later referred to as the 'Second Battle of Chattanooga.'"[29] The meeting was marked by heckling and disorder, making the selection of a route impossible. But the conference did result in the formation of the Dixie Highway Association, modeled after the Lincoln Highway Association. Gilbreath was named field secretary and Tennessee Circuit Judge Michael Morrison Allison was elected president. The governors of the states represented at the meeting were to appoint two delegates each for a commission to select the route the highway would take. The fourteen commissioners would meet in May to make a decision after communities had had an opportunity to make their cases. Carl was appointed one of the delegates from Indiana.

The meeting convened on May 20, 1915, under the chairmanship of Clark Howell, an Atlanta newspaperman. He and Carl were at odds over the timing of the route selection. Carl wanted a decision made right then; Howell preferred to allow counties who were competing for a route to construct their portions of the highway first and then make a decision based upon the quality of these roads. The commission was concerned that if one group's choice was rejected, they would lose so much support that the entire project would be threatened. They settled on a compromise suggested by Carl: two routes, the eastern route passing through Cincinnati and Knoxville to Detroit, and a western route through Louisville, Nashville, and Chicago. Before two years passed, there would be changes even in these routes.[30]

Just as the Hoosier Tour had publicized and gained support for the Lincoln Highway, a motorcade from Chicago to Miami did the same for the Dixie Highway in the fall of 1915. It reached Miami on October 14, with thousands on hand to welcome them. Carl participated in the motorcade, but reached Miami early to be part of the welcome. The Dixie Highway was in the works, but it would be more than ten years before it would be completed.

The previous October work had begun on the Fishers' new home on Lincoln Road, "the largest home to be constructed in the area at the time."[31] Its building was to encourage other large estates nearby — Frank Wheeler chose a site, as did T.J. Nolan of Omaha.[32]

Carl was also in the midst of preparations for the Mid-Winter Regatta, scheduled for January, 1915, in conjunction with the Mid-Winter Festival. His intent was to have two days of world-class boat racing in the Bay, already dredged in preparation. Belle Isle (formerly Bull's Island) was being readied for the event. Grandstands, press boxes, and judges' booths were built.

The inspiration for the regatta had come from a race held in the summer of 1913, when Carl raced his 66-foot cruiser *Shadow* against the 77-foot *Skeejacks*, owned by A.Y. Gowen, president of the Lehigh Portland Cement Company, who had spent $20,000 on two new engines.

The terms of the race were that the loser would pay all the expenses to bring the winner's yacht to Miami for the season. Carl lost. Gowen was the first of many sportsmen "whose hobbies Carl used as bait to lure them to Florida,"[33] according to Polly Redford. The Gowen-Fisher race received

Carl and Jane Fisher's first Miami Beach home was on Lincoln Highway Road, facing the ocean. (Chase Family)

(Matlack; HASF)

Fisher's mid-winter regattas drew the top names in racing.

national attention. *"Motor Boating* called it the biggest one ever held outside of international competition."[34]

The first regatta was a success. Crowds came over Collins Bridge to watch. Carl raced four boats, and this time the *Shadow* won. He also won two new residents for Belle Isle. Yachtsmen Charles Kotcher and Robert Henkel of Detroit decided to build homes there.[35]

By March, the three development companies decided it was time to incorporate into a town. On March 26, they met in the offices of the Ocean Beach Realty Company, and decided on the name "Miami Beach." There were now 150 inhabitants, and 33 registered voters. J.N. Lummus was elected mayor. Most of the inhabitants lived in the Ocean Beach development, which Polly Redford described as having "the look of a lowbrow resort."[36] Because the new town had no finances, the Lummus brothers paid the costs of incorporating and obtaining a charter. Their realty company "Realizing that a recreational park and bathing beach of sufficient area, extending along the ocean, was absolutely essentail [sic]"[37] offered to sell to the new town twenty acres of land, 421 feet long at ten dollars per foot, while the going rate, Lummus said, was $100 per foot. Their proposal was approved at the price of $40,000. "We graded the park, planted Bermuda grass and coconut palms, built a ten-foot concrete walk the full

Carl G. Fisher driving a speed boat — 1920 Regatta. (L.P.)

length, and paid for the upkeep of the park until 1917,"[38] Lummus wrote.

Two weeks after incorporation, one of a long line of celebrities graced Miami Beach. Indiana poet John Whitcomb Riley was spending the winter in Miami and frequently visited Carl and Jane in their Brickell Avenue house. At the Fishers', he found freedom from his housekeeper, Mrs. Holstein, who would not allow him to drink alcohol or tell off-color stories. Carl, Jane wrote, would tell Galloway to "shake up a stock of toddies"[39] whenever he saw Riley arriving. The toddies were left in the butler's pantry so Riley could leave the room and imbibe discreetly if Mrs. Holstein was there.

On one visit, it was planned that Riley should plant a tree to celebrate the founding of the new community; he decided that he should also write a poem. It was not a big public ceremony — only a few friends. He read the poem, planted the tree, and they returned to Miami. The poem:

> We plant this tree
> Beside the sea
> In trust, that it yet may wave
> Through shower and shade
> In sunny hours
> For other eyes as glad as ours.[40]

The Fishers moved to their new home on Miami Beach for the 1915-1916 season. There were no neighbors. The house was not completely finished, and like the other early residents, the Fishers had to obtain all of their food and supplies from the mainland.

There were 300 square feet of ceiling-high window frontage, and sea green carpeting. Carl again sent Jane to Grand Rapids to buy "the biggest things you can get."[41] She bought sofas and chairs that were padded with down and covered in pale green cotton damask. There was a curved twin stairway and fireplaces large enough to walk into where they burned cypress logs. Carl's requisite brass cuspidors were placed in the drawing rooms and Carl's bedroom. Both the Lennox china and the silverware had an orange tree design. It was truly a Florida seaside home.

Pets were there, too, including an Airedale named Rowdy, who "hated every living human except Carl, whom he adored.. Rowdy bit everyone who came to the house unless Carl held him back."[42]

With no hotels or restaurants on the beach, the Shadows became the central meeting place for business and social affairs. Carl asked Jane to "be ready to entertain anyone who might come to Miami Beach,"[43] especially as many of them were potential buyers. He wanted a well-run household, and Jane endeavored to fulfill his wishes. At times the number of staff was as high as 20 to accommodate last-minute lunch or dinner guests. Jane ordered canned food by the crate.

There were other "visitors" to contend with. "Among my domestic duties was the daily warfare against the insects, land crabs, and snakes that retreated toward the Shadows in advance of the dredge filling in their marsh retreats."[44]

(I.S.N.)

Of their 26 homes, Jane said the Shadows was the "most lived-in."[45] On Sunday nights, they held open house, serving fruit punch and sandwiches.

Still, in 1915, the Shadows and Carl's real estate office building were the only buildings on Lincoln Road, the major thoroughfare that Carl wanted to be Miami Beach's Rue de la Paix.[46] Sales for all three real estate companies were slow.

World War I was seriously affecting the economy in early 1916 when Carl went to see J.N. Lummus. They both lamented that Carl and the Ocean Beach Realty Company had each already spent at least

A young Jane Fisher in Miami Beach

182

This photo of the County Causeway (now MacArthur)
taken on November 30, 1918. (Parks)

a $1,000,000 on developing their properties. "But the fact that each of us had already spent millions and had very little cash on hand did not prevent us from carrying on with even greater enthusiasm. We still believed in the future of Miami Beach, so we employed more salesmen and ran auction sales regularly for a period of two months,"[47] Lummus wrote. Their auctions were held until mid-April. Both also gave away lots, hoping that new buildings would encourage more sales, but even this did not increase lot sales.

Carl and Lummus also conferred on a new causeway in 1916; Collins Bridge was becoming congested. Dredges began to deepen the ship channel between Government Cut and the Miami River, creating a sandbar across Biscayne Bay that could be used as the roadbed. Also, if the shallows between the ship channel and the speedboat basin were dredged, "all South Beach could be open to ocean-going yachts."[48]

The new causeway was Lummus's idea. He owned the land where the causeway would reach Miami Beach and secured an option on land on the Miami side. Lummus approached the County Commissioners and was appointed campaign chairman for $600,000 in county bonds. Carl donated $2,000 and the Lummus brothers $4,000 to promote the bond issue. The county electorate approved the bond issue five months later.[49] But some residents of the northern part of the county filed injunctions and lawsuits until the following March, when World War I interceded and postponed the whole project.[50]

In April of 1916, Carl, the Lummus brothers, and others formed a new real estate company: the Miami Ocean View Company. The *Miami Daily News* on April 13 identified the other members of the firm: John Levi; James Allison; Carl's friend, James H. Snowden; Edwin P. Lent; and others from Atlantic City and New York. Snowden was president, J.N. Lummus, vice-president, and Levi, secretary-treasurer. The article said that the corporation planned to pave streets, install water mains and sewers, and plant larger trees. "All of this work will be done this summer."[51]

Lummus claimed that he had "saved" Carl, Collins, and Miami Beach by selling his land at a loss of $330,000 to the corporation. Lummus, however, admitted that "we all had plenty of land, but had no cash..."[52] and it is possible that he would otherwise have had to declare bankruptcy.

Carl was busy building that year. The Lincoln Hotel on Lincoln Road with 32 rooms was the first building in his development offering public accommodations. The Atlantic Beach Hotel, later known as Brown's Hotel, had opened for the 1915/1916 winter season in the Lummus development.[53] Carl built a golf course near his new hotel. He was also building a glass-enclosed tennis court.

The new hotel was a showplace. August Geiger, who had also designed Carl's home, had designed it in the Italian Renaissance style with decorated stucco and marble insets. The $40,000 hotel opened on January 20, 1917.[54]

With a view to making the beach even more attractive, Carl purchased Collins Pavilion from the Miami Beach Improvement Company. At a cost of $350,000, Carl added a second swimming pool, a restaurant, stage, ballroom, and a shopping arcade. He had an Indianapolis contractor build a

Aerial view of Miami Beach in 1918. (HASF)

Dutch windmill to pump water from holding tanks into the two swimming pools. The whole complex, now called the Roman Pools, quickly became a popular spot. There were swimming classes, diving exhibitions, lectures, concerts, parties, dinner and dancing.[55]

Together with Charles W. Kotcher and James Snowden, Carl bought two small islands in the Florida keys in 1916. With excellent fishing in the area, they founded a fishing club — but for millionaires. The Cocolobo Club, named for a native tree, the pigeon plum *(Cocoloba diversifolia)*, was only a one-day excursion from Miami Beach. It was an ideal fishing spot. "In calm weather the water was so clear then even without a glass-bottom boat one could see bright tropical fish and marine gardens below."[56] There were dolphins, marlin, and shellfish in the Gulf Stream five miles from shore; and grouper, snapper, barracuda, mackerel, and kingfish in the reefs. Bonefish, ladyfish and tarpon were there in other areas.[57] Later, Carl would argue that the yachts he used to take prospective buyers on these fishing trips were business, rather than personal property as he sold millions of dollars' worth of Miami Beach property to wealthy men who were his guests.[58]

In December of 1916 Carl and Charles Kotcher challenged "the world at large" to an express-cruiser race in February, 1917, on the Biscayne course. Carl not only won, he set a world speed record of 29 miles per hour in his *Shadow II* on February 16; the next day he broke it with a speed of 30.1.[59]

That 1916-1917 winter season was the best ever. World War I brought tourists who would have otherwise gone to Europe. Carl chose that time to announce that Miami was now his principal home, although he would retain a summer home in Indianapolis and his business interests there. "I expect to see Miami in a very few years as prosperous as Los Angeles. We have everything that they have and much that they can never have."[60]

Chapter 17

World War I

Carl's reactions to the United States involvement in World War I were predictable to those who knew him. He suspended all racing at the Speedway and notified the government that its facilities were available for military use. In addition, he offered his personal services to help in any way he could. Carl's poor vision would have kept him out of any war, but he had definite ideas about the best way to win. To Carl, there was no question that it was air power that was the key to victory. He had observed the development of the airplane since he had flown on the Wright brothers' airplane when they had come to help promote the Speedway, and he had maintained his U.S. balloon pilot's license.

In July, 1915, Carl had set forth his ideas in "A Proposal for National Defense," a privately-published article citing the importance of an air force in war. He maintained that if France had had thousands of airplanes, rather than hundreds, at the beginning of World War I, they could have assisted Belgium and delayed the German invasion.

Carl felt that America's geography made it imperative to invest in airplanes to repel an invasion.

With Atlantic, Gulf and Pacific coast lines of thousands of miles extent and with a very great proportion of the nation's population lying along and comparatively close to these water frontiers, most especially the Atlantic sea-board from the Potomac north, the problem of adequate defense in repelling invasion cannot be solved solely in terms of naval arms, battle-ships through the list to submarines, nor in terms of adequate ships supplemented by a vast enrollment of militia....

What must be provided for in every detail is an aviation fleet of aeroplanes — not a few hundred or even a few thousand — in plain English, not less than ten thousand of them.[1]

The cost of the large fleet of planes would be kept down by standardization and mass production by car makers, who had already managed to produce hundreds of thousands of cars annually. Altogether, Carl wrote, the planes would cost about as much as one superdreadnought — twelve to fifteen million dollars. He advocated training centers near important cities up and down the East and West coasts. Level twenty-acre fields thirty miles apart would be landing fields in war time and pilot training centers in peace time.

Such level fields would not cost much for lease and mainte-nance and could be used for pasturage without affecting its military use in any degree. In the center of each field could be erected a cheap telescoping tower 100 to 150 feet high, carry-ing lights at the top to serve as guide posts at night and signal stations by day; at the base in suitable shelter could be kept reserve supplies of fuel and oil, and in the event of war, possi-bly other materials as well.[2]

The type of airplane Carl advocated was a "well designed" biplane with multiple cylinder, water-cooled engines. There would be a two-man crew: a pilot to operate the plane and another man "to either make observations or manipulate ex-plosives for attack."[3] He noted that experiments with drop-ping explosives from planes had not been very successful, but:

Given the need for the immediate production of proper meth-ods, suitable speedometers could be designed to indicate not only actual but relative speeds as affected by wind velocity, sighting apparatus and all the mechanism calculated to ren-der the aeroplane efficient from the standpoint of a projectile carrying and dropping machine.[4]

The targets for the explosives would be transports carry-ing the enemy troops. Carl maintained that the airplanes would be preferable to enlarging the navy as "even this country must somewhere draw the line on unlimited naval expenditures."[5] The airplanes would also have the advantage of being faster and more mobile than ships.

A gradual phase-in of an air defense was his recommendation. While an initial 2,000 planes were being built, car drivers and mechanics would be recruited. Men would be trained and then go back to their homes, with a new group replacing them until a trained "Aviation Corps" of 25,000 would be ready to respond when needed.

Carl's closing words were a call to the country to awaken to the danger of invasion.

> To blindly hold invasion impossible, or if attempted that the invaders could be driven back into the sea between "sunrise and sunset" is to be indifferent to all the experience of war as it is being conducted on the greatest scale in history and worse, to ignore all our own military history from 1775 to 1898, all of which is calculated to make an American grieve that so much blood and money had to be wasted in each of our wars, solely because in not one instance have we ever been prepared, though lack of preparation has not kept us out of war.[6]

With the United States entering the war and Speedway racing suspending, Carl wrote to his old friend George Bumbaugh on March 29, 1917, about plans for furthering aviation education in Indianapolis.

> I am making an application to get an Aviation School in Indianapolis and I think I am going to succeed — and if so, I will have a job for you in both divisions, the balloon corps and the flying squad.
> Say nothing about this until I hear from the Government. Will be home about the 20th of April.[7]

George Bumbaugh saw Carl's plans as not only a military effort, but also as an opportunity to gain some publicity. Carl made clear in a letter to Bumbaugh on April 9 that this was not a promotional scheme.

> Replying to yours of recent date : I haven't any companies to promote and nothing to sell — and I want you to keep your mouth absolutely closed regarding any plans that I may mention to you.

My principal effort will be to lend such services as I can to the Government, without charge: of course I realize that I will have to make arrangements to pay men of your caliber for your work, but don't get mixed up on the idea that this is a promoting scheme.[8]

In the same month, Carl contacted the government for approval for temporarily using the Indianapolis Speedway as a military airfield. He not only received approval for his suggestion, he was also appointed to the National Advisory Committee in Aeronautics, becoming chairman of the Landing Fields and Flying Routes Subcommittee of the Civil Aerial Transport Committee.[9] Their goals were to locate emergency landing fields and to devise some system of aerial navigation in the Midwest.

The committee succeeded in having large arrows painted on the roofs of barns and other large buildings to guide pilots. They also had small town officials sign signal lights between 7 and 11 p.m. These actions resulted in the first regular airplane route in the United States, between McCook Field in Dayton, Ohio, and Chanute Field in Rantoul, Illinois.[10] The Speedway was midway between the two. Carl spent thousands of dollars of his own money on this project, and in the process became acquainted with prominent and wealthy men who shared the same beliefs. He also tried to interest them in investing in Miami Beach property.[11]

The infield of Speedway became a landing field for military airplanes on the route. Other land at the Speedway was used to grow oats, wheat, and timothy. While there was no racing, the Marmon Company used the Speedway oval to test 2,998 passenger cars before delivery, paying $1.25 per car.[12] Without any income from racing, the four Speedway partners had to assess themselves for taxes and maintenance. Frank Wheeler, who had lost money in another race track, sold out his interest to James Allison.[13] An aviation repair depot was built at the Speedway by the government to service planes. In 1918, England sent a fleet of planes, under the command of General Charles Lee of the British Royal Flyers, to make Americans more aware of the importance of airpower in war. This fleet "staged sham battles through the Middle West..."[14] Carl, James Allison, Frank Wheeler, and Arthur Newby took it upon themselves to build hangars for the British planes.

After the war ended, Carl appealed to some of the outstanding race drivers to put on an exhibition for 700 wounded soldiers from the Fort Benjamin Hospital. On July 22, 1919, Carl wrote to legendary race driver Ralph DePalma, who had won the Indy 500 in 1915 with a Mercedes and who set the world land speed record of 149 mph. in 1919.

Dear Ralph:

The hospital here at Fort Benj. Harrison has about 750 badly shot up young men from this last war. There is one thing that these young fellows want to see more than anything else in the world — at least they say they do: they want to see a match race at the Speedway and they want to see Ralph DePalma, Barney Oldfield, and Wilcox together [Howdy Wilcox won the Indy 500 in 1919 driving a Peugeot].

I told the Colonel in charge of the fort the other day that the Speedway would donate the Track and the Officials, and that we would get the Motor Corps to donate the automobiles to haul these poor devils out to the Speedway. I also told him that I would try and get you fellows down here to drive an exhibition for these boys.

We have a couple of Peugeots and one premier that are in good shape — and we would like to have you come down with your Packard. Wilcox can drive one of the Peugeots and if you can't bring your Packard along, you and Barney can drive the other two cars of ours.

I [think] that for a program, if we could get your consent and Oldfield's, we would have a ten (10), twenty (20), and thirty (30) mile race for a Gold Medal. In the twenty-mile race we would have a stop on the fifth lap for a tire change. This is about the only program I could think of that would not run into considerable expense for tires, mechanics, etc.

I feel that we can't do too much for these poor devils who are all shot up. There will be about seven hundred of them in the Grand Stand and it will take about four hundred automobiles to haul this number, as in some cases it takes an entire automobile to haul one cripple. There will also be a large number of officers, nurses, etc.

On receipt of this letter, won't you please wire me if you will come. The tentative date is August 12th.

I would like to get Joe Boyer to come with a Frontenac if I could, or Louis Chevrolet, and make it a four-cornered affair. But we can't give them a real thriller unless we can get you and Oldfield to come down.

Let me hear from you.[15]

On August 6, 1919, the *Indianapolis Star* reported on the upcoming event:

Speed Program Fixed for Wounded Soldiers

The spell of silence that descended upon the Indianapolis Motor Speedway when the roar of the last exhaust died away at the conclusion of the last world's championship battle under this historic oval will be broken next Tuesday afternoon when a special speed program will be staged for the entertainment of convalescent solders at Fort Benjamin Harrison.

The details of the program have not been announced. However, it is reported that General Manager Theodore E. Myers is endeavoring to pit two of the country's foremost racing stars against Howdy Wilcox, winner of the last Indianapolis five-century, in a gasoline tourney that is expected to bring out some of the fastest competition that has ever been witnessed on the Hoosier track.

Speculation is rife as to the identity of Wilcox's opponents. However, Myers is noncommittal on the subject merely stating that they would be stars of the first water, with a record of victories equal to, if not greater, than that of Wilcox himself. Accordingly, a real contest may be expected, and not merely an entertainment of the exhibition variety.

It is the endeavor of the Speedway management to give the country's wounded heroes a show worth remembering, and it is a safe bet that the pilots engaged for the occasion will do their best to demonstrate that when it comes to fearlessness and a cool display of bravery they are second only to those who so gallantly and courageously went over the top in France.

Music for the occasion will be furnished by the Indianapolis Military Band, through courtesy of the Indianapolis Musicians Union, under the management of W. F. Mitchell.

It is significant of the spirit of the occasion that everyone connected with the enterprise, from the owners of the Speedway to the musicians, are furnishing their services free of charge, as a mark of appreciation of the services rendered by the guests of the day during the late world conflict.[16]

On August 20, 1919, the *Indianapolis News* reported the results of the races held for the wounded soldiers.

CHAMPIONSHIP STYLE

About 1,600 soldiers from Ft. Benjamin Harrison witnessed exhibition automobile races at the Indianapolis motor speedway yesterday afternoon. Many of the men were wounded soldiers in convalesce at Ft. Harrison Hospital.

T.E. Myers, general manger of the speedway, acted as starter. The events were put on in true championship racing style.

The drivers were paced in the famous white speedway automobile by N.H. Gilman, treasurer of the Allison experimental company. With Gilman rode Colonial Robert Tyndall, commander of the field artillery, Rainbow division.

The first race, a five mile event, was won by Joe Dawson in a Peugeot. It marked the reappearance of Dawson on the speedway track after a number of years in which he had been out of the racing game. Howdy Wilcox, who won the 150-mile Liberty sweepstakes here in May, finished second. He also drove an Indianapolis owned Peugeot. Tommy Milton, in a Premier, was third. The time was 3:33, an average of 84.5 miles an hour.

In the ten-mile race, Milton had engine trouble and did not finish. Wilcox crossed the tape first and Dawson finished second. The time was 7:19, or an average of 83.53 miles an hour.[17]

World War I had given Carl a new hero. Hanging above his bed were pictures of Lincoln and Napoleon. He added to this a newspaper photograph of General Gallieni, Military Governor of Paris. When the German army was advancing on Paris, General Gallieni commandeered all of the French taxis and used them to rush army troops to meet the Germans and save Paris. On the photograph, Carl wrote: "The man who kept his head."[18]

The 1917-1918 Miami winter season was the only season that was seriously affected by World War I. Construction slowed or ceased; transportation shortages restricted travel. Meanwhile, Carl had developed a new interest — polo. Now in his forties, he had never ridden a horse before. Five weeks after the Armistice was signed on November 11, 1918, the first polo ponies arrived on Miami Beach. "...the Great Florida boom was on its way."[19]

Fortunately, Carl's interests coincided with many of the other wealthy men in America. Financier Harold Talbott, Jr., who was to become Secretary of the Air Force thirty-five years later, introduced Carl to polo. Talbott, from Dayton, Ohio, even helped Carl make Miami Beach a winter center for polo by urging his polo-playing friends to bring their polo ponies for the 1918-1919 season just as he had done.[20] Talbott's parents were early Miami Beach residents and had built a winter home, "Fieldstone House," on the bayfront.

The new Flamingo Polo Grounds, which had cost $40,000, opened on February 20, 1919. An estimated 2,000 fans were there to see the first match when Talbott's "Reds" team defeated the "Whites." Carl did not play, but he had prepared well for the crowd. He had seats and parking for the spectators, with reserved places for his new polo club. Carl had

Carl G. Fisher, right, playing polo. (LP)

also built stables, a blacksmith's shop, mess-room and stablemen's quarters.[21]

The new arrivals expected the best. Because well water on Miami Beach was brackish, Carl had built tanks to catch rain water. Laddie Sanford, one of the owners, didn't think the water was good enough for his ponies (one of which had cost seven thousand dollars), and shipped down fifty bottles of water from New York every day.[22] The Fishers had a stable of thirty ponies, most of them used by Carl's friends.

European polo players were also enticed to Miami Beach, through a lucky break. Tom Dryborough, a seventy-two-year old English polo writer, came to spend a winter and played polo. His glowing report of the new Miami Beach facilities appeared in England. Sensing an opportunity to raise the quality and reputation of Miami Beach polo, Carl paid the expenses of the entire English team to come and play at Miami Beach. The English team included players with titles, as well as money. Two of them, Lord Cromwell and the Marquis

Carl Fisher looks down from polo balcony. (HASF)

Carl G. Fisher on one of his polo ponies. (Matlack; HASF)

of Waterford, paid seventy-three thousand dollars for Miami Beach land. When they were given the tax assessment for the land, they naively tried to pay the evaluation, rather than the actual taxes.[23]

An international polo player, Colonel C.T. Melville, accompanied the English team. Miami Beach received more accolades when he wrote a book and mentioned his pleasant surprise at having "strawberries for breakfast at Christmas and being driven around by a lady [Jane] wearing pajamas"[24] By 1923, Carl had spent two million dollars just on the polo facilities. In a reply to Thomas Pancoast, who had complained about Carl's spending on polo, Carl gave him a financial explanation.

> ...as long as these people are willing to ship their ponies down to Miami at an annual expense of several thousand dollars, it is the proper thing for us to provide barns for them, since they afford us a big part of our attractions there during the Winter, and draw the kind of people we want to sell houses to. Eventually nearly all these people will own houses at Miami Beach where they can have their own ponies and their own barns...[25]

Although Carl was not a golf afficionado, he appreciated the fact that many others were, and he provided well for them. When one golfer told him that the courses were "too flat,"[26] Carl brought a golf engineer from Scotland to lay out a new course. This time there were hills, composed of ground from the Everglades, at a cost of thousands of dollars.[27]

Carl liked to honor his friends by naming things after them, as he did with the LaGorce Golf Course. John Oliver LaGorce, of Washington, D.C., served as associate editor and later editor of the *National Geographic.* In 1918, LaGorce published *A Little Journey to Altonia,* an effusive account he had written about Alton Beach. Carl sent the pamphlet to prospective customers.

Boat racing, Carl's favorite sport according to his wife Jane,[28] did more than give enjoyment to him and his friends and attract more people to Miami Beach. Regattas, like the Indianapolis Speedway, were a testing ground for engines. His friend Gar Wood "said of Carl that he did more for the refining and development of motor boats than anyone in the business."[29]

The large number of sports enthusiasts that began pouring into Miami Beach found an important deficiency — a lack of accommodations. In 1919, Carl announced plans to build a new and elegant hotel — the Flamingo. Also in 1919, he began a policy of raising prices on Alton Beach property ten percent a year. One of his advertisements said: "We try to give our customers an investment in a house site or a business site that substantially and steadily gains in value."[30] To demonstrate his belief that beach real estate values would appreciate steadily, he offered to return the purchase price with six percent interest to anyone "not well pleased with their investment."[31] As it turned out, his ten percent estimation was too conservative. The Roaring Twenties would bring prices far beyond what the early residents would ever dream. No one ever took him up on his offer.

Sales figures for the Alton Beach Realty Company reflect the escalation in sales in just five years. The total dollar amount of sales were as follows: 1916 – $40,000; 1917 –

$52,000; 1918 – $132,000; 1919 – more than double the previous year; 1920 – $1,966,000![32]

The post-war building boom was well underway. Carl and Jim Allison had planned to spend $750,000 on the hotel, but their architects' design would cost more. The bids were in the range of two million dollars. Labor and material costs were rising sharply because of the postwar construction boom. Jim Allison bowed out to concentrate on an aquarium he was building.[33] This $200,000 investment would open at the same time as the Flamingo. When each winter season ended, Allison would release his specimens back to the sea.

For the first time since his bicycle-selling days, Carl was forced to borrow money. To save money, he had Indianapolis architects design a more modest hotel. In April of 1920, he organized the Flamingo Hotel Corporation with Cecil G. Fowler, owner of the National Bank in Lafayette, Indiana. Fowler invested $5,000 in the project. Carl was planning to finance the hotel by selling seven and one-half percent bonds.[34]

The name and theme of the Flamingo hotel were the result of a cruise Carl took with Allison, LaGorce, and Levi to Andros Island in the Bahamas. "They saw a cloud of flame they took to be a sunset. Then they realized it was in the wrong direction for the sun. The pink cloud lighted and they saw the wings of thousands of gloriously colored flamingos."[35]

Carl wanted to have live flamingos on the hotel grounds and made an attempt to bring some from Andros Island. With the help of John LaGorce and the *National Geographic,* he managed to include in the party artist-naturalist Louis Agassiz Fuertes, as well as LaGorce, John Levi, Jim Allison, and fishing guide Charley Thompson. They had to take skiffs and canoes to traverse the creeks and then wade for miles to the nesting grounds. A group of sponge fishermen had arrived before them, killing as many flamingos as they could for food. Charley Thompson was immediately sworn in as a deputy game warden and arrested the fishermen. The rest of the men took movies of the hundreds of flamingos with equipment they had brought with them. They also captured some

Gondolas in front of the Hotel Flamingo, (Albertype; S.P.A.)

gave three flocks from Cuba to the Hialeah Race Track did any flamingos manage to survive in Florida.[36]

But there were plenty of flamingos to be seen in the paintings and plaster reliefs of Louis Agassiz Fuertes in the lobby of the Flamingo. These became a bone of contention between Carl and Charles S. Krom, who was to manage the hotel for 28 seasons. Krom had come highly-recommended and oversaw construction of the 200-room hotel, with luxury cottages on the grounds. Krom wrote Carl "that he did not feel murals highlighting flamingos were proper, that he had consulted with decorators and architects and that the planned murals and plaster casts were not in keeping with the architecture of the public rooms."[37] What Carl wanted, Carl got. In a reply on May 29, 1920, Carl told Krom that he wanted the flamingos and that was that.

The new hotel featured one of Carl's favorite architectural features — a tower, this one eleven stories high with a glass dome. At night, multi-colored spotlights shone far out over the sea, visible for seven miles. The hotel had its own docks, a boathouse, laundry, men's club, brokers' office and shops. To provide the guests with the freshest of dairy products, Carl spent $7,000 on round-trip transportation to bring forty Guernsey cows from Milwaukee, Wisconsin.[38] For all this, guests paid $15 and up for a single room or $20 and up for a double room.[39] Carl anticipated that the hotel would have an income of $125,000 to $150,000 per season.[40] A private party on New Year's Eve, 1920, preceded the formal opening on January 1, 1921.

Chapter 18

Carl Scores a Coup with President-Elect Harding

Even before the opening of the Flamingo, Carl was planning to score a publicity coup with the most-desired hotel guest in America — President-Elect Warren G. Harding of Ohio. Achieving this coup was not easy.

On December 6, 1920, Carl wrote a letter to then-Senator Harding, inviting him and his wife to be his guests at the hotel, "...where a suite will be at your disposal, I assure you that every possible privacy and comfort will be yours, and no overdraft on your time and good nature permitted." He presented Miami Beach as the ideal spot for a vacation.

> Miami Beach has become the real garden spot of the sub-tropics and is especially attractive to lovers of outdoors because the bathing, in the surf or in the great Roman Pools nearby, the eighteen and nine-hole golf courses, the polo, tennis, and, last, but not least, the splendid sport-fishing, all make for health and a thorough enjoyment of every hour.[1]

The letter assured Harding that his stay there would be "for rest and relaxation."

According to Polly Redford, the letter "was actually written by John LaGorce, who had it transcribed to Carl's personal stationery and delivered, along with an Alton booklet, to Harding's personal secretary."[2] Harding did not reply.

About a month later Carl received a letter from Ohio State Senator William M. Miller. Miller obviously did not know that Carl had already extended an invitation to Harding.

> You know I am enthusiastic about Miami Beach and I felt that if Senator Harding could visit there and be entertained in a home there that it would be a wonderful boost for the Beach and without displaying this part of my eagerness to get him there to Mr. Daugherty [Harding's campaign manager], I told him fully of your marvelous work on the Beach and of your wonderful public spiritedness and stated to him that I felt assured you would be only too glad in conjunction with your friends there to entertain the presidential party.[3]

Miller wrote that he had already conferred with Harry Daugherty about Harding's planned trip to Florida, telling him that Miami Beach had "the finest golf course...of any place in Florida," and learned that Harding planned to stay on Senator Freylinghuysen's houseboat. Miller told Daugherty that Carl would certainly be glad to offer accommodations to the President-Elect.

> I have the assurance of Mr. Daugherty, the man who has made Mr. Harding president of the United States and the man President Harding looks to for advice more than any other man in our country, that he, Daugherty, will use his influence to convince Mr. Harding that he ought to accept the invitation, if it is tendered.
>
> Should you write, I wish you would state in your letter to the President that you are making this offer of entertainment upon the suggestion of his friend, Senator Wm. M. Miller of Ohio.[4]

Miller wanted Carl to wire the President "immediately" and send him information in a letter, copies of which were to be sent to Daugherty.

Carl did telegram Harding, offering two cottages for his use, a total of eight rooms and six baths. The hospitality, he said, was being furnished by the city of Miami Beach and the Flamingo Hotel Company. He also told Harding that he was sending Ann Rossiter, his secretary (and mistress) with drawings and blueprints so that Harding could choose the cottages he preferred.[5] Carl also telegramed Miller, notifying him of what he had done.[6] He wrote a letter telling Miller that he was sending him copies of a telegram and letter from the Mayor of Miami Beach and the City Council, which invited Harding as "the guest of the city."[7]

Miller telegramed Carl that he had spoken to Daugherty and cautioned Carl to "Take only your most intimate associates into your confidence on this until you receive my letter."[8]

All of these plans seemed to be fruitless when John LaGorce wrote Carl on January 11 after talking with Senator Freylinghuysen. LaGorce urged Carl to stop his efforts to try to have Harding stay overnight at Miami Beach.

> Freylinghuysen said that it was the wish of Harding that no invitation be accepted to stay on shore for they do not wish to incur obligations to speak to a select bunch of lifelong Republicans over in the town hall or anything of that kind — which was his way of putting it.
>
> I recalled to him our conversation about you and that you were the last one in the world who would stand for anything like that or try to perpetrate it, and then made your offer of either a suite at the Hotel or the cottage. He said once again that Harding was steadfast in his determination to live on board the boat and that he just wanted to play golf and fish. He said that Senator Harding would very gladly avail himself of your offer of the glass bottom cruiser and fishing tackle and would also wish to play golf at Miami Beach, and that both Harding and himself would always be grateful for your courtesy in this connection.
>
> To sum the matter up, they deem it advisable not to accept any invitations on shore where in all likelihood they would be surrounded by people looking at them and interfering with their enjoyment in spite of all that could be done to protect him from it. That's why I suggested in the wire that it would be inadvisable for you to further press the invitation, for I feel positive that it would be declined.[9]

A letter from Miller on January 12 reflected the same opinion. Miller had met with Harding and gave this reason for Harding's declining the offer: "...he would have been glad to avail himself of this opportunity had he not thought that Miama [sic] Beach was too far removed from New York and Washington for people to reach him with whom he must necessarily keep in touch and confer with prior to his inauguration." Daugherty, he wrote, wanted to accept Carl's invitation, and felt that anyone who wanted to see Harding "could have afforded to come to Miama Beach..."[10]

Harding himself wrote Carl on January 12, declining Carl's offer.

I wish I could come and make a long stay. The simple truth about the matter is, however, that my plans will not admit of such an enticing program. We are coming South soon and I am expecting to get a rather hurried glimpse of Miami and the Beach. We shall not be able to stay, and the nature of my travels is such that I will not be in a position to accept any courtesies of a public nature. I very deeply appreciate your interest in extending your tender of courtesy and hospitality. If the circumstances were different I should certainly rejoice to accept.[11]

Carl had not received Harding's letter when he wrote to John LaGorce, rather disgusted with the whole matter.

This is the second time I have gone after a President and it is the last. From now on Miami Beach is going to be so hell-fired attractive that the Presidents and the rest of the newer politicians will telegraph for accommodations. We certainly will never make another effort to get one of them here.

I feel like a "NUT" and I certainly don't think a hell of a lot of Harding because he has not answered either one of my letters and telegrams so between you and me and the gate post Harding and the whole outfit can go to Hell as far as I am concerned.[12]

LaGorce answered Carl's letter on January 21, indicating that Carl's efforts had "completely overwhelmed the man and his office force." LaGorce said he had learned that Harding had received about a dozen other such invitations.

There is no hotel in the country that wouldn't break its neck to offer Harding and his party every accommodation and entertainment gratis for the publicity and advertising value of such a thing is well known. Just glance at the layout a moment. Here's a new hotel just opened in an expensive winter resort; why wouldn't it be the best kind of an investment of a couple of thousand dollars — the cost of a page in The Geographic — to have every paper in the country carry the fact that the President-elect of the United States was stopping at the Flamingo! Secondly, would you personally accept such a thing from anybody, thus placing yourself under some kind of an obligation — nay, I think not.

...Now if they do show up down there and want to be friends with you, for Heaven sakes don't go hide in the corner and get mad. The very fact that Harding has kicked the whole inaugural program in the pants and has absolutely refused to permit his induction into office to be the occasion for these hotel profiteers to gouge the American people, and has called off even the parade, to say nothing of the Inaugural Ball, and everything going with it, certainly shows that he's in earnest about sidestepping the spotlight.

I understand that his real reason for doing what he did was because a number of his friends had told him that the downtown hotels in Washington were refusing to rent a room for less than the entire week with a minimum of $300.00 a room, and he just wouldn't stand for it.[13]

Only Ann Rossiter had positive feelings. After her visit to Harding at his home in Marion, Ohio, she wrote to Carl. In the January 11th letter, she told him that she had been given preference above the others who were there to see Harding.

He gave us a full half-hour in the midst of his rush, was most courteous, asked me all about the Beach... He leaves for the South within the next ten days and will be in Miami probably two days on Senator Freylinghuysen's houseboat — but in that time will surely visit The Beach, play golf and make your acquaintance.[14]

The city of Miami had also planned to greet Harding and reap some publicity for themselves. Harding arrived a day early from Fort Lauderdale aboard Senator Freylinghuysen's houseboat. A small flotilla of boats from Miami was in the middle of the bay, loaded with dignitaries. Freylinghuysen's boat started moving east, completely avoiding the flotilla, and continued to the Lincoln Hotel. That night he did go to Miami to have dinner at the Royal Palm Hotel. Before that, however, he had lunch with Carl and then played 18 holes of golf.[15]

Carl's hospitality and the charms of Miami Beach prevailed. Harding stayed at one of the luxurious bungalows on the grounds of The Flamingo. The next day Carl showed him the sights of Miami Beach, including the Roman Pools, where Harding swam in the pool and the ocean. There, Harding told reporters: "Because of the attractiveness of Miami and Miami Beach, I hope to come here again. The beach is wonderful. It is developing like magic."[16] Photographers had a field day. Harding spent the next two days fishing with Carl on the *Shadow VI* and visiting the Cocolobo Club.

Carl had succeeded again and garnered a bonanza of national publicity. LaGorce sent him clippings from newspapers in New York, Philadelphia, and Washington.[17] On January 31, 1921, David Jameson, President of the American Automobile Association, wrote A. G. Batchelder, chairman of the executive board of the American Automobile Association in Washington, D.C.

> Everybody is laughing at the way Fisher put it over Miami. Miami had made great preparations for the entertainment of the President-elect, had gone so far as to procure guides and arrange all the essentials. When Mr. Harding got in sight of Miami and the highly decorated boats, ladies, etc., he shied off to the east. He never stopped shieing until he had landed at the Lincoln Hotel. Mayor Smith did succeed in delivering some

Carl G. Fisher waits to greet President Harding on January 31, 1921. (Matlack; HASF)

sort of an address of welcome on the way to the Beach, and the Senator did come over and have dinner at the Royal Palm in the evening. He is now down at Cocolobo, the guest of Fisher Allison and Thompson, just the same as you were when you were down here. They may slip him over to Bimini to get him a drink, but if they do, Miami will never know it.[18]

A.G. Batchelder wrote to Carl on February 4 about the newspaper stories in Washington.

Make allowance for the usual hot air messages which pass between our worthy president and me. Having done so, you will be interested in his summation of recent happenings in your midst.

The dispatchers up here didn't leave out anything: Fisher, Allison, Flamingo, Lincoln, Shadow, L'Apache, Cocolobo, and of course Thompson, besides etc., etc.

You certainly handled the job in great shape, and I again take off my hat to the firm of Fisher and Allison.[19]

Batchelder wrote a similar letter to James Allison on the same day.

Carl continued to correspond with the President, sending him a book and inviting him to spend the holidays at Miami Beach. Now that Harding had become President, he sent his replies to Carl through his secretary, George B. Christian, Jr.

THE WHITE HOUSE

The President has received the little book which you have been good enough to send to him, and he asks me to thank you heartily for your courtesy in the matter. He is most appreciative of your thought of him.[20]

Another letter from Christian was sent on October 21, 1921.

Please accept my thanks for your letter of October 18th. In reply I beg to say that there is no chance of the President visiting Miami during the holidays. There may be a chance late in February.

With best wishes, believe me,[21]

President-elect Warren G. Harding stands holding a child for a political photo op while playing golf in Miami Beach during his 1921 visit. (Matlack; HASF)

Chapter 19

Personal Tragedy

Even though Carl's parents had been divorced since he was a young boy, Carl had never ceased to hope for their reconciliation — to unify his family. His two brothers had died young. Earle, at 34, had died October 27, 1910, of diabetes. Robert (Rolla), at 32, died in 1912 of Lympho-sarcoma cancer. Carl was generous to his parents, supporting them financially and providing a home for his mother since his marriage. He had given her a house of her own on his Blossom Heath estate. In 1919 he was building her a house on Miami Beach. The closeness between the two is evident in the letters Carl wrote to her concerning the progress of the new house. He wrote on January 13, 1919, shortly after the death of Theodore Roosevelt.

Dear Mother,

I am sure the loss of Roosevelt is the greatest individual loss America has had since Lincoln. People will finally commence to appreciate Roosevelt, and build monuments and name canals, etc., after him in the next few years, and will keep it up for the next five hundred years.

Bastian is getting along with your house rather slowly. We had to pull him off houses to build pole barns. They will be completed in two weeks, and then we'll get the carpenters back on the houses. Don't forget. I am going ahead with your house just the same, and will furnish it up complete.

If there are any colour schemes you would like for the different rooms, buy me some pieces of ribbon or something in the shades you want, and send them down.

Much love,[1]

Carl's mother, faced with the task of buying gifts for some-one who could buy himself anything he wanted, still found ways to please him. Carl noted such gifts in a letter to her on February 10, 1919, that also updates her on the house.

Dear Mother,

I have yours written on a rainy day, also the flower. It was a little bit out of shape, but it still gives some perfume.

I will have the Indianapolis News sent to you at the St. George Hotel every day. I think you should have it daily, and not once in a while. We, also have had some bad weather, about the worst winter I can remember in Florida.

However, the city is turning away a good many people, all hotels and houses being full. Everything looks very bright for us. I am very much in hopes we will clean up your house in another two weeks. From this time on, at least, you can have your own grounds. I am going to plant you some very pretty flowers and trees.

Do you need any money?

Thank-you very much indeed for the salted peanuts and the candied fruit. They are very good, and it was a sweet thought to send them. They were so nicely packed; they arrived in per-fect condition.

Love from,[2]

Unfortunately, Carl's mother did not always receive his letters and complained about what she thought was his fail-ure to write. Carl responded to her complaints on March 24.

Dear Mother:

Enclosed please find check for three hundred dollars.

I wrote you last on February 29th and March 18th. Am sending you a telegram today, asking you if you received these letters. I can't understand why you don't get my letters un-less there is some crook who is opening the letter expecting to find money or a check in them. Wire me on receipt of this letter.

There is no reason why I shouldn't always write you promptly, and whenever you don't hear from me promptly, you step over to the telegraph office and send me a telegram.[3]

Two days later Carl wrote again about the problem of her not receiving his letters. The problem might have been caused by her move from the St. George Hotel in St. Augustine, Florida, to the Hotel Seminole in Jacksonville.

Dear Mother:

I have just wired you as follows: "Have written you a half dozen letters to the St. George Hotel at St. Augustine. Your check was mailed to the St. George at St. Augustine on Monday. Remain at the Hotel Seminole until you receive your check. I will wire the St. George to forward your check and mail today. I cannot understand why you don't receive my letters if you have been at the St. George. Wire me at once advising if you receive this telegram. Am writing. Love."

I cannot understand why you do not receive my letters. You see it takes two or three days to get mail down here from St. Augustine and I have just returned from a two days trip down the Bay with Mr. Vincent of the Packard Company.

I think the weather at home will be very fair. I have wired Galloway and Al Heath that you are coming — so that they can have the house all ready.

I am sorry you lost patience and write me as you did because you know there is no use of doing this, with the telegraph office within a block of you. When you don't receive prompt mail there is no reason why you shouldn't go right over to the telegraph office and send me a wire. You must always know there is something wrong when you don't receive answers to your letters because I always answer them. The mail situation is terrible all over the United States. Sometimes we get a letter here that has been delayed on the road for ten days.

Write me. With love and kisses,[4]

By April 2, Carl's mother was staying at the Windsor Hotel in Jacksonville, and Carl wrote her to tell her that her new house in Miami Beach was finished.

Dear Mother:

I enclose you another check for two hundred dollars, which you can keep separate from your other account.

I...had Van make out a lease to you, during your life time, of the new house which has just been finished. We had it painted a light yellow and it is a beauty. It is light and airy, has a big living room and the prettiest fireplace you ever saw. It has a fine yard and Tashiro is putting all sorts of flowers around the place. We are going to have Bougainvillae [sic] over the gate and up the side of the porch. It is an old fashioned English house, and I am sending you a booklet with a marked picture of it and the plans. It has a dandy garage with two servants' rooms and bath upstairs — a garage and two automobiles and a laundry. It has a big light, airy bathroom; and a side porch that you can sit on. I think we will put yellow awnings on it and finish it in light wicker.

Now all you have to do is pick out who you are going to have live with you next Winter.

It looks now as tho' I wouldn't be able to get away for the road meeting in Jacksonville, Saturday. Will wire you if I am coming.

Lots of love,[5]

In contrast, Carl's correspondence with his father reflected a strained relationship. Usually signed with a more formal "Yours Very Truly," Carl's letters at times sound like a father advising an errant son. On April 25,1918, Carl wrote his father about a plan that would bring his father to Florida.

Dear Father:

I have yours of the 15th: Personally I think you are very foolish to stay put in Illinois, in the mud and sleet. You have very poor weather in Illinois and in this part of the country generally. For a big part of the season it is either hot or cold.

I am figuring on a trade for some property near Vero, Florida, where they have good climate the year round, particularly in the Winter months. If I make this trade there is about 10-acres of good property that raises potatoes and cabbage to the tune of three to four hundred dollars an acre — and you might have some fun fooling with it. I will let you know if I make the deal.

Yours,[6]

Less than a month later, Carl had changed his mind and showed some concerns with his father's handling of the money he sent him.

Dear Father:

On June 2nd, 1917, I gave you $600.00 for a Ford, which you decided not to purchase. You advised me that this money was in the bank.

212

I am willing to give you annually, sufficient funds for you to live on without booze — but I have to know that the money I give you is properly used.

Regarding the Florida land, I have decided that I am not going to bother with it. I already have enough troubles without having a farmer on my hands in northern Florida who is more or less green with the conditions there.

In your letter of the 20th you state that you are making expenses. Am I to presume by this statement that the $600 I advanced you on June 2nd, 1917, just a year ago, has been expended?

Let me hear from you.

Yours very truly,[7]

By the next year, Carl had concluded his father could not handle large sums of money and decided a change was necessary in his method of advancing money. The letter was written February 7, 1919.

Dear Sir:

Enclosed find check for $100. I think it best for you to go back to the farm, and stay there. You can take better care of your health. It isn't necessary for you to pound around on the road.

I will send you $60 the first of each month if you will send me the address of just where you are permanently located. This letter is addressed, as you see, to: General Delivery, Mason, Warren County, Ohio. Let me know as soon as it reaches you.

Yours sincerely,[8]

In March, Carl received a letter that only confirmed his father's financial irresponsibility. H.A. DuBois of Cobden, Illinois, whose letterhead identified him as vice president of H. A. DuBois, maker of fruit and vegetable boxes and baskets, informed him of a debt his father had long owed.

Dear Sir:

I hold a note against your father A.H. Fisher for $50 with ten years interest due.

I have been wondering if you will be willing to take up this note. I will take the face of the note for it.

This note was given by your father and the money advance

213

[sic] him when he was down in Oklahoma out of work and out of funds.[9]

Carl replied to Mr. DuBois on March 22.

Dear Sir:

Replying to yours of the 17th: I have written my Father a letter asking him regarding the account to which you refer and advising him to pay it, and have also sent him the money to take care of the matter.

Thank you kindly,[10]

Carl also wrote his father on the same day.

Dear Father:

Enclosed herewith I am handing you [a] check for one hundred dollars. I have a letter from H.A. DuBois of Cobden, Illinois, in which he says that he has a note of yours for $50.00 with ten years interest due. He says he would be willing to take the face value of the note. At 6% there would be $30.00 interest due on this note, making a total of $80.00. If this account is correct you should immediately send check for $80.00 and pay the account.

A man who will loan fifty dollars should be taken care of.[11]

By December of 1919, Carl's parents were living together in Jacksonville, Florida.

Carl wrote his father there on December 26.

Dear Father:

I have waited to get our automobiles in good shape to send one of them up for you, and I think now that Fred, the driver, will start day after tomorrow and drive thru to Jacksonville, and he can drive you and Mother down. It will take two days for you to come all the way down, but it will be quite an interesting ride.

Yours very truly,[12]

Although Carl's parents were reunited, it did not last. According to Jane, it was Carl who had brought them back together. But after living with Ida for a short while, Carl's father "drifted away as unobtrusively as he had arrived. Carl never mentioned him again,"[13] wrote Jane.

Of all the news that Carl was to hear in 1921 there was

certainly none more surprising and exciting than Jane's announcement that she was expecting their baby in the fall. After twelve years of marriage, they were starting a family. Jane was elated.

> We were in Miami Beach when I knew that at last we were to have a child — the only thing we had asked of this rich life that had not been given. I don't think any man was ever so happy as Carl. His name waited for his son, Carl Graham Fisher, Junior, for of course Carl's child must be a son.
>
> In my little red velvet chair by his side I embroidered and hemmed and feather-stitched the little white dresses — no lavish layettes from Paris for our child! His clothing would be prepared for him by his mother's own hands. I was so proud — proud of my sense of well being and my sun-polished body — proud that at last I was giving Carl what he most desired.[14]

Carl and Jane Fisher happily anticipated the birth of their first child, but tragedy was to precede the event. On the morning of May 27, 1921, after showering and shaving, Frank Wheeler, Carl's long-time friend and partner in the Indiana Speedway, shot himself in the head with a double-barreled shotgun. Wheeler had been despondent over health problems — advanced diabetes and gangrene in his foot and the loss of Seymour Avery, secretary-treasurer of the Wheeler-Schebler firm, who had also committed suicide.[15]

On the morning of June 25, 1921, Carl's father, Albert, died at the age of 75. When Frank Shutts wrote Carl a letter of condolence, Carl replied: "Thanks for your letter. The hardest blow was on Mother, and she is coming through all right."[16] Mrs. Fisher moved in with Carl and Jane.

A depression that summer of 1921 forced Carl to sell his automobile company and obtain a bank loan, using his interests in Globe Realty and the Speedway as collateral. It was not a good time, especially with a baby coming. "Carl's restlessness increased. Tired of Indianapolis — summers were too hot and became unbearable for him in the hay-fever season — he considered moving to Detroit, then changed his mind. Money got tighter and tighter; he had to forfeit his annual pledge to the Lincoln Highway Association."[17]

Henry Ford, left, posed with speedway founders Arthur Newby, Frank Wheeler, Carl Fisher, and James Allison. (I.M.S.)

On August 1, Carl canceled his plans for a new hotel. To the architect, he wrote: "This summer is very discouraging. One day the stock market takes a small turn for the better and people feel encouraged, only the next day to go to the dumps with all sorts of losses on stocks and shut-down of industrial plans."[18]

Carl had another building project in mind, but this one was to be built in Indiana. Carl had purchased property on June 29, 1916, to build a mausoleum in Crown Hill Cemetery. Now, he decided to build the mausoleum. "Every body should have a place ready...."[19] he told Jane. Carl wasted no time. The mausoleum was under construction within a week.

But the birth of the baby was quickly approaching. Carl was convinced it would be a boy — Carl Junior. Another polo player, he said. The baby was to be born in Indianapolis.

It was not an easy birth. Jane endured four days of labor before a Caesarian was performed on October 13. The baby was a boy, as Carl had said. Jane thought he was the picture of Carl, "the dimples, the half-shut, amused baby look."[20]

When Jane awoke after the operation, she found her room full of American Beauty roses from Carl, but Carl was crying. After seeing her go through the ordeal, he said, "Never again, Jane honey. I'll never let you go through this again."[21]

Carl was truly happy about the baby. He brought his friends "in swarms"[22] to see him and sent telegrams to all his friends.

To Edward C. Romfh, president of The First National Bank in Miami, he wrote: "...I suppose you will be surprised to know that Mrs. Fisher presented the family with an eight and a half pound polo player. Both are doing very well."[23]

Romfh responded: "I am glad it was a boy, because now you can see yourself live over again. As you know, I have three, and every day I am reminded of myself when I was a 'kid.' Children are the greatest institution on earth, and furthermore, this is just the beginning."[24]

In a telegram, Frank Shutts sent his congratulations:

Please inform Junior when he wakes up and quits crying long enough that he has innumerable friends in Miami including ourselves and all our subsidiaries who will be glad to welcome him here this winter and who now offer him any services which may be desired stop. We all congratulate Mrs. Fisher and yourself and hope that the young man's life may be long and happy in this wicked world.[25]

On October 21, 1921, Julius Fleischmann wrote Carl from New York.

Very glad to hear the news of the arrival of the boy. My very best wishes to you and Mrs. Fisher. Will you please extend to her my very kindest regards with the hope that she is as well as mothers possibly can be under the circumstances.[26]

After a few weeks' time, Jane and Carl, Jr., returned home to Blossom Heath, Jane still recuperating from surgery. But all was not well.

...a few weeks later, I felt my baby grow quiet in my arms. I felt his coldness and screamed for the nurse. She leaned over us, professionally soothing.

"Don't be frightened, Mrs. Fisher. Little babies get cold so quickly!"

The ambulance came again to Blossom Heath and went away with our baby. I was too ill to go to the hospital. Carl rode with him. There was an emergency operation, and all day I waited word while Galloway prayed beside my bed. It was pyloric stenosis — our baby had literally starved to death and we had not known. Fifteen miles by ambulance with snow streaking its windows, I was driven to the new mausoleum on the hill overlooking Indianapolis. In its shadowy coldness, under flowers, was the little jewel-case casket that held our son...."[27]

Carl Graham Fisher Jr. lived only 26 days. Of her marriage, Jane wrote: "That was the real ending. We would never be complete again."[28] Carl and Jane spoke little. But he did tell her, "I never want another — never another baby, Jane."[29]

Carl's announcements of his son's death and burial were terse. To his uncle, Amos Fisher (author's grandfather) of Frankfort, Ohio, he sent this telegram:

Carl Junior died last evening. Quiet burial tomorrow. No funeral.[30]

The obituary notice read:

Carl Graham Fisher Junior, infant son of Mr. and Mrs. Carl Graham Fisher. Funeral Thursday, 3:00 p.m. For family only.[31]

It was Carl's sad duty to send the following letter of authorization to the superintendent of Crown Hill Cemetery:

This will authorize you to open my Mausoleum this date, Thursday, November 10, for Mr. Flanner, to receive the body of my infant son, Carl Graham Fisher, Jr.[32]

After the death of Carl Jr., Jane and Carl never again lived in Blossom Heath. In 1928, the 4380-square-foot house became the campus of The Boys Preparatory School of Indianapolis, which obtained a 90-year lease on the property with an option to buy. They purchased the property in 1949 and changed its name to the Park School for Boys.

Carl's mother had an operation shortly after Carl Jr.'s death. She recovered well, and Carl returned to Miami Beach. A week before Christmas, Jane stripped the nursery and gave away all of the baby things before she returned to Miami Beach, where she continued the Christmas celebration she had been conducting there every year for other people's children. "Carl and I were again together. But our lives would not touch again. Carl's terror while waiting for our child to be born, my operation, and the death of our baby had left him determined never to allow me to carry another child. This very real fear forced back the customary caresses and kept him from my room at The Shadows."[33]

Although Jane was at first negative to Carl's plans to develop Miami Beach, the rapid progress that had been made had changed her mind. But it had not been an experience that had drawn them closer together; if anything, they were gradually drifting apart, their twenty-year difference in age perhaps more pronounced than ever before. It was not that they fought or had confrontations. She wrote of Carl's kindness and generosity; he never questioned the amount of money she spent on the household. Whatever she wanted, she received. She had personal maids, a social secretary, her own speedboat, yacht, and stable. He had built her a bridle path. But, she wrote, at the beginning of the 1920's, "Carl and I were seeing too little of each other, for business and social demands came between us."[34] Whether she suspected that his secretary, Ann Rossiter, was also his mistress is left unsaid. Carl seemed preoccupied. Sometimes, she wrote, he never went to bed but instead lay on the rug in front of the fire with Rowdy, "planning, working, building in his mind the night through."[35]

She was free to travel — alone, or with friends. While he was building The Flamingo, she went to Europe and sent him a gondola from Venice. It immediately struck Carl that gondolas would add a wonderful touch to Miami Beach.

Before her pregnancy, Jane had led an active social life. She resumed it. Inadvertently, she also started on a writing career. The first newspaper in Miami Beach had just started publication. Her letter wishing success to the editor, Clayton Sedgwick Cooper, prompted an offer from Cooper for her to write a social column for the *Daily Tribune.* At night in her bedroom she would type her column. She continued writing for the paper until it ceased publication four years later. [36]

Carl's grief over the death of his son was deep. "Long afterward, Art Pancoast [Collins' grandson] told a curious little story: at the Roman Pools on the day Pancoast was proudly handing out cigars to celebrate the birth of his first child, he gave one to Carl, who smiled, took the cigar, congratulated him, and burst into tears."[37]

Carl had his businesses to keep him occupied. He would seek the physical intimacy he no longer shared with Jane with other women. He would also find solace in what would soon become a constant companion — alcohol.

Mrs. Carl G. Fisher and Mrs. Ida M. Fisher
on March 23, 1922. (Matlack; HASF)

Chapter 20

The Dixie Highway

Progress on the Dixie Highway was much slower than Carl would have liked. In 1916, Michigan was admitted to the Dixie Highway Association. "...promoters than claimed that the route linked two of the most remote and culturally different places in the country: Sault Sainte Marie, Michigan, and Miami Beach, Florida."[1] Altogether, the highway now linked ten states, in what Howard Preston called "a complicated network of roads."[2] Preston says that after it was announced that the Dixie Highway would include such cities as Detroit, Chicago, Cincinnati, and others, "Miami Beach came to life."[3]

It would be a long haul before the highway was actually completed; parts of it were not improved until the late 1920's. "Completion of the project was slow because it involved the coordinated efforts of more than fifty counties in ten states, state and county bond issues, federal subsidies, along with local contributions from owners of hotels, restaurants, and automotive supply stores along the route, which paid for the highway,"[4] Preston wrote. Also, instead of a coordinated effort to obtain federal aid for the highway after it became available, communities tried to get the money for themselves. The publicity given the Dixie Highway encouraged others to build roads and capture some of the tourist trade. Between 1915 and 1920, hundreds of new interstate highway associations were formed in the South.[5]

It was the duty of Michael M. Allison, the president of the association, to inform Carl of the setbacks that were to prove discouraging to both of them. On April 16, 1919, Allison broke the news that Tennessee's fifty-million-dollar bond issue had been defeated. Allison had spent almost a month in Nashville, gaining what he thought was positive support for the issue, but at the last minute,

> ...right on the eve of the adjournment politics got into it good and proper and gummed up the cards.
>
> The Governor is in politics and wound up by fixing a place for some of his friends on the Highway Commission, which would have made the bill a failure if we had gotten it thru [sic]. When we saw the ship going on the breakers we tried to salvage as much as possible, but we did not get much.
>
> The bill passed by the Legislature provides for a one mill direct tax, and a tax of fifty cents per horse power on automobiles, trucks, etc., but the two bad features of the bill are — first, that it permits politicians to be appointed on the State Highway Commission, and second, it fails to provide for any permanent or through highways. The road tax is apportioned out to all the counties of the state and will result in building a few miles of road in each county which cannot be connected up.
>
> I am straddling the fence wrestling with conflicting emotions. I do not know whether to give up in disgust, and wash my hands of the whole damn business, or try to put on an educational campaign of two years, and try to elect representatives in the Legislature who have some sense and are substantially honest, and a governor of like proportions.
>
> We could get some little good out of the present law if we had the right kind of Highway Commission but since I have taken the trouble to tell the governor in no uncertain terms what I think of him, any suggestion along that line from me would not have much weight.[6]

Carl, back in Indianapolis, replied on April 25:

> I have your letter of the 16th and certainly it has sent a big gloom around this office. I have always felt that Tennessee as much if not more than any other state in the South needed interconnecting roads — first, for the people who live in Tennessee and use these roads, and secondly, to let the other people in the United States who want to get into that beautiful

country have a chance to see it and spend more of their money in Tennessee. I would be in Tennessee this month myself if there was any road to get in and out that was fit to drive over. Thousands of other motorists are in the same boat.

You have a long hard fight and you must feel very much discouraged. You know more about the situation than I do and I will be governed a great deal by your advice. I will drag along with you to the end of the road or let them all go to Hell — whichever you say.

I have been home for a week. The weather is no good and I miss Miami, or any other part of the South that is warm and pleasant.

If you are up this way, don't fail to stop over with me for a few days. I have one bottle of Scotch left and we might be able to forget our troubles.[7]

There were other people in Tennessee who were interested in improving roads. A.F. Sanford, president of the *Journal and Tribune* in Knoxville, wrote to Carl that some month for same financial support for a section of the road. Carl refused.

Personally I don't see any use of either the Detroit organization or myself spending money on a job that is not complete and leaves us with seven or eight miles of unimproved roads.

Just now I don't mind telling you that I am pretty thoroly [sic] disgusted with the situation in Tennessee. Certainly a lot of good people have spent a lot of valuable time and hard work and a great deal of money trying to help out Tennessee and lift them out of the mud, and it seems to me the hardest state in the Union to get going. With all the rock in the world in Tennessee for the building of roads, they have some of the poorest roads.

However, I won't say "No" entirely to the situation but want to hear from Judge Allison first.[8]

Carl did, however, donate money where he thought it would be well spent. In May he sent Allison a thousand dollars for the survey of the link between Cincinnati and Chattanooga.[9] He was not so willing to contribute to a semi-permanent road in Charlton County, Georgia. In a reply to William T. Anderson, editor of the *Macon Daily Telegraph,* Carl instead offered to donate five thousand dollars, fifty percent of the cost of a half mile of concrete highway, if federal aid or some other source would pay the remainder. The idea was similar to the "ideal" sections of the Lincoln Highway.

> I think that a half mile of concrete road in that country where thousands of people have never seen a concrete road, would give them a splendid idea of the wearing surface of a concrete road and a comparison in the next few years of the actual cost in road building.[10]

Anderson discussed Carl's suggestion with Judge Patterson, chairman of the Georgia Highway Department. A cement company offered a $500 discount if the project used its cement, saying the half mile was too small to be profitable because of the cost of moving heavy equipment.[11]

Although the Dixie Highway was progressing very slowly, Carl had great admiration for the association president, Michael Allison. On May 26, 1919, he wrote his friend A.G. Batchelder of the American Automobile Association.

> If there ever lived a hard-working, painstaking road builder, it is Mike Allison of Chattanooga. If we had selected any other man of a million for President of the Dixie Highway, we probably would have gotten nowhere. The people in the South are rather clannish and they have to have one of their own folks preach to them, curse them and exhort them.[12]

Carl felt strongly that it was important to put a "first class" road crossing the Cumberland Mountains between Cincinnati and Chattanooga. "...this road over the Cumberlands passes thru poor territory, with poor people who haven't seen the light, and not only haven't seen the light but haven't the cash."[13]

Just as Carl had wanted to enlist Henry Ford's help in building the Lincoln Highway, he thought of him again in building this section of the Dixie Highway. He even appealed to Batchelder for some assistance.

> I have often thought that if the right fellow would present on paper an attractive and true picture of the Cumberland Mountains and what could be done to the South by opening up the road across them — if handed to Henry [Ford] at the right time, he might himself build this road. Ford has been waiting for a long time to spend five, ten or fifteen million dollars in

some memorial to himself and the Ford Company. He promised me at one time ten dollars on every Ford car that he built for three years or until the Lincoln Highway was finished — and then somebody talked him out of it. I almost had his signature to this proposition. Haven't you somebody in your office who could prepare the proper papers to be submitted to Ford for consideration? Pictures of the roads as they are and as they could be, would have to be fitted into a pamphlet, or an album, say. You have plenty of photos that will fit the occasion without taking a single extra one.

The biggest part of the South might just as well be a foreign country as far as the automobile is concerned. The average automobile is almost a wreck by the time it gets over the Cumberlands.

I would like to donate two or three hundred dollars for some longheaded gumshoe artist of about your calibre to pick out of a bookworm to handle this proposition — and then let me go up to Detroit and take another whirl at Ford. In other words, I would like to gamble two or three hundred dollars against a ten million dollar road that is probable. Hardly probable, but still possible.

Some day somebody will get Ford to sign his name to something that will cost ten or fifteen million dollars — and he will pay it gladly and be tickled to death. It may be a hospital or a college — and it may be a road across the Cumberland Mountains.[14]

Nothing ever came of the Ford idea, but Carl was willing to donate money for this section of highway, under certain conditions. He wrote Allison on July 22, 1919:

Of course I would be delighted at any time to deal out five thousand dollars to that Highway between Cincinnati and Chattanooga to help make a permanent piece of road that can be used in the winter time — and any time they have to have five thousand dollars for one particular spot when the balance of the road has been completed, you can call me for $5,000 and get it. *But I'm damned if I am going to give up five thousand dollars to a bunch of people who won't help themselves.*[15]

Carl thought little of the inhabitants of Tennessee who appeared to be unconcerned about the condition of their roads.

You know what I think of all the rock and all the material they have in Tennessee for the roads and the fact that the people there won't even pick up the rock along the road and throw it into the holes — and when I think of all the mudholes we went thru before we got to Jellico — well — it wouldn't do for me to put it on paper.

I am going to switch my donation of $5,000 to that county in Georgia that voted every damned cent they have and are actually going to do something. Really, some of the people of Tennessee ought to be ashamed of themselves at the roads they have.[16]

There was an opportunity for investment in road building, and Carl took advantage of it. He bought about a twenty percent interest in the Kentucky Rock Asphalt Company, which produced six to ten thousand tons per month. He regarded asphalt as an excellent material for the Southern states because they did not receive heavy freezes.[17]

After so many setbacks, Carl was elated in January of 1920 when William Anderson, editor of the *Macon Daily Telegraph* of Macon, Georgia, informed him that a Georgia road plan had been approved.

I will meet you at any point on that road any day in the year, day or night, and drink that champagne with you, after you get a first class road between Waycross and Jacksonville, and I will not only furnish the champagne but I will furnish the ice.

I am glad your road plan came through without the use of the Five Thousand; but we always have this Five Thousand to make a crack at any community that cannot build its own roads, and I have found in a good many cases it really does some good to offer to help them, although they don't always accept.[18]

There was also good news that month about sales of lots in Miami Beach; Carl predicted one million dollars in sales in January.[19]

Carl's interest in the success of the Dixie Highway had been so great that he planned to will them one-third of his wealth. In August of 1920 he changed his mind and instead offered to subscribe $2,500 or more each year for ten years, with a promise to raise that amount if Miami Beach prospered.[20]

When Dixie Highway Association President Allison replied to this news from Carl, he revealed his own feelings of discouragement about the highway.

Do you believe in mental telepathy? If you do not, then how do you explain the fact that for two or three weeks I have had in mind to write you, suggesting a revocation of that clause in your will covering your bequest to the Dixie Highway Association.

While I can think of no greater service to the general run of humanity, I get disheartened when I consider the lack of interest in this proposition.

A year ago we passed a resolution to dedicate at least one of the divisions this fall. Clark Howell secured the acceptance of the governors of all the states to accompany us on this trip of dedication, and we have been hammering at the people along the line to get ready, trying to appeal to their civic pride and show them what it would mean to fall down, and in most cases they have pursued the even tenor of their way, showing that they don't give a damn whether roads are ever finished or not.[21]

A few months later, in January, 1921, Allison wrote Carl, indicating his decision to resign as president. Carl immediately replied:

I think you are making amistake [sic] to resign as President. You are the healthiest President of a Road Association that I ever heard of and you have accomplished wonders. The main thing is that the people in the South have not the money to give and they are not anxious to give for roads, they are slower in doing things generally than we are in the North.

The Lincoln Highway Association has of course great funds from the automobile manufacturers and those same automobile manufacturers ought to help us out but somehow or other they just don't do it.[22]

In June, the association's Board of Directors refused to accept Allison's resignation; he agreed to stay on until the next meeting in September. Allison had some optimistic news for Carl, who had been unable to attend the annual meeting of the Board of Directors.

The old enthusiasm seems to be reviving and we had a very interesting and enthusiastic meeting. A live delegation of about fifty from the civic organizations of Cincinnati was in attendance pledging the hearty co-operation of the City of Cincinnati in opening up the eastern division through the mountains of Kentucky and Tennessee. A great number of our friends from various sections were present pledging further co-operation and renewed efforts toward the completion of the highway at an early date.

You have been re-elected as one of the Directors for the State of Indiana. We have some new blood in the Board of Directors and they promise to make us step lively.[23]

Carl did not attend the September meeting either. He suffered from hay fever. He wrote W.H. Gilbreath, manager of the Detroit Auto Club: "I have had a terrible time this summer and hope to get out of the hay fever district next year."[24] Carl also revealed to Gilbreath his financial problems and his dissatisfaction with auto makers and road builders.

I have had considerable trouble on account of the financial market to raise sufficient money for my financial program at Miami Beach and have been compelled to shut down on progress, until next Spring so that my donations to the different road building programs are cut to the limit.

I might incidentally tell you that I am damn good and sore at the various automobile companies, sundries companies, etc., who are making millions out of the automobile business and who will not help support road building programs. There is absolutely no inducement, nowadays, for people to purchase touring automobiles and to tour in various parts of the country. Why should I, entirely out of the automobile business, waste a lot of time and a lot of money in promoting touring roads for the automobile companies who are too selfish to do their share. I am just about to the point where I would like to tell them all to go to Hell. If it wasn't for a few people like Bill Metzger, I certainly would tell them all to go to Hell.

The automobile business has a long and rocky road ahead of it in the next few years unless we got some good touring National roads and speaking on this subject, the greatest favor the Detroit Automobile Club could perform would be to promote a law to make contractors and road builders provide a temporary turn-out where small bridges are being constructed and also to provide suitable detour signs. I am quite sure that 90% of all detours in America are silly and ridiculous. In France and England you don't have detours for a small piece of construction work and larger detours call for only five or ten miles drive over mud roads, narrow roads and rotten roads.

...Last night I was on one detour of seven miles thru some perfectly hellish roads in order to get around a little concrete culvert that would probably cost about $1,800 — the culvert crossing a stream which was six feet wide and dry seven months in the year. I made a careful estimation what it would cost to provide a go around, and I would be willing to take the contract tomorrow to do the job in first class shape for $150.

Now, if your Automobile Club has a damn bit of influence and is not wasting time or money in your salary or other people's salary, why not get behind this detour business and settle it or at least start to settle it. Of course, I don't refer to large construction work where tremendous expense would be necessary but on the little road between here and Dayton for the last fifteen years there has been between five and ten detours and there is only one detour in the whole road that is necessary that I can think of and that is at Knightstown. It took them over two years at Knightstown to build a bridge that should have been constructed in four months.[25]

Carl's bouts with hay fever, his father's death, financial setbacks, and the death of his son made 1921 a very difficult year. Despite Carl's troubles, he saw hope in the future of the Dixie Highway and even in passenger air travel across the United States. For financing these hopes, he looked to federal money, particularly money appropriated for defense. Carl wrote Allison on November 17, informing him of the death of Carl Junior and of his ideas.

We lost our little boy last week and it will not be necessary to fool with the will, at this time.

I have been delayed leaving for the South for thirty days but am leaving tonight and will go thru as quickly as possible as I have a lot of things that must be looked after immediately. I will see you when you get down this winter. In the meantime, I read a lot in the Dixie Highway magazine regarding the big progress you are making. You certainly deserve a tremendous amount of credit for the manner in which you handled this road campaign in Tennessee. For a long time I thought that Tennessee and Kentucky was [sic] absolutely hopeless and that the people did not want good roads but it begins to look like we will yet see the time when we can drive thru in some comfort.

It seems to me that it would be a good time right now to jump into some publicity regarding the amount of roads that could be built in America if only one fifth of the money appropriated for the Navy could be applied to roads. Nowadays a first class battleship costs about fifty million dollars. With the grades already established the Dixie Highway from Mackinac to Miami, Florida could be a boulevard for the cost of one battleship. Three complete boulevards from the Atlantic Coast to the Pacific Coast and two boulevards from the Great Lakes to the Gulf of Mexico could be built with the war appropriations for only two years, and the tax on automobiles and gasoline could pay back to the nation in five years all that these boulevards cost.

One sixth of the present appropriations for war purposes if applied to the promotion of air control would give us not less than five aerial dirgibile [sic] liners carrying one hundred passengers each, traveling from New York to San Francisco in two days. And these expenses of government moneys would be distributed thru out the United States where the masses of the people would get real benefit of this. You can elaborate on what could be done with even a portion of these moneys properly distributed for the benefit of the people. It would not be necessarily wise to cancel the war deed and spend the same amount of money at this time in internal improvements but it certainly would be the proper thing under present conditions of business to cancel war expenditures and immediately appropriate for road building in the United States something like one fourth of the proposed budget for war purposes.

With an additional fourth of the present budget appropriated for aerial navigation, the United States in five years could be far ahead of any other countries in the world both in air navigation and permanent road construction.[26]

Picking up on Carl's idea for some publicity, Allison suggested a cartoon:

showing the general outline of one branch of the Dixie Highway from the Lakes to the Gulf with the greater part of it shown as a completed permanent boulevard with some horrible gaps here and there with farmers stuck in the mud on their way to the market, school children climbing out of [the] bus because the bus is stuck in the mud and having to walk to school, with a picture at the top of Uncle Sam and a battleship and these farmers and children begging Uncle Sam for the price of one battleship with which to fix these gaps in the highway... I could get this reproduced by the press practically from Michigan to Florida.[27]

Allison also reported on complaints from the city of St. Petersburg that they had not been included on the route of the Dixie Highway. He planned to invite the Florida directors to the next meeting of the executive committee so that they could discuss the possibility of including St. Petersburg. He wanted Carl's advice on the matter.

Carl deferred to Allison.

I have yours of the 1st: Any changes you want to make in the location of the Highway will be, I am sure, much better controlled from Chattanooga. You are more in touch with the different local conditions than anybody I know of and your judgment is bound to be better than the judgment of outsiders.

It seems to me that it would be quite easy to have a very effective propaganda just now if, for instance, a battleship could be traded for either 1000 or 10,000 miles of good highway. Some of the up-state battleships cost fifty to seventy-five million dollars so that one good one would be enough to build a first class highway clear across the United States. This sort of propaganda might take very well with the farmers — and if we could once get the eyes of the Nation concentrated on a North and South Highway and an East and West Highway, it would be a good thing.

It doesn't seem to me that it is practical to make any Paradise Loop in the Florida part of the Highway. The Highway is crooked enough as it is now. If you have a map completed, it seems to me that the best thing to do is to stick to it. However, as I stated, I suggest leaving the matter up to you as you must be better posted than any of the rest of us.[28]

Unfortunately, progress on the Dixie Highway continued to be excruciatingly slow. Three years later, on December 11, 1924, Carl indicated in a letter to Allison how bad things still were, years after they had begun their attempt to build a north-south highway.

I wouldn't go over the Dixie Highway, or any other highway from here to Chicago in an automobile for the whole state of Indiana, or Tennessee either for that matter. The road from here to Jacksonville is much worse than it was five years ago; and it is almost as bad as it was when we came over it. Of course, the bottom of the road base is there, but the top surface in a great many places is gone and on account of new building there are a great many terrible detours. I am satisfied that any attempt at new road building should be with a permanent type either concrete or Kentucky Road Asphalt, otherwise a big part of the money spent on the road is soon gone.[29]

Completion of the Dixie Highway would take until the late 1920's. Regardless of the delays, the South's desire for economic development, mainly through tourism, ensured that the project would not be abandoned.

Carl Fisher's promotional brochure for the Dixie Highway enticed people to Miami Beach. (Parks)

232

Chapter 21

"It's June in Miami"

In the winter of 1922, men and women slogging through the snow and cold of New York City were brought up short by a large new illuminated sign on the corner of Fifth Avenue and Forty-second Street flashing the message: "It's June in Miami."[1] Carl's penchant for publicity was at work, bringing to one of the largest groups of potential customers the appeal of the warmth of the South when they were most vulnerable. The new sign "created a sensation,"[2] according to Polly Redford.

"...Carl's Miami Beach development was the first of its kind in Florida, the first to make something new, bright, expensive and fun out of what to most Americans had been nothing, a wilderness. Of all Florida resorts, Miami Beach was the most publicized and, most important, it best reflected the spirit of the decade that later came to be known as the Roaring Twenties,"[3] Redford wrote.

Those who went south found a concerted effort by the four real estate companies — the Miami Beach Improvement Company, Alton Beach Realty Company, Miami Beach Bayshore Company and the Miami Ocean View Company — to sell land. Carl had arranged for a "super salesroom" in downtown Miami, so inviting that tourists walked in to inspect the Spanish-style living-room-like salesroom with its 6 foot by 35 foot painted panorama of Miami Beach. Miami real estate brokers, who had previously largely ignored Miami

Beach sales in favor of sales on the mainland, found this new competition so threatening that they, too, began to sell Miami Beach properties. The office remained open for only two seasons; after that, there were more customers than lots.[4]

It was Jane Fisher who inadvertently helped fuel the Miami Beach bathing beauty appeal marketed throughout the United States. Women's bathing apparel had been exceedingly modest: bathing suits as long as street dresses, long black stockings, bathing shoes, and caps covering their long

(Matlack; HASF)

Miami Beach was publicized as the year-round perfect climate.

hair. Jane's motive for changing such attire was, she said, prompted by her learning the new Australian crawl, and she "longed for greater freedom in the water."[5]

Jane's modifications — though considered scandalous at the time — were hardly lascivious. Her new bathing suit was form-fitting, but knee-length. In place of the long black stockings, she wore anklets. "The following Sunday a minister in a church on the mainland used my bathing suit — and me in it — as a symbol of the brazenness of the modern woman. Miami Beach was compared to Sodom and Gomorrah, and I to a female biblical character I prefer not to name."[6]

The bathing suit became a new draw. People made their way over the bridge to see it.

Carl, who avoided personal publicity, "Usually... was very strict in all matters pertaining to his wife — if not to other women,"[7] Jane wrote. But this time he saw an opportunity. "'Honey, that's the first sensible bathing suit I've seen,'" he told her. "'You hold your head up and keep right on wearing it. I don't see why in hell a woman with a damn pretty figure hasn't a right to show it.'"[8]

It took only a few weeks for other women to discard the black stockings. Carl was elated. "'By God, Jane, you've started something! Why, damn it, I've been trying for months to think up an idea for advertising the Beach nationally. We'll get the prettiest girls we can find and put them in the goddamned tightest and shortest bathing suits and no stockings or swim shoes either. We'll have their pictures taken and send them all over the goddamn country as "The Bathing Beauties of Miami Beach"!'"[9]

Bathing beauty contests began in Miami when Everett Sewell, head of Miami's Chamber of Commerce, started an annual bathing beauty parade and contest about 1920.[10] The national publicity, however, was a promotion of Steve Hannagan, who had been in charge of publicity at the Indianapolis Speedway. He had been recommended to Carl in 1920, but lost all chance for the job when he took it upon himself to set the terms. Four years later he inquired about working for Carl at Miami Beach, but all Carl could give him was a referral to someone else, as he had already hired a publicist. The next season however, he went to work for Carl.[11]

The Miami Beach community was more than willing to assist in the publicity effort. The high school allowed Hannagan to photograph their female students in bathing suits, resulting in pictures that appeared in newspapers throughout the U.S.[12] Slogans accompanied posters of beautiful girls pictured bathing in the ocean: "It's always June in Miami Beach." "Where summer spends the winter." "A paradise for sport lovers, a playground for youth, a haven of peace and beauty for the aged."[13]

Carl's promotion of Miami Beach had taken a whole different turn from his original attempts to lure tourists and prospective customers with promises of a peaceful, relaxing getaway. Carl wrote much of the advertising copy, just as he had done at the Speedway.[14] Alton Beach was portrayed as a "subtle refinement of homelike restfulness where high strung nerves could relax." His posters "pictured Spanish palaces fretted with grill work, troubadours singing under palm trees, lovers drifting under sails on moonlit lagoons."[15]

The campaign was not very successful. Other wealthy people were no more interested in merely taking it easy than Carl had been when he first came to Miami. In 1923, he explained his misguided campaign to *Business* magazine. "I was on the wrong track. I had been trying to reach the dead ones. I had been going after the old folks. I saw that what I needed to do was go after the live wires. And the live wires don't want to relax."[16]

Carl's new tack was sports. Golf matches, polo games, and regattas were events that attracted tourists and celebrities. Miami Beach was now "America's greatest winter playground." Carl told *Business* that he was spending $350,000 annually on boat races, golf and tennis matches, and swimming and diving exhibitions at the Roman Pools.[17] Sports champions Bill Tilden, Gene Sarazen, Johnny Weismuller, Gertrude Eberle, Jack Dempsey, and Gene Tunney came to Miami Beach.

In 1928 when business had slowed down, Carl devised a new way for the LaGorce Golf Course to produce publicity for Miami Beach. He proceeded to name each of the eighteen holes after a celebrity, all of whom had visited Miami Beach. To Reinald Werrenrath, whom Polly Redford described as a "popular concert baritone, a long-time friend and drinking companion of Carl's,"[18] he announced the honor in a telegram on February 28, 1928:

A UNIQUE HIGHLIGHT OF GOLF HISTORY WAS WRITTEN TODAY ON LAGORCE GOLF COURSE MIAMI BEACH OF WHICH YOU ARE AN IMPORTANT FACTOR STOP HOLE NUMBER 9 ON WHICH YOU HAVE DISTINGUISHED YOURSELF HAS BEEN NAMED IN YOUR HONOR AND A BRONZE PLATE BEARING YOUR NAME WILL BE PLACED THERE FOR ALL TIME STOP WE BELIEVE THIS IS THE FIRST TIME SUCH A THING HAS BEEN DONE AND THE PIN WILL BE FOREVER BRIGHTER BECAUSE OF THE ASSOCIATION WITH YOUR NAME STOP MORE POWER TO YOUR SWING.[19]

The honorees seemed genuinely touched by the unusual honor. Poet Edgar A. Guest wrote a poem and on March 8, 1928, sent Carl the sports page from the previous Sunday's *Detroit Free Press* "containing a complete account of my reaction to your very friendly telegram regarding the bronze tablet." Guest said he "greatly appreciated the honor."[20] Carl replied on March 12:

Thanks for yours of the eighth. It certainly was a nice write up in the Free Press. I don't know how much time it took you to roll off that poetry stuff, but I know what a terrible job it would be for me to even try to do it.

I hope to see you some time this summer at Montauk.[21]

Gene Tunney was equally pleased to be honored as he wrote to Carl on March 14.

It is impossible for me to express the gratitude I feel at the great distinction you have conferred upon me in naming Hole Number 1 of the LaGorce Golf Course after me.

I have always been opposed to the idea of personal immortality, but for some reason which I cannot analyze, I feel a great sense of gratification at your most considerate and thoughtful act. I can assure you no favor of fortune or man has ever pleased me more.[22]

Carl replied to the recipients, thanking them for accepting the honor. To Thomas Meighan of Paramount Studios he wrote:

Thanks for yours of the 29th. I am sure you are not going to be ashamed of the other names that will stick on this golf course.

We thought at first we would make these names on cast iron, but we finally figured that they would rust out and we would have to do it over again, and that real bronze in the long run — maybe 150 years, would be cheaper.[23]

To Tex Rickard, owner of Madison Square Garden, he wrote:

Thanks for permitting us to honor the LaGorce course and you by the permanent affixing of your name.

As far as we know, this is the first time such a thing has ever been done and I hope that you will feel a sort of God-fatherly interest not only in your particular hole but for the LaGorce Course.

There is one little joker in connection with it that I can tell you, now that you have accepted — we feel it is only right that you should give a stroke to your opponent when playing it, in view of the fact that this is your hole. If your partner does not know this rule, he may not claim it, so that it rests entirely with your conscience.

With renewed appreciation of your very nice reply, and all good wishes, I am [24]

Carl received this letter from sportswriter Grantland Rice.

I just wanted to tell you how much I appreciated the news received in the telegram from you and the Hon. John Oliver LaGorce. I can't tell you how deeply gratified I am.

Here's hoping the coming tournament is going to be the biggest in the country.[25]

John Golden, Broadway playwright, wrote on March 24.

I arrived here this morning and my first and happiest duty is to acknowledge that wonderful letter which you both signed.

I don't want to appear too sentimental, but this further evidence of your friendship, has really touched me deeply.

I would rather have that proof of the regard of two such men as yourselves than any other thing that I can bring to my mind.

Your statement that a bronze plate, bearing my name, will be placed there for all time, suggests the thought that if it were possible I would like my ashes to be placed beneath that plate, so that some day some passing golfer jester might say "Golden finished with a hole in one."

Anyway, seriously, I love you and I appreciate the thought and the sweetness of it all.[26]

New York Evening Post sportswriter Walter Trumbull was as pleased as the others who had been honored.

The signal event of any return to this village was the finding of a letter signed by you and John Oliver LaGorce notifying me that Hole No. 13 on the LaGorce Course had been named for me.

I have an impression that this may be news to you, but nevertheless I must tell you that words are but feeble instruments to express the pride I feel. On reading the news the chest buttons of my vest flew off with a popping sound and that garment is now at the tailors having new buttons wired on. Gentlemen, I thank you. Never again shall I labor in a trap guarding a thirteenth green without pausing to brag. My only regret is that I was not present at the christening to break a hogshead over the pin.

We have you to thank for much of our pleasure at Miami Beach and we sure had a bully time there. Please don't forget us for we, like everyone who visits the place, hope sometime to return. It's the only place in Florida I ever saw where I'd like to own a house.

Mrs. Trumbull joins me in appreciation of all your kindness and in asking to be remembered to Mrs. Fisher.[27]

The honorees were as follows, as described by Polly Redford:

1. GENE TUNNEY — world heavyweight boxing champion, soon to retire, marry an heiress, and disappear forever into High Society.

2. GRANTLAND RICE — dean of American sportswriters.

3. HARVEY FIRESTONE — President, Firestone Tire & Rubber Company, whose estate later became the Fountainebleau Hotel.

4. TOMMY MEIGHAN — Paramount Studios, Hollywood, California.

5. WILLIAM KISSAM VANDERBILT — "Willie," one of the few Vanderbilts to grace Miami Beach, was an auto racer, amateur explorer, big-game fisherman, and holder of a merchant marine Master's Ticket (all oceans, unlimited tonnage) which he obtained at the Seamans' Church Institute's night-school courses after leaving his offices at the New York Central Railroad. The lavish estate he built on Fisher's Island is now occupied by Gar Wood.

6. TEX RICKARD — fight promoter and owner of Madison Square Garden.

7. EDGAR A. GUEST — newspaper and greeting-card poet made forever famous by Dorothy Parker's critique, "I'd rather flunk my Wassermann Test than read the poems of Eddie Guest."

8. WILL ROGERS — cowboy, vaudeville comedian, movie star, and syndicated columnist — one of the best-liked men in America.

9. REINALD WERRENRATH — popular concert baritone, a long-time friend and drinking companion of Carl's.

10. GAR WOOD — millionaire inventor and speedboat champion.

11. EDDIE RICKENBACKER — race car driver, World War I flying ace, owner of Indianapolis Speedway, later president of Eastern Air Lines.

12. RING LARDNER — sportswriter, raconteur, short-story artist whose baseball stories captured the American vernacular as no others have ever done, before or since.

13. WALTER TRUMBULL — sportswriter for the *New York Evening Post*.

14. JOHN GOLDEN — Broadway playwright and producer of many hits: *Seventh Heaven, Susan and God, Skylark*.

15. GLENN CURTISS — aircraft pioneer, owner of large tracts of land north of Miami.

16. ARTHUR BRISBANE — leading news columnist of the day, and a great booster of Carl's Montauk development. His ar-

ticles appeared daily on the front page of the *New York Evening Journal.*

17. GEORGE ADE — Indiana humorist, author of *Fables in Slang.*

18. ARTHUR CHAMPION — developer of Champion Spark Plugs, and a great friend of Carl's, his was the only posthumous name at LaGorce. He had died the summer before on a trip to Europe.[28]

Sometimes Carl reaped a harvest of publicity from something serendipitous. One such boon came in February of 1921 as a gift from Ed Ballard, an old friend from Indiana and a former owner of the Ringling Circus who knew that Carl loved animals. Ballard wrote Carl to inform him that when the weather warmed up, he was going to send him a young elephant he had named "Carl II." "He is a great little pet and I am sure you will become attached to him."[29] Carl was elated. He replied to Ballard:

> I am going to have a lot of fun with him and I am going to get a lot of publicity out of him too. I am going to send to Ceylon for a regular trainer of elephants and I am going to make this elephant do stunts or know why. I have already sent for the trainer who ought to arrive in two months.[30]

To John LaGorce he wrote about his plans.

> I never saw so many possibilities for advertising and I am certain I am going to get a million dollars worth of advertising out of this elephant. One of the particular things we are going to do with him is to make him tamp down the polo fields between games, also carry trees, haul ice and work in the garden. I have sent to India for a special Mahaut, red cap, brass collar, camel smell and all. We are going to teach him to swim in the sea and pull gondolas, etc.[31]

Although Carl had enlisted the aid of his friend M.U. Salie of Ceylon, a gem miner and importer, in obtaining a suitable trainer, Carl II arrived before the trainer did. Carl entrusted his care to Aaron Yarnell, a black assistant gardener, who had proven himself to be adept in handling mules. Yarnell was also capable with Carl II. Getting Salie and Sernal Isnarol

241

Carl Fisher used his elephants in many different ways. (F.I.A.)

into the United States was complicated by the U.S. government, which considered Salie a bigamist. He was also suspected of smuggling.[32] Carl asked John LaGorce, who lived in Washington, D.C., for help. LaGorce contacted the Secretary of Labor, who was instrumental in securing a bond and work permit.[33] Even with a permit, the trainer was delayed. Isnarol, suffering from a high fever, had to be admitted to a hospital in New York for several weeks.

Before Isnarol arrived, Carl had an opportunity to handle the elephant himself. The experience prompted him to write again to LaGorce, this time requesting an elephant hook.

> I went up to the barn the other day and the trainer was not around, so I took the elephant out to show him to some friends of mine. I did not know whether this elephant was kidding me or not, but he certainly did make a monkey out of me. He knocked me down and ran off and when I grabbed hold of him by the tail to stop him, he hit me a jolt with his trunk and almost broke my ribs — then I grabbed him by the trunk and he locked his trunk around my arm, and if you think that a three year old elephant has no particular strength in his trunk,

you should let him wrap it around your leg or arm and give you a yank — Anyway, I am black and blue, and the funny part of the whole affair is that I finally discovered I could pick up a short stick and stab him lightly and make him behave, but without that stick I certainly did have a swell time. The caretaker tells me that I got off lucky and that I should never go near him without the hook or something that looks like a hook, as he understands thoroughly that he is to obey the hook.[34]

When Isnarol finally arrived and attempted to take over from Yarnell, Carl II made it quite clear that he preferred Yarnell. According to Jane, Carl II "...chased him up the newly built water tower and tried to shake it and the new trainer to the ground."[35] Only Yarnell could recall him and calm him before he butted over the tower. "At a single command the elephant calmed down and hung his head like a wayward pup,"[36] Nash wrote. Carl acceded to the reality of the situation and made Yarnell the permanent trainer.

Carl II hauled rocks and lumber, mowed the golf course, and pushed down trees. He was later renamed "Nero." As he grew older, he became too difficult to handle and was finally given to the Detroit Zoo.[37]

In 1923 Carl received another young elephant, "Rosie," as a gift. Carl later raved about her: "...kind and gentle as a Newfoundland dog... [She] hauls her own food in a cart. She gives herself a bath from a hose, and she can do the Black Bottom better than most Harlemite entertainers. She has been photographed in possibly millions of films; rotogravure pictures by the thousands of feet have been run by all the newspapers in the country."[38]

Carl had a special two-wheeled boxcart, green with six-foot-high red wheels, made for her in Indianapolis.[39] Every morning she would give children rides. She worked on the golf courses and construction sites with Carl II and Yarnell, whom she followed around like a dog. For publicity purposes she was invaluable. "The elephant became a legend around which Miami Beach publicity prospered," wrote Howard Kleinberg. "Her publicity value ran for almost a decade — and her legend even longer!"[40]

Rosie the elephant delighted local children at their parties. (HASF)

One of Rosie's most famous escapades was the deposit she made in the Miami Beach First National Bank. Having an elephant open an account at the bank was meant to publicize the bank as well as Rosie. Accompanied by Yarnell, Rosie arrived at the bank, Rosie carrying a passbook and a five-dollar bill in her trunk. Things did not go as smoothly as planned.

> Unfortunately, animals become frightened in unfamiliar surroundings and tend to react in the same way; Rosie was no exception. In this strange marble barn where people flashed lights and cameras at her and put pieces of paper on her trunk, Rosie eased her anxieties with a long loud defecation that drove customers helter-skelter from the bank. It was, say all the old-timers, the biggest deposit that Miami Beach First National ever had.[41]

This incident caused no real damage, but Rosie did cost Carl $5,000 in a lawsuit when she made an innocent attempt to find something to eat. Yarnell and Rosie were standing near a trolley car while Yarnell talked with a friend. Unnoticed by Yarnell, Rosie found the trolley car's open windows an invitation to forage for food. In the window seat was a man apparently sleeping off a drinking binge. When Rosie's trunk landed in his lap, he abruptly awoke, screamed, "Snakes! Snakes!" and jumped out of the car, breaking his leg in the process. The subsequent lawsuit he filed won him the $5,000.[42] Newspapers delighted their readers with the continuing elephant stories.

Chapter 22

The Boom Begins

ALL OF THE MILLIONS Carl had received from the sale of Prest-O-Lite had been spent on building Miami Beach, and it still was not enough. He was in debt. It was time for his investment to start paying off. World War I was over, much of the construction was done, and the publicity machine for Miami Beach was in full operation. As early as 1919, tourists had to be turned away because of the shortage of hotel rooms. Carl was about to recoup his fortune with the Florida land boom of the 1920's that would come to an end only with a natural disaster.

Carl had spared no expense in making the new resort as inviting and beautiful as one would wish. He personally supervised the landscaping and made suggestions as to what should be planted. Kotano Suto, a Japanese national living in Miami, worked as a landscaper for Carl for 25 years. He and Shige Tashiro were two of four Japanese gardeners employed by Carl and living on Carl's estate. Carl brought Fred Hoerger, who had worked for him in Indianapolis, to Miami Beach. Hoerger became the landscaper engineer who introduced new methods of planting at Miami Beach.[1]

With most of the native species gone, Miami Beach had become a home for flowers, trees, and shrubs from all over the world: Australian pine, Arabian jasmine, Brazilian pepper, Chinese holly, Canary Island date palms, Hong Kong orchids, Mexican flame vine, Rangoon creeper, and Surinam cherry.[2]

Carl advised Thomas Pancoast, his partner, to plant at least ten coconut trees on every lot sold in his subdivision. In a letter written May 11, 1920, Carl suggested:

A large number of your small and ragged avocados be replaced by coconuts, Royal Palms, Bougainvillea and other ornamental trees — particularly flowering trees like the Bougainvillea so that people driving thru the trees will note the beautiful vista of flowers and palms.[3]

Carl brought birds from the West Indies, and built a 30-by-300 foot exhibit cage. Some birds were released in hopes that they would prosper. When hurricanes hit, many were blown to the mainland, where they remained. An exhibit of birds and animals from the Everglades lasted only six months.[5] The inhabitants were released to fend for themselves after complaints from neighbors about the smell. Many birds simply disappeared, with Polly Redford speculating that many may simply have been captured and cooked by laborers working on the Beach.[6] As Charles Edgar Nash concluded about Carl's attempts to create a bird sanctuary, "The idea was good but a bit impracticable for the situation."[7]

There were other picturesque and colorful sights to be seen: sailboats for hire on Biscayne Bay with red, lemon and turquoise sails. At the Roman Pools, Italian troubadours in bright costumes sang and played for the tourists.[8]

Carl's attention to detail and quality was an intrinsic part of the building of Miami Beach. "His incessant demand was for the best in materials and workmanship. I believe he personally inspected every foot of pipe line and every inch of scaffolding. I would see the familiar slouched hat bobbing through a newly dug drainage ditch in a torn-up street, or silhouetted from a skeleton structure against the blue, blue sky,"[9] wrote Jane.

To ensure the freshest of dairy products at the Flamingo Hotel, Carl had paid $7,000 in railroad fares to bring 40 Guernsey cows from Milwaukee for the winter season. They were kept on Collins' farm. He furnished the hotel with $218,709 worth of furniture from Wanamaker's.[10]

Pete Chase, Carl's chief salesman and sales manager,

credited Carl's influence as being responsible for bringing many of the customers.

> "People up north were making money hand over fist. Fisher had all these acquaintances up north: they began to come down here and they saw what Fisher was doing — what a great place it was and how it was being built and beautified and everything.
>
> They told their friends, 'Come down to Miami Beach. It's marvelous, it's wonderful!'
>
> And they started coming. Many of them were making big money, so they bought homes and bought property."[11]

Carl and his real estate salesmen directed their sales efforts at potential buyers with deep pockets. Yet Fisher's policy toward hotel guests was firm; no guests were to be harassed by salesmen in any way.[12] Every morning the salesmen checked the hotel registers, looking especially for the famous and the wealthy. These persons received free polo tickets and invitations to the Shadows or Carl's yachts, where Carl himself solicited their business. Jane wrote that "On the deck of the *Shadow K* he sold Albert Champion half a million dollars worth of property at the flip of a cigar. Men who bought from Carl now, bought without seeing the land they were buying."[13]

Sometimes the prospective customer was not who the salesmen thought he was, as Jane recounts in a story of one such case of mistaken identity.

> ...what was thought to be the name of a billionaire copper king was found in a hotel register. Carl drove the "tycoon" around his tropical paradise and took him aboard the *Shadow J* for a day-long cruise. All day Carl sang in his most persuasive tones the beauties of Miami Beach and the wisdom of buying early.
>
> The man was brought to The Shadows, feasted and wined, and later, on the veranda facing the ocean, Carl got down to brass tacks.
>
> "Well, sir" — his best approach was always on the personal side — "how are things in your business?"
>
> The honored guest puffed on his dollar cigar. "Tell you the truth, Mr. Fisher, the haberdashery business isn't what it was.

You've been mighty nice, and I'm going to send you a couple of neckties from my shelves."

The following morning the Fisher properties' personnel received a stern memorandum signed by Carl Fisher. "Avoid in the future all errors resulting from a similarity of names."[14]

Carl's concentration on selling to the wealthy — wealthy whites because segregation was the law in the South in the 1920's — provoked some criticism. Aside from the fact that selling estate land to millionaires was the fastest way to recoup his investment, Jane Fisher, in her biography of Carl, felt the need to explain the strategy. She wrote, "The millionaires who bought gave the more moderate buyers a feeling of security."[15] She added, "He did not want Miami Beach to be the exclusive playground of millionaires. He wanted a family city with pleasant homes, but knowing the value of famous names to a new community, he concentrated during those first years upon the distinguished and the wealthy. They, he knew, would bring others."[16]

Because of the enormous amount of money that Carl was spending developing Miami Beach, others seemed to think that his funds were limitless. Eventually, when even his fortune was running low and he had to borrow to complete the project, Jane recalls how she began to feel the pinch: "...I would tell Galloway to have Carl's last year's suits repaired and would scramble through my own wardrobe for geegaws to freshen up hats that were three years old!"[17]

Jane tells a story that demonstrates not only how others considered them fabulously wealthy, but also how casually Carl reacted to theft of his property.

> The public point of view toward us was summed up by an aged native Carl discovered on the Beach piling building materials on his rickety wagon. The old man was grumbling to himself because he couldn't get a bathtub aboard his wagon — a tub waiting to be installed in the Lincoln Hotel! Carl stood watching the old codger before he asked him what he was doing.
>
> "I can't load this danged thing on my wagon," the old man answered testily.
>
> "Who does it belong to?" Carl wanted to know.

"That man Fisher," snapped the native. "I figure I've as much right to it as he has. No one has a right to be as rich as that man Fisher."

"You're perfectly right," Carl agreed amiably, and he helped the old man pack the loot onto his wagon.[18]

The Beach was unquestionably attracting customers. In February of 1922, more than 2,000 prospective customers had to be turned away at the Flamingo Hotel, whose lowest rate was $15 per day. Still in debt, Carl urged other investors to come and build more hotels, suggesting that a dozen first-class hotels were needed.[19]

In 1923, he expanded the Flamingo, adding six more rooms. He also built the Nautilus Hotel, which opened on January 10, 1924. At a cost of $870,000, the Nautilus, as Howard Kleinberg described it, "offered the ultimate for wealthy guests: posh rooms, and swimming pool with cabanas, beautiful stairways and chandeliers, a gourmet dining room, and, of course, the adjoining polo fields..."[20]

The hotels, Polly Redford notes, were built on cheap land that would not otherwise be developed. The hotels then raised the land values. "Carl's business at the Beach was never hotels; it was land. The hotels were only a come-on, a necessary nuisance to draw customers and hold them long enough for his salesmen to sell them house lots. His plan for Miami Beach was a city of winter homes."[21]

The increasing demand for rooms lengthened the tourist season. Instead of January 1, during the 1923-24 season the Lincoln Hotel opened on November 1, the Wofford Hotel on December 6.[22] Land sales escalated. In 1923, the Fisher-Collins interests sold a total of $6,000,000 in new sales; in 1924, it was $8,000,000, but in 1925, sales almost tripled to $23,419,782.[23]

By 1925, there were 56 hotels with 4,000 rooms, 178 apartment houses, 858 private residences, 308 shops and offices, eight casinos and bathing pavilions, four polo fields, three golf courses, three movie theaters, an elementary school, a high school, a private school, two churches, and two radio stations.[24]

The dredges continued to pump sand, creating more land. Islands were created in the bay and sold to the wealthy. All of south Florida was booming. "Miami was transformed from a sleepy little town on the edge of Biscayne Bay into a Magic City of modest skyscrapers and legendary real estate profits,"[25] wrote Kenneth Ballinger in *Miami Millions.*

There were enough celebrities living in Miami Beach to create a market for sightseeing buses. Guides used megaphones to identify the homes of the rich and famous. Carl was called the "Prest-O-Lite King." Guides could point out the estates of Harvey Firestone, Julius Fleischmann (Fleischmann's yeast), Gar Wood, Albert Champion, Harry Stutz (the Stutz Bearcat), Roy Chapin, and C.F. Kettering (Delco). Jane and Carl were called the "king and queen" of Miami Beach. "Nothing annoyed Carl more," wrote Jane. "He hated personal publicity. The only publicity he wanted was for the new city."[26] "Some day, if the migration of celebrities continues," reported the *Miami Beach Register* on January 16, 1924, "it won't be necessary to publish 'Who's Who in America.' The Miami Beach city directory will be all that's needed."[27] J. C. Penney owned a mansion on Belle Isle; he brought Arthur Rubenstein and violinist Paul Kochanski to entertain his guests there.[28] Carl and Jane hosted Jascha Heifitz, who played the pipe organ, and Irving Berlin, who played the piano. Will Rogers and George Ade told jokes. Henry Watterson, editor of the *Louisville Courier-Journal,* was another of their guests at the Shadows, as was Indiana governor Winfield T. Durbin.[29]

By the mid-1920's, Carl had become immensely wealthy, some estimating his wealth on paper to be $50,000,000. He was called "the Barnum of real estate."[30] Will Rogers called him "The midwife of Florida." Rogers' wry humor made fun of Carl, while recognizing his achievements. He devoted his October 11, 1925, weekly article to stories about Carl:

America has about a hundred and ten million people. Now, out of all this herd there are about $99^9/_{10}$ percent of us that just drag along and what we do or say don't have much effect on any of the rest of the mob. But, scattered among these $^1/_{10}$

percent, every once in awhile you run into some odd individual, some queer Bird, that is out of the natural beaten path of human beings. We all go up the main road, while they take the trails.

I fell afoul of just such a duck. Henry Ford? No. He is not the one I am talking about...

But this other one that I want to tell you about has, next to Mr. Ford, been responsible for causing more dissatisfaction and unrest among contented people than anybody I know of. He is Carl G. Fisher, the man that took Miami away from the alligators and turned it over to the Indianians.

Had there been no Carl Fisher, Florida would be known today as just the turpentine state...he rehearsed the mosquitoes till they wouldn't bite you until after you bought.

He was the first man smart enough to discover that there was sand under the water. So he put in a kind of dredge, "all-day Sucker" arrangement, and he brought the sand up and let the water go to the bottom instead of the top. Up to then, sand had been used to build with, but never upon.

Carl discovered that sand would hold up a Real Estate sign, and that was all he wanted it for. Carl rowed the customers out in the ocean and let them pick out some nice smooth water where they would like to build, and then he would replace

Will Rogers relaxing on Lecture Tour at Miami, January 21, 1926.

the water with an island, and you would be a little Robinson Crusoe of your own. And today the dredge is the national emblem of Florida.

This guy has done more unique things, even before he ever heard of Florida, than any man I ever met, and I met Al Smith, Al Jennings, Calvin Coolidge, Rudolph Valentino, Senator Borah, Ben Turpin, and the Prince of Wales.[31]

Carl's emphasis on constructing expensive hotels presented a dilemma for office and construction workers. There was no room for them in the hotels even if they could afford them.

To provide housing for office workers, Carl built the Dade Hotel.[32] Carl was well aware of the importance of good affordable housing in retaining workers. He had faced difficulties in Indiana with employees of the Prest-O-Lite Corporation and the Speedway. In a letter to M. J. Carney of New York City on June 21, 1920, Carl outlined what he thought was needed.

> Recently I have been looking into the labor turnover situation here at the Speedway. I find that this situation is not improving and at certain times of the year is worse than it was last year or any year previous.
>
> With the large interests that you have here, together with the interests of the Allison Experimental Company, it seems to me that it is absolutely necessary that some arrangements be made for the better housing of a large number of mechanics, and also for the Saturday afternoon, Sunday afternoon and evening amusements of the mechanics who live here, and who work at the Prest-O-Lite Company, or who board in the neighborhood.
>
> The fact of the matter is that there are no boarding houses in this neighborhood which will accommodate a hundred to a hundred and fifty men, and these boarding houses are not conveniently situated.
>
> I am satisfied that the Prest-O-Lite Company loses annually in the labor turn-over more than enough money to construct at least one $150,000.00 hotel. With the construction of two such hotels, I am thoroughly convinced that the labor turnover problems would greatly improve, and that your hotels could be so handled that they would pay a small interest on the investment.

We should have here at the Speedway a small moving-picture show. We should have a swimming pool, also a small gymnasium, a basket ball court and a handball court, as well as a billiard room and cafe with up-to-date soda fountain attachments.

All the big companies in Akron, Cleveland, and most of the other large cities have learned that it is a necessary part of their equipment in order to keep the best labor.

Just recently several large companies have begun operations in Indianapolis and these companies are drawing and going to draw heavily on the skilled labor, as well as the unskilled labor.

If you make plans immediately, and start to build for the care of the workmen, you can retain a large number of the skilled men until these improvements are made. In the meantime, you can have a line out for a great many others that would like to have a permanent location in the neighborhood where they are employed.

Kindly let me hear from you.[33]

Providing accommodations for blacks was a more daunting task. Domestic servants, like Carl's own William Galloway, could be housed in their employer's homes. Laborers,

A largely black work force helped build Miami Beach's streets and public facilities. Carl Fisher created a black village in Miami Beach in 1920 to ease the busing of workers back and forth to Miami. (Matlack; HASF)

essential to the continuing construction, had to travel back and forth from the mainland. One young man was fined while doing so. Carl responded by writing a letter to Judge A. Frank Katzentine in Miami on December 19, 1931:

Dear Frank:

I enclose you a statement from a colored boy who works here on the Beach. He has been hauling three servants back and forth to the Beach to work, in his Ford car. It is a great accommodation for these people to be hauled over here and back to town. Of course they divide up the expense.

I know that indiscriminate jitneys are no good, and that there should be some control of them, but no law can be made to stick, that will fine a workman under these conditions. This has been tried in other courts and will not stick, and while I don't want to buck the law and have an argument, I do think this fine should be remitted, and this boy should be given a license to haul these employees to and from the Beach.

The young man works here at the Maren Apartment, 1543 Michigan Avenue, and if you wish him to, he can come down and have a talk with you.[34]

When building the Nautilus Hotel, Carl provided a temporary solution by housing workers in a "tent city" on his property.

As early as February 25, 1919, Carl had written to Thomas Pancoast concerning the need for black housing.

Something must be done and done at once!...I think it is up to the Miami Beach Improvement Company, the Schilling Company, who employ a good many laborers, and ourselves, and to immediately erect fifteen small houses suitable for negro laborers, furnish them with suitable sanitary arrangements...[35]

A few months later Carl publicly announced his plans for the black community. A story in the *Miami Herald* on June 12, 1919, entitled "Carl Fisher to Establish Industrial Center at Beach for Colored People," revealed the details. It was to be built on a three-acre site. Twelve concrete houses were to be constructed immediately. A school house, play yard, movie theatre, and church would complete the community. Some cottages were built near Forty-first Street and Pine Tree Drive in 1920, but they were torn down in 1927 when the area was being developed.[36] Carl's self-contained community never fully materialized.

Allowing blacks to use the ocean beach was another concern. Blacks from Miami were bathing and swimming in the ocean. In 1918 a wealthy black Miamian, D.A. Dorsey, the primary owner of Terminal Island, had wanted to make the island a black resort, but there were so many obstacles he abandoned his plan.[37]

When Thomas Pancoast wrote Carl about what could be done concerning blacks' use of the Beach, Carl was in favor of their being able to use the beach but realized that segregation laws did not at that time permit intermingling of the races. He replied to Pancoast on September 28, 1920.

> The negroes should have a place of their own to bathe, where they can get suits and bathe in the ocean the same as white people, and if I knew where we could build such a place for them at not too prohibitive a cost, it would be to our advantage to build it. We certainly should not allow people to come here from the city without being properly clothed — nor should we allow them to dress or undress in their cars along the Beach. This business is going to be a great deal of trouble and cause us a lot of damage... It is really a matter that should be handled by the city of Miami and the city of Miami Beach.[38]

No separate area was set aside. Blacks were not allowed to use the ocean beach.

Another group that could use the beach found themselves restricted in other ways. Jews in the first decades of the twentieth century found prejudice increasing against them, from wealthy leaders like Henry Ford to hotels restricting their clientele to "Gentiles Only." Anti-Semitism in the United States had been growing since the late 1870's, marked by the Saratoga Springs Grand Union Hotel's turning away New York banker Joseph Seligman and his family.

There was a financial basis for the rejection. America was rapidly changing from an agrarian to an industrial nation. Many had gained their wealth during the Civil War.

This fast-growing and managerial class was beginning to close ranks against the German Jews who had immigrated in considerable numbers since 1848 and found their talents and energies ideally suited to the "Second American Revolution" — the building of industrial empires that changed the United States from a nation of farmers to a commonwealth of railroads, heavy industry, large corporations. What native-born Christian parvenues could not forgive their Jewish counterparts was not their religion or national religion...but their success.[39]

Carl's friend John LaGorce had a strong prejudice against Jews, so much so that he did not want the *National Geographic*, of which he was an editor, to distribute films. In a 1920 letter to Gilbert Grosvenor, founder and president of the *Geographic*, he wrote that

[the film industry] is known to be practically in the hands of some of the most unscrupulous men and associations in the country, — mainly Jews who have by a process of elimination and massacre absorbed or done away with the smaller fry, and their business methods have been an unpleasant odor in the commercial nostrils for a long time.[40]

Although Howard Kleinberg notes that "typical" deeds for Carl's properties did not have restrictive clauses against Jews, his hotels did practice restricted policies. Carl's treatment of Jews appears to have been based on the financial status and personal qualities of individuals. Kleinberg says that "Fisher's thinking... reflected the attitude of a considerable portion of the nation's non-Jews."[41] Kleinberg cites a letter Carl sent to financial advisor Lyman Kendall in New York on May 11, 1921, when he was trying to sell bonds for the Flamingo Hotel:

At the present time I have a $350,000 Bond Issue on same, but I am going to have to make some big sacrifices soon to complete my work there, and I don't want this hotel to fall into the hands of Jews.[42]

But Kleinberg writes that Carl "...numbered Jews among his friends and often broke his own rules to admit Jews whom he felt met his acquired standards of social elegance."[43]

257

When Eugene Stahl, who owned the Helene apartment house, sent Carl brochures he was planning to send to prospective customers with a "No Hebrew" card, Carl advised him against including the card. On October 6, 1921, he wrote:

> You can usually tell by the names of the people applying for apartments and their occupation whether they are desirable or not.... There are some Hebrews who are very high class people, and it does seem a shame to injure their feelings unnecessarily if it can be avoided. The average run of Hebrew trade at a Hotel is not desirable, particularly at a resort hotel, and it is quite a question of knowing just how to handle the undesirable ones best.[44]

Harry Klein of Peoria, Illinois, wrote Carl when he read in the paper the following story:

> John Hertz, president of Yellow Cab Company and other companies including the Hertz U-Drive-It, has purchased a house on the ocean north of the Firestone estate, formerly owned by Eugene Coutoure of New York. The purchase was made through Fisher Properties Company for $115,000.[45]

Klein, who had been personally affected by the restrictive policy at one of Carl's hotels, wrote Carl the following letter:

> Mr. Carl Fisher:
> Enclosed find clipping which speaks for itself. Mr John Hertz is a Jew. I don't believe he denies it. Evidently you are the type of man who has a prejudice against the Jew if [he is not rich] enough. Christ, who was a friend of the poor and lowly and not the rich, could not buy at your end of Miami Beach, nor would he be allowed to play golf, because he was a poor Jew. I [who] employ about two hundred Christians and have always been considered by them a friend, was denied the privilege of playing golf on your links because I did not deny I was a Jew.... This was my first experience in that form of prejudice. A bit out of date don't you think — simply not of a true Christian spirit. Your Glenn Adams told me he was sorry. I told him I would not care to play where Jesus Christ, St. Paul, and St. John would not be allowed to play because they were Jews.
> Regretfully Yours,
> [Signed] Harry Klein[46]

Carl promptly replied.

I have your letter of recent date regarding Mr. Hertz. Mr. Hertz is a very high class type of man and we have several men here on the Beach who are very good friends of mine who are Jews, and they are not all necessarily rich. In fact, I have two Jewish friends in the banana business in Lafayette, Indiana, whom I loaned a thousand dollars to nine years ago, and on account of several severe troubles they just finished paying me last year, which was entirely satisfactory to me.

The next time you come to Miami Beach, drop up and see me.

The late Julius Fleischmann was a very good friend of mine. Both Charles and Dave Summers of Indianapolis, also Dr. Sam Row are friends. So I think you are mistaken in some of your viewpoints.[47]

Carl sent personal requests to Miami Beach clubs, on behalf of some of his Jewish friends, for the clubs to offer memberships or the use of their facilities. In January of 1923, he wrote to the Cocolobo Club on behalf of the Fleischmanns.

Please extend the courtesies of the Cocolobo Cay Club to Mr. and Mrs. Julius Fleischmann, for two weeks, making a memo charge of anything they may want to me.

We have asked Mr. Fleischmann if he desired to join the Club, but he has been absent for some time in Europe and until he returns, I would prefer to have his accounts made as a memo against me as my guest.[48]

Julius Fleischmann returned the favor in May of 1924 at his own golf club.

Mr. Julius Fleischmann
takes pleasure in extending to
Mr. Carl Fisher
the privileges of
his golf course at
Middle Neck Farm
For the season of 1924 [49]

Carl and Fleischmann remained close friends until Fleischmann's sudden death.

Fleischmann sent Carl a thank you note on February 2, 1925, shortly before his death.

I was just about to write you and thank you for the beautiful, tall coconut tree which I found planted right next to my house, upon returning from New York.

It is really very wonderful at my place and the tree fits in perfectly with the atmosphere. We are having moonlight now and some evening I am going to ask you to come over and sit up on my terrace and take a look at the moon through the tall tree. I cannot tell you any more than that I certainly appreciate your thought. I have a caretaker on the place now and I will see that the tree gets plenty of water. There are many things we can replace. Trees, however, most difficult.[50]

Julius Fleischmann died suddenly that February right after dismounting from his polo pony at Miami Beach. His wife Gettie sent a letter of thanks to Carl.

I have not answered your letter of February ninth 'ere this, as I have been unable to write. Julius's death, as you can well imagine, is such a crushing blow that I was obliged to rest as much as possible and was not permitted to carry on my correspondence; I am sure you will understand.

I deeply appreciate your sympathy in the great loss that Julius's death means to us, and to all of his friends; it has indeed left a tremendous void, and I know full well how much he will be missed.[51]

Bernard Gimbel, owner of Gimbel's Department Store, was another recipient of Carl's friendship. He sent the following request for Gimbel in February of 1924 to the Miami Beach Golf Club:

Mr. Bernard Gimbel wishes to play on our golf courses and I would like to have you extend to Mr. and Mrs. Gimbel the privilege of becoming members.

Our Board meeting this morning passed Mr. and Mrs. Gimbel unanimously.[52]

In January of 1927, Carl sent another request to the same golf club.

Please issue a complimentary ticket to Mr. Bernard Gimbel and guests.[53]

Another letter was sent to Glenn Adams by Robert Tyndall,

(Chase Family)

Carl G. Fisher recommended Jewish department store mogul Bernard Gimbel for membership in the Miami Beach Golf Club.

one of Carl's managers in January of 1930, on behalf of Mrs. John Hertz's brothers.

> At the request of Mr. Fisher will you please issue a season membership to each of the following, sending their cards to their respective addresses today, together with invoice:
>
> J.L. Kesner — Season membership for LaGorce Club Residence Room 601 Roney Plaza Hotel.
>
> S.H. Kesner — Season membership for Bay Shore Club Residence — Bowman Hotel.
>
> These gentlemen are brothers of Mrs. John Hertz.[54]

Carl also leased houses to other Jewish gentlemen, such as Mr. Nathanson, head of all the Paramount moving picture interests in Canada; Mr. W.V. Hartman, vice-president of Gulf Refining Company of Pittsburgh; Mr. H.L. Rauch, paper manufacturer of Monroe, Michigan; and others.

Mitchell Wolfson credited Carl as having been a major factor in his being elected to the Miami Beach City Council in 1939. Wolfson, with his partner Stanley Meyer, had founded

(HASF)

Mitchell Wolfson's City Council campaign headquarters was on Washington Avenue. Elected to the council in 1939, with help from Carl G. Fisher, Wolfson became Miami Beach's first Jewish mayor in 1943.

a movie theater chain. Wolfson was not the first Jewish member of the city council. Baron De Hirsch Meyer had been elected to the City Council in 1932. Wolfson became Miami Beach's first Jewish mayor in 1943, after receiving the unanimous vote of the city councilmen.[55] In a 1970 interview, Wolfson gave his account of the 1939 election:

> He [Fisher] found there were others on the Beach who were his contemporaries...who were very much opposed to me because they didn't think they'd want a Jewish member on the council. Mr. Fisher had quite a fallout with some of them as a result of supporting me, but I would think that I probably owe my election more to Carl Fisher than to almost anyone else... At the time there were not sufficient Jewish votes on Miami Beach to elect someone like myself.... Without Carl Fisher's support, I would have had a difficult time receiving sufficient votes from the Gentile community to have been elected.[56]

Miami Beach residents plant trees in the new county. Community activist Rose Weiss, sits on Rosie the elephant. (Parks)

Wolfson was an honorary pallbearer for Carl, who died later in 1939.

The Lummus development, an area of modest cottages and small apartment houses in the south part of Miami Beach, had no restrictions against Jews. There was some ill feeling by those in the south side towards the northern, wealthier part of the beach. Community leaders like Rose Weiss prospered in business there. When the Miami Beach Chamber of Commerce opened, Rose was one of the first to join and became membership chairman after she enrolled sixty members from the South Beach area.[57] Rose, called the "Mother of Miami Beach" because of her welfare work for poor children, had come to Florida because of her asthma. She and Carl were to form a friendship that lasted until his death. Pete Chase had started the Miami Beach Chamber of Commerce. Thomas Pancoast was the first president of the new Chamber, with Chase serving as secretary-treasurer. Soon the new organization had 300 members paying $10 per year, including businesses south of Lincoln Avenue.[58]

In the early 1920's, Jews were only a small minority on Miami Beach, but their numbers rose steadily. Not until financial reverses hit the Beach and forced a less selective attitude would the Jewish population be able to buy freely.

Chapter 23

The Binder Boys Arrive and Carl Heads North

In 1925 Carl's fortune was immense, perhaps ten times as much as the amount he had received for Prest-O-Lite. That year, he opened two new hotels — the King Cole and the Boulevard. By the end of the 1925-1926 season, only 246 of his 3,000 developed lots remained unsold.[1] However, two of the projects that he had planned in Florida had not come to fruition: a deep water seaport and a steamship cruise line between Miami Beach and Havana, Cuba.

As a site for the seaport, in 1919 Carl had bought what had been the southern tip of Miami Beach until 1905, when a ship channel named Government Cut had been cut through it to the ocean. The thirty-three acres, then called Rabbit Island, were made up of mangrove and sandbar. Carl planned to enlarge the island by dredging and filling, asking the city of Miami for half a million dollars to carry out the work, including bulkheading and building piers. The island would become Miami city property, controlled by the city.[2] The Peninsula Terminal Company was incorporated to carry out his plans; he renamed the island Terminal Island.

The city of Miami, which preferred to dredge a deep water channel through Biscayne Bay so that ships could travel through Government Cut up the bay to Miami, was unwilling to cooperate with Carl's plan. Miami Chamber of Commerce president Everett Sewell was adamantly opposed. Carl did obtain a government permit to enlarge the island, but Miami remained intransigent. In a letter to Thomas Pancoast in 1921, Carl expressed his reasons for thinking that his site for the seaport was a better choice.

> I was in hope that the people of Miami would realize how much cheaper it would be for them and how much better to have the harbor away from the most beautiful part of the city and away from Miami Beach. I am quite sure that we don't want the docks at Miami Beach and I am also quite sure that Miami doesn't want the docks on their water front. The real estate on the Miami water front — for hotels and apartment houses — is worth five times as much as it would be for fish houses, dock houses and storage warehouses.[3]

Deadlock over the harbor's location continued for decades. When the seaport was finally built in 1965, it was not located at either city, but instead mid-way between them.[4]

Carl's other failed project, the Havana-American Steamship Corporation, was initiated in the summer of 1920. One of Carl's polo friends, Harold Talbott, Jr., became partners with Carl in the venture. Carl enthusiastically described to Talbott why he thought trips to Havana from Miami Beach would be a popular tourist attraction.

> We have people down here by the thousands with lots of money and no place to go — and there is no reason why a high-grade, bang-up steamship shouldn't be loaded to the decks every trip. It will be one of the interesting things to help people get acquainted with that part of the country and will help Miami and the Beach wonderfully.[5]

There was a basic problem. Because Cuba was a foreign country, tourists would be required to have passports. To his friend Antonio Giraudier, Jr., of Havana, Carl wrote on March 25, 1920, that he was considering sending a representative to Cuba to discuss the steamship plans with government officials and financiers.

> Don't forget that the most necessary thing for the welfare of Cuba is proper connection by steamship between Havana and Miami or between Miami, Havana, and Jacksonville, or possibly Havana, Miami, Jacksonville and New York — but there must be proper boats of at least 20 miles per hour, and the

passports must be practically eliminated. On account of the passports it is entirely too much trouble for the average American to bother with a trip to Cuba. If you could do away with the passports and have a twenty mile per [hour] boat between Havana and Miami, it would mean millions of dollars to the Cuban people. Undoubtedly you would have had 25,000 additional visitors from Miami alone this Winter, with proper steamship connections, and each one of these visitors would have spent in Cuba from $100 up to $1000 or $2000 each.[6]

Because neither Carl nor Talbott had time to manage the new corporation, they had to rely on others. A steamship was purchased, but it was mortgaged heavily. When the economy faltered in 1921, the corporation went down with it.[7]

But neither of these unfulfilled projects affected Carl's success in Miami Beach to any real degree. Ironically, it was the success of Miami Beach and the rest of southern Florida that attracted land speculators in and ultimately caused harm to Florida's reputation and economy.

By 1920, *Harper's Weekly* reported that the roads to the South had improved so much that tourists no longed needed to ship their cars by train.[8] The number of cars entering Florida was increasing dramatically. The secretary of the Jacksonville Motor Club said that he was keeping records of the number of out-of-state cars passing through Jacksonville. In 1922, 80,640 out-of-state cars reportedly arrived in Jacksonville, traveling down the Dixie Highway, with 20,160 cars arriving in Florida through other cities. In 1923, it was estimated that tourists spent $300,000,000. More than one million tourists, traveling by car, boat, and train, were said to have arrived in 1924.[9] Howard Preston, in *Dirt Roads to Dixie*, points out the importance of the literature written about the South from 1900 to 1920. There were hundreds of articles published during the period, many of them giving "uncritical romantic description of the South."[10]

Kenneth Lewis Roberts, the historical novelist who in 1921 was a writer for the *Saturday Evening Post*, "...in the early 1920's... was credited with initiating what became popularly known as 'The Florida boom.'"[11] *Saturday Evening Post* editor George Lorimer sent Roberts to Miami Beach to report on Northerners vacationing there. Roberts's first articles appeared in the spring of 1922, the first of a total of eleven appearing between 1922 and 1926.

> ...Roberts, better than any of his contemporaries, sold twentieth-century Americans on the belief that no matter what their profession, assets, or status in life, Florida was for them. He argued with confidence in the previous forty years, few Americans had been able to travel, but in that short time, the affordable automobile had been produced, and southern roads had improved enough to make a motoring excursion feasible.[12]

Between 1922 and 1925, newspaper and magazine articles began featuring stories of wealth being made buying and selling Florida land. In 1924, Roberts wrote an article claiming that real estate values in Florida were increasing 100 percent every day.[13] "Roberts later assumed the blame for starting and spreading these far-fetched rumors of average Americans becoming fabulously wealthy overnight,"[14] Preston wrote. "Both Roberts and Post editor George Lorimer assumed responsibility for the phenomenal overnight popularity of the state. The Florida craze of the 1920's, however, had roots that went back to Reconstruction, and Roberts's vital contribution was that he reported the Florida boom like no other journalist."[15]

When the Miami Beach tourist season ended in March of 1925, the usual decline in population did not occur. Many decided to stay on, causing a shortage of tourist accommodations. About the same time, the "binder boys" arrived from the north. They were so named because they made their living by selling and reselling binders, written agreements to purchase property after making a down payment. They were easily identifiable because they dressed, as Polly Redford wrote, in "baggy golf knickers" or "greasy linen suits."[16] For a ten percent down payment, property was sold and resold, sometimes as many as eight times in one morning, prices escalating that rapidly.[17] Their frenetic activity continued from March through August of 1925. A lot on Fifth Street and

Washington Avenue in Miami that was purchased for $800 in 1914 brought $150,000 in 1925.[18]

By June, the price of land was escalating wildly. Jane Fisher wrote that the binder boys were using Carl's name when they sold land elsewhere in Florida. Carl was forced to take full-page newspaper advertisements, telling the public "No dollar of mine will be invested in Florida properties outside of Miami Beach."[19]

While the rest of South Florida was experiencing the land speculation, Miami Beach managed to keep the binder boys at bay. Carl and his associates owned the large developed tracts of land; Carl's sales policy had been to raise prices ten percent each season. This raised Miami Beach land values at a steady pace and served as an incentive to those who left at the end of each season to buy land before the price rose. In 1925 Carl continued to require 25 percent down, with the remainder due in three years. A ten percent discount was given for cash sales.[20] Finally, Carl took much of his land off the market.

Carl also took steps to ensure that Stephen A. Lynch of Atlanta could not bring speculation to Miami Beach by selling land he owned which extended into Biscayne Bay. Carl offered to buy the land, but Lynch refused.[21] Carl then had a canal cut between his land and Lynch's land, turning Lynch's land into islands with no bridge to the mainland. Permission to bulkhead the islands was refused.

Carl was well aware of the disastrous effects the land speculation would have on Florida. To his friend James Cox, publisher of the *Miami Daily News,* he wrote on July 29, 1925:

> Some of the property now being sold in Florida will not bring as much money in thirty years as it is selling for now. An enormous amount of money is coming from small speculators who invest nearly all they have. There is a tremendous amount of misrepresentation.... there has been at least a dozen million and five million dollar hotels mentioned that have not been built or even started. Land has been sold in Florida that will take many years to reclaim. We are bound to have a big flareback and Miami and Miami Beach are bound to suffer as a result of some of the exploiting schemes that have been car-

ried on around Miami and further North.... The city is literally flooded with "sharpers" who are pulling all kinds of schemes. The sales made at Miami are nothing as compared with the sales made thru [sic] the north.[22]

Even though Carl's realty companies did not participate in the land speculation, they sold more than $23,000,000 worth of property in 1925.[23] By October, sales began to decline, and so had the reputation of Florida in the North, where many buyers had lost money in land speculation. Howard Kleinberg, in *Miami Beach*, recounts some of the damage that had been done.

> Northern institutions, including the press, claimed that most of the Florida land being sold was under water and made allegations that soon the Boom would bust and, thus, leave the investors holding much devalued assets. Ohio passed a law that made it illegal for certain enterprises to peddle Florida real estate in that state. Miami attorney R. Freeman Burdine, son of the department store founder, went on a 10-week fact-finding tour. He found that New York newspapers, when writing about Miami, referred to nonexistent bread and milk famines. He cited one New York businessman returning from a trip to Miami and telling a newspaper that Miami dairies all were unsanitary, the milk watered and selling at 90 cents a gallon. The result was a counter-campaign by prominent Florida businessmen and developers.[24]

To reassure owners of property in the Fisher development, Pete Chase sent them a letter and enclosure, including statistics of the increases in building permits, postal receipts, municipal collections, railroad tonnage, and bank deposits.[25]

Some of the losers tried to recoup their losses. Polly Redford reported on one attempt.

> "Did you or did you not tell my client he could *grow nuts* on this land?" asked a lawyer cross-examining a Palm Beach developer in one of those lawsuits that crowded court calendars when the big spree was over.
>
> "I did not!" replied the developer. "I told him he could *go nuts* on it."[26]

The binder boys did more than cause the inflation of land values. Isidor Cohen, a Jewish merchant from Miami, asserted that they increased anti-Semitism: "These indiscreet fellow Jews had made themselves obnoxious to the local non-Jewish conservative realty operators, and to the rest of the community, who manifested a hostile spirit toward them which spread toward their local brethren as well as toward Jewish tourists who came the following season."[27] Indeed, in 1926, the Bath Club, a restricted private club, was started by non-Jews who had formerly frequented the Roman Pools. Even with membership fees of $1500, plus annual dues of $200, its 200-member limit was reached in its first season of operation — 1927-1928.[28] Other clubs were subsequently formed.

The 1925 boom proved to be too much for transportation facilities. Building materials were pouring in by rail so fast that 2200 freight cars jammed the railroad yards in Miami, where there were not enough laborers to unload them.[29] The Florida East Coast Railway issued an embargo on all building materials in an attempt to bring the situation under control. Construction was delayed because of the delay in delivering materials. "Then ships began to be used, and the Miami and Miami beach waterfronts were filled with schooners, steamers and any kind of vessel that could carry building material. In fact, they were so close together that unloading was a problem,"[30] Lummus noted. Dock facilities were not adequate. Dockworkers struck to raise their wages to sixty cents an hour, from forty-five cents, causing additional delays. The steamship companies put their own embargo on furniture, machinery, and building materials on September 12. Enterprising seamen rejuvenated old boats, loaded them with building materials, and sailed them to Miami, further complicating the situation. A new channel had to be dredged next to Bayfront Park for these vessels.[31]

The harbor was completely blocked in January of 1926 when the *Prins Valdemar,* an old Danish Navy ship, capsized after it was stranded on a sandbar while being towed into the harbor. It took 42 days to clear the harbor.[32]

The 1925-1926 tourist season was good, but Carl found that at his Nautilus Hotel, business had declined. This time, when the season ended, the tourists went home. Construction of houses, hotels, and office buildings continued, finishing up what the freight embargo had delayed. Essentially, however, the boom was over.

A few years before the land speculators arrived, Carl had embarked on a new project. Having sold his Indianapolis home, Carl rented a cottage in Port Washington, Long Island, in the summer of 1922, hoping to escape both oppressive heat and the hayfever that had plagued him in Indianapolis. He had also established an office in Manhattan on Fifth Avenue and 57th Street, to be "near the seat of war,"[33] in his words. At that time, he was still seeking financial backing for his Miami Beach hotels and the seaport he hoped to establish.

Deciding that Long Island was the place he wanted to be in the summer, Carl purchased a house on Manhasset Bay. In the next two years he built a shipyard for the Purdy Boat Works, who built his yachts. He also planned a development called Bay View Colony, with 45 restricted home sites. A private club would oversee recreational activities. He refurbished an old house into an office and formed a realty company for the new project.[34]

Carl advertised his new project as "a yachtman's paradise." Manhasset Bay, only twenty miles from New York City, was a well-established residential community with three yacht clubs: Carl started a fourth, the Bay View Colony Club. A full-page advertisement, written by Walter F. Bailey, claimed that the land being sold was "the last available waterfront property near New York."[35] All of the 100-foot, professionally landscaped lots were on the waterfront with a view of the bay. The amenities included tennis courts and a swimming pool. "...Mr. Fisher's idea is to create a home community of kindred souls who know how to enjoy life to the utmost in every sort of activity,"[36] Bailey wrote.

The success of the Bay View Colony and Carl's preference for Long Island summers led to one of his most ambitious ventures. In 1925, a real estate broker took Carl to Montauk, 30 miles past Southampton, to show him a vast tract of 10,000 acres, "empty, windswept dunes and beaches"[37] on the easternmost point of Long Island. Carl was following in the footsteps of an earlier buyer, Arthur W. Benson, a millionaire who saw it as an opportunity to indulge in his love of hunting and fishing. Benson, who planned to build summer homes for his wealthy friends, paid $151,000 for Montauk in 1879.[38]

Like Carl, Benson believed in only the best. Frederick Law Olmsted, the designer of Central Park, was hired to do the landscaping. Architect Stanford White designed the shingle buildings, featuring large porches, wide staircases, fireplaces in most rooms, and wood-paneled ceilings. The Montauk Association, composed of Benson and his wealthy friends, lived in an enclave of seven cottages, with a clubhouse where meals were served, a laundry building, stable, and private beaches. The site was not accessible by railroad; private yachts brought members, with additional baggage shipped by railroad to the nearest station in Sag Harbor and then carried by wagon to Montauk.[39]

The land was previously owned by heirs of "The Proprietors," seven men who had obtained the land from individuals and trustees of the town of East Hampton by 1712. The Montauk Indians, who had sold the land in 1687, made an agreement with the Proprietors in 1754, allowing them to live in Montauk "under certain conditions."[40]

Benson hired a Mr. Dominy "to persuade and move"[41] the Indians still living in Montauk to Freetown in East Hampton. The families moved in May of 1885, after Benson's buildings were completed. Some of their homes were also moved; those that remained were burned.[42]

The Association used the resort for several years into the twentieth century. By 1910, many of the houses were uninhabited. Carl bought many of them and modernized them for friends. The cottages, whose original costs were about $12,000 or $13,000 each, are on the National Register of Historic Places.[43]

Austin Corbin, Jr., president of the Long Island Railroad, and Charles M. Pratt purchased 5,500 acres from the heirs of Arthur Benson. Corbin had extended the railroad to Montauk and hoped to make it a port of entry, saving trans-Atlantic passengers time. He was successful in getting a proposal in Congress, but it was not passed. Corbin was killed in 1896 in an accident involving a run-away horse.[44]

Carl's purchase of the property was announced in the *East Hampton Star* on September 18. The *Star* described the land as having "several miles of ocean shore front, the land formation being high rolling hills, different from that found anywhere else on the eastern coast."[45] Much of the land had been used for cattle pasture, with one hundred head still pastured there.

Carl and his associates, Howard Coffin, Charles Hayden, and Richard Royt, bought 9,632 acres at Montauk in 1925 for two and a half million dollars.[46] In one day, Carl drew up the plans for his new development; he planned to dredge a fresh water pond and a channel to the sound for ocean-going yachts. There would be golf courses, tennis courts, polo fields, a large resort hotel, and a tall office building similar to the one in Miami Beach from which prospective customers could view the land available. Carl planned to entice Miami Beach residents to summer in Montauk.[47]

George LeBoutillier, president of the Long Island Railroad, persuaded Carl that Montauk could become the port of entry that Corbin had envisioned.[48] The plan was that boat trains would meet ocean liners and save trans-Atlantic passengers one traveling day.

The announcement of Carl's purchase had an immediate effect on land values. A lot measuring 57 by 120 feet in the village of East Hampton was reported to have sold for $16,000, having been purchased for only $9,500 the year before. The *Star* reported on October 2 that the Sunday after Carl's announcement, five automobiles had come to Montauk, their occupants inquiring about available property. The prospective buyers were from New Jersey and western Long Island.[49] In the same edition, the *Star* gave its

Blasting — to make the inlet channel. (M.L.)

readers a view of Carl Fisher, quoting from an article by George F. Lyndon in the *Eagle*.

Surrounded by a coterie of Florida land millionaires, a former Indiana newsboy, incongruously clad and chewing a ragged cigar end, sat in the luxurious offices of the exclusive Beach [sic] View Colony, near Port Washington, today, and placidly announced that within the next five years he would be responsible for investments in Long Island real estate amounting to $100,000,000, and nobody smiled.

...Mr. Fisher's holdings extend from State park on the shores of Napeague Harbor to the tiny strip of park land at Montauk Point, the tip of the island, and includes what was until today Lake Wyandotte and Big and Little Reed ponds. Lake Wyandotte now is Lake Montauk. Mr. Fisher accomplished that transformation with a brief direction to one of his secretaries as the result of a decision reached on the instant.

That is the way his development projects proceed by leaps and bounds, lightning-like decisions. His secretaries are in a state of constant dizziness trying to keep up with things that are happening around them.

There is a seventy-acre island in the middle of Lake Montauk

— formerly Wyandotte — and Mr. Fisher was asked what he proposed to do with that.

"I am going to put a spa there, and one of the finest surgical hospital [sic] you ever heard of," he replied instantly, while a secretary gasped and reached for a memorandum pad. That was the first time the secretary or anyone else had learned of that plan, because it hadn't existed a minute before. Hence the dizziness epidemic.[50]

Lyndon gave his viewers a physical description of Carl that conveyed the appearance of an eccentric millionaire. At the press conference, Carl was "wearing mismatched coat and trousers, a floppy Panama hat, a weird-looking pair of extremely low dancing pumps, evidently his own invention; a pair of regulation Ed Wynne horn-glasses and an air of having from now to eternity in which to do nothing at all, with a disposition to do it thoroughly."[51]

If not impressed by Carl's appearance, Lyndon certainly was by the Bay View Colony offices. "Expensive hangings drape the windows. Enormous Oriental rugs cover the floors with rich color, and massive furnishings are offset by graceful floor lamps. The broad veranda of the office faces the sail-dotted waters a hundred yards away...."[52]

Carl was described as appearing almost uninterested in the extensive plans he had just announced. "He just strolls around talking to whomever gets in his path, but not talking about Montauk or Bay View Colony or newsboys necessarily. Apparently he is the least interested individual in the place until an idea strikes him. Then he turns it over to whoever happens to be nearest and then seems to drop it from his mind."[53] Carl's associates assured Lyndon that Carl stood by his decisions and carried them out.

Carl's plans for Montauk, which was about three times the size of his Miami Beach holdings, were very different from his Miami Beach project. "At least, I don't have to make the land,"[54] he said. Jane wrote that he envisioned "a northern resort city that would have the charm of the old world. Montauk would be a city of medieval cottages with thatched roofs, windmills, blooded sheep with shepherds and dogs to herd them, splendid hunters, hunting dogs. Roads and streets, business buildings and hotels would be hidden behind low hills and grassy moors."[55]

Jane had reservations about Montauk, just as she had had about Miami Beach. It was, she wrote, "swept by fogs in summertime, by storms in winter..."[56]

Before the end of September, engineers and surveyors were at work laying out what would be thirty miles of roads. Carl was quoted in the *East Hampton Star* on September 25: "No attempt whatsoever will be made at this time to sell property or invite investors. The development itself will be made in cooperation with the Long Island Railroad Company. When it has reached a satisfactory stage, there will be two and one half hour service between New York City and Montauk Bay in the finest club car trains."[57]

Carl also announced plans for boat service to New York City and New London, Connecticut, and an 800-foot channel

Engineers — Carl G. Fisher hired a team of engineers to cut the inlet through from Long Island Sound to Lake Montauk, to create a harbor for yachts. (M.L.)

that would be dredged to Lake Montauk for the use of steamers and yachts. Although he said that he would bring 1,000 workers from Miami Beach to Montauk each spring, he also made provisions for year-round residents with plans for a skating pond, a radio station, schools and churches.

There was one dispute over 1,750 acres of land in the parcel purchased by Carl. Robert Moses, president of the Long island State Park Commission, had convinced New York State Governor Alfred E. Smith in 1924 that sites for state parks should be selected and parkways should be constructed so that they would be easily accessible. A bond issue of $15,000,000 that was going before the voters in November of 1924 would fund the system. Moses began to negotiate with the then-owners — the Benson estate — to acquire the land for approximately $75 per acre. Carl made a higher offer for the land before the deal was signed, and the Bensons decided to accept Carl's offer. But Moses had the authority under the state's conservation law to condemn the land and proceeded to use it. On December 4, 1925, a story in the *East Hampton Star* said that Carl "contemplates an action to upset the appropriation... The reason for the action, the *Star* reported, was the assumption "that a public park will injure the prestige of the high class of development that he is planning at Montauk...."[58] Nothing became of this; Moses had the law on his side, and the tract became Hither Hills State Park.

In an adjacent story, the *Star* reported that a "great amount" of real estate had been sold within the past two weeks. After enumerating the sales, the paper pointed out that the sellers were trying to avoid land speculation by demanding one third or one-half of the selling price in cash for a down payment "and are insistent that in all contracts a nontransferable clause shall be inserted."[59]

The cost of the first phase of the project would be more than $7,000,000. In 1925, Carl was worth over $50,000,000, at least on paper.[60] His past successes would be an incentive for investors. Carl was ready again to go full speed ahead.

Chapter 24

Moving Towards Divorce

Aᴛᴛᴇʀ ᴛʜᴇ ʟᴏss of their son and the cessation of physical intimacy in 1921, Carl and Jane drew further and further apart. Their age difference seemed more pronounced; she was only 27, he was 47. She wanted more children; he did not want to subject her to another painful labor. She loved gracious living and social affairs; he loved sports and practical jokes. More and more, Carl chose alcohol as his companion of choice.

In 1922, Jane was prevailed upon to adopt the three-year-old son of a poor Indianapolis woman. She was happy to agree. Jackie would be the child she wanted. Carl was willing to let her take the child on a trial basis before they made the decision of adopting. It was Carl who corresponded with the boy's mother, Mrs. Mazie Rattay. On May 20, 1922, he wrote to the natural mother, who apparently had requested money so that she could go out west.

Dear Madam:

Replying to your letter on the 17th, I am willing to take the little boy on trial commencing June 1, for 30 or 60 days. At the end of that time I can tell you definitely whether I wish to take him or not.

I will not advance you any money to go to California or any other place during the trial. At the end of 30 or 60 days if I decide to keep the little boy I will then talk to you about some arrangements to pay your way out west.

If this is entirely satisfactory to you I wish you would advise me by return mail.[1]

By December, the Fishers had made up their minds that they were willing to adopt, and Carl wrote his Indianapolis attorney on December 2, asking him to make arrangements.

Sometime last fall, Mrs. Mazie Rattay, of 11 Hampton Court, Indianapolis, but now in employ of Mrs. August Bohlen, came to us and was very anxious that we adopt her little boy.

We thought we would take the boy on trial for a few months to see if we wished to keep him. We now have had him with us for one month, and if the Mother is willing and continues anxious that we adopt the little fellow, I wish you would make such arrangements as are necessary to her.

If there is any doubt at all in her mind now after the boy has been away from her one month, we would prefer to send the boy back to her now rather to have an attachment broken later. We are very fond of the little fellow and he is well and happy.

You may say to the Mother that I will settle on her five hundred dollars a year, annually. It will probably be best to make these payments twice each year; half of this sum the first of April and the other half the first of February. This amount will at least insure the Mother against want of the necessity of working. The Mother has not asked for this payment and I don't want to get into a complicated arrangement, but you may handle the matter in the form of a contract, which would be easier for me to handle then to deposit securities.[2]

Denny replied by telegram on December 6.

YOUR PLANS FOR A BOY FULLY UNDERSTOOD AND ACCEPTED BY MOTHER. ADVISE CORRECT ADOPTED NAME. WILL ADOPTION BE BY YOU AND JANE JOINTLY OR ONE OF YOU. ONE OF YOU SHOULD BRING BOY HERE FOR PROCEEDINGS. CAN CLOSE ON YOUR ARRIVAL[3].

By December 9, Carl had heard from Mrs. Hothay, for whom Mazie worked as a housemaid, and wrote Denny again to give him further instructions.

We have received letters from Mrs. Hothay in which she states that she is very well satisfied, and that while she misses the boy considerably, she thinks he is in good hands. If we are going to have any trouble on account of this adoption, I would rather give it up now than later.

Jane thought that instead of making the adoption just for her that you had better make it for both of us, and this is entirely satisfactory with me. I thought at first that she was so fond of the little fellow that it would be a compliment to have the adoption papers made out in her name, but she prefers it otherwise and this will be satisfactory with me.[4]

Less than a week later, Carl had second thoughts about having his name on the adoption papers and so advised Denny on December 14.

I enclose herewith the papers which you sent down the other day, signed by Jane, and witnessed by notary.

After talking the matter over, we thought best to let this adoption go through as it is by Jane, for a year or so; after that time, if no complications arise, we can change it to a mutual adoption.[5]

The adoption was finalized in December, 1922. Jane described Carl's behavior with little Jackie and their first Christmas as a family.

Jackie was to me the baby we had left in Indianapolis; but Carl, fond though he seemed to be of Jackie, and kind though he was to him, could not fully accept him in the place of our son. Sometimes I would see his eyes darken with pain and he would push the little boy away. I knew Carl was pushing back the memory of his own son because he loved all children, particularly little boys; but how to explain that to a child!

The second Christmas after our baby's death was our first with Jackie. Carl joined me in making it a fairy-tale evening.... Under the tree Carl had tied his Christmas present for Jackie — a beautiful little black pony resplendent in red saddle and bridle. As an added surprise on Carl's part, into the room paraded Rosie the elephant in her gayest harness, and after her Caesar the great Dane, Laddie the collie and Flambeau the airedale, all decked for Yuletide.... Through the hullabaloo came the bubbling of Jackie's laughter. He, at least, was amused by the antics of his new father and mother.[6]

Carl continued to correspond with Mrs. Rattay about Jackie and financial matters. On February 22, 1923, Carl wrote:

I am sending you a check herewith for $250, and I wish you

Carl and Jane Fisher pose with her adopted son Jackie for the Miami Beach Register. *(Parks)*

would drop me a note giving me your street address about August 1st, and I will send you the additional check about that time. Jack is well and looking fine.[7]

On August 6, 1923, Carl responded to a letter from Mrs. Rattay inquiring about Jackie.

I have yours of the 1st. Mrs Fisher is in Europe with Jack, and she has been there for several weeks; and will return probably the later part of September. I am very glad you are well, and beg to remain

Yours very truly,[8]

Later that month Mazie wrote Carl, asking for some financial advice.

I have been away over the weekend with the people I work for and upon my return received your letter containing the check. Please let me thank you for the same also for the advice given in regards to buying a lot. Will do as you suggest as of course you know best. How much money must I have to buy the lot you have out at the speedway? Or can you suggest some way to invest the money I have, it now amounts to $500.00. I have placed it with the Fletcher American Bank and I am saving a little on the side out of my wages. What do you think I ought to do with it. I do so want to have enough to build a little house of my own. Then my dream would be realized. I will close hoping you are all well and happy. Send my love to little Jack. With kindest regards and best wishes I am. Yours Sincerely Mazie Rattay[9]

On August 23, 1923, Carl promptly replied:

Replying to yours of the 21st. If you will call on General Tyndall, of the Fletcher American Bank, he will advise you how to deposit your money so that it will be earning interest; and then when you have saved enough money to build you a small house I will provide the lot.[10]

Mazie replied on August 27, 1923:

I further wish to thank you for your kind offer in regards to the lot. It will be many years before I get that little house for building seems to be going up all the time and would take at least $5,000 to build the little home I have planned. It only consist of five rooms and a bath but I would want it brick veneer to save up-keep expenses. But it doesn't matter I am very grateful to you for what you have and are doing for me and little Jack and as long as he is well looked after and happy nothing else matters.

I remain with love to all.[11]

More than a year later, on December 3, 1924, Carl received a letter from Mazie in which she described how she traded off a bungalow inn for a vacant lot and wanted to "borrow $6,000 at the regular interest to build a house on the vacant lot."[12] A few days later, Carl answered her letter:

I have your letter of the 3rd. We cannot loan you the amount you refer to, or any part of it. We are borrowing large sums of money ourselves in order to promote our property here.

I think you have made a mistake in trading your cottage off; and I am certain you are making a mistake in putting your money into vacant lands at his time.

Mrs. Fisher has been abroad for one month and Jack was very well and seemed to be growing rapidly.[13]

Jane's trips to Europe with Jackie, as mentioned in Carl's letters to Mazie, reflected the growing rift between Jane and Carl. Jane now had Jackie as a companion and spent most of her time with him. During their marriage, Jane had fulfilled the role of hostess to Carl's guests and friends that he expected of her. When Miami Beach was in its first stages of development, she called on all of the new residents. On Sunday nights, the Fishers entertained at the Shadows, serving fruit punch and sandwiches. It was Jane who made their guests welcome. "Often Carl would not even be downstairs to greet our guests. Tired from playing tennis or polo, he would stay upstairs in bed with a book. Or he would take two or three cronies out on the glass-enclosed porch and smoke and tell stories."[14] When she complained of his lack of attention to their guests, he replied: "That's your job, Jane. I have no talent for social business and no time."[15]

Even though he was not very social, he liked a house full of people, thinking nothing of inviting everyone at the tennis court or polo field for lunch, whether he knew them or not. Jane would be informed an hour before dinner that he had invited up to twenty guests. Knowing his ways, she was prepared. When she went upstairs after the party was over, Carl was frequently already in bed, "propped against his pillows reading, with Rowdy and the peanuts on one side of the bed and the bright spittoon on the other.... He would know I was angry and would grin up at me, the dark, kind eyes slitted with mirth behind his reading glasses. 'Now, honey, you handled them like a champion. I was tired and I knew I could depend on you.'"[16] At times Carl excused himself midway through dinner and did not come back. Because of his impatience, he would often have his entire meal served at once, rather than waiting for the individual courses.[17]

Carl fought against accepting dinner invitations. When

they accepted one dinner invitation and dinner was late, Carl went home, ate, napped, and returned to spend the evening.

Neither the size of the parties nor the importance of the guests or entertainers had much effect on his behavior. On one occasion, 350 guests dined at the Shadows, enjoying the view of the ocean, the palms, and the stars from the Fishers' dining room. Honored guests were the Cuban Army polo team, who had brought Jane an Arabian horse, Cuba Bebe, a gift from Cuban President Machado. The guests were serenaded by Cuban songs, sung from the balcony by Sybil Cromer, and arias sung by Metropolitan Opera star Reinald Werrenrath. The party lasted till dawn; Carl went to bed long before it ended.[18]

One elaborate party — a polo ball — was held at the Roman Pools. The ballroom had been decorated as a miniature polo field complete with papier-mâché horses. Carl had asked Galloway to use a mechanical counter to record the number of handshakes Jane made. "Mrs. Fisher," Galloway reported when the party was at its peak, "you have just shaken the hand of the four hundred and fiftieth guest."[19]

Formal dress was out of the question. The only time Carl agreed to wear a tuxedo was for a wedding. He refused to buy it and had Galloway rent one. Carl didn't like the "shepherdess bonnet" Jane wore as a member of the wedding; he tried to throw it out the car window.[20]

Just as Jane had been the first in Miami Beach to wear a new kind of bathing suit, she often was the first in other areas, claiming to have had the first Irene Castle bob "south of the Mason-Dixon Line,"[21] the first lipstick, the first knee-high skirt, and the first pajamas.

Her fashion daring was not always welcomed by Carl. He was in Indianapolis when Jane won a silver cup at a Hawaiian ball by dancing barefoot in a hula outfit made of hundreds of velvet ribbons. The hula skirt was ankle length. Jane said of her appearance: "Not an inch of me showed from throat to feet. It was as demure a costume as can be imagined."[22] The hostess, Mrs. John Hanan of Narragansett Pier where the party took place, told her to wear only flower anklets and not the red slippers she had brought. The next day, a photograph of her in the hula outfit was on the front page of the Indianapolis newspaper with the headline: "Social Leader, Mrs. Carl G. Fisher, Dances at Ball Barefooted."[23] Carl immediately sent a telegram: "Shocked over pictures front page this morning. Return home at once."[24]

That was not the end of it. She went to Indianapolis with the cup. Carl went to the news agency in New York and paid $5,000 for the photographic plates to ensure that they would not be distributed anywhere else.[25]

Jane did worry about other women in Carl's life. She called Miami Beach "the playground of millionaires and the happy hunting ground of predatory women."[26] She was particularly concerned about Carl's employing hostesses from respectable families to accompany lone male visitors and keep them away from golddiggers. One in particular annoyed her because Carl had invited her to their dinner parties, "upsetting my seating arrangements and temper."[27] Jane thought the woman favored Carl.

As was her wont, Jane had a new hairdo — a bob by Antoine of Paris. The girl, with "artistically untidy hair,"[28] made the mistake of complimenting Jane's bob. Jane offered to give her a bob, took her upstairs, and proceeded to cut her hair with dull manicure scissors. When the girl looked in the mirror and saw her hair, she "ran screaming from the house and never came to the Shadows again. That night I was scared,"[29] Jane wrote. After their guests left, Carl's reaction was a chuckle. Without looking at Jane, he told her, "'You're the goddamnedest woman I ever saw,'"[30] went to bed, and never referred to it again.

Before Prohibition started in 1920, Carl seldom drank, and he and Jane did not serve liquor in their homes. There were no bars in Carl's Miami Beach hotels.. Dade County had been dry since 1913, but the law was not enforced strongly, "...and few who wanted a drink went without one,"[31] Kleinberg noted. After Prohibition, Carl began serving liquor at the Shadows. "'Prohibition made a rummy outa him,'"[32] said Cloyd Hewes, skipper of many of Carl's boats. "Not even the United States Government could tell Carl Fisher what he should or should not eat or drink!"[33] wrote Jane.

For a supply at Blossom Heath in Indianapolis, Carl had purchased the University Club's wines and liquor. He kept it in their cellar. In Miami Beach, where he also had a goodly store, Carl grew nervous when many of his friends' cellars were raided by revenue officers. His friend Jim Allison kept his supply at the aquarium. In 1921 it was discovered when Allison's former chauffeur was arrested for bootlegging. The chauffeur told police about Allison's liquor supply, from which he had already stolen 35 cases.[34]

On a tip that his own supply would soon be discovered, Carl, with the help of William Galloway and Carl's chauffeur Garrett, buried all of his liquor in Jane's rose garden by night. This was not enough to allay Carl's fears. One night, a week later, he dug it all up and made several trips in his car to the yacht-club landing, where he loaded it on the *Shadow F*. He drove the yacht to the Gulf Stream and threw it all overboard. To Carl's surprise, the revenue officers never came to the Shadows.[35]

There were other sources of supply that fed Carl's increasing appetite for liquor. The Bahamas and Nassau were close enough to provide as much as was wanted. Bootlegging was widespread. In *Miami, USA*, Helen Muir writes: "Some of Miami's best citizens were engaged in rumrunning. Downtown salons operated on an open-door policy and tourists accepted this freedom as part of the June-in-January setting. In Miami it was not so much that people did not observe Prohibition. They blatantly ignored its existence."[36]

Bootleggers had huts in the palmetto forest. Jane said it "became smart"[37] for people to gamble and drink there. Carl provided liquor for guests and customers on his yachts and in his home. The bar was always open on the yachts. "... he plied his guests with the best booze money could buy; and, like a good fellow, he drank it along with them."[38] The cruises were described as "one long party from the time they set sail."[39]

The gracious dinner parties at the Shadows were no more. People gradually discovered that a drink could be had at any time of the day there. Women who smoked and drank and told jokes with the men frequented the house. The atmosphere was more like a night club than a home. And yet Carl would boast that Jane never drank.[40]

Carl's constant swearing and more frequent outbursts of temper were reflected in scenes with some of the servants. "His cursing habit grew until every other word was an oath. He flew into quick rages that were as instantly forgotten,"[41] Jane wrote. Carl and Danny, the cook, had a volatile relationship, she quitting and he rehiring her many times. On one instance she left a message for her successor on the kitchen wall: "'This is the way Mister Fisher orders his meals: "Goddammit to hell, why in Jesus' name don't I get my goddamn breakfast?"'"[42]

Once Carl walked into the kitchen, saw a large T-bone steak on the table, and accused the servants of keeping it for themselves. "'Goddamn it, you kitchen folks have a nerve eating choice cuts when you're probably going to serve me stew!'"[43] With that, he picked up the steak, walked outside, and threw it into the sea. When his temper quieted, Galloway said to him, "'You didn't give me time to tell you, Mister Fisher, that was the steak I hunted all Miami for you especially and we were preparing to serve it for your dinner.'"[44] Jane called him "unpredictable," adding that "He never admitted he was sorry after a tantrum, yet he always made atonement. His kindness was a legend among his friends but it was kept as secret as if it were something to be ashamed of. He never talked about the people he helped, and he never let anyone else do so.... He once gave Jack LaGorce a five-thousand-dollar check to send the *National Geographic Magazine* to various penitentiaries."[45] The men who worked for Carl, especially those with prison terms, knew Carl believed in privacy and that a man's past was his own.

Jane linked Carl's deteriorating eyesight with his temper outbursts. Carl was now middle-aged with a worsening drinking habit. Jane began to spend more time with Jackie and more time away from Miami Beach. With Jackie, Jane traveled, favoring Paris. Her description of Carl's friends as "successful," "rich," and "old,"[46] reflected her desire to find friends of her own age. "Life with Carl was an unending succession of records set and building accomplished, rewarding and enduring, but tormenting to the nerves of those who raced and those who built."[47]

Carl lost the three most important women in his life in 1925. His mother died that August in his home on Long Island. He replied to a letter of condolence sent to him by Mrs. E. J. Kyle of Brooklyn.

> Thanks for your kind letter of the 9th. I have had a great loss in Mother. I am glad that she was not ill long, and that I could be of comfort to her in her last days. I wish you a long life and happiness.[48]

Carl's long-time secretary and mistress, Ann Rossiter, married a minister and left his employ. And Jane and Carl decided to divorce. In 1925, Jane was in Paris, away from the land speculation going on in Florida. "Because of the boom, the races, the regattas, Carl's new interests at Port Washington and Montauk, the building and the tension that never ended, I was feeling myself to be that sad product of the money-mad twenties — a deserted wife."[49]

Carl seldom wrote, but he did send her a letter in Paris the winter of 1925 demonstrating a sincere concern for her future.

> I don't blame you, Jane, for any of our trouble — I only want to make you happy. I do not have much to live for nowadays except to help someone else. I don't think you can be happy all the time — excited and on the go. Your nerves will soon snap as mine have done. Then you will know for the first time the real punishment nature gives for high pressure. It is very hard for me to write in long hand again. This is the first letter I have written in two years. I am having trouble with my eyes, a blood vessel snapped in one and I have spots over that eye which makes it very difficult for me to read. I am leaving on the boat today for a short trip with Doctor Edwards, Jim Allison and John Levi, and we are going to see what can be done about the treatment.

Carl G. Fisher (I.M.S.)

From your letter I take it you have found someone. Be careful, Jane — for your own future. You may be only [jumping] from the frying pan, etc. — and too late to get out. Don't hurry. No reason why you should. Lots of thought on a long jump like this. But just the same I want to help you — can't you give me a chance to check up on the young man? Let me see if I can help you without in any way causing you embarrassment. You know I only want to help you and not cause you an atom of pain if I can help it. If you have some real man and want to marry, then perhaps you may be happier — but most men you would have are not much better than I am or have been. Will write you again soon. Twenty-four days for a letter from you to me! Mails are very slow. Love and good-bye until next spring — get Jackie a Christmas present for me and send me the bill.

Yours, Carl[50]

The separated couple showed no signs of acrimony. Jane said of Carl that he "was my closest confidant. I could tell him anything."[51]

She took advantage of her independence when Carl cabled her that someone had offered $86,000 for a lot he had put in her name. She wired back that he should sell the lot. Claiming that Carl never bought her jewelry, she said she traveled with a jewel case holding only imitation pearls. In one afternoon Jane spent the entire $86,000 in a Paris jewelry store.[52] Unlike the rest of the Miami Beach millionaires' wives, Jane did not possess much jewelry. "From the beginning, he had told me the only jewels a woman needed were clean hair, a sun-scrubbed appearance and sparkling teeth. Later I learned he did not want me to wear gems because of the very real danger of thieves."[53] The Fishers had suffered a burglary in 1912 when they were living in the original Shadows in Miami. They lost $2,000 in jewelry and cash, including a ruby ring, two diamond rings, a garnet necklace, and a black opal and diamond ring.[54]

Jane soon discovered that someone had designs on her new jewelry. Her cook told her that the chauffeur was plotting blackmail and had already written a letter to Carl. When Jane cabled Carl, he sent Hugh Davis, his attorney, to bring her back. When Davis arrived, he told her that Carl "wants your way of living around him."[55]

When they arrived in New York, she was delayed on suspicion of smuggling jewelry. This she blamed also on the chauffeur.[56] Because it was late, she stayed overnight in a Fifth Avenue hotel. She telephoned Carl the next day, and he urged her to come out to Long Island so that he could show her Port Washington and Montauk Point. When she arrived at his new house, she found Galloway at the door to greet her, but Carl in bed. She attempted a reconciliation by urging him to go away with her for six months or a year. His reply: "'Whoever heard of a woman asking a man to leave his business for six months?'" Jane said, "'You don't want me back, darling.'"[57] Jane left to return to New York. He rang for Galloway, who brought him a scotch and soda.

The next morning, Galloway called Jane. Carl was leaving for Miami Beach on his yacht and wanted her to move into the Long Island House. She did move there, but concluded that this was the end of their marriage.

> I knew at last that I could not help Carl. The habit formed during prohibition had its hold over him, and Carl hated being chained, even by a habit. He had been the most strong-minded and determined of men, and this was the first weakness to which I had seen him give in. Drinking, he brought into our homes the sort of people that in sober moments he despised. When sober again he cleared them out with the abhorrence he would show a nest of cockroaches. But the craving always came back, and with it Carl's drinking companions. The other women — I was no longer jealous of them. I was only bitterly sad.[58]

She received some disturbing news when he sent her a telegram from Miami Beach — he had sold the Alton Beach waterfront and the Shadows to developer N.B.T. Roney in 1925 for two and a half million dollars. She was not totally surprised. He had previously given away their furniture, their rugs — even some of her Paris dresses.[59] He wrote that he had a "pretty little apartment"[60] for her to stay in at Miami Beach and invited her to come down for the season. She was to discover later that it was the penthouse of the Flamingo Hotel. He did not share the penthouse with her but had built a palatial home for himself on the rim of Biscayne Bay with an elevator to his apartment in the tower.

Carl visited Jane in her new apartment every day. She said he was "kindly, smiling,"[61] often with gifts: toys for Jackie, deeds to land, stocks and bonds. He offered her advice about how to handle her investments. He told her, "Don't let anyone fool you with sweet talk, Jane. Lots of fancy pipsqueaks are on the Beach these days smelling after money."[62] He showed her his plans for Montauk and brought plans for the new house he was building for her on Miami Beach and a deed to the house under construction for her at Montauk. Carl even asked her advice about the new houses at Montauk and the hotel furnishings.

When he inquired about the man she had been interested in in Paris, she told him that she had been rejected because the suitor wanted her to live in Paris — away from Carl.[63]

Every afternoon Carl's friends came, sometimes staying for dinner. Carl and Jane were host and hostess, Carl often staying after everyone else had left. At one point he told her, "'I'm sorry about the Shadows, honey. I didn't know you loved the old house so much.'"[64]

Carl and Jane even gave parties together. As a surprise for her, Carl had hired Paul Whiteman and his 35-piece orchestra for one party to which only 50 had originally been invited. Hundreds came, as Carl invited many more. He had to open an adjoining apartment to accommodate the overflow crowd. Prima donna Mary Garden was the guest of honor, as well as Gene Tunney. At the party was Jane and Carl's divorce lawyer, Dudley Field Malone. Jane had told Carl that she had decided to marry someone else. When the party was over, Jane said Carl gave her a bear hug and told her, "'Honey, that was the nicest party we ever gave.'"[65]

Carl did not object to her remarriage. Instead, he acted the part of a generous, doting father. Jane had chosen a man younger than she: Bob Johnson, "gay, untroubled and very young."[66] He had been a fellow passenger on the boat that brought her home from Paris. Carl told her, "'...why in hell don't I meet him? Goddamn it, Jane, I'll be damned if I'll let you marry some stranger. You bring him down here I'll pay all his expenses — and I'll let you know if he's any good.'"[67]

Bob came and was invited for lunch with Jane and Carl. Carl cross-examined him about his purposes and desires and told him Jane's faults as well as her virtues. About six, Carl offered them the use of the *Shadow J* for a moonlight cruise. Unbeknownst to Jane, Carl had ordered champagne and dinner for two as well as American Beauty roses.[68]

A divorce was not easily obtainable in the United States in 1926. Carl consulted his lawyer, Frank Shutts, who advised him about what to do in a letter on February 24, 1926.

I am of the opinion that French divorce is absolutely legal in this country. Over there the grounds can be anything; that is, the French Court will grant divorce decrees upon the general proposition that two people do not want to live together any more. All you would have to do would be to write a letter, which would be prepared for you in which you would state that in your judgment it is impossible for you to remain as man and wife with any degree of happiness and content, or words to that effect.[69]

Shutts added that the divorce process was estimated to take five to six weeks. Dudley Field Malone specialized in French divorces, charging about $15,000.

Carl passed Shutts' letter on to Jane, with the note: "Think this is best way to proceed and save much time and trouble for both of us. P. S. return for my files: Do you wish to talk to Frank Shutts. C."[70]

The divorce was arranged by Malone, who accompanied Jane to Paris. Carl was back in Montauk and had asked her to see him before she left. She was taken aback when she saw him there. His bed was on the sun porch, the bed on a platform so that he could look over Long Island Sound. "No question of his illness now. The doctor's warnings that he could not continue drinking were ignored. Bottles of scotch almost crowded out the medicine bottles on the table beside him."[71] He told her that the houses in Montauk and Miami Beach would be ready for her when she returned. When Jane left, Galloway, waited to say goodbye, wearing dark glasses. She thought that he was trying to hide eyes that were red from worry.[72]

Twenty years earlier, Galloway had been working as a waiter in an Indianapolis restaurant when Carl Fisher had hired him, nearly doubling his salary. The event changed his life from a routine of drudgery to an adventure. He was party to the victories, the defeats, the quarrels and infidelities. He had been there while the money flowed in by the truckloads, and he was still there when it was all gone. Galloways's career with Carl and Jane not only secured his future but let him jostle with the rich and famous of the Roaring Twenties. From his vantage point, as Carl's aide and confidante, Galloway had seen it all.

After Carl and Jane's divorce, Carl cabled her, wishing her happiness, and cabled her money, which he called a "honeymoon gift." She prepared for her wedding.

Chapter 25

"Miami Beach of the North" and a Hurricane

CARL RETURNED to Montauk in May of 1926, the first time he had been there since he completed the purchase. Carl arrived on his new 150-foot yacht, the *Shadow K,* with James Allison; W. A. Kohlhepp, a director of the Fisher Company; Charles Chapman, editor of *Motor Boating;* and Caleb Bragg, a well-known speedboat and race car driver.

Noting that "few people on this end of the island... have ever seen Fisher," the reporter in the May 21st issue of the *East Hampton Star* gave readers a glimpse of the new yacht and its owner. The *Shadow K* had taken only 59 hours to reach Sandy Hook, Long Island, from Miami Beach. The reporter was impressed by the twelve-passenger yacht's "home-like atmosphere," noting the coal-burning fireplace in the lounge, paintings of pirates on the walls, and books on the table and in a bookcase. Books on the table "were worn with constant handling." To reveal Carl's taste, he noted their titles and authors: two books by Carl's poet friend, James Whitcomb Riley; *Everywhere, The Memoirs of an Explorer* by A. Henry Savage-Landor; and *Through Southern Seas with Jack London.* On the after deck, there were wicker chairs, Oriental carpets, and cigars, cigarettes, candy, and nuts available for guests.

Although it was well-known throughout Carl's public life that he was very difficult or almost impossible to interview and refused to name any of his projects after himself, the

296

reporter thought him an example of the "bigger the man, the easier he is to reach and talk to." He described Carl: "Dressed in a loose-fitting tweed suit, with low cut pumps with a strap fitting over his instep, a negligee shirt open at the neck, tweed cap, glasses with one black glass (an ardent tennis enthusiast, Fisher was hit in the eye recently with a tennis ball) Carl Fisher presented a very picturesque appearance. Far from giving the impression that he is a millionaire developer who has performed miracles in the business world, Carl Fisher looks more like the sport and outdoor living man that he really is."[1]

He did get a report from Carl about progress at Montauk: "...there is a great deal of work going on here. In spite of a bad winter here, which delayed operations a great deal, things have gone ahead very nicely. With the nice weather we are having, there will be a great deal of work going on from now on. Although our party is going back this evening, I expect to be back in about four days and will probably be coming out this way after that at least once a week."[2]

Carl probably could not have had a more flattering portrayal of himself if his own publicity man had written the article. Carl's relationship with his employees was described in a similar manner:

Carl Fisher's yacht "Shadow K" in Montauk. (M.L.)

Carl G. Fisher office building with penthouse on top when he tempted the wealthy to purchase real estate at Montauk Beach. (M.L.)

It is interesting to find how all of Carl Fisher's, men, whether they be at Miami Beach, New York, Port Washington or Montauk, are for him to a man. Everyone speaks well of him as an employer and all emphasize the fact that "he's a regular guy — nothing up-stage with him, he sure is alright [sic]." The men on his motor boat are loud in his praise; "He is a peach of a boss to have on board, thinks of his men all the time — Our crew quarters are better on the Shadow K than owners' quarters on some yachts are." Not long ago an East Hampton man, in talking with one of Fisher's Montauk engineers, asked this direct question, "Tell me, is there anything doing at Montauk on this development or is it just a lot of bull?" The Montauk engineer, a huge man, grabbed him roughly, shook him a few times, and replied, "Where do you get that stuff? Carl Fisher does what he says he'll do." That, and the way that the Montauk boys rushed into the Inn during the recent fire to save all of the records and maps only shows the wonderful esprit de corps of the Carl Fisher organization. To command such loyalty as that he undoubtedly has done much for the boys to earn his reputation.[3]

Carl planned to open Montauk in the summer of 1927. In 1926, as many as 800 people were working to make it possible. He was building miles of good roads, an electric plant, water mains, and nurseries in which to grow the trees and shrubs for landscaping. There would be a seven-story office building, docks, a yacht club, polo fields and a golf course. Carl's own house would be built on a hill on a fifteen-acre site. Eventually, bathing casinos, cabanas, an ocean boardwalk, hotels, apartment houses, a laundry, churches, schools, and a business block would complete the project. Carl's first planned hotel, the 200-room Montauk Manor, would be ready for its first guests.

By June 8, 1926, work was well underway when the *East Hampton Star* reported on the progress that was being made. Carl had chosen English Tudor as the architectural style with the Montauk Struck Company doing the building. To provide housing for the hundreds of workers, a small development called Shepherd's Neck already had five completed houses, with 20 more under construction and a contract let for 30 more. Near what would be Montauk Manor, bunk houses were completed with housing for 240 and a dining room for 280. The engineers and surveyors occupied three other buildings, with a separate house under construction for employees of Conhall, Inc., which prepared meals for the workers. An 800-foot pier was almost complete. In the planning stage was an emergency hospital that would include an operating room, a ward accommodating six, and at least one private room. There would also be an ambulance. A thousand sheep were on order, and the *East Hampton Star* reported that "It is thought that a Basque shepherd will be brought to this country with a batch of thorough-bred sheep dogs to look after the flock."[4] A dredge had arrived at Fort Pond Bay.

Aerial view of early development was used in brochures to attract people and buyers to Montauk. (M.L.)

The one unexpected glitch in construction of the roads was the discovery of a 200-year-old cemetery comprised of 20 graves that had not appeared on the maps. A detour was made to leave the cemetery undisturbed.

The first stage would cost more than seven million dollars. Carl formed the Montauk Development Company in May. As in his other ventures, Carl invited his friends to participate, helping to make their fortunes. "From the beginning he had planned Montauk so his friends who hadn't made it on Miami Beach would have a second chance to get rich. His friends had always been the dearest thing in life — he would not, could not, let them down,"[5] Polly Redford wrote.

Not everyone shared Carl's vision of "The Miami Beach of the North." Irving Collins, his long-time partner in Miami Beach, gave Carl five reasons for his belief that Montauk would not succeed. Then he asked, "From a monetary standpoint, you don't need it, and why do you do it?"

Carl replied, "Just to see steam shovels throwing dirt and buildings going up!"[6]

Jane said John LaGorce tried to talk Carl out of developing Montauk, making him angrier than he had ever seen him before. "Why do you want to make more money? You have more than you need now. Why can't you take things easy?" LaGorce asked. "And Carl, Jack said, turned on him with black fire in his narrowed eyes. 'Damn your soul, who said I'm building Montauk for money? What the hell do I care about money? Miami Beach is finished and there's nothing left for me to do there but sit around in white pants looking pretty like the rest of you goddamn winter loafers.'"[7]

One of Carl's salesmen analyzed the Long Island market. In a five-page report, he cited the summer resorts and luxury homes that already existed there as they did all along the East Coast, competition that Miami Beach did not have.[8] But Carl could no more be dissuaded from continuing with his new project than he could when people called him crazy for developing Miami Beach.

Progress on Montauk continued full speed until the middle of September, when Carl received news from Miami Beach that had a far-reaching effect on his Montauk project. On September 16, the *Miami Daily News* reported on three tropical storms at sea, affecting Bermuda, Nassau, and St. Kitts. A large hurricane had struck Puerto Rico two days earlier. A 19 mile-per-hour wind began to blow the morning of Friday, September 17, on Miami Beach. By 11 a. m. the hurricane signals were up on Miami docks. The Weather Bureau began to telephone warnings to southern Florida.[9]

Most residents of Miami Beach were almost completely unprepared to deal with a hurricane. They had not been living there when the last big hurricane hit the area in 1910. Only a few long-time residents and weather forecasters understood the nature and consequences of a hurricane. One pioneer, Ralph Munroe of Coconut Grove, realized that something should be done to minimize possible hurricane damage. That spring, he testified that a plan to build islands south of Cape Florida could cause a tidal wave that would wash everything out to sea. The plan was not approved.[10]

The arrival of the hurricane was described vividly by Miami author Marjory Stoneman Douglas:

> Late that night, in absolute darkness it hit, with the far shrieking scream, the queer rumbling of a vast and resistible freight train. The wind instruments blew away at a hundred and twenty-five miles. The leaves went, branches, the bark off trees. In the slashing assault people found their roofs had blown off, unheard in the tumult. The water of the bay was lifted and blown inland, in streaming sheets of salt, with boats, scows, ships, the *Rose Mahoney*, coconuts, debris of all sorts, up on the highest ridge of the new land. Miami Beach was isolated in a sea of raving white water.[11]

For eight hours the wind blew from the Northeast, "covering the causeways, sweeping schooners across Bayfront Park and into Biscayne Boulevard, drowning the new lowland developments on the Miami shore, filling streets with flying debris, peeling plaster from the walls of half-finished buildings."[12]

At 6 a.m. the wind ceased. The sun shone — for half an hour. It was the eye of the storm. The residents, unfamiliar with the progress of hurricanes, thought it was over and congregated in the streets. Weatherman Richard Gray knew; but when he rushed out to warn that the storm was not over, people would not listen to him.[13]

Suddenly the winds returned, gusting up to 128 miles per hour. Unfortunately, some of the man-made additions to Miami Beach contributed to the damage because natural channels had been blocked by the new islands and causeway. Had these channels remained, some areas would have escaped flooding.

Electricity, the telegraph, and telephones were out on Miami Beach; those on the mainland feared the worst. The day after the hurricane a special one-page edition of the *Miami Daily News* reinforced these fears.

> Miami was laid waste Saturday by a raging hurricane attended by a gale of more than one hundred and thirty miles an

hour and followed by one of the most disastrous tidal waves experienced on the Atlantic Coast.

Miami Beach was isolated from the mainland and no word has been received as to the effect of the storm there. It is feared that a monster tidal wave has been swept across the entire island city.

Newspaper men called from Miami Beach at three a.m. with a story of pounding surf, broken communications and distressed boats. It was the first information to reach Miami. All boats on the Miami waterfront except one, *Adventure II,* were sunk. The *Nohab,* former yacht of Ex-Kaiser Wilhelm, was split in two.[14]

On Long Island, construction was in full gear. The 1,000 sheep that Carl planned to have graze on the golf courses had just arrived. With him on Long Island, John Levi received a telegram: "STORM IS OVER. DID A GREAT DEAL OF DAMAGE. MUCH PROPERTY LOSS.... SEVERAL PEOPLE KILLED AND MANY INJURED." Carl immediately made plans to return to Florida on Monday morning. The *East Hampton Star* reported in its September 24th edition that "Mr. Fisher is said to have taken the news of the hurricane calmly and philosophically and refused to be hurried into a special train..."[15] The paper quoted Carl when he left for Florida: "We are leaving for the devastated area to offer all the physical and financial aid of the Fisher interests. As soon as the homeless are cared for the work of reconstructing Miami Beach will begin. Miami Beach was built from a mangrove swamp to an artists' picture of reality. What was once done can be done again."[16] Before leaving, Carl instructed Tom Ringwood, his construction foreman, to halt the Montauk project.

In Miami, recovery work was well underway by Sunday night, September 19. A Citizens' Relief Committee was in operation. They fed the hungry and organized a medical service. Hotels and apartments were opened to the homeless. Already, 300 volunteer plumbers were working on restoring the water supply.[17] Martial law had been declared on Miami Beach, with a 6 p. m. curfew. Anyone selling food or water had to obtain a permit. City Manager Claude Renshaw asked for volunteers to clean up the city and serve as volunteer policemen.[18] Soon relief trains from all over the country were sent to Florida to help in the emergency.

Carl found that there was far less damage to his properties than had initially been reported. Carl's hotels had no structural damage, but the glass dome on the Flamingo had been blown out. Part of the roof on his new house had also blown off. The major expenses were for repairs to the docks, bulkheads, and tennis courts, new roofs and windows, painting walls, replacing carpets, and saving trees. The Roman Pools, close to the water, needed much work.[19]

Leo F. Reardon, executive editor of the *Miami Tribune,* toured the area and described South Beach as having the most damage. "It took the Coney Island of Miami Beach, twisted and gnarled it into an unrecognizable mass and flung it down on the sands.... Not an apartment block, hotel or storage on South Beach escaped the ravages of the storm."[20]

The city was a mess: two feet of sand on Collins Ave., sand in hotel lobbies, cars abandoned in the streets, debris everywhere. Thomas Pancoast wanted Collins Ave. to be raised two feet to prevent deposits of sand from such storms, but no action was taken.[21]

More than a hundred people died in the Miami area, three of them in Miami Beach. Hundreds were injured, and thousands homeless.[22]

Another casualty of the hurricane was a board racetrack Carl had built on land he owned in Miami in 1925. Ray Harroun designed and oversaw the construction of the speedway, named Fulford. Fulford featured high-banked turns. "...the 50 degree banks of Fulford were so steep that a car had to run at least 110 mph. to stay on them, any slower and the car would slide off."[23]

The track had opened on February 22, 1926, sanctioned by the AAA. The feature race was the Carl G. Fisher Cup Race, with a $30,000 purse. On the day of official time trials, 1600 spectators paid to watch cars with speeds averaging more than 130 mph. "Making it the fastest field ever to race in America."[24] Attendance for opening day was 30,000 people. "It seemed all had witnessed the birth of a speedway that would bring big time auto racing to south Florida. Fisher's dream seemed to have come true."[25]

When the hurricane hit only seven months later, the track was destroyed. The one million board feet of lumber were used in rebuilding Miami, and the land was sold as lots.[26]

With the hurricane following almost upon the heels of the damage done to Florida's reputation by the land speculators, Carl wasted no time in trying to rebuild confidence in the Beach. His sales manager, Pete Chase, in a letter dated September 24, acknowledged the three deaths but could even find good in some damage, such as the large number of trees that were destroyed.

The reports of our recent storm printed throughout the north exaggerated actual conditions greatly.

For instance — Hundreds were reported killed in Miami Beach. There were three deaths of Miami Beach residents.

Reports also stated that practically every Miami Beach home was demolished. In a careful inspection from 10th street to the north end of Miami Beach, I found not over three per cent of the homes so badly damaged that they cannot quickly be repaired. On Star Island, where over a million dollars had been spent in homes, the total damage will not exceed $5,000.

The chief property damage consisted in tiling blowing off roofs, and rain damage caused by awnings breaking holes in windows.

Possibly one tree out of every six or eight is badly bent or down; many of which can be raised satisfactorily. This summer we cut down 1,900 trees at Miami Beach at a cost of over ten dollars per tree. Last summer we cut down 15,000 trees and had planned to cut down 10,000 more this winter. We felt there were too many trees there.

There is no shortage of food or water. Neither is there an epidemic.

Stores are all open and no raise in prices.

Our Flamingo, Nautilus, Lincoln, King Cole, and Boulevard Hotels are none badly damaged and will all be open on schedule for the winter season.

Possibly you want first hand information on any property at Miami Beach. Whatever we can do for you, please feel it's our pleasure.[27]

Two weeks later, Carl wrote to his friend John LaGorce, summarizing the cost of damages.

...You might be interested to know that the total amount of our damages at the Beach, as far as our own Company was concerned, including the Bay Shore Company and The Alton Beach Company, will probably be around $400,000, of which we will collect insurance, I imagine, of about $200,000. Considering the wind velocity, we were probably lucky. However, a great part of all the damage was on tile roofs and awnings tore loose and beat all the windows out and the wind got under the edge of the roof and blew them off. No shingled roofs on the Beach were injured, although they were right in the path of the storm. The houses that stood best were those we purchased from Sears Roebuck.[28]

Jane read the news of the hurricane in the Paris edition of the *Herald-Tribune* as she was preparing for her wedding. Her first letter from Carl afterward was reassuring.

Dear Jane, — Don't worry about the hurricane. It will prove to be the greatest blessing to Miami Beach in the long run. Miami Beach will be more beautiful and bigger and better than ever before. After we get rid of this shyster boom trash there will be only hurricane proof structures allowed to be built. Miami Beach will ride all tides of time and change and coming through this storm will only make her the winner and the gainer in the end. As old Jess Andrews said, "Nothing much happened to Miami Beach — but a hell of a lot happened to the weather! "[29]

By the time the tourist season began a few months later, repairs were completed, except for a wrecked amusement pier near Government Cut. Repairs were delayed by another, much weaker hurricane that hit on October 20.

Tourists did not flock to Miami Beach in 1927 the way they had in previous seasons. This was no surprise to the inhabitants after the hurricane. Real estate sales were down, defaults were up. The Flamingo Hotel enticed prominent people with free rooms and meals to fill the hotel.[30]

Carl's financial losses from the hurricane were far more than the one million dollars he spent for repairs. Within weeks, his income from the sale of Miami Beach properties dropped precipitously; buyers just stopped making payments. The value of his holdings dropped one-third, from $30,000,000 to $20,000,000. He and other investors in Montauk, including Collins, Levi, and Allison, found their cash flow drying up. New York banks were reluctant to loan money until the Long Island and Pennsylvania Railroads interceded with their plans to connect with a deep sea harbor. Even then, the bankers were given lots in Montauk as an incentive.[31]

With Miami Beach no longer a reliable source of cash, Carl was forced to look at his other assets. Major among them was the Indianapolis Speedway. He had thought of selling his interest in it in 1923, when auto manufacturers seemed to be losing interest and the track needed to be refurbished at a cost of $200,000.[32] That year, a law that would have prohibited any commercialized sports on Memorial Day was passed by the Indiana legislature, only to be vetoed by Governor Warren McCray. "On the day after the 1923 race, Fisher let it be known he would accept any reasonable offer for his interest in the track and, if such an offer was not forthcoming, he would recommend sale of the land for other purposes unless the automotive industry definitely wanted the big outdoor proving grounds to remain in operation."[33] Henry Ford and other industrial leaders responded quickly. Carl, however, gave up the presidency of the speedway but served as a director.

Carl again tried to sell the track when his Miami speedway opened. He tried to sell it to retiring race driver Tommy Milton, the first driver to win the Indianapolis 500 twice. Carl offered to sell to Milton for $100,000 less than an offer he had received for the land from a group who wanted to build a real estate development. Milton was not interested.[34] Carl was determined to continue the speedway as a raceway. Fortunately, he was able to find another racer — Eddie Rickenbacker — who was interested. Carl wrote him on July 12, 1927.

> I have a copy of wire that Jim sent you a few days ago. We have to be careful and not have this proposition shopped around as though it was a second hand automobile.
>
> You are the only real life looking customer at this time who

307

understands the business and could handle the proposition and there is no reason why, if we have not sold it, you should not continue to see if you can get together a bunch to buy it.

In the meantime, I suppose you are acquainted with Lindberg and I would like to have you take up the matter with Lindberg for you and he in the same car to pace the race. It would, of course, be best for us to feature Lindberg [sic] and I think the combination will be a good thing for the Speedway. If, in the meantime, you should purchase the Speedway, it would be good for you.[35]

A letter from T. E. Meyers to James Allison on December 7, 1927, indicated that the price was $650,000 plus interest, for a total of $672,690.92, with $100,000 paid on September 1, $540,418 on November 1, and $32,272.92 on December 6. Elmer Stout, the trustee, withheld $29,156.51 for 1927 income tax, property tax, attorney fees of $1,250, etc.[36]

Carl continued as a director of the speedway for a few more years, but as his correspondence indicates, he was ready to resign. On June 10, 1929, Vice President "Pop" Meyers wrote to Carl:

On Saturday following the race Captain Rickenbacker called a meeting of the Directors of this Corporation without notice. It was possible for all of the Directors to be present except you so the Captain asked me to get from you a waiver of notice, which you will find attached. If you will be good enough to sign this and return in the enclosed stamped and addressed envelope, we will attach it to our minutes and our records will then be complete.[37]

On June 12, Carl replied:

I am returning the Waiver of Notice.

Don't you think you had better accept my resignation as one of your Board of Directors? I never get out that way and I am sure you don't need me, and certainly some of those Indianapolis people would be very proud to be one of the Board of Directors.

You can always depend upon my cooperation and any help I can give.[38]

Pop Myers answered Carl's letter on June 15.

Thanks very much for your letter of June 12th, enclosing the waiver of notice for the Directors meeting.

I note your feeling that you had better retire as Director of the Speedway. Personally, I would regret very much to have you sever your relations with this institution after having been associated all of these years. I just wonder if you have recalled that it will be twenty years this August since the first automobile race on the Speedway. I know that Captain Rickenbacker will not want you to retire but will bring the matter of your resignation before the Board at the next meeting, which, is set for July 23rd.

With all good wishes and best regards, I am[39]

The Board of Directors did not accept Carl's resignation until the following February.

With further reference to your letter dated June 12;

At a meeting of the Board of Directors of the Indianapolis Motor Speedway Corporation held on February 24th, the following resolution, acting upon your resignation was passed:

"RESOLVED, That the Board of Directors of Indianapolis Motor Speedway Corporation view with keenest regret the resignation of Mr. Carl G. Fisher as one of their number.

"RESOLVED, Further, that the officers be directed to express to Mr. Fisher their appreciation of his services as a Director and his helpful and constructive suggestions looking to the betterment of the operation of the Speedway, and their sincere regrets that he felt it was necessary to discontinue his association after so many years in the interest of this organization and automotive development."[40]

Having sold the Speedway, Carl personally guaranteed the continued development of Montauk with $5,000,000 in stock of the Carl G. Fisher Company, his holding company with assets of about $23,000,000. Some subscribers, such as Howard Coffin and Caleb Bragg, were able to advance more money.[41] He sounded optimistic in a letter written in March of 1927 to one of the investors.

Unless you have been in the business, you have no idea of the wonderful influence that is corralled through friendship and purely sporting instincts. Montauk is bound to appeal to people from a sporting standpoint and I believe it is going to be one of the big developments in America. I would not be disappointed if we only sold one and a half million this summer. On the other hand, I would not be surprised if we sold three million, but if we do not sell them this summer, we have next summer and several other summers to sell, and finally Montauk will develop into the great summer resort in America, and I am very much pleased to have you in the development and to talk over plans with.[42]

Back at Montauk in the summer of 1927, Carl went to visit Jane and her new husband at the three-story Victorian home he had purchased and furnished for them in East Williston. The twenty-acre property would be "perfect," Jane said, except there was no brook. Carl replied that instead he would build her a glassed-in swimming pool. Construction began the next day.[43]

Financial troubles or not, Carl continued to shower her with gifts on his almost-daily visits: a new station wagon, sterling silverware. "Completely ignoring the fact that I now had another husband to take charge of my affairs, Carl added improvements to our farm without my knowledge or permission as if he were still lord and master of my household and my destiny."[44] He built a garage where he thought it should be, regardless of her protests. He built a practice polo field, although she never played polo. She rented the place to Will Rogers for two seasons because he loved the polo field. Jane and her husband remained at Miami Beach.

Carl showed them blueprints of the house he was building for them on Miami Beach. When she argued that it was too big and suggested changes, he replied, "Hell, why do you want to change anything when I tell you it's all right! Besides, it's practically finished. I'll have it all furnished, ready for you to move in to when you come down."[45]

Carl's drinking hadn't stopped; whenever he had breakfast with them, he had to have a glass of whiskey first. Sometimes he would bring a bottle of scotch for him and her husband Bob to share. Easygoing Bob had no objection to Carl's presence or gifts. When she offered to give him back all that he had given her because of his financial situation, he indicated how welcome he felt in their home. "Hell, honey, keep your pin money. If I lose everything, why I'll just move right back in with you. Bob wouldn't be jealous of an old bow-legged has-been like me."[46]

Meanwhile, Carl was not alone. His secretary, Margaret Collier, had become his mistress and moved in with him. One June morning after a leisurely breakfast with Jane, he casually announced that he had to leave — he was being married at noon. The officiating minister was the husband of

Carl G. Fisher gets the full treatment. (HASF)

Carl G. Fisher enjoys a friendly game of croquet. (F.I.A.)

Ann Rossiter, his previous secretary-mistress. This marriage was not destined to be a happy one.

Some say he [married Margaret] only because New York bankers objected to the very open way she was living with him, but Wall Street has never objected to sin as long as it paid 6 percent, and Carl was paying more than that for Montauk money. More likely, say others, he was influenced by his friends Albert and Edna Champion, who made a frequent foursome with Margaret and Carl. They liked her, and thought Carl needed a woman's hand to steady him; he had no family, his mother had died in 1925. Everyone agrees, however, that the marriage was not a happy one. Margaret shared Carl's fondness for liquor, and did nothing to discourage his drinking. He was by this time too old to fall for that comfortable combination of sex and domesticity that can tame even the wildest man, and Margaret, a good secretary and shrewd businesswoman, was not the type to do it anyway. Perhaps that's why he married her. For Carl was never a family man; he was completely undomesticated, and refused to change. To him, a woman was still only a woman; a good cigar was a smoke.[47]

Carl was 53 in 1927. "A tennis ball had hit him in his good eye, making his vision worse than ever. Physically he was still a bear of a man, tremendously strong, and when he was sober his smile and personal magnetism still made him seem more alive than anyone else; but his body, no longer hard from exercise, was running to fat. His face was lined and heavy. He breathed hard."[48] In physical decline, Carl was soon to face some of the most difficult circumstances of his life.

Hunts were frequent at the Montauk Manor, and the Manor's stables were used to house patron's horses. (M.L.)

Chapter 26

Montauk Opens and Capone Comes to the Beach

O<small>N</small> J<small>UNE</small> 1, 1927, Montauk officially opened. It was imperative for Carl that his new venture succeed. For maximum publicity, Carl had invited members of the New York State press for a two-day visit. Montauk Manor, the Tudor-style hotel built at a cost of one million dollars, had 200 guest rooms ready for occupancy. George LeBoutillier, representing the Long Island Railroad, served as toastmaster, welcoming town, county, and village officials from throughout Long Island as well as Long Island and Pennsylvania Railroad officials. A total of 2,846 cars, carrying about 10,000 people, traveled over the cinder road on their way to Carl's Montauk. development and the two new state parks.[1]

A brochure a few years later celebrated the amenities of Montauk Manor.

> THE MANOR... proud Tudor gables rising from a lofty hill, overlooking the Sound, with a vista of sea and green, rolling knolls to the south... gay, gracious, suave...it boasts an enviable reputation as a hotel of distinction, with its 200 light, airy guests' rooms, painstaking service and unexcelled cuisine... Friendly and warm, yet with a formality bred of good taste, the Manor is of the moment, but its appeal is enduring. Its hospitality is the gracious anticipation and gratification of the preferences of its guests, an alluring roster of games, well-known; its atmosphere the protection of a finely-conducted home.
>
> Children are given special attention in a dining room provided especially for them, while chauffeurs and servants are

accommodated in quarters especially provided for the purpose.

The Manor is operated on both American and European plans and includes in its house facilities, broker's office, beauty salon, house physician, valet and fireproof garage.[2]

Carl had invited many of the well-known guests. On April 22, Carl had written to C. W. Barron, president of the *Wall Street Journal*, and invited him to accompany Carl on his yacht on a trip to Montauk and also to the opening.[3] On July 12, Carl personally invited United States Vice President Charles G. Dawes, who had already visited at Miami Beach, to

...see our new hotel and catch some real fish at Montauk Beach. I will guarantee that you will catch larger fish than President Coolidge or any member of his cabinet will catch this year if you will come out as my guest to Montauk Manor.

This is an open invitation; any time it is convenient to you. Hope you can come.[4]

Explorer Robert E. Byrd was away when Carl invited him. He replied on February 11, 1928:

I have just returned here [Boston] from an extended speaking trip and found your letter about the cottage. Want to tell you again how much I appreciate your kindness and thoughtfulness.

I know it is going to be the greatest fun to be in your house at Montauk Beach. I am looking forward with pleasure to seeing you.[5]

Business was good that first summer. On the July 4th weekend accommodations were filled to capacity. The Manor was "jammed."[6] Hither Hills State Park was a virtual "tent city."[7] The Napeague Beach road had been used by 10,000 cars that weekend, carrying about 25,000 people to the east end of Long Island. The heavy traffic brought about a movement to improve the road, culminating in East Hampton residents approving a $100,000 proposal for a new road on July 29.[8]

Another advance in transportation to Montauk had been announced in April of 1927 when the Long Island Railroad

*Montauk Manor — a hospitable inn — with the
enduring beauty of all distinguished things. (M.L.)*

said they would build a $100,000 terminal at Montauk. There
would be train service between Pittsburgh and Montauk from
June 1 through September 6.[9]

Carl needed to sell land to enable him to continue the
project. His friends invested just as they had on Miami Beach:
Albert Champion; Fred Moskovics, president of the Stutz
Motor Car Company; Howard Coffin of General Motors; Caleb
Bragg and George LeBoutillier.[10]

Plans for a trans-Atlantic harbor had been dashed earlier when a study commissioned by the Long Island and Pennsylvania Railroads estimated that it would cost $12,000,000
for piers and a breakwater. Passengers, the study concluded,
would probably prefer a trip through New York Harbor to a
three-hour train ride.[11] Interest was revived when newspapers reported that ten new ocean liners that could cross the
Atlantic in four days would be built with government help.
Eastern Long Island or New England were cited as the probable location for docks. Adding to the speculation, Army engineers arrived in 1928 to evaluate Fort Pond Bay as a possi-

bility. Representatives from the North German Lloyd Line and the French Line came as well. The Long Island Railroad was planning to build four 1,200-foot piers extending into Fort Pond Bay.[12]

While the summer tourist seasons were busy, the year-round population was to grow very slowly. Montauk was 125 miles from New York City and had no real industry of its own. In September of 1927, Carl wrote Parke G. Haynes, informing him that he had decided that he wanted Montauk Manor to remain open all winter, but with a "very small crew,"[13] with 18 to 20 rooms available for guests.

Winters Carl spent, as usual, at Miami Beach. There the end of the boom had meant less real estate business, but a boon in a different kind of business. When rooms were no longer at a premium, hotels could not be as selective. A criminal element began to manifest itself.

There had been gambling in Miami since the days of Henry Flager, who built "discreet, high-toned gambling houses along with his hotels. All these clubs were open to tourists only, and were considered respectable, necessary parts of a rich man's resort..."[14] Carl had refused to allow any gambling rooms in his Miami Beach hotels although, Jane, recalled, "I have seen him shooting craps with his friends in the living room at the Shadows at a thousand dollars a throw. He would gamble on anything. But he hated the gambling dens, as he hated all that was cheap and unscrupulous."[15] Other hotel owners were not so particular. Local residents in the 1920's had illegal gaming operations, but they had arrangements with the sheriff and city police.[16] After Carl sold the Shadows, it became the Beach and Tennis Club, offering dinner, dancing, entertainment and gambling, none of the physical sports its name implied. Jane went to see it and found that the veranda had been made into a bar, slot machines had been placed in the living room, and a roulette wheel had taken the place of the bed in Carl's bedroom.[17]

"Everyone played hard and fast at the Beach in 1928 and 1929,"[18] Polly Redford wrote. Instead of buying real estate, people invested their money in the stock market. Miami be-

Mobster Al Capone purchased this private Palm Island estate in 1922 for $40,000. (MN; HASF)

came known for its "free and easy" ways. In 1929, a new Florida law allowed pari-mutuel gambling, and to Carl's great disapproval, Tex Rickard opened a dog track on the southern part of Miami Beach.[19]

The depths to which the area had sunk were personified in Al Capone, who, having been run out of Los Angeles in December, 1928, decided to seek warmth in Florida. Using the pseudonym "Al Alcosta," Capone rented the top floor of Miami's Ponce de Leon Hotel for the season. Capone found plenty to interest him: fishing, the race track, even shopping, buying thousands of dollars worth of suits and silk underwear at the haberdashery owned by Miami's mayor, Ev Sewell.[20]

Capone liked the area so much that the next season he purchased a Palm Island estate originally built for Clarence M. Busch. His use of intermediaries guaranteed that it would take local residents a while before they realized who was living in their midst. But bodyguards and lavish parties soon made them aware. Some locals tried to solicit business or contributions. Roddey Burdine, head of the Miami Chamber of Commerce, called on Capone and was given a check of $1,000 for the Community Chest. There was a stipulation: Burdine was supposed to arrange a party for Capone and his friends at the country club. The check was returned when other members of the Community Chest threatened to quit.[21]

By 1929 night clubs had proliferated. Gambling was the new lure for tourists. When the Sharkey-Stribling prize fight was held in Miami Beach in February, Capone invited the nation's sportswriters who were covering the fight to lavish parties at his home.[22]

When the St. Valentine's Day Massacre in Chicago occurred in 1929, Capone did not need an alibi: he was in the office of Robert Taylor, Dade County solicitor, where, at the request of New York's District Attorney, he had been summoned for questioning about the murder of extortionist Frankie Yale. Yale had employed Capone as a bartender in New York when Capone was only sixteen.[23] It was Yale who sent Capone to Chicago in 1919 after Capone had beaten a member of the White Hand gang and gang boss William Lovett was after him.[24] Yale had been murdered on July 1, 1928, after Capone's friend, Filesy DeAmato, was killed because he had informed Capone that Yale was double-crossing him and hijacking Capone's trucks carrying illegal liquor in Brooklyn.[25] Questioning of Capone did not result in an arrest. But Capone, who had never served any jail time, was removed from the Miami Beach scene for ten months when he was imprisoned in Philadelphia in May of 1929 after pleading guilty to being a suspicious character and carrying concealed weapons. There was some speculation that Capone had deliberately chosen to be imprisoned to escape revenge for having brutally beaten three gang members who had betrayed him.[26]

Like other Floridians, Carl was deeply concerned about the criminal element surfacing in the area. Unfortunately, he could not claim the title of "Good Law-abiding Citizen" for himself; Prohibition had made him and many of his well-connected friends lawbreakers for its duration.

The Volstead Act went into effect on January 17, 1920. Newspapers headlining "Prohibition Begins at Midnight" outlined what passage of the 18th Amendment meant to the American public.

January 16, 1920– The party is over. Enforcement of the nationwide prohibition against drinking alcoholic beverages-the 18th amendment to the Constitution-begins at 12:01 A.M. tomorrow morning.

"After that hour," a government official said, "not a barrel of intoxicating liquor, a case of wine, or a keg of beer can be legally manufactured, sold, or transported anywhere in the United States."

In the past few months, many Americans have been buying up cases of whiskey and wine. It will still be legal to store liquor at home, where drinking will continue to be allowed. Federal authorities say private homes will not be searched.

The latest figures on the impact of the 18th amendment are impressive. These figures show that 236 distilleries, 1,092 breweries and 177,790 saloons will go out of business.

Most saloons are being turned into restaurants or candy stores, their owners report. Breweries, in many cases, have been turned into malt sugar factories, automobile factories, or meat packing warehouses. And an "army" of bartenders have found jobs at soda fountains.

Passage of the 18th amendment into law did not come as a surprise. Antiliquor campaigners have been fighting for the Prohibition law for a number of years.

"The false charge is made that Prohibition was 'put over' on the country while American soldiers were fighting in France," said William H. Anderson, a leader of the Anti-Saloon League.

"The truth is that in December 1914, the question was voted on in Congress and received a majority in the House of Representatives.

"Prohibition was consummated by the moral element in American citizenship," Anderson added. "And that includes the business element which recognized that alcohol, even when moderately used, lessened efficiency."[27]

Not only liquor, but also books on the manufacture of alcoholic beverages, were banned. An article entitled "New York Library Will Not Ban Books on Liquor" pointed out the differing reactions of different libraries.

Books on the manufacture of alcoholic liquors will continue to be available in the references department of the New York Public Library, said Edwin H. Anderson. Anderson said he was surprised by reports that libraries in Massachusetts and Connecticut had removed such books from their shelves. "We would no more think of forbidding readers to consult those books than we would books on flying," he said.[28]

It was not the manufacture or sale of liquor, but the transportation provision of the 18th Amendment that Carl and his friends would violate. Carl's drinking problem grew progressively worse. His correspondence during the years of Prohibition reveals a trafficking in illegal liquor not only for himself, but also for his guests and clientele at Montauk and Miami Beach.

At first, Carl was greatly concerned with being arrested for his possession of liquor, as shown with his dumping his liquor supplies at the Shadows into the ocean. In 1921, he requested George Denny, his Indianapolis attorney, to determine the legal status of the liquor he owned. Denny assured him that there was no problem.

As I understand it, this stuff is at your house here under lock and key, there is nothing in the last Government Regulations which either requires or authorizes the registration of liquor by the owner, possessed in his private dwelling while such dwelling is occupied and owned by him, providing said liquor is held only for the personal consumption of himself and his family and bonafide guests to be entertained in such dwelling.[29]

Denny did note that since Carl did not live in Indianapolis year-round, there might be some question about whether Blossom Heath could be challenged as his legal residence.

Until Prohibition ended in 1933, Carl and his friends warned each other about possible raids and helped each other obtain liquor. There were times when Carl narrowly escaped being arrested. His good friend Jim Allison sent Carl a warning in a letter dated April 5, 1920, from Indianapolis.

> By the way, when I was in Washington, I got a tip from Jack [LaGorce] that there are about a half dozen Secret Service men in Miami looking around and trying to get a line on any information as to the location of any wet goods. So it might be a pretty good idea to have anything that your friends may own placed in a safe place. I think that Peterson is putting everything I am interested in in the new storage place, where I think that it will be all right.

Jack LaGorce was right. But it was a year before there was a raid on Allison's own store of liquor in "the new storage place," the Miami Beach Aquarium. Carl didn't dispose of his liquor until the raid on Allison's, and he wrote Allison with all the details of what had happened on April 28, 1921.

> The Revenue Officers came over yesterday afternoon with a diagram of the entire lay-out of where you had placed 'your' liquor. You will note I say 'your' liquor. They were very nice, very polite and completely thorough. It seems as tho' your former chauffer [sic] (and this is confidential) had stolen 35 cases from the place before you had it sealed up: he went back to steal all of it and found it sealed. He became frightened and left, not attempting to break into this sealed part. However, they caught him for bootlegging, probably gave him the Third Degree, and he told just where he got the liquor. The first information came from this chauffer telling a hired stool pigeon. This dope we got from people friendly to us.
>
> The first officers, local men, came over and made a thorough search but could not find anything. Just as they were leaving, after Mowbray had taken them thru [sic] the place, the Federal outfit came along — and they knew exactly where to look for it. We also got a tip that someone knew of a vault over here that had several bottles in the vault belonging to friends who had left them here for safe keeping. I got on the job at once and

broke it all up. We didn't even have time to take a drink — and believe me, it was quite a job as we thot [sic] we only had about thirty minutes in which to work.

John suggests that we immediately advise you regarding the offense, which is not particularly serious — only $500 for the first offense.

The *Herald* treated the matter very decently this morning, I thot, considering that the Revenue Officers said this was the second largest haul they had ever made.

There is a wild scurrying of automobiles on the Beach this morning. We are expecting these pleasant gentlemen to stop in any minute and ask to look thru our property — but we have broken up all of it and for some time to come, I personally don't care if I don't see any more liquor. Jack just writes me, in a letter received this morning, that if I stop off in Washington he wants me to bring him a dozen bottles of Mitchell's Imperial. He is just a little bit too late.

Don't take the matter too seriously, as other people don't, and even the Revenue Officers think it is more or less of a joke, but rather hard on the owner of the liquor, especially such a good assortment. John is just about to send you a bill for a case of fine champagne left in your vault for safe keeping. Safe? Not too safe![30]

In the early months of Prohibition, on May 7, 1920, Carl was already active in arranging illegal shipments of liquor. Carl wrote to Cecil G. Fowler of the Fowler National Bank in Lafayette, Indiana, about one such transaction.

When Olaf A. Erickson gets to New York he will go to the Gas Engine and Power Co. and ask for Mr. Potter. Mr. Potter is a friend of mine there — and he will have this material in a small boat. I don't know what to advise in regard to the shipment — you will have to handle that yourself. If anything turns up that you don't get the material, let me know. I am enclosing you my check for $2500 to help pay for it. The full amount will be $5200, delivered there.

Mr. Potter will be very glad to give you some unusual help, and I would suggest that we give him about two dozen bottles, half a case, for his own use. I am writing him a letter today.[31]

A few years later, on April 16, 1923, Fowler warned Carl about the danger in bringing liquor into Indiana.

I would be a little careful in bringing back much liquor. I got through with two cases O.K. in trunks and suit cases but the enforcement officers are very active all over the state. They have recently sent ten of our bootlegger citizens to the penitentiary, out of this county alone.[32]

Later that year, on November 6, Carl commiserated with another Indianapolis friend, Herbert Duckwell, who, like Allison, had "lost" his liquor supply.

I have just learned of your sad "accident." I am indeed sorry to hear of such a loss, because it is a calamity in these times. A carefully selected stock of liquor — which you must have had — is not only a very difficult thing to get; but is a difficult thing to keep. It is like an expired life insurance policy. Something Abe Lincoln said at the battle of Gettysburg about "At this time words fail me — "[33]

In 1926, although Carl had managed to evade the law, he began to actively seek a change in it; if not a repeal, then at least fewer restrictions for beer and light wines He wrote Representative Robert L. Bacon of New York State on November 5, having earlier made a campaign contribution.[34]

If you folks in Washington do not wake up to the fact that the people want light wines and beer, you are crazy.

I am going to be a Democrat, if you don't turn over. I am one of a million who are going to do the same thing. Once you birds get out and the Democrats give us light wines and beer, you will have a hell of a long road to hoe before you get back.[35]

Carl entertained Virginia Representative Joseph T. Deal on his yacht and lobbied him about repealing the 18th Amendment. Deal acted, addressing Congress on the subject of changing the law. He sent Carl a copy of his speech but did not give much hope of a quick repeal.

I am... enclosing, as promised, a copy of my remarks before Congress, setting forth my views on the subject of the Volstead Law. I do not think that we will obtain relief until this wave of fanaticism has in some measure subsided, but as for myself, so long as I may live, I shall continue to antagonize, and endeavor to bring about a change in, these fanatical laws. I am resolved further that I shall never waiver in the face of apparently insuperable obstacles.

I trust that this may be the feeling of yourself and others. Let us not lose hope because results are not obtained as soon as we desire.[36]

Carl thanked Deal two weeks later, on January 31, 1927, but he was not as patient and complacent as Deal was about Prohibition.

Something will have to be done soon to help this Prohibition situation out. It is wrong for the Government to make criminals of hundreds of thousands of our best citizens, and the Government can no more stop people from drinking beer and liquor than they could stop them from drinking water.[37]

Carl specified a citizen who had become a criminal in a letter to William Anderson of the *Macon Daily News* the month before.

You remember some time ago you sent down a young man by the name of Hart to me and, recommended him highly as a very intelligent and aggressive young man who would surely make his way in the world. I am just reminded of this letter of yours by seeing Hart go by in a Rolls Royce Car. He undoubtly [sic] is the most successful bootlegger on the Beach and carries a fine stock of the best liquor.[38]

Convinced of the wrongness of the law, Carl continued to obtain and serve liquor in Miami Beach and Montauk. In April of 1927, he informed George LeBoutillier of some choice liquor that he had for him.

...there are twelve bottles of Usher's Green Stripe which a friend of mine bought for me in Scotland nine years ago and we have had it in the Bahama Islands since. Please divide it up with Mr. Atterbury and tell him that the last railroad president I was out with drank a full quart of this Green Stripe in one evening with no bad results except that he had steam coming out of his nose for three days.

After drinking a lot of White Mule for the last two years and then going on a beer diet, it['s] just my tough luck to dig up some of this old time Scotch. We brought this old Scotch from Nassau about nine years ago and hid it on Cat Key and it has only been recently we had [the] opportunity to get a man to deliver it to us.[39]

Carl did not like the quality of the beer he managed to obtain and in July of 1927 asked his friend Albert Champion, head of the A. C. Spark Plug Company in Flint, Michigan, for some help. In letters, he and his friends could speak freely about their illegal dealings, but in telegrams they had to be more circumspect. A bad phone connection the night before prompted this letter.

I wanted to tell you that good beer that is fit to drink is practically impossible to get here; at least, I have not found any place to get it, and all at once the demand for ale has been so great there is none of it around here. The number of guests I have consume a lot of liquor.

Do you know a good reliable bootlegger in Detroit who can get a truck to me either by shipping it in separate trucks every four or five or six days or driving the truck through? I am, of course, willing to pay for the expenses and a good price for a man to bring it through.[40]

Champion answered Carl's letter nine days later, having made all the necessary arrangements to try to avoid being caught.

Regarding the beer you wanted, I was in Detroit yesterday and got into that proposition. The following is what may be done:

Arrangement can be made to ship a carload of 500 cases which would be packed in vinegar barrels at $8 a case. They will guarantee to deliver to any siding that you name. That would come from Canada, go right through Buffalo, and they are set all along the line.

The other proposition which costs more per case would be a truck load of 100 cases that would be delivered to your place at approximately between $12 and $13 a case.

Of course with the latter proposition you would not have to worry about handling anything from the siding to wherever you want the beer. Let me know whatever you decide. You can wire me simply stating "Ship a carload or truck load", and I will see that the matter is taken care of. It would take about three days for a truck, and somebody should be on the job when it arrives. I will try to be posted when they start so I can advise you.[41]

Carl quickly telegraphed "Send truck,"[42] as he did not want to have to make arrangements for delivery if the beer was left at a siding. Champion confirmed the arrangements on July 29, informing Carl that the carload would arrive near New York the following week and then be trucked to him. Champion also offered his assistance for "any other things you want..."[43]

Carl was soon to lose his good friend. On October 1, 1927, Albert and his wife, Edna, sailed from New York to attend the London and Paris automobile shows and inspect his new factory in Paris. On October 27, Champion had just entered the Hotel Maurice banquet room when he collapsed into the arms of a business friend. Only 49, he died from an embolism. Six months before his death, Champion wrote a letter to Carl about the importance of work.

On my arrival home I received your telegram and like yourself we have not felt the weather any more comfortable in Detroit than you did in New York compared to Miami, but it will not be very long before we get good weather and I will be busy enough so I will not have time to worry as to whether the weather is good or bad.

I know that you do not like the statements I make in that line but work is really the greatest thing in the world because when we are not busy we certainly can make trouble for ourselves in many ways. In addition to that we find so much time to be sorry for ourselves and the more money a man has the more chance he has to find himself in that position. Activity also helps so much to keep young and it has been proven many times that we are only going to stay as young as the amount of activity we have.

On reaching here I certainly find any amount of work in every branch of our business that is going to keep me hustling from early morning to late evening. This is my first morning at work and I had people come to the house because this afternoon I must be at Chrysler and Packard, but I do not take it as work — I take it as a game and if I did take it as the people who work for me do I certainly would be very unhappy. I make myself happy by enjoying the things that I have to do and by trying to do a good job I enjoy myself so much more.

I will be interested to have a note from you regarding the result of your trip in New York and am writing this to Miami as I presume you will be back by the time this letter arrives.

You have my very best wishes in all kinds of ways.[44]

During Prohibition there was always fear of discovery. In the fall of 1927, when Carl decided to keep Montauk Manor open all winter on a limited basis, he was very concerned about the way liquor would be handled there. It would be available, but he explained in a letter to Parke G. Haynes exactly the way it must be served.

> The Club House job is going to be most difficult as most of our players will want a drink after playing. It will be all right for our man to furnish them with drinks, but under no circumstances to sell it to them. He will give them drinks with his compliments and if they pay him for it, all right, and if they don't it is entirely his loss and up to him. You can advise him that if we catch him selling liquor we will fire him in a minute.
>
> I think you should drop in there occasionally and see how things are going; also ask our guests how things are going, until we are satisfied this man thoroughly knows his business. I don't want you to fire him until you take the matter up with me and tell me what is wrong.
>
> ...I am going after all the people who are employed now very hard on the drinking question. I do not care how any of our men drink or when they drink out of office hours, but I am certainly going after any or all of you very strong from now on, if I hear of anything wrong down there during office hours.[45]

Carl always demanded quality, whether it was the liquor he served or the construction of his buildings. (In 1941 the Army Corps of Engineers considered razing Montauk Manor but decided that "...it was virtually indestructible and would take so much dynamite it would take down the hill upon which it stands."[46] It was used as an Army barracks instead.) The liquor that Carl was buying in the Bahamas during the 1927-1928 season he found so unsatisfactory that he wrote A. G. Burns, the Colonial Secretary, to complain.

I recently purchased some beer that was brought directly from Nassau, and found that it was not good. It had not been tampered with between Nassau and the States. Also I bought a half dozen bottles of Scotch that did not test well.

The only really good liquor people around here believe in now-a-days is Bicardi from Cuba. Don't you think it is a bad thing to have poor Scotch or poor beer coming through your clearing house or your country? At one time not long ago the reputation for pure liquor coming from Nassau was splendid. Right now it is considerably damaged and I am very sorry of this condition as I like to have a glass of beer occasionally and a Scotch highball and, of course, I would like to have good Scotch and good beer. I believe one of the best things your country could do would be to put a very strict prohibition on anything except good liquor coming through the country.[47]

Carl received a reply from Charles E. Bethell, apparently alerting him to the difference in various brands, and wrote to thank him for the information.[48] Later that season, in March, Carl had more to worry about. His good friend C. F. Chapman, editor of *Motor Boating*, wrote to warn him about information he had gleaned from a friend, a Lieutenant Commander who was an aide to Admiral Billard, head of the Coast Guard. Chapman had been on the same train with the aide when he left Miami Beach and learned that Admiral Billard was "particularly hard boiled against yachting and yachtsmen.... "[49]

Chapman's friend had been the Admiral's personal representative in Miami in charge of investigating "the question of yachts running liquor into Southern Florida and particularly to watch *Shadow K* and yourself, as well as one or two other prominent yachtsmen.

The Coast Guard has dozens of secret service men in Miami and Miami Beach on this particular mission and what they know about the yachts and yachtsmen is almost unbelievable. They have data on the action of various yachts during the past six weeks and the names of the owners and Captains that have brought liquor in, or have had any on board. They followed Shadow K to Jacksonville recently and had a man an board while Shadow K was hauled out and know the complete layout of the yacht.

329

The Coast Guard authorities are particularly antagonistic to the yachtsmen as they believe besides running liquor themselves, they have assisted the rum runners and particularly on account of testimony and evidence given by them at the recent trials... which have been tried recently at Miami.[50]

Chapman wrote that the Lieutenant Commander had tried to mitigate the negative attitude of the Coast Guard towards the yachtsmen before he returned to Washington and that he would attempt to "try to prevent the order which he believes will go out soon to seize and inspect all yachts at Miami and Miami Beach.... I do know that Shadow K is being watched closely and is the boat at the head of the list for seizure when the proper time comes."[51]

Chapman also noted that some of the Coast Guard antagonism seemed to be the result of their feeling slighted, particularly as only one officer had been invited to the Yachtsmen's Ball, while Miami Mayor Ev Sewell and his friends from Miami had paid them much more attention. Another problem Chapman identified was the Miami Beach Harbor Master, Colonel Bailey. Chapman suggested that he be replaced.

This man has had several run-ins with the Coast Guard, both this year and last year and they are all down on him. On several occasions he has reported to the Coast Guard officials, the fact that he has seen Coast Guard enlisted men with liquor in their possession and this has caused court martials and several men have been fined and reduced in rank, with a result that a number of the cutters and picket boats are out to get this man or any of his friends. As Colonel Bailey is pretty close to a number of the Captains who have yachts at the Boat Slips, the situation is none too good.[52]

Carl answered immediately, denying using his yacht for carrying liquor. According to Polly Redford, however, Carl's yachts had special compartments between decks for carrying liquor from Bimini.[53]

Many thanks for yours of the twenty-fourth. I will look into the matter of the man, Bailey, right away. However, there is another side to this situation, and that is, if Bayley (sic) was not rather hard boiled the Coast Guard outfit would take advantage of him.

I knew that the man at Jacksonville had called on the captain, but in a rather friendly way and Captain invited him to look the boat over. There was nothing on the boat, and there never is anything on the boat except a few bottles of beer, some sulphur water and a few other things of that nature. We don't make a practice of bringing in liquor on the boat.[54]

By 1928, organizations had formed to try to at least loosen the restrictions on alcohol. The Association Against the Prohibition Amendment had incorporated in Washington, D.C., and solicited money from businessmen, including Carl, suggesting $5,000 contributions from individuals and groups. They hoped to have the law changed to allow "mild" liquors, taxing liquor sales to reduce income and corporation taxes.[55] The cost of repairs after the hurricane and the development of Montauk had severely depleted Carl's cash holdings. He supported them, but could offer only $100 cash as part of a subscription plan he proposed, whereby a letter from the association would solicit contributions in his hotels and club houses.

The prohibition effort, of course, is a farce, and a greater one every day. I am tomorrow to witness to almost a real murder right in front of my eyes in the bay here of an unarmed bootlegger who had come to a stop to surrender before he was shot. In several cases here the prohibition men have been very nasty, but we have not had so much trouble this year as we had last year — but just the same, it is a very vicious law.[56]

Chapter 27

Old and New Friends and a Confrontation with Capone

FROM HIS early days on the racing circuit with Barney Oldfield, to Miami Beach, where John Levi, Jim Allison, and other old friends from Indianapolis came both in business and friendship, Carl had always managed to make and keep good friends. William Galloway, his friend as well as his servant, remained loyal to Carl from his first employment in Indianapolis until the end. Even the Collins family, whose Quaker origins and upbringing made them more sedate in character and behavior, admired Carl for his honesty and integrity, if not his social graces. "He was not the sort of man we entertained much in our homes,"[1] Art Pancoast said. A grandson of John Collins commented: "His word was as good as any contract he'd put in writing. There was an integrity there that should be recognized, and I don't think it always is."[2]

Carl respected the opinions of his subordinates, asking them to let him know when they thought any of his decisions were wrong. When he instructed Parke Haynes about what was to be done at Montauk in September of 1927, he ended the letter with the following:

> You can talk this letter over with Drumpleman and General Tyndall. If you do not thoroughly agree with these instructions, do not hesitate to write me immediately why not. In any instructions you receive from me, you will always remember that you are permitted and asked to comment on them. If you do not agree with the instructions, I do not want you and do not

expect you to fulfill any orders you may receive with an idea in your own head that they are wrong. In other words, I always want you to feel that you have a right and you are asked to do so, to comment from your point of view. Undoubtedly many instructions come from this office that are wrong, but they go to employees who have not sense enough to criticize them.[3]

Carl, however, was firm about employees' behavior. In that letter he told Haynes that no employees were to use the golf course before 5:30 p. m. "We are not running the place at Montauk to teach a lot of our employees how to play golf."[4]

From the beginning of his success with Prest-O-Lite, it was James Allison who had been Carl's friend and confidant, a friend who had been a needed tempering force on Carl's endeavors.

On August 3,1928, Carl received a telegram at Montauk from Indianapolis:

JIM IN CRITICAL CONDITION   END SEEMS ONLY A
MATTER OF A FEW HOURS
        DR E H ADKINS.[5]

Allison passed away that day at the age of fifty-five. He had died of bronchial pneumonia at his home in Indianapolis. Allison and his wife Sara had divorced earlier that year. He had married Miss Lucille Musset, who had been employed at the now-closed aquarium, just three days before his death at Carl's home in Montauk.

The relationship between Carl and Allison was an easy-going one, as can be seen in this letter Carl wrote to Allison.

Attached is a letter from Jack [LaGorce]: I have suggested to Jack that you might like to be an angel for a botanical garden. I will give them four or five acres of good land for them to locate the damned thing on — and I thought maybe you might be interested in these strange and peculiar plants, to the extent of five or ten thousand bucks.

If this investment doesn't appeal to you, don't let it hurt your feelings. Some other nut will come along who will take it up.[6]

A letter from Allison to Earl Kiser, whose friendship dated back to Carl's racing days, indicates the generous natures of both Carl and Allison:

"Old Salts" — Carl Fisher with James Allison. (HASF)

Carl and myself have just had a hell of an argument about splitting the expenses of the Nassau Havana trip and I told him in advance that I would be glad to go along if I could stand half of the expenses, and in Carl's office this morning he told me to "Go to Hell" and threw the check at me. He and I rather compromised the matter after a heated argument by my not accepting the check and Carl not accepting it — and both of us agreeing that we owed a lot to you and there was no one in the world that we know of that we would rather have the check turned over to, and stop the argument.

So — you will find the enclosed check payable to Carl and endorsed by him; and it is up to you to do whatever you damn please with it…. but I would suggest that you get a good supply of liquor, also about twelve gross of sauerkraut.[7]

Another of Carl's long-time associates, John Collins, died in 1928 at the age of 91. Carl was to continue his business connections with the Collins' family at Miami Beach until his own death.

Two years earlier, Carl had acquired a new, if somewhat unlikely, friend who would be as loyal a friend as Carl had ever had. Father William Barry, born in Ireland in 1886 and ordained in Baltimore in 1910, was one of three priests who had been sent to the Miami area to minister to the growing Roman Catholic population. Father Barry made friends with Carl soon after he arrived. The priest was eager to establish a new parish and needed land on which to build the first Catholic church on Miami Beach. Carl was receptive to Father Barry's needs. The first Mass was said in one of Carl's polo stables, with the first classes of the parish elementary school held in another of Carl's polo stables.[8]

Negotiating with Carl for land for a real church took longer. When the priest visited Carl at Port Washington in the summer of 1927, they discussed details about the land. After Father Barry returned to Miami Beach, he wrote Carl with the stipulations they had discussed. Carl was to give him deeds to the land where the temporary chapel, schools, and Sisters' home were located. Father Barry also mentioned some possible other donations of land, including the Lincoln Hotel tennis courts, leaving the decision about this to Carl.

> ...What I want to make clear is that I am not desirous of more than the minimum requisite. Neither do I want to impose on your goodness and generosity characteristics I have reason to believe to be just as much part of your nature as your intelligence and business acumen.
>
> You will understand why I am anxious that this matter be speedily executed. I have waited now over one year to begin building. I hope that two or three weeks will see me breaking ground. I am sure this is in accord with your own spirit.[9]

Carl was willing to give the church the land, but he wanted the church to buy the tennis court, which had cost him $45,000 to build. He replied to Father Barry on August 24.

> Now I would suggest that you let the matter drop until I get down there, which will be about the first or second of November.
>
> I don't see any reason why we could not take 125 feet from the corner of the golf course for church purposes. As I remember you want about 125 feet. We could do away with one tennis court for your building purposes, or possibly two tennis courts if necessary, leaving the corner free. Let me hear from you right away as to the exact needs, in size and not lots. This corner, as

you know, is very valuable and we should have enough of it left to help pay for what we give away.[10]

Father Barry replied on September 14, sending a sketch and specifying a 150 foot by 220 foot requirement. "...if possible I hope to have the building under way when the tourists arrive, and the building well advanced at the height of the season."[11] Carl assured him that they would be able to find the right piece of property, but not on Lincoln Road, unless the city allowed the appropriation of part of the golf course. In a memo to W. A. Kohlhepp, a director of the Carl G. Fisher Company, Carl noted: "I think we could easily give them, for instance, the location of the present golf club, which would be quite central... I realize any property we give them is very valuable, but on the other hand the church is valuable."[12] In the end, Carl gave the church six lots and the church purchased six more for $4,233 each.[13]

Carl enjoyed the priest's ebullient personality. "With your kindly smile and the blarney you always have on your tongue," Carl wrote to him on February 11, 1928, "you are bound to win out. I am satisfied if you set out to try you can make a bronze door knob grin."[14] In turn, Father Barry wrote that he was caring for the "department of religion" in the "busy little republic" of Miami Beach that Carl had created.

The new St. Patrick's Church was dedicated on February 3, 1929. In the same letter in which Father Barry invited Carl to the dedication of the new church, he felt secure enough in his friendship with Carl to ask for the use of Carl's yacht to entertain the seven Bishops who would be attending.[15] Carl was very receptive to the request.

> I have yours of the 29th. We will get some boat for you for February fifth. We will be very glad to accommodate the visiting Bishops. Also, will you tell me personally a little more about refreshments.[16]

In January of the following year, Carl issued an open invitation for the use of the *Shadow M* to Father Barry and showed a concern for the nuns who staffed St. Francis Hospital on Allison Island. The hospital had been built by Jim Allison and offered gourmet food and other amenities for the patients. Unfortunately, Allison Hospital had opened on January 1, 1926, when the Florida boom was ending and there was little demand for such luxury. Allison, already in poor health, asked for help from Father Barry and Carl, who used their contacts and resources to obtain an agreement with the Sisters of St. Francis of Allegheny, New York, to run the hospital. The sisters took over in the fall of 1927, but Jim Allison, then in a wheelchair, had a hard time accepting the economies of Mother Alice and the other sisters. Gone were the landscape gardeners. Allison's resident manager's car was transferred to the sisters for use in their motor pool. Despite Allison's threats to end the agreement, Mother Alice managed to place the hospital on a more sound financial basis. After Allison's death, the Franciscans purchased the Allison hospital.[17]

Carl recognized the hard work of the sisters and offered his yacht for their enjoyment.

Will you please see Mother Alice and arrange to take all the nuns and nurses for a boat trip on the "Shadow M"? They need a breath of fresh air.

St. Patrick's Church dedication, 1929. (S.P.A. – Parks)

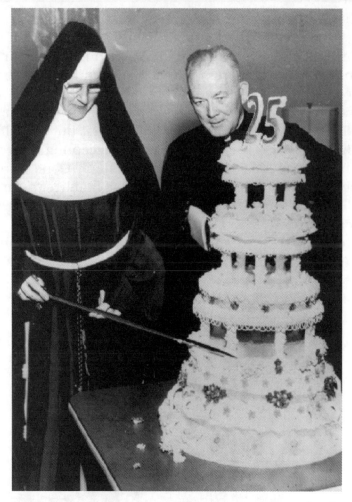

Msgr. Barry and Mother Magdalena cut the cake for St. Francis Hospital's 25th birthday. (Parks)

I would like to have you consider that once each month by engagement we can make arrangements to take all the guests you would like to invite for a trip. This trip can be around the Bay and Miami Beach in protected waters and nobody will get sick. To make a regular party out of it, they should make up sandwiches and some lemonade, leaving about ten o'clock in the morning and return about twelve o'clock. However, it is up to you to arrange the details.[18]

Carl was not so fortunate with some of his associates at Montauk as he had been in Indianapolis and Miami Beach. On March 16, 1929, he wrote to George LeBoutillier from Miami Beach: "I am beginning to realize very seriously that it is difficult to operate six months of the year here and six months at Montauk without a strong organization."[19] Carl had learned that one of his Montauk employees, C. F. Redden, had written what LeBoutillier had called "a very indiscreet and uncalled-for letter to Mr. Rankin about the Company's affairs..."[20] LeBoutillier advised against taking any action against Redden because of his "ability."[21] The problems at Montauk went further than Redden, as LeBoutillier revealed in a letter of March 29.

> It must be admitted that Redden has not received the support of the organization — but then again, who has, of Talbot, Kohlhepp, Davis, McCaffery and Sheedy, and, to some extent, "yours truly."
>
> It is very important to get the discordant element of an organization such as yours outside as soon as possible, so that the petty jealousies that are constantly cropping up do not become common gossip and hurt the whole situation.
>
> You and your group of friends have a wonderful proposition at Montauk, as you well know, and you will come into a sales time when it will be satisfactory to all. But the many rumors that are flying around New York and other places about the organization and financial status must be quieted in order to make the development a success, and this can only be done by having high type, conscientious men in the organization.
>
> I hope you will take what I have said in the spirit in which it is written and that you will agree that no hasty action should be taken in this matter.
>
> I feel that Redden wrote this letter under great stress, after he had talked to some of the officers after the last meeting at Sapeloe.[22]

There was no question that Montauk was having financial problems. Carl had personally guaranteed the financing, and his cash was running out. He agreed with LeBoutillier that Redden was very capable. "However," Carl wrote in his

March 16th reply, "I do deeply resent one of our assistants spreading rumors with our own pen and ink and stamps."[23] Carl also gave his reasons why he thought there had been a lack of cooperation.

> There are many reasons why Talbot, Kohlhepp, Davis, McCaffrey and Sheedy did not have cooperation. With the exception of Talbot and Davis, I could easily show you why the others did not deserve cooperation, and by taking them out of any control at Montauk I undoubtedly saved several hundred thousands of dollars in expense. Davis told me he did not want the job, and Talbott [sic] could not cooperate with Kohlhepp and the rest of the organization without wrecking the organization at that time which would have been serious. McCaffrey was not competent; and Sheedy on account of his association with the Government, was letting contracts that were very expensive to us.[24]

Carl did agree to wait until a new president of the Montauk Beach Development Corporation had been installed and reviewed the Redden situation. But he suggested as a replacement a friend of his, Daniel J. Mahoney, who had managed newspapers in Miami as well as Ohio. Mahoney was the son-in-law of Carl's friend, James Cox, former Governor of Ohio who had been the Democratic party's Presidential candidate in 1920 against Warren G. Harding. Carl had invited Cox to Miami Beach in 1923, and, at Carl's suggestion, Cox bought the *Miami Metropolis.*

Cox already owned newspapers in Dayton and Springfield, Ohio.[25]

Carl tried to bring Henry Ford to Miami Beach, just as he had tried to interest him in supporting the Lincoln Highway. In 1921, Carl wrote to Harvey Firestone, president of the Firestone Tire and Rubber Company, whom he was trying to interest in coming to Miami Beach, and he also inquired about Henry and Edsel Ford. Both Firestone and Ford had been active in the Indianapolis Speedway, Firestone with the development of tires and Ford as an umpire for the Prest-O-Lite trophy race when the track first opened.[26] Ford was also one of the automotive industry leaders who had helped to save

Old Timers — this picture taken in 1924 shows some of the colorful characters known to the racing world. Those present were Carl G. Fisher, Speedway founder, Louis Chevrolet, for whom the General Motors car is named, Barney Oldfield, famous racer, and others. Seated is Henry Ford, founder of the Ford Motor Company. (HASF)

the track when Carl announced in 1923 that he wanted to sell it.[27] Carl wrote to Firestone:

> Sometime since Mr. Duffee left with you a booklet of one of our best places at Miami Beach. This booklet is our "Traveling Salesman" and we have two or three other prospects now that we want to try and sell this place to. I am in hopes the reason you have kept the booklet is that you are interested in this place...

Carl added a postscript.

> P.S. We heard indirectly the other day that Mr. Henry Ford and Edsel Ford might spend some of the winter at Miami Beach. I would like nothing better than to take my boats and show them that part of the country. It is certainly interesting and there are a lot of the Keys that you have never seen that are wonderful, especially in the Bahama banks. It is probably the most wonderful place in the world for fishing and boating and there is some unusually fine scenery there. If you can, in any way, help us interest Henry and Edsel Ford to come down, please

do so and don't hesitate to call on me for assistance in making them have a good time.[28]

Carl had some correspondence with Firestone, but Firestone was interested in leasing, rather than purchasing, a home. The following year, W. D. Hines of Firestone's office inquired about such a place.

Mr. Firestone is planning a trip to Florida this winter with his family and may spend a couple of months there. Recalling the correspondence that he had with you a year ago about your house at Miami he thought that possibly you might know of a suitable place that he could lease for that length of time.

As you will probably recall in his correspondence with you last year he mentioned the fact that one of his boys is troubled with asthma and he believes that Miami would be a good climate for him to spend the winter.

Mr. Firestone would appreciate it very much if you could give him any information concerning a well located home at Miami.

He sends his personal regards.[29]

Carl again had no luck in interesting Ford. Ford, however, on September 22, 1924, did send him a postcard with a

Great figures in early automotive and racing world. Second row center Henry Ford and Carl Fisher looking aside. (F.F.A)

photograph (but no message) of Ford sitting in a race car at the Speedway. When Ford was in Fort Myers, Florida, in March of 1926, Carl sent him a day letter.

> I'll bet you an innertube against a rubber patching outfit that I have a fiddler here that can beat yours Stop Why don't you come over and see this country Stop If the roads are too rough I'll send my boat around for you in the next few days.[30]

Carl had better luck with Ford's son Edsel. Edsel and his wife did lease one of the Flamingo Hotel's cottages in 1930.[31]

William K. Vanderbilt II, grandson of Commodore Cornelius Vanderbilt, was another of Carl's friends who was an avid sportsman and frequent visitor to Miami. Carl admired Vanderbilt's 250-foot yacht, *Eagle,* and, the story goes, offered to exchange Fisher Island for the yacht. Their correspondence, however, indicates that the deal was for only part of the island. Vanderbilt promptly accepted and wrote Carl a thank-you note. "I am in receipt of Warranty Deed for piece of your property on Harbor Terminal Island, for which I thank you, and remain."[32]

Carl's secretary replied to Vanderbilt.

William K. Vanderbilt's yacht. (F.I.A.)

W. K. Vanderbilt poses with his wife aboard his yacht. His stately mansion on Fisher Island is now the equally elegant clubhouse for the sumptuous Fisher Island development. (HASF)

Mr. Fisher has received your letter of December twenty-seventh, with which you enclosed check for ten dollars.

As you had previously sent check for one dollar, the agreed price of land at Terminal Island, Mr. Fisher directs that this check be returned to you. I enclose the check with Mr. Fisher's endorsement.[33]

Two months later, Carl made a suggestion about Vanderbilt's new property.

I inspected the work on your island property the other day, and I noticed you are spending considerable money on the place in shrubs, trees, etc. I just want to be sure that you know that the surrounding property is quite liable to be commercial. I don't see how it could be anything else except that we could and would be glad to reserve some of the property adjoining your property, possibly a quarter mile of it, for others who might want to purchase private dock landings.

I hope to see you on your return.[34]

When Vanderbilt returned to Florida in November, he was very pleased.

I arrived at Miami some days ago on board the ARA and made fast to dock, which has proved a great success. The work has been splendidly done and comes up to my expectations in every way....

As I shall in all probability not have the pleasure of seeing you ere my departure for a trip around the world, allow me to take this opportunity of wishing you and Mrs. Fisher a Merry Christmas and a Happy New Year.[35]

Vanderbilt built an elegant home facing the Atlantic. The Mediterranean-style mansion, with its imported English oak, Victorian mahogany paneling, and marble fireplaces, later became one of Dade County's registered historical landmarks.

Vanderbilt knew of Carl's love for animals and decided to send Carl some pets for his new home on Montauk. He cabled Carl from the West Indies that he was sending him a honey bear, a seal, and a boa constrictor. Carl replied: "Send honey bear and seal but keep boa constrictor. I can see one of those any day with a two-dollar bottle of gin."[36] The honey bear was to cause some difficulty. Carl had a cage constructed for him and a pool for the seal, and enjoyed watching the bear's antics. Just as flies are attracted to honey, they were attracted to the honey bear. Since the cage was near the cafeteria, the flies began to bother those eating there, especially Caleb Bragg. Carl refused to move the bear. Bragg consulted with Tom Ringwood, who succeeded in getting the bear moved. Ringwood went hunting with the Board of Health Inspector who subsequently condemned the bear cage. The seal Carl took with him to Miami Beach when he returned at the end of the season.[37]

Other livestock problems at Montauk occurred with Carl's polo ponies. Restrictions on property at Montauk included a ban on all livestock. Carl wanted his ponies near him and proceeded to build a stable for four horses on his new estate. The ponies and a pile of manure were a direct violation of his own rules. Carl was adamant when this was pointed out to him: "It's up to you fellows to straighten this thing out — I'm not going way down to the polo barns every time I want to ride a pony."[38] Ringwood solved the problem by obtaining waivers from the other owners in the section so that Carl could have his way.

Besides polo, Carl enjoyed deep sea fishing with his friends at Montauk. He telegraphed this request to Captain Charles Thompson.

ARTHUR BRISBANE AND BERNARD GIMBEL MAY COME WITH ME TOMORROW FOR SATURDAY AND SUNDAY FISH-ING. CAN YOU GO WITH US. IF YOU ARE ENGAGED GET SOME OTHER GOOD FISHERMAN FOR ME PENDING CON-FIRMATION THIS REQUEST TOMORROW NOON[39]

The stock market had not yet crashed by the summer of 1929, but Carl was already receiving bad financial news from Miami Beach, where property values had not recovered and assessments were falling. On July 12, 1929, Thomas Pancoast wrote him with some bad news:

We had to foreclose the third mortgage against the Lauder-dale Memorial Hospital and had to buy it in, which we did this week in the name of the Allison Realty Co. These hospitals are nightmares. I understand the City of Miami pays $1,000.00 a day to keep up the Jackson Memorial Hospital.

...so it does not look as though all of our Florida troubles are over yet. This [a bank failure] very unfortunate for it makes everybody nervous and wondering whether their money is safe anywhere or not, and many of them draw out and put in safety deposit boxes. However, our bank at Miami in about in the best condition of any bank that I know of in Florida.[40]

Carl's reply reflected a rather resigned attitude towards the Florida situation.

A lot of bad news from Florida, but I don't see any possible thing we can do except keep sticking money in our own bank.

I am going to bring the seals down this fall. We are now teaching them to sing bass. Vanderbilt sent me a Honey Bear from India that is the funniest thing you ever saw in your life. I believe I will bring it along. I always did figure I should have a circus so I am making a small start.[41]

The summer of 1929 was a good tourist summer at Montauk. Celebrities came; Johnny Weismuller appeared at the Montauk Beach Casino. But at the end of the summer, there was a gambling raid at the Montauk Island Club, with a waiter arrested, and wheels and a $25,000 table seized.[42]

The development was still hampered by the lack of cash. In early July the Montauk Beach Development Company had laid off some construction workers. Later, the dredging of Lake Montauk was halted. Then a page one story in the *East Hampton Star* of October 18, 1929, revealed more bad news:

A lay-off which practically means the curtailment of all activity during the winter was announced on Wednesday of last week by the Montauk Beach Development Company.... the announcement of last week exceeded the expectation of most of the people here and left many without employment unexpectedly.[43]

On October 29, the stock market crashed. In response to a wire from Carl about the effect of the crash on reservations

Montauk Island Club, on Star Island in Lake Montauk. (M.L.)

at the Flamingo Hotel, Manager Charles Krom estimated on November 18 that "...if the break doesn't go any further I don't think we will be hit more than ten per cent."[44] The 1929-1930 season at Miami Beach went surprisingly well. The stock market temporarily rebounded in the first three months of 1930. The second week of March, however, marked a sudden exodus; the Flamingo closed quite soon after, although, according to Carl, "we finished somewhat ahead on our season in spite of the stock market crash."[45]

The Depression that ensued was to destroy any hope that Carl could rescue the Montauk project from financial ruin. Mortgaging and selling his devalued assets on Miami Beach in a depressed market would not be enough. In March of 1930, Carl still believed he would be able to do so. On March 21, in a letter to New York banker Clem Keys, he sounded very optimistic. "We will be entirely out of debt within the next sixty days. I won't have any spare cash, but I have other assets that you might be able to use."[46] In May of that year, when it was clear that he could not get enough money out of his Miami Beach holdings, he tried unsuccessfully to have the bank accept the holdings as assets of Montauk.[47]

With mounting financial problems and a steadily worsening drinking problem, Carl 's future did not look very bright. However, just as he frequently deserted the parties that he and Jane had held at the Shadows, preferring to go upstairs to read, in 1930 he remained a voracious reader, perhaps as solace and escape from the troubles that beset him. He ordered hundreds of books for himself and his friends, but as a good customer, he was not happy with the marketing policies of book publishers. He complained to his friend William Anderson of the *Macon Telegraph.*

> I have yours of the 10th. Of course, the only way I would accept the $5 back from the publishers would be with interest.
>
> I often wonder how some publishers and some newspaper men ever have a chance to get by. For instance, I probably buy more books as presents than any other man in the United States. I received just last week over 300 books. Three years ago I bought 3,000 copies of just one book. I have bought Tom Masson's Annual until the copy is exhausted. Yet, with all the

books I buy, I have never yet had a letter from any publisher advising me of a certain book that is good or that is new. Most publishers I buy books from are either independently rich or apparently have no sales policy whatever.

If you want to write something about these publishers, you can give them a little hell for me. We have done this much; we have organized a company for all of our purchases, so that we do buy books at a discount from the publishers. If the publishers only knew their job, they could get a list of the buyers of their best "sellers" and continue to sell new issues. Most of the publishers I have come in contact with would starve to death selling automobiles or bicycles.

Hope to see you soon.[48]

Carl was generous with the use of his library, asking friends, like Major George E. Brown of Miami Beach, to make full use of it.

I am leaving the early part of next week. Won't you come over to the house and pick up some books you would like to read this summer.

I have four or five hundred books and a certain percentage of these I am sure would be interesting to you and I would like to leave them where they would be used.[49]

Having hosted Warren Harding before his inauguration in 1921, Carl was particularly interested in a book about him. Harding had died in 1923. On April 19, 1930, he sent the following memo to his business manager, A. W. Howe.

Send the following books:
"The Strange Death of President Harding" (Guild Publishing Corp)
1 to John Oliver LaGorce National Geographic Society, Washington DC
1 to Governor James M. Cox 11 Miami Beach, Florida
1 to Arthur Brisbane, 220 South Street, New York City
1 to Albert D. Lasker 400 North Michigan Ave., Chicago, Ill.
1 to John Hertz, 231 South LaSalle Street Chicago, Illinois.
1 to V. H. Ehrhart, P. O. Box 669, Miami Beach, Florida.
3 to Carl G. Fisher, Miami Beach[50].

Carl apparently expected to have plenty of time to read in the summer of 1930. He requested an extensive list from Mr. Howe.

Send the following books to me at Montauk.

Behind the Monocle	J.S. Fletche	Doubleday
The Lighted Lantern	John Lebar	D. Appleton
Devil Drums	Clements Ripley	Brewer & Warren
It's Still Boloney	Joseph F. Fishman	Doubleday
Open House in Flanders	La Grange	Stokes
Jefferson Davis	Allen Tate	
The Memoirs of the Comte de Gramont		
Green Ice	Raoul Whitfield	Knopf
The Woman in the Shadow	Louis J. Vance	Lippincott
Science Remaking the World	Caldwell & Slosson	Doubleday
A Book of Operas	Krehbiel	Doubleday
Edge of the Jungle	William Beebe	
Cleopatra	Claude Ferval	
Francois Villon	D. B. Wyndham Lewis	
Zola and His Time	Mathew Josephson	
Haunch, Paunch and Jowl	Samuel Ornitz	
The Outline of History	H. G. Wells	
The Story of Philosophy	Will Durant	
The New Book of Etiquette	Lillian Eichler	
Bird Neighbors	Neltje Blanchan	
Now it Can be Told	Philip Gibbs	
Adventures of an African Slaver	Brantz Mayer	
Six Years in the Malay Jungle	Carveth Wells	
The Saga of Billy the Kid	Walter Noble Burns	
Famous Trials of History	Brikenhead	
The Conquest of Fear	Basil King	
Nature's Garden	Neltje Blanchan	
Beggars of Life	Jim Tulley	
A Laugh a Day Keeps the Doctors Away	Irvin Cobb	
Murder for Profit	WilliamBolitho	
Psychoanalysis and Love	Andre Tridon	
Creative Chemistry	Edwin E. Slosson	
Gentlemen Johnny Burgoyne	F. J. Huddleston	
The Fruit of the Family Tree	Wiggam	
The Doctor Looks at Love and Life	Joseph Collins	
The Red Knight of Germany	Floyd Gibbons	
Rasputin, The Holy Devil	Rene Fulop-Miller	
The Great American Bandwagon	Charles Merz	
The Son of Man; The Story of Jesus	Emil Ludwig	
Shanty Irish	Jim Tully	
Trader Horn	Horn-Lewis[51]	

Even this list was not enough. Carl continued to send requests to Mr. Howe.

Send me at Montauk the following books, also the books on the enclosed lists.

The Cruise of Kron Prince Wilhelm, by Luckner
My Friendship with Roosevelt, by Wister
The World's Fastest Rider, by Major Taylor (This is published in Indianapolis and may not be in the regular stores. It is an autobiography of a colored bicycle rider.)
The Strange Death of President Harding.[52]

In August, Carl had apparently acquired a taste for John R. Oliver.

Send at once to me at Montauk.
   "Fear"
   "Victim and Victor"   [all] by John R. Oliver
   "Four Square"[53]

Clements Ripley became another author whose books Carl wanted to read.

Send to me at Montauk:
"Dust and Sun" by Clements Ripley. (Brewer & Warren)
I have "Devil's Drums" by Ripley. Get any other books he has written other than these two.
"The Pig is Fat" by Lawrance Maynard
Please have these sent out as promptly as possible.[54]

Two books that Carl ordered in November of 1930 had a particular reference to his life. One, *Al Capone, The Biography of a Self-Made Man,* was of certain interest because Miami Beach had not seen the last of Capone. Another was Frank Buck's *Bring 'Em Back Alive.*[55]

Carl wrote Rube Goldberg, recommending *Bring 'Em Back Alive,* a few weeks later. He had found in it a situation similar to his own.

There is just one more book I want you to read, which I don't believe you have read, and that is entitled "Bring 'Em Back Alive" by Frank Buck.
Particularly I want to call your attention to the feeding of the king cobra, which is about the way I feel, that, "I am being

swallowed up by general circumstances".

Hope to see you down soon.[56]

In that spring of 1930, Miami Beach saw the return of Al Capone. After ten months in prison, with two months off for good behavior, Al Capone came back to his estate on Palm Island. Even before his return, there was a concerted effort to keep him out or have him arrested immediately. Capone had been released on March 16, but he had gone first to Chicago. Florida Governor Doyle E. Carlton, thinking that Capone was coming directly to Florida, sent the state's 67 county sheriffs the following telegram:

IT IS REPORTED THAT AL CAPONE IS ON HIS WAY TO FLORIDA. ARREST IF HE COMES YOUR WAY AND ESCORT TO STATE BORDER WITH INSTRUCTIONS NOT TO RETURN. HE CANNOT REMAIN IN FLORIDA. IF YOU NEED ADDITIONAL ASSISTANCE CALL ME.[57]

This telegram, according to Capone biographer Robert J. Schoenberg, was "orchestrated" by Carl, at the "instigation"[58] of Dan Mahoney, son-in-law of James Cox. Cox's newspaper, the *Miami Daily News,* had begun to crusade against Capone in front-page editorials even before he was released. "The decency of the community is now asserting itself [in the] form of a movement to drive Capone out of here, if he should come.... [He] should be escorted to the county line and told plainly that the compass points north."[59] Another editorial said a "generation or two ago a man guilty of crime and regarded as guilty by the appraising sense of the community — even though he might have been acquitted — would have been hanged to the first tree."[60] The *News* referred to him as "Scarface Al Capone, alias A. Acosta, alias Al Brown, the notorious beer and brothel baron of Chicago."[61]

Dan Mahoney was delighted with the Governor's stand against Capone. He wrote Carl on March 20.

I have been looking over the Miami papers very carefully and have been noticing with a great deal of pleasure the blast that the Governor is directing at the gamblers and racketeers in Miami. If the community as a whole responds as it should to the efforts of our paper we should, in a very short while, be able to clear Miami and Miami beach of this undersirable [sic] element. I need not dwell at length in telling you what would happen to the Beach if these people were allowed to continue. You probably realize that better than I do. I suppose John and the Beach police are cooperating one hundred percent. If not, grab him by the neck and give him a sock for me. The news bulletins of yesterday stated that Governor Carlton has issued an order to the county sheriffs in Florida to arrest Capone on sight and move him out of the state. Drastic action of this kind is a sure cure for all the bad babies.[62]

The Board of Governors of the Miami Beach Chamber of Commerce sent Governor Carlton a congratulatory telegram on March 27, saying that they were going "on record as commending Honorable Doyle E. Carlton Governor in his efforts to relieve the state of Florida of one Alphonse Capone."[63] Carl had telegraphed Carlton the day before, and the Governor thanked him for the news that "the best element of Miami Beach endorsed my action with reference to Al Capone. I wish to say that this is very encouraging."[64]

James Cox credited Carl with Capone's brother Albert being sentenced to jail for vagrancy.

THE EXPRESSED DECENCY AND COURAGE OF MIAMI-BEACH [sic] THROUGH YOUR POLICE JUDGE THIS MORN-ING... IS THE MOST EPOCHAL EVENT SINCE YOU DECLARED WAR ON THE MOSQUITOES AND THE SWAMPS SEVENTEEN YEARS AGO STOP IT MAY TAKE TIME TO GET THE OLD SKIP-PER GOING BUT HE IS HELL WHEN HE GETS A GOING[65]

Capone was not deterred by the Governor's telegram or by a raid on his Palm Island home. "All that fuss about keep-ing him out was all politics — and a newspaper trying to sell papers."[66] Capone had hired two Miami lawyers to protect his interests: Vincent C. Giblen and J. Fritz Gordon. In re-sponse to the Governor's telegram, the lawyers sent their own to him, asking

BY WHAT AUTHORITY OF LAW YOU OR THE SHERIFFS OF THE STATE MAY SEIZE AND BANISH FROM THE STATE A CITIZEN OF THE UNITED STATES WHO IS NOT CHARGED WITH ANY CRIME?[67]

Halstead L. Ritter, a federal judge in Florida, found that the Governor had no authority to issue the order, rendering the Governor's order meaningless.[68]

The Florida campaign continued, even though southern Florida was already rife with gambling and bootlegging. Schoenberg noted why the desire to rid Florida of Capone was not mere hypocrisy or a desire to keep the illegal business to themselves: "In all of Miami's local vice and corruption there lurked no hint of racketeering or extortion, no bombs or wholesale beatings (except by the police). That was it: homegrown corruption was consensual and lacked all sense of menace. Its practitioners operated without evident capacity for, or easy recourse to, violence."[69]

The March 20 raid on Capone's Palm Island estate was based on a warrant that the sheriff's department had issued in a search for Ray Nugent, who had jumped bail on a second degree murder charge. Several months earlier, when Miami police had picked up Nugent on a speeding charge, he gave the Palm Island estate as his address. Nugent was not there, but illegal liquor was. The raid resulted in caretaker Frank Newton and Al's brother John being charged with possession and vagrancy. The end result was a $500 fine for Newton, who said that all of the liquor belonged to him.[70]

Capone himself arrived on Easter Sunday, April 20. On April 22, a suit was filed by N. Vernon Hawthorne, Dade County's state attorney, to padlock Capone's estate for being a nuisance, "a place frequented by common gamblers.. habitual loafers, idle and disorderly persons..."[71] The suit claimed that the house was "kept and maintained as a harbor for criminals, crooks, gangsters, racketeers, and fugitives from justice."[72] Consequently, it was "a menace to the safety and well-being of residents."[73]

Meanwhile, a photograph taken of Al Capone appeared in newspapers throughout the country. The caption read: "Spends his first day fishing from the deck of his house boat." James Cox in Ohio cut out the picture and enclosed it in a letter to Carl:

This is the kind of publicity this bum is getting in Miami (from The World Rotogravure section). Please show it to John Levi and Renshaw. I don't send this to you in any facetious spirit — the thing is simply sickening.[74]

Until the matter was settled in court, Capone enjoyed himself, fishing and visiting Cuba. He was picked up a few times by Miami police, as Miami's director of public safety ordered the police chief to arrest Capone whenever he set foot in the city of Miami. Capone's lawyers readily got him off, although Capone and his friends had to spend one night in jail because it was too late for his lawyer to get a judge to issue writs of habeas corpus.[75]

Circuit Judge Paul D. Barns presided over the hearing concerning padlocking Capone's home on May 16. Carl was the only witness to testify before the hearing was adjourned for weeks for the judge to consider motions.

Carl had delayed leaving for Montauk in order to testify. On May 13, he wrote to his Uncle, Victor Ehrhart of Pittsburgh.

I am still staying on a few days because I don't want to run out on the Capone suit. They think perhaps they could take my deposition but the other side does not want a deposition; they want to delay as much as they can until I leave town. We are having quite a stormy time down here with the various interests on just how to get rid of Capone, but the sentiment is growing very much every day to get rid of him but at the same time to do it legally, if possible.[76]

The *Indianapolis Star* covered the hearing and Carl's testimony.

CAPONE ASSAILED BY CARL FISHER
Gangster's Residence Cuts Realty Values,
Capitalist Tells Florida Judge.

MIAMI, Fla. May 16 — (AP)-Testimony of Carl G. Fisher, former Indianapolis capitalist and now widely known real estate operator, that decreased property values and a reign of fear among Miami Beach citizens had resulted from presence in the community of Alphonse Capone, was introduced today into a hearing...

355

FAR FROM THE RACKET, SCARFACE AL CAPONE, generally credited with the title of Chicago gang czar, returns to his palatial winter quarters in Miami and spends his first day fishing from the deck of his houseboat. (International News)

Capone Watches Witness

Capone and his wife, named as co-defendant in the petition, attended the hearing. The Chicago gang lord gazed fixedly at Fisher throughout the latter's testimony. The record was filled with objections by Vincent C. Giblin, attorney for Capone, to questions asked by Hawthorne in an attempt to show that the presence of Capone had had a disturbing effect on residents of the wealthy winter colony.

Firestone Mentioned

Fisher testified that at least one hundred residents of Miami Beach had held fifteen meetings in an attempt to find some way by which the gangster's home could be closed. He mentioned Harvey S. Firestone, capitalist, as one concerned about Capone's presence on Palm island, and said he could name many others.

The real estate operator said his information concerning Capone and other men whom he described gangsters, living at

Al Capone was constantly harassed by public officials and newspapers. (MN; HASF)

Capone's home, came through newspaper reports and police reports.[77]

Vincent Giblin questioned Carl, described as "unfazed"[78] by Capone's steady stare. Asked whether it was he who had ordered the Miami Beach police force to station police outside the Palm Island home, Carl replied: "No sir, it wasn't my order or request; it was my suggestion."[79] He testified that property values had declined and protest meetings had been held because of Capone's presence. Carl denied that he had any gambling interests or had any financial interests in any place serving illegal liquor. When asked to name Miami Beach residents who were intimidated by Capone's living in Miami Beach, Carl named Mrs. Earl Kiser and Harvey Firestone.[80]

Carl's Uncle Vic had followed the news about the hearing and wrote Carl on May 21: "I also notice in the news that Capone stared at you for five long minutes trying to get you disconcerted. I hope you were wise enough to turn that bum eye of yours at him."[81]

The hearing adjourned until June 10. Meanwhile, Carl, who had returned to Montauk, directed Michael J. Glenn, in charge of security at his hotels, to investigate to see what evidence he could get on Capone.

The Miami police continued to arrest Capone. After the fourth arrest, Giblin "advised him not to go along except under compulsion."[82] The police left. Capone's lawyers proceeded to charge Miami's mayor, Commissioner John Knight, Sam McCreary and Jim Cox with conspiracy. The charges were dismissed at a hearing, but Justice of the Peace Warren L. Newcomb threatened to arrest the police if "they bothered Capone while under subpoena as a prosecution witness."[83] The practice of arresting Capone on sight was dropped. Capone tried to win public sentiment by inviting his 11-year-old son's classmates to a party and inviting 50 adults to a banquet.[84]

In Montauk on May 27, Carl wrote Glenn about some beer that he had ordered from Tom Harbin in April but which he had never received. He wanted Glenn to check into the matter, fearing "there was some sort of set up that might cause trouble...." He instructed Glenn not to leave any of the beer at his home. Carl expressed his concern at the end of the letter: "You will have to handle it rather carefully so we will not get in a jam. I am afraid with the Capone situation as it is, we might get into a tough hole. Take it up with Harbin and see what you can do."[85] Carl also called about the matter the next day.

On May 29, Glenn wrote back, saying he had been in contact with the parties concerned and was disposing of the beer.

He also told Carl that Capone reportedly had driven through Miami Beach at night more than once. Glenn was pessimistic about the local authorities being able to deal with Capone.

> As I have previously mentioned, I do not believe this thing can be handled by the local courts, as Capone seems to have too much money for the local authorities. I understand he has been paying for protection to somebody in Miami as well as Miami Beach. Am investigating this, and hope to be able to find out who it is before I leave here. Am enclosing clippings from the *Miami Daily News* and *Herald* regarding his trial before Judge Newcomb, whom I understand is on his pay roll.
>
> The only sensible solution I can see is to have a special United States District Attorney appointed to investigate Capone and his activities here. In that way all local political influence could be eliminated, and at the same time we could find out who is behind the movement to keep him here.[86]

Carl was concerned enough about the report that Capone had been seen driving around Miami Beach that he contacted John Levi to find out what he knew about it.[87] Levi confirmed that Capone had done so once or twice, but told Carl that he didn't think it was a good idea for the police to pick him up.

> ...the way I feel about it, and I am sure the Judges feel the same way, is that they are just muddying the water by picking him up before his case comes up, which is on the 10th, as every time they pick him up he is just getting a point on the authorities. It was awful publicity that went all over the United States that the Mayor, Chief of Police and one of the Councilmen had to appear before the court and put up a $1,000.00 bond for molesting Capone.[88]

Dan Mahoney also wrote Carl, indicating that Capone had driven through Miami Beach on his way to Palm Beach because "the Miami side was heavily guarded."[89]

Glenn's next report to Carl on June 6 specified instances of Capone's being involved in gambling.

> The Island Club opened this past winter January 15th under a new management, and Capone has one-fourth interest for which he paid $25,000 to the present owners. He also had a one-fourth interest in the Floridian Hotel gambling room, in which

he installed crooked gambling devices. He had two Chicago gun men stationed in this room at $40.00 a night to protect it from any outside interference. He also owns the controlling interest in the South Beach dog track, and Carters gambling house, as well as Albert Bouche's Villa Venice. He tried to muscle in at the Deauville Casino, but was refused, and after some kind of a threat, some men were brought from New York to protect Deauville from Capone's crowd.[90]

Glenn also named officials who were taking payoffs: Dan Chappel, the district representative "collector from the Sheriffs's [sic] office under the guise of attorney for his clients,"[91] and City Manager Renshaw and other Councilmen who controlled gambling house openings. According to Howard Kleinberg, author of *Miami Beach,* the accusations made by Glenn were never "substantiated,"[92] nor were any of the officials "publicly charged."[93]

Glenn gave other instances of corruption. When the Roman Pools Casino was raided and gambling materials removed, owner Frank Dineed complained he had been paying $1000 a week for protection; all materials were returned the next day. Bootlegger Ralph Kervens was

> ...highjacked of 300 cases of whiskey by the Sherrif's office...the whiskey being taken to Hialeah, stored in a barn where the bootlegger who lost it, located it and went with his own trucks and gang to recover it. While they were loading it the Hialeah police arrived and placed them all under arrest and took their liquor to the Hialeah police station where the Sheriffs office came and took 100 cases, and sold it to the Biltmore Hotel in Coral Gables. This was reported to the government and they made an investigation, but somebody bought them off.[94]

When the Capone hearing resumed on June 10, other residents testified about Capone's possession of liquor and the fear he instilled in the community. Edward Robinson, who lived on Palm Island, said, "Every time an automobile tire explodes on the causeway people wonder if a gang war hasn't started." [95] Some residents were embarrassed on the stand by confrontations concerning their own wrongdoing. Thomas Pancoast admitted that there were slot machines in the Paricoast Hotel. Roddey Burdine admitted drinking champagne with Capone.[96]

Judge Burns found for Capone, indicating that the evidence was not sufficient, but the community was in part to blame.

> It is apparent that the popular action to take in this matter would be to enjoin Al Capone from further occupancy of the premises... but if I am to abide by my oath, I can not do it, believing that... the only cause of annoyance is the mere presence of Al Capone upon the premises... [T]he law does not provide for the expulsion of undesirables, as such.
>
> If a community is embarrassed by the mere presence of any particular individual, it certainly does not have to deal with him either socially or in business, either of which would of course encourage his residence being continued. However, to some, the smell of money is good, regardless from whence it cometh.[97]

Capone continued to reside on Palm Island, until he was finally sent to jail by the federal government for income tax evasion in October, 1931. Capone was released in 1939. He returned the next year to Miami Beach, where he spent his remaining years until his death on January 25, 1947.

Capone had contracted syphilis years before and the final years of his life showed a progressive mental and physical deterioration. On January 21, he suffered an apoplectic stroke, and then contracted pneumonia. James Cox, publisher of the *Miami Daily News,* refused to make Capone's death a front-page story, but instead treated it as an ordinary obituary. "I don't want that son of a bitch on my front page,"[98] Cox said.

Chapter 28

Depression

THE SUMMER OF 1930 at Montauk was described by Ralph Hausrath in *The Long Island Forum* as seeming to fly in the face of the financial depression that was gripping the country.

> Of the July 4th crowd, the *[East Hampton] Star* reported that the Montauk Manor was "filled to capacity" and that many more were flocking in by yacht. Fisher's friends in the world of the priviledged [sic] were either undaunted by the times or determined to help him put on a good face and bluff it out. They continued to come to the Manor in droves, the yachts came on and on and gambling added spice to the revelries. The Long Island Rail Road ran special trains and arranged for a steamer to take fans to the America's Cup Races off Newport where one of Sir Thomas Lipton's "Shamrocks" was again trying to take the cup from the Americans.[1]

The almost-unreality of the continuing revelry at Montauk continued in 1931. Early in the year there were announcements that the U. S. Atlantic Fleet was coming for maneuvers and the Gold Cup speedboat races would be held at Montauk that summer. A horse show, a visit by the Navy dirigible *Los Angeles* and perhaps even by the *U. S. Constitution* would be other events that season. Aviators Wiley Post and Harold Gatty stopped over at Montauk after setting an around-the-world record.[2]

The arrival of the 35-boat scouting force of the U. S. Atlantic Fleet sparked some controversy, particularly because

Carl's friend, Representative Fred Britten of Illinois, Chairman of the House Naval Affairs Committee, was a guest at Montauk Manor and owned stock in the Montauk Beach Development Corporation. According to the *New York Times*, it was Representative Britten who had "suggested" the visit to the Chief of Naval Operations.[3] The fleet usually spent the summer at Newport, Rhode island. "...some newspapers such as... saw in it the distinct possibility of political logrolling to advertise the Carl Fisher development,"[4] wrote Hausrath. The force stayed for one week, the sailors mostly staying aboard ship. Shortly after, thousands came to see the Gold Cup Races. The winner, Victor Kliesrath, was a member of the Montauk Yacht Club, entitling the club to host the races at Montauk in 1932. Montauk Manor closed on September 14.[5]

For all of the activity and tourists during the summer, Montauk still had a small year-round population: only 350 voters were registered for the 1931 election. Although the tourists were still coming to Montauk, there were not enough to save Carl from his financial troubles. Two weeks after Montauk Manor closed, Carl wrote to the Long Island State Park Commission, offering to sell his holdings at a loss. There was no sale.[6]

Carl wrote to Representative Britten the following February, indicating the precarious financial situation of his Montauk holdings, as well as the slow season in Miami Beach.

His letter indicates that Britten had been using his influence in Carl's behalf.

> I hope you have more success in patching your political fences than I have in holding up my financial fences.
>
> By this time you have had copies of our Brief on the harbor, and sooner or later of course this job must be done for the general benefit of this part of the country, and at such time as it is done, the affairs of the Penn Terminal will work out O.K.
>
> ...I was in hopes you and Alma could run down, as there are some points I wanted to talk to you about regarding Montauk. Its [sic] a certainty that we cannot meet our bonds in May, and our season is so bad here that we are a million dollars short in receipts that we had every reason in the world to expect. It may be a good plan for you to seriously consider being ap-

pointed Receiver for the Company in May, if it can be so arranged, at least I would like to talk to you about it, and I hope you will have a chance to fly down for a few days.

...I am sending you a deed for a lot on Alton Road. I know you have had a good many expenses in looking after some of my various calls on your time. At the present time this lot is not in great demand, but it will some day be valuable. Two lots have been sold this year on Alton Road for $6,000, but the demand generally, all over the property has been slow, and when and as you can, I will exchange this lot with you for anything on the Island that looks more desirable, and of the same general value.

A great deal depends on some action in Congress for deep water situation here, and I will appreciate any specific advice you can give me to help get some immediate action. We need deep water here, if there is any place in the United States that needs it. We have the entire city, and county officials now with us in this plan, and all we need is the rest of the representatives of the United States Government, Including yourself.[7]

The Montauk Beach Development Corporation did go into temporary receivership on May 6, 1932. Britten was not appointed as a receiver. Instead, on May 26, 1932, Federal Judge Robert A. Inch in Brooklyn appointed William H. Robbins of Bay Shore and Chris Carroll of Brooklyn as permanent receivers. The assets of the corporation were estimated as worth about $9,000,000 with liabilities of $6,000,000.[8] The corporation went through a series of reorganizations in the 1930's, with Carl remaining on the Board of Directors.

Carl wrote the news to his Uncle Vic on April 30, 1932. He also had plans for a new venture in building.

We turned the Montauk Development Corporation over to the bond holders yesterday in a very friendly and equitable manner. It was through [sic] best to do this in order to protect the stockholders and the company, as per a letter which will be mailed to all stockholders on Monday.

I have been trying to get in touch with a real official of the Jones & Laughlin Steel Corporation in Pittsburg [sic], but want to locate a steel company that makes a specialty of angle iron and small $2^1/_2$" or 3" channel irons. We have a prospective order for one hundred houses at Montauk and perhaps the same will go through at Miami Beach. At least we are not spending a great deal of money in preparing our plans, but we are in hopes that we can get, at the present time, quotations on steel that will more than allow these houses to compete with wood.

I will be glad to show you one of these houses when you come up, as we are going to build one right here in the yard.[9]

Montauk Manor was open the summer of 1932; celebrities came. Thousands viewed the Gold Cup Race. But when the season was over, Suffolk County sold 3,760 acres that fall for taxes, bringing in $13,431.77. In February of 1933, the Bankers Trust Company foreclosed on a debt of almost $3,000,000.[10]

Carl continued to spend summers at Montauk and winters at Miami Beach. Besides the construction efforts that were mentioned in his letter to Uncle Vic, he had made other attempts at new business. In the late 1920's, he actively tried to sell the Aerocar, a vacation trailer whose suspension was supposed to be a real advancement, to the major car companies. Carl wrote J. G. Vincent of the Packard Motor Car Company on August 3, 1928, explaining some aspects of the Aerocar's construction.

I hope you will have a chance to drop in when you are down, and see this trailer, particularly to have a ride in it. It is not the looks of the trailer that counts, It is the way it rides. I am sending you a picture of the trailer hooked to a Hudson light runabout. This is the second model made. The third, fourth and fifth are coming through. The next model will be attached to a Hudson coupe. The following model will have the roof of the trailer extended to the tractor so that the completed job will look like one job instead of two.

The three point suspension is the big feature of the trailer. The third point in the trailer is hung in an airplane wheel in the tractor and this wheel absorbs all shocks through the rubber tire on the wheel. It is rather difficult for me to give you an explanation, but the entire hitch-up is simple with no mechanics of any kind.

The trailer is built with airplane construction with airplane wires for stiffening and holding the sides, floor and the roof. The complete trailer only weighs 1700 pounds.[11]

In September of 1928, Frank Seiberling of the Seiberling Rubber Company in Akron, Ohio, wrote Carl after a demonstration of the Aerocar, saying "...am well convinced you are on a good lead."[12] Seiberling thought the coupler needed improvement and offered to have his engineers work on it at his own expense. Seiberling noted that the market for the Aerocar was "limited,"[13] naming such uses as touring and school buses.

Seiberling's company would also profit if the project were a success: "This effort will doubtless cost us several thousand dollars, but, as stated, we are willing to do the work without expense to you, taking our chances on the success of your project and our being able to furnish you rubber connections when you are in commercial operation."[14]

Carl replied on September 12.

> I have yours of the 10th and I am indeed glad you are impressed with the Aerocar. There does not seem to be very much we can improve on at this time in the coupling for light jobs such as you saw, but our engineers are going ahead as fast as they can and I had hoped that your engineers could work out a plan for heavier couplings for light railroad cars up to, say, 10,000 pounds.
>
> ...we have a new car coming through and I will try to get the blue print of same at that time. I believe the future of this coupling will warrant your assisting in its development.[15]

On September 2, 1928, Carl wrote R. A. Havey, vice president of the Mack International Motor Company in New York City, about the Aerocar, telling him that they would have different classes, from a light body weighing 900 pounds to school buses.

> Then we will have a specially designed car that will be a complete road boudoir and open car with bridge-tables, revolving seats, toilet and all the little things that go with a high grade touring car... Such a car will probably sell with the tractor for something around $8,000.
>
> We are going to use three 'Aerocars' at once at Montauk in connection with our hotel. We are going to offer all the buses we have at Miami Beach at twenty-five cents on the dollar to get rid of them and replace with these cars.

Mr. Arthur Brisbane was in the Aerocar the other day. He wants one immediately for a traveling office where he can carry two secretaries and dictate and have room enough to go over his other papers he wants with him. He made the statement that it was the nicest thing he had ever ridden in in road transportation and that he wanted a car as quickly as could be delivered. We are getting out a model now which we think will save him having folding typewriter tables and a lot of stuff that he will want.

I think that considering you already have a large tractor outfit, you might be interested in the large type of sleeping car and large passenger car for up to as many as 36 passengers.[16]

R. A. Haver was less enthusiastic. "We all have been thinking a great deal about the trailer operation we rode in a month ago at Port Washington. We still have no definite idea what we can do about it."[17]

Carl wanted to add an Isco refrigerator to the Aerocar's attractions, and was trying to get Charles Kettering to determine what battery and equipment would be necessary. In September of 1928 he was not ready for "general demonstrations" of the Aerocar; he wanted it "more completed and more thoroughly dressed up...."

Carl also planned to use a special Aerocar to present to the President of Cuba.

I have promised as a present to the President of Cuba one of these Aerocars and we will have to fix him up one with a lot of gold paint and feathers and an interior layout that will knock all those rich Cuban Spaniards for a loop.

The Cuban government sent their polo players and their horses and a band of 180 musicians, sword swallowers, dancers, and about four carloads of champaign [sic] and Baccardi Rum over to Miami Beach to call on us a few years ago. Between their musicians with their snaky dance music and the Baccardi rum and the champaign, they almost put Miami Beach on the bum. They then gave me a pure Arabian horse that has jumped right square from under some of the best riders in the United States; so that while I feel I am not returning their courtesy in actual dollars and cents I will be giving him a very practical outfit that will not stir up another revolution in Cuba.[18]

Instead of selling stock in the project, Carl invited individuals, such as Walter F. Chrysler — friends of his who were manufacturers, engineers, or salesmen — to join him. Carl did not intend to build the Aerocar himself, but instead planned to have the holding company license the manufacturers of the cars and the tractors. He also wanted "to limit the body builders' sales to those manufacturers who will distribute the Aerocar in conjunction with their tow cars and who pay a lump sum of $1,000 for the contract and an agreement to turn over to the Aerocar Corporation patents on improvements, all to the end that they may be a co-operative effort in the development of the idea."

Carl continued to promote the project into 1930, writing Roy Chapin of the Hudson Motor Company on November 28 about an Aerocar bus that he and Glenn Curtiss had been working on before Curtiss' death. Carl claimed that there was a "demand for hundreds of thousands of light buses...."[19] The six-wheel bus seated 27 people, getting 11.5 miles per gallon. The city of Miami was using the buses on a 30-day trial. "Not only as a bus does the new outfit appeal, but it is the most complete and elaborate road coach imaginable. With some refinements, you could turn out a road coach that would make a Rolls Roice [sic] disappear from competition." Carl enclosed a photograph that demonstrated that his bus could "turn in a narrow street where no other bus ever seen could make the turn." Carl also commented that there would be "splendid profits as compared with the close figures you are selling at today."[20]

On December 24, Carl wrote again to Chapin, telling him that the week before he had sent an Aerocar to Washington to transport Congressman Britten and his wife to Miami Beach. Carl also informed Chapin that he had driven a six-cylinder Hudson more than 32,000 miles, the entire time pulling an Aerocar. He also pushed the bus again. "I know that you can't help being interested in the bus matter. The outfit can be built and sold against any competition in the field, and easily out-perform anything I have seen."[21]

Potential markets and performance for the trailer and

the bus seemed to amount to little in the face of the Depression. Travel trailers eventually were built, with refrigerators and other accessories, but they were not going to rebuild Carl's fortune in the 1930s.

To add to Carl's troubles in the fall of 1930, Margaret fell ill and stayed in New York while Carl went on to Miami Beach. It was "the same old goiter trouble," he wrote Jess C. Andrews. "It is getting to be much more serious and I have been quite worried."[22] Carl was upset before he left for Florida, as Margaret had moved to the St. Regis Hotel in New York City for treatment. He blamed her doctor, Scott Edwards, for her move, which, he wrote her on September 27, "annoys me continuously." Carl told her that:

Scott Edwards will never let you get well as long as he can get a nickle [sic] out of you. I am consulting my lawyer and notifying Scott Edwards that I will not be responsible for any physicians debts; also I am consulting with my lawyer on what we can do to avoid a scandall [sic] and get you out of his hands. In most things you are unusually bright but in this particular case you seem to be very, very dumb. The tactics we find used by Edwards are almost illegal. He has lied to you repeatedly and to me.[23]

He gave her a choice of leaving with him that Monday when he went to visit her or to stay, in which case he would go ahead with his lawyer.

...as soon as Scott Edwards finds you will not pay him five hundred dollars a week, you will also learn you have no doctor; then you will be compelled to get another doctor.

You have no idea how much thought and worry I have had over this subject; in fact, so much that I am very anxious now to leave for the South after Monday and forget the entire situation as much as I can; except that I don't want you to feel that I am running away from you, but I do put it up to you fairly — if you are so bull headed to imagine that Dr. Edwards is the only doctor who can do you any good, then I am satisfied I have done everything in the world I can for you and you can stay with Dr. Edwards.[24]

Carl informed her that he would have his yacht ready at the 52nd Street dock with two doctors from Johns Hopkins if she were willing to see them. "Otherwise I am finished and leaving for the South and shutting up the house here just as quickly as it can be done. My love to you dear, and you must immediately make a decision that will influence both you and myself for the rest of our lives."[25]

Margaret stayed at the St. Regis. Carl went to Florida. On October 22, a letter to her was much friendlier.

> We got back from the fishing trip in great shape. It was really very smooth and lovely. I pulled a couple of very fast ones on Jack and Ed Romfh — in fact, Jack left here blushing to his ears. He will probably tell you all about it. He and Esther are coming down in about ten days to stay some time. Jack has not been very well.
>
> Your tom cats are causing a lot of trouble, also the poll parrot. I have tied a little bell on his tail and he shakes his tail, and hauls for Galloway at the same time. Will phone you tonight if our phone is working.
>
> The grounds look beautiful. I am building a sixty-five foot tower on the edge of the house next to the old organ room with a small elevator so you can go up and sit on top of the tower and look over the sea to Bimini. It is a small job and will have it finished in ten days.
>
> I found my old high wheel here when I arrived and I am going to take it out the first of the week and ride it. Many people here never have seen a high bicycle and I expect I will have a lot of fun. Think I will be able to play tennis tomorrow.
>
> Best regards, dear, and will try and telephone tonight.[26]

Margaret was still in New York when Carl wrote her on November 3, indicating that things were quiet at Miami Beach. "Life is not very exciting here, as we play bridge almost every evening and nothing much else to do. Almost everybody around the place is on the water wagon. You will be surprised when I tell you that all the guests in the house put together since we arrived, have not used a quart of Scotch. We got a good case of tropical beer which seems to fill the bill."[27]

Carl also seemed far more conciliatory about Dr. Edwards. "I wish you would tell me what arrangements, if any, you have made with Scott Edwards regarding your bills. I think you should have some understanding, and if you will let me know, I will be prepared to take care of them."[28]

In addition to paying Margaret's bills, Carl was helping relatives who were having a hard time of it during the Depression. His Uncle Amos Fisher (author's grandfather), to whom Carl had given some land in 1924,[29] had lost his farm in 1930. Another uncle, John Fisher from Greenfield, Ohio, had received $100 in June with which he was able to pay for his car. He sent Carl some potatoes and told Carl how to plant them.

> The potatoes are called the White Michigan. They are a fine potato. Sure, now, Carl, I plant them potatoes the 20th of June. I plowed close and deep the first and second time; that keeps the ground loose for the young potatoes to grow when it rains the ground will hold a lot of moisture and will not get hard. A potato wants soft ground to get big.[30]

Carl's reply sounded facetious: "We have taken careful note of your remarks about how to plant the potatoes and we are going to plant a few. I bought a new hoe for Margaret and she is out about half the time hoeing the garden."[31]

Uncle John wrote a letter of thanks for another $100 Carl sent him in August during a drought.

> Say, Carl, I can't thank you too much for your kind help. I was so glad when I went to the mail box and saw a long envelope from Montauk. I went home and opened the envelop [sic] and saw there was a check for $100, say, say, you don't know how glad I was and what I said about you to your Aunt Kate for your kind gift. We want to go to town the 9th for our groceries and get your check cashed.... There has been, Amos said, so much dry hot weather that the farmers won't have a half crop... We have the dryest summer here I have seen for 20 years, so hot and dry every day.[32]

Uncle John wrote again on September 12. "There are a lot of farms breaking up, some can't pay out, too high living. Well, Carl, I am trying to do the best I can for everything we buy is so high."[33] Uncle John was 79 in 1930.

Uncle Amos and Aunt Maude had wintered in Florida, staying until June 1. Carl had regularly sent them money there. After Uncle Amos wrote to him about returning to Ohio, Carl replied: "I don't believe I would go back for several days yet. Tell Aunt Maude in order to accustom herself to a change in climate, she should take deep breaths."[34] Uncle Amos was 68 and wanted to buy a farm "...so we could have chickens and our good sausage that we once had and I would have something to do and the time would not drag as long as it does. I am not satisfied of lazing around. It is not my nature to do so. I know several small farms for sale."[35]

Carl, in financial straits, wrote Amos on August 30. "I think it would be much better to find a ten or twelve acre

(F.F.A.)

Amos M. Fisher and Carl G. Fisher in their later years.

place that you can rent. I am certainly in no position at the present time to buy any farms. I am very hard pressed for cash myself and will be for another year."[36]

When Amos finally found a farm, Carl sent him a check and a letter.

I have yours of the 22. I am enclosing a check for $25.00.

Am glad you found a farm. I don't know just what you need with a six room house, but perhaps you do need it. At any rate, I am glad you will be out in the country, where you can get plenty of fresh air, raise a few chickens, etc.

Merry Christmas and Happy New Year![37]

In May of the following year, Carl arranged for more permanent help for Amos in a memo to Paul Kunschik: " Please arrange, until further notice, to send a check for $25.00, the first of each month to Amos Fisher, Leesburg, Ohio."[38]

Both uncles were grateful for Carl's help during the Depression. In November of 1930, Uncle Amos had a walnut table made for Carl from a tree cut down on the farm 35 years before.[39] Uncle John promised to send Carl something when he was at Montauk.[40] Both uncles sent news as well as their thanks when they received checks. Uncle Amos in Chillicothe, Ohio, in July, 1930, wrote: "Business is very dull here. Factory has closed. Farmers are in bad shape. No crops this year to speak of on the account of dry weather. No rain but one since the 26 of March.... Highland County Bank closed up last week. One at Sabania and one at Good Hope. Maybe one or two in Chillicothe will close up. "[41]

It was from his Uncle Amos that Carl acquired his fondness for the name "Rowdy." Uncle Amos sent Carl a newspaper article about his prized horse that was sold in 1902.

"Rowdy" Came Home

Last January, Amos Fisher sold his 12 year old Wilkes gelding, "Rowdy," to Luther Cooper of Spargursville, a small town 30 miles distance on the D. T. & I. railway. Last Wednesday morning "Rowdy" escaped from his owner's stable and started for his old home south-west of this place. Although the horse had never been over the road since the night he was taken away, he covered the distance between Spargursville and Amos

373

Fisher's barn — 30 Miles — in one hour and forty-five minutes. This certainly illustrates the great instinct of a horse, as well as his fleetness in covering the distance in the record time as stated.[42]

Although Carl was able to help family members in 1930, he had to turn down requests from others. On March 14, he replied to Mrs. Keyes Winter of New York City, who had asked him to contribute to a hospital: "In the past few years I have donated to a lot of hospitals and other funds in Long Island, and during 1929 and 1930 it has been necessary to borrow money to take care of our own obligations, so I am in no position to make a donation at this time."[43]

From his early days in Indianapolis, Carl had a history of generosity not just to his family, but to friends and institutions he thought worthy. There was the yacht that Carl gave to Pete Chase; the $10,000 ring to his favorite fishing guide.[44] He had provided so generously for Jane that even though he went bankrupt, she was still comfortable during the Depression. In 1928 Carl contributed $10,000 to a fund drive conducted by Sergeant Alvin York, World War I hero, for a school in his native Tennessee. When a black women's college burned in the South, Carl wired to them: "Rebuild college at my expense."[45]

Carl did not forget the kindness of those who had helped him get a start. George Erland took a chance on Carl and helped him establish himself in the bicycle business. Carl gave the deed to the first house finished at Montauk to Erland. Erland refused. "You don't owe me anything, Carl!" Carl told him, "I owe you everything I have in this world."[46]

Before leaving Indianapolis, Carl had been generous to his community, contributing $10,000 worth of Union Carbide and Carbon stock to the Young Men's Christian Association War Fund in November of 1917. However, he wanted them to get as much value from his contribution as possible. He valued the stock at $60 per share, and was concerned that they wanted to sell it immediately.

> Stocks are hammering down now on all sides, and the immediate sale of this ten thousand dollars worth would only mean that much more of a downward trend to Union Carbide & Car-

bon Corporation Stock. I will be very glad to give you this stock with the idea that it cannot be sold or placed on the market for less than a year — and in doing this, I am satisfied in my own mind at least that the stock in less than a year will net your company considerably more than the value at which I am turning it over to you.[47]

The stock was given the following year, with the agreement it would not be sold for less than $70 per share.[48]

In October of 1920, Carl wrote to Frank D. Stalnaker of the Indiana National Bank in Indiana about providing "a place for colored women and colored children of this town to be properly taken care of."

I had a talk today with Mrs. Ellinwood and I am very anxious to help, in some manner, provide a place for colored women and colored children of this town to be properly taken care of. It is a job that the city and citizens together could combine on, make a thoroughly first class place that would be properly managed, and large enough to furnish several branches of assistance.

I have noticed recently that the old work-house is vacant. This is a very large and substantial building that could be really worked into a wonderful Community Wellfare [sic] House and particularly for the colored people as it is in about the proper location. Do you happen to know whether this building could be secured for this purpose, and do you think it would be possible to got the co-operation of the city and a substantial number of business men to complete the job?[49]

A letter written on May 31, 1927, from John Bankett of the *Indianapolis World,* a weekly newspaper, read: "Thank you again for your contribution to the colored Y.W.C.A."[50]

William Galloway's daughter Karlena appealed to Carl in April of 1926 for a scholarship. "You were very liberal to the small school in Louisville, Ky; a scholarship of about one-fifth that amount would enable me to study several years in New York. My ability lies directly in two fields; physical training and aesthetic dancing; and art."[51] Karlena was a student at Tuskegee Normal in Alabama, and even with her job of being in charge of aesthetic dancing could not afford summer school.

Carl responded in a letter to Karlena, "I enclose you a check for $200, which will give you a lift on your education."[52]

Karlena was very grateful for Carl's help, as she wrote in June of 1926.

> I hope that you will not assume that my delay meant any lack of gratitude! Your letter was forwarded to me in Indianapolis; I cannot adequately explain how thankful I was to receive it. You have made it possible for me to attend a Physical Education School, this summer. This will enable me to qualify for a larger field.[53]

Money was not as important to Carl as the principles behind its use. This attitude was illustrated by an incident that occurred in Florida, when Carl leased Soldier Cay from the government. On the cay he built a house and dock at a cost of $25,000. When the government put the Cay up for auction, Carl was outbid. The government gave him permission to remove his house and dock; the new owner offered him $3,000. Carl did not remove his property; he went to the cay and blew it up instead.[54]

Chapter 29

Final Years

THERE WOULD BE no more high-profile projects for Carl Fisher. The 1930's would only intensify his financial, marital, and drinking problems. Thanks to his financial connections with the prudent family of John Collins, he would never be penniless, but there was no fortune to leave to posterity, or even a project bearing his name. He had chosen to promote the Lincoln Highway, the Indianapolis Speedway, Miami Beach, and Montauk, rather than himself.

As far back as 1919, *Motor Boating* magazine had tried to publish an article on Carl and his participation in motor boating. Associate Editor Harwood Koppel appealed to Carl's secretary, Ann Rossiter (mistakenly believing that "A. A. Rossiter" was a male), for help in this regard.

> MoToR BoatinG [sic] is particularly anxious to publish a personality sketch on the life and more particularly that part of the life of Mr. Carl Fisher which has to do with his yachting in general and motor boating in particular. We are aware of Mr. Fisher's modesty in this connection, and know that it would be almost next to impossible to get him to write this story for us or even to furnish us with the necessary details so that we might have it written in this office. It is to you, therefore, that we appeal for assistance in our dire extremity.
>
> Will you not be good enough to write for us this sketch of Mr. Fisher of say 2,000 or 2,500 words and forward it at your

earliest possible convenience along with a late photograph preferably one in more or less yachting togs.

Mr. Fisher's importance in the motor boating world is second to none, and we really believe that the motor boat lovers of the country will be stimulated and inspired with further efforts in developing the sport by learning all that one man can do and has done in furthering motor boating.

Assuring you of our very thorough appreciation of whatever you may do for us in this matter, we are with all best wishes, and with very kindest regards,[1]

Ann Rossiter sent the letter on to Fred Wellman, as indicated by a handwritten note on the top of Koppel's letter: "FW PL. SEE ME AAR." On July 3, 1919, Wellman sent an article to Koppel, with the following letter.

Miss Rossiter referred to me your letter of June 27th asking for a biographical sketch of Mr. Fisher, and I have endeavored to meet your requirements in the manuscript enclosed. I am also sending you a number of photographs under separate cover, with the request that you take good care of them and return them promptly, as they are from Mr. Fisher's private collection.

I found it rather difficult to condense Mr. Fisher's intensely varied and interesting career within the 2,500 compass that you outlined, and you will find that my story runs 500 to 750 words over that figure. You are at liberty to do any cutting that you like, of course, to meet your space requirements, selecting those portions that are of greatest interest to you.

Permit me to state that this article was prepared without consulting Mr. Fisher, as he would have put his foot down on an attempt to give him publicity, and that I would prefer it if no mention were made of me in this connection, as I am in his employ. Once this article is in print, I don't think he will have any objection to it, however.

Kindly send me a copy of your issue in which this article appears, and if there is anything further that you want at any time, do not hesitate to call on me.[2]

Carl remained opposed to publication of biographical information about himself. In 1933, George Derby, managing editor of the *National Cyclopedia of American Biography*, made a second request for biographical material.

Receiving no reply to our recent letter, I write to repeat our request for information to complete a biography of yourself for this Cyclopedia. You may have thought it unnecessary to respond because of possible accounts already published. The National Cyclopedia, however, fulfills historical functions in no way duplicated by other reference works and the data we particularly need have not been found elsewhere.

What a person has done or is doing in his profession or particular line of activity, is really the most important part of his life story and those details are being stressed in this Cyclopedia. Therefore, won't you kindly send us the information under paragraph ten of the questionnaire sent in my previous letter, with full details.[3]

The Cyclopedia was still trying to obtain the information seven years later, after Carl's death. Margaret, his widow, had been more cooperative than Carl. John Dickson was now managing editor.

Thank you very much for the courtesies extended to Mr. Fisher, of our editorial staff, who reports checking with you the outline biography of your husband, the late Carl G. Fisher, as prepared for The National Cyclopedia of American Biography. At Mr. Fisher's request we are enclosing the manuscript of the article for your further correction and amplification, and we trust you will return this at your early convenience.

We are very pleased that you are considering the question of a portrait to accompany this biography of Mr. Fisher, and enclose a brochure describing this feature, which is one of the most outstanding and interesting of the Cyclopedia.

The Cyclopedia is a national and permanent work of reference whose purpose is to supply the world with authentic information on American achievement in every line of activity and in the fifty years of its existence the distribution of its published volumes has been world wide. There is no other work of its kind which so thoroughly covers the entire field of American history and is considered by the librarians as the most comprehensive reference work available. There could be no more satisfactory or permanent memorial than a portrait of Mr. Fisher accompanying his biography in The National Cyclopedia of American Biography, which will always be the first place consulted by those seeking information about his career.

We hope you will consider this favorably and decide upon

the halftone portrait costing $130.00, and is placed in the column with the text. Payment may be made at your convenience, or, if you prefer, in small monthly installments.

When you return the biography we hope you will also let us have your husband's best photograph and your authorization to proceed with the work on the engraving.

Your interest and cooperation are very much appreciated.[4]

For whatever reason, Margaret never completed the process, and Carl's biography did not appear in the Cyclopedia.

Just as Carl had little or no interest in submitting biographical information about himself for publication, he had little interest in the genealogy of the Fisher family. Two separate attempts were made to encourage him to help in completing a genealogy. The first was by Betty Carter of Washington, D.C., who had written Carl in July. Carl's secretary wrote a response.

I am enclosing herewith the data which you sent in your letter of July 8th.

Mr. Fisher has decided not to pursue this matter further at the present time, and wishes me to thank you for your interest in same.[5]

Betty Carter, who had been out of town, made another appeal in August.

On my return to Washington I requested my sister who attends to all my correspondence to forward you a duplicate of the first statement I sent you regarding the Fisher line which she failed to do. I had resumed the search and had hoped to complete it in a month or two. I was quite disappointed when returning after a few days absence to find your letters. If it is due to the neglect of forwarding the statement which I now inclose, I hope that you will allow me to conclude the search.[6]

Dr. William G. Alexander fared no better in October of 1925.

I spent this morning in Newberry Library looking over the old family records. I wish you would send to me any information which you may have regarding the Fisher family — all that either of your father's brothers can give you. I find that the Fisher families are apparently of about three distinct groups, and if I could only locate the group in which you belong it will help greatly in the handling of this.

If your father's brother whom I met in Indianapolis this summer could be reached I think he might give you some information which would help us in locating this proper genealogy. With this information at my disposal I believe I can help things out with you.[7]

Carl knew Dr. Alexander, but was not more cooperative.

I have so much other business right now, that I can't think much about this "jinnyology" proposition. I will leave it up to you who have nothing else to do, except cut out appendixes.[8]

In 1932, Carl had more important concerns than genealogy. He began to try to sell off personal property in order to raise money. One valuable painting that he owned was "Battle of the Forty-Fives" by Charles Russell. On February 18, 1932, Carl wrote to R. F. Garland in Tulsa, Oklahoma, offering to sell the painting but using the title "Smoke of the Forty-Five."

I am as hard up as the devil for cash! We are having a very poor season here, and not making any sales. Do you know somebody among your friends who will buy 'SMOKE OF THE FORTY-FIVE'? You would do me a favor if you would dig around and find me a buyer.

I also have a marvellous copy of a Remington, the title of which is "SELECTING A POLO PONY."

I want to sell it, and will take $1500.00 for it. I refused $15,000 for the original, and when I thought I was very rich, I presented it to the Detroit Athletic Club. The duplicate, however, is a better picture than the original and has been so stated by a lot of experts.[9]

No buyer was found. Later Carl wrote to a Chicago art dealer about the painting. Mrs. J. W. Young had requested a photograph of the painting, but had not received one. She wrote Carl on May 6, 1936, informing him that she had sold an "important" painting by Russell very quickly, and had eight other persons who were interested in it "...which is a good indication that if I had eight more Russells, there is a strong possibility that I could have sold one to each one of these gentlemen."[10] She wanted all of the information about the painting, including a photograph.

Carl replied on May 13, saying he had given a previous letter to his wife "who probably overlooked the subject of sending you the photograph...."[11] He was referring to a May 6 letter to Margaret. Mrs. Young received the photograph, but never was able to persuade the Fishers to set a price. On August 30, 1938, she finally wrote to Fred Humpage, Carl's friend and business associate, to see if he could help her.[12]

Carl replied on September 20, setting a price of $6,000, giving her a ten per cent commission. "The picture appeals to horsemen, or men from the Middle West, or men who like this type of picture. I wish I could afford to keep it,"[13] Carl wrote.

On December 15, 1932, Carl wrote to Charles E. Sorensen of the Ford Motor Company. Sorensen had planned to build in Miami Beach, but Carl thought this could be an opportunity to sell his home. He enumerated the various features of the home he had built: 900 feet of water front; a $35,000 swimming pool; a tower with an elevator; a $30,000 pipe organ; a sitting room at the top of the tower with fireplace, a Frigidaire, and bathroom; six servants' rooms; a four-car garage. Altogether, Carl had paid $300,000; he was willing to sell for $185,000, but asked Sorensen to keep the price confidential.[14]

In April of 1933, Carl assured banker Clem Keyes in New York City that "...we are making every effort to dispose of any assets that we can dispose of at even reasonable prices."[15] The *Shadow K* was priced at $33,000 to the "only real buyer that appeared this season." It was not yet sold. His house, for which he considered even $200,000 a "sacrifice price," he would sell for $130,000. He thought he could sell the covered tennis courts, costing $1,000 a year to maintain, for $25,000 to H. E. Talbot for a convention center.[16]

Carl complained about Miami Beach taxes in a letter to J. N. Lummus, Jr., on April 10, 1933:

> Some of the most valuable pictures in the house have been sold, and as I explained to you a part of the furniture is over

twenty years old, being shipped and originally from Indianapolis. The rugs in the house are the principal item of value. You know the depreciation in yachts.

I am very frank to tell you if you will give me $50,000 for the furniture and the "K" you can have them, and I will be glad to make a deal with you.[17]

Carl could no longer afford to give much assistance to his relatives. On March 27, 1933, Carl sent money to his Uncle Newt, A. N. Fisher of Houston, Texas. "I am enclosing you herewith check for $20.00 which is all I can spare at the present time. Will send you additional amounts from time to time, as and when I am able to do so."[18] Carl wrote a memo to Fred Humpage to send his uncle a $20 check on the first of every month "until further notice."[19]

He received a letter in March, 1934, from A. E. Stark of Houston, informing him that Uncle Newt was seriously ill and had asked him to notify Carl. Stark also asked if he could contribute to the nurse, "as she is very much underpaid."[20] A postscript to the letter indicated that Stark had since been notified of A. N. Fisher's death.

Carl could do little more than send money for the burial.

I forwarded $100.00 for the burial of Mr. A. N. Fisher. It seems as though his two sons could not help him and at the present time it was not possible for me to do any more than I did.

I have the other relatives to look after and my own finances have been very much tied up. It seems that most of my relatives are old, and all of them in trouble at once.

I cannot do anything now for the nurse you refer to, but might be able to do something in the fall or spring — a little something to help her along.[21]

Carl could not avoid bankruptcy. In 1934, the Carl G. Fisher Company went into bankruptcy, with Carl declaring personal bankruptcy in 1935. Carl still had some income from the Bay Shore Company. At first he received $50,000 in salary, but as the Depression deepened, it decreased to $10,000. He maintained his office in the Bay Shore Company, continuing to go there regularly until the end of his life.[22]

His financial condition adversely affected his drinking. "Carl began drinking more and more heavily, beer by the case in the long lovely afternoons at home, and at night, reading in bed beneath the portraits of Lincoln and Napoleon, a can of peanuts on one side and a bottle of Scotch on the other. By morning, both would be gone,"[23] Polly Redford wrote.

In a letter to a friend, Claude Mercer, Carl wrote of his situation.

> Your letter of October 1st is received and I am glad to hear from you and to know you are getting along as well as you are.
>
> As to the depression, do you know of anyone it did not leave an imprint on? I myself lost about twenty-five million, but am still able to eat, up to this evening.[24]

Carl had marital as well as financial problems. His womanizing had not ceased with his marriage — both Carl and Margaret had been unfaithful.[25] On August 3, 1935, he sent her a particularly scathing letter. He warned her about some financial contract she was planning that he thought was a big mistake.

> You are no more fit to carry on a deal than is a dead cat — against the people you are dealing with. Take this or leave it and from now on cut me out and row your own canoe and we will split. You go your way and I will go mine
>
> ...I would like ½ of the furniture and my office stuff and then we will split. Dont [sic] think I am sore but I am tired of being a dray horse — Now if you have some one so damn smart — to give you advice — lets split and divide up 50/50 and call it a day: I will start from scratch and you can start with a good lead — after Sept 1st I am through....
>
> I move out of here [Montauk] on the 10th of Oct — or before and I want a divorce as soon and as easy as possible. No noise — No publicity.
>
> Its [sic] lonesome as hell to work and furnish the cash for such an existance [sic]. If you don't care neither do I.[26]

Carl also noted that Margaret was "well fixed for life if you have any brains." He had made arrangements to provide for her in a pre-nuptial agreement. He asked her to make a decision before November 1, and ended the letter: "Yours — Love, Skip. "[27]

The two separated. Margaret remained in New York when Carl returned to Miami Beach. He had lost his house there and moved with his faithful servant and friend, William Galloway, to a small house on 51st Street. Before long, Carl could not afford to pay Galloway; he owed him $2,600. According to Jane, Carl fired Galloway, using the excuse that Galloway had paid too much for watermelon. Later, he repaid the back wages in bonds.[28]

Carl had regarded Galloway's services so highly that he had written to Galloway in 1920 to ask him to leave his family in Indianapolis and come to Miami Beach, offering a substantial salary that would enable Galloway to save money as well as support his family.

Since we have come down here we have had several people in the house trying to fit in and run the place, but none with satisfactory results. The man and wife we brought could not and would not do — and it was necessary to let them go right away. They were only here two or three days. The housekeeper we brought down is a nervous sort of a woman without the ability to direct, so we have let her go. We have found one very good colored boy who has had lots of experience. He is very good and very willing. We also have a fine maid — Victoria is a

Carl Fisher (in white overalls) stands with his friends. (HASF)

peach. We have a cook and a butler coming Monday and I believe that this cook is Swiss and that he will be alright.

However, I have enough work here and will have for the next five or six months to use you on the job to good advantage, particularly in making drinks and doing the buying of vegetables, meats, etc. When Wyckoff gets here he will furnish us with all of our meats, our ice, and water. In a short time we have our own gardens. If you come down, I will give you a salary here of $200 a month so that you can send $100 a month to your family while you are here — and this same salary will carry thru next year at Indianapolis.

But in paying you this salary I want to make an agreement with you that you will put at least $50 or $60 in the Bank each month and not invest it in the enameling business or in another business, for I am afraid that you cannot give enough time to the business to watch it properly — and I think in the long run you would be better off with this money accumulating and drawing interest. You will then be saving and sure of your investment — and could make your investments in property instead of businesses. At almost any time and without warning a thousand things can come up to wreck a small business, particularly if you are not in position to be in the job and to attend to it yourself. I have thought over the matter considerably and I think this is the best thing for you to do — it will give you an assured income and a saving account.

On receipt of this letter, wire me.[29]

Three years later, Galloway was concerned about being so far away from his family. Carl had sold his house in Indianapolis, where Galloway's family lived. Working for Carl meant being away from his family the entire year, either in Miami Beach or Long Island. Carl understood Galloway's dilemma.

When Mrs. Fisher gets ready to shut up the house, I think you might as well take a good vacation in Indianapolis, as you have had a hard summer.

I don't blame you a bit for feeling that it is a long way from New York, and possibly it might not be the best thing for you to move down there. If you decide it would be best to stay in Indianapolis, I will give you one thousand dollars a year.... just for old times sake. I am enclosing here within check for one thousand dollars. However, I want it distinctly understood that you are not to invest any of this money in business or in an investment of any kind....... you are certainly the original easy mark when it comes to "gold brick" articles.

Drop me a line once in a while, and let me know what you have in mind and what is on your mind.

Don't say anything to the folks that I have sent you this check.[30]

Galloway was very appreciative of Carl's thoughtfulness.

Dear Mr. Fisher

I received your letter. Also the check Tuesday. I cannot tell you how I felt when I saw the check, for it filled my heart, but I can only say in letter, that I thank you from my heart, also for the consideration you have shown me for at least 20 years. I will take the vacation you have given me, after closing up the house. I will write you again soon after I go back to Indianapolis. Again thanking you for the letter and that wonderful Thanksgiving.

I remain yours truly
        Galloway
P.S. No more investments for me. You hit the key note.[31]

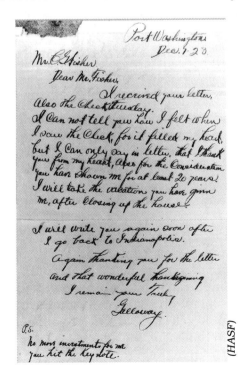

(HASF)

When the Galloways celebrated their twenty-fifth wedding anniversary on October 4, 1926, at their home on Edgemont Avenue in Indianapolis, they invited Carl to the celebration.[32]

After Carl was forced to fire Galloway because of his financial straits, the two remained good friends, but this was to be a permanent separation of friends of many-years standing. Carl showed the high regard he had for Galloway in a letter of recommendation he had written for him, dated May 22, 1933.

To Whom It May Concern:

Mr. William Galloway has been in my employ for over twenty years as cook and butler.

He is first class in every particular, writes a splendid hand, can keep very accurate accounts, is familiar with any branch of housework.

He does not drink or smoke.

Mr. Galloway is a man of excellent character, and I can recommend him to anybody who can use his services.

He has handled moneys for years for me, and handled my entire household more satisfactorily than anyone I have ever had in my employ.[33]

Late in 1935, Carl heard that Galloway was ill. He inquired about his old friend and received the following news.

Yes, Galloway has been ill, quite ill, in the Post Graduate Hospital, New York, suffering from an absessed throat and threatened at one time with pneumonia. Fortunately he escaped the threatened pneumonia, in time recovered from the throat affliction and is now back at his duties in the McIntosh household in New York City, the family having moved to the city for winter.

Upon receipt of your note I called the Port Washington estate of the McIntosh family and fortunately got in touch with the house-keeper. She gave me the facts and I told her to tell Galloway you had heard of his illness and had written to inquire as to the facts. She said she would see Galloway that evening and would tell the Old Boy of your interest. In case you wish to drop him a line the address is Care Allan J. McIntosh, 740 Park Avenue, New York City.[34]

Even after he had been fired, Galloway visited Carl. Jane Fisher wrote, "They were more than servant and master. They had long been friends. It was impossible, as Galloway said, not to love him."[35]

Carl put the best face he could on losing his palatial home in Miami Beach. In a letter to Jane on June 3, 1935, he told her: "I wouldn't have another big house if you gave it to me. The houses that I gave Margaret have turned out to be lemons — nothing but expenses — cannot either rent or sell them nothing but work and worry with big houses."[36]

He did require household help. In a letter to Margaret on June 9, 1936, he mentioned that he needed someone to drive and also to take care of the insulin.[37] On September 23, he wrote and told her that he had hired a "bright colored boy who reminds me a good deal of Galloway.... he has had experience in giving insulin."[38] Business was also apparently picking up at Miami Beach: "quite a little property is being sold and leased."[39]

Carl spent the summer of 1937 in Miami Beach, but not happily. "I never expect to spend another summer here, as long as I have the ability to walk out of town," he wrote Margaret on September 15. "I want some of my furniture up there, to furnish up a small cottage."[40] He was also concerned about what belongings he still had. He was particularly concerned about his brother's Toledo sword that was missing. It was worth about $500; Carl was willing to offer a $25 reward for its return.

There are only a few Toledo blades in existence. The last I saw it, it was standing in the corner of the settee. Of course somebody has stolen it because it couldn't fly out the window; and this is liable to happen to your better small pieces, unless you store them. This is one reason I want to get my books out of the house and down here where I can keep an eye on them myself. I have some very rare books that I enjoy reading, and I can pick you out a few for your library down here.

House burglaries have increased about 25% in the last few years.

But I have lost all confidence in your being able to get anything down here to me that I want. Now that the sword is gone, if this other stuff isn't shipped next week I want you to leave the keys with Ringwood and he can go up and get them and see that they are shipped. This could have been done long ago.[41]

Carl worked on some promotions during his last years, one for a store mannequin that rolled its eyes and another for non-skid tires, but both efforts were futile. His last project was an attempt to build a fishing club on Key Largo. He purchased waterfront property on the key at a cost of thousands of dollars. The dues would be a modest $25 a year. "Carl G. Fisher dreamed of a club where the man of moderate means could enjoy the pleasures and privileges of the wealthy,"[42] according to C. W. Chase, Jr., secretary-treasurer of the Caribbean Club.

By 1938, it was evident that Carl's continued excessive drinking and refusal to follow doctors' orders had left him in precarious health. He worried about his doctors' bills. On January 7, 1938, he complained to Dr. E. B. Maxwell about his bill.

> I have your bill and to say that I got a shock at the size of this bill puts it mildly. It would have been cheaper by far to die.
>
> Quite seriously, I want to tell you that the bill, in my estimation, is out of reason. I do not know how many trips you made, but I do know that you stopped in once in awhile towards the last two or three days. Well, anyway, I think the bill is out of all reason, and it was not necessary to ask Dr. Walters to come in (who also handed me a bill for $25.00, for saying 'Hello').[43]

Both Margaret and Jane were concerned about Carl's health. On June 28, Jane wrote from New York, telling Carl that she thought he might come north because Montauk had been reorganized.

> I did so hope that you would come up to Johns Hopkins and see what they could do for you — they have such marvelous Doctors there and have made such wonderful advancement in treatment of stubborn cases. I am afraid the Doctors down there are not doing very much for you. I asked Mr. Purchase to go and see you and tell you about the man he knows in John Hopkins who does such wonderful things with cases of your

kind. He tells me that he has seen you but that you think all is being done for you that can be — surely not — do go and try them. PLEASE.[44]

Jane added that she wanted him to give Emma, his house-keeper, her regards..."and tell her she had better take care of you — or else."[45]

Carl's reply on July 8 assured her that he had "the best of advice." He also wrote: "There isn't anything you can do for the liver. If it was any other part of the body, they might do something to help. Thanks just the same for your interest."[46]

On August 11, Carl wrote to Dr. Frank B. Vorhis, who was on vacation in Wisconsin. Carl had been retaining fluid that had to be drained regularly.

> I should have written you several days ago, but I really have not been feeling any too hot for a marathon, and I have had a lot of other work to do.
>
> I was tapped last Friday — 20½ pounds. The new opening sealed up immediately, but she 'busted' open on me day before yesterday — almost blew my suspenders off. It has sealed up again this morning and I am feeling pretty fair. I am up to 180 pounds again.
>
> From Friday evening until Thursday noon, I gained 10 pounds — just about the same as last time.
>
> I have been down to Key Largo and things are coming along slowly there. The dock should be finished Saturday of this week. I am leaving here Saturday for Key Largo.[47]

Even with his medical problems, Carl retained a sense of humor. He told the doctor: "I bought me an almanac and I am reading the stars now, to see if there is any connection with my star and these frequent interruptions. I haven't found anything yet in the almanac that is worth while. It seems to be a continuous advertisement for some sort of pills."[48]

Fred Humpage wrote Margaret on August 18 with a not very encouraging view of Carl's health. "He seems more languid and more willing to remain home and in bed... I asked [the doctors] particularly if they could give me any idea as to what, if anything, might happen and when. Their answer is there is no way to determine..."[49]

Carl was so concerned about his health in November that he wrote LaFayette Page in New York City. Page's brother was a veterinarian.

> What veterinary colleges is your brother associated with? I understand he makes a specialty of livers and lights, and general internals. My liver don't work.
>
> The proper diagnosis of my case is that I feel fine and am in very good health — all blood tests, urine tests, etc., are right up to the standard, but liquids I cannot handle, and every six days I have to go to the hospital and they take out between 18 and 19 pounds.
>
> This only takes an hour and I feel very well after the job is over.
>
> Is there anything new in treatment of liver troubles of this kind? Of course, you don't know anything about livers, but you can ask your brother.
>
> Why don't you run down and I will talk to you about some insurance — on livers only. I have no property to insure.[50]

Page did ask his brother, who diagnosed Carl from the letter but had no positive outlook.

> I judge from Carl Fisher's letter that he has developed a case of alcoholic cirrhosis of the liver. Unfortunately, there is little or nothing that can be done under the circumstances if the liver is irreparably damaged. I would consider it a mistake to seriously try to change his present life. He might as well be happy even though the disease will inevitably progress. The only other alternative would be to put him in a hospital on the assumption that the diagnosis was not correct and give him a long course of treatment, the outcome of which would be highly uncertain.[51]

Carl still went to his office, which was next to that of Irving Collins at the Bay Shore Company. He did have his bad days. "I used to be able to make dreams come true," he told his friend Walter Myers, an Indianapolis attorney who had moved to Florida. "I can't do it anymore. I'm only a beggar now. The end can't be far away."

His old friend Rose Weiss stopped by to see Carl and the two commiserated over their financial losses. "Rosie, I wish I was the Carl Fisher of yesteryear," he told her. "You wouldn't have to worry about losing your building."[52]

Carl spent some of his time writing long letters to old friends. "I am getting up a little den and lining the walls with pictures of old-timers — which saves wallpaper," he wrote to Barney Oldfield on November 7, 1938. "I would like to have one of your old time pictures, with a cigar. If you have new front false teeth that are shiny, you can darken them up a bit, or I will have the picture touched up so that it would look natural."[53]

He wrote Oldfield, then living in California, some details of his treatment that December.

I am not doing so well these days — I mean my health. I go up to the hospital every seven days and they bore a hole in me with a fence augur and let out about 18 pounds of excess fluid. The operation isn't that painful and I am out and flying around in a couple of hours afterwards. While I don't drink liquor nowadays, I keep a little 'Mountain Dew' in a jug. I look on while my friends drink it, and I let the tears from my eyes roll into a cocktail of tomato juice and Listerine, diluted with some Vitamin B's in capsules, and wild goose liver oil. If you get cirrhosis of the liver, try this remedy. It won't do you a d — bit of good, but it is a terrible punishment.[54]

Of course, Carl had not stopped drinking. He ignored his doctors warnings and joked to Oldfield in the following letter he wrote April 25, 1939 when he said he was "trying to get my liver copper-plated so that I can continue to enjoy life and still have a drink occasionally."[55]

Sometimes he turned to the radio for a diversion, but he found it frustrating. "It seems that every time I turn on the radio some gigolo is trying to sell corn medicine or second-hand automobiles or cathartics; or I tune in on a bunch of swing music or liver-lip crooners. Of course, if I stick to it long enough, I get into some good stuff eventually. My secretary just informs me that she heard you and it was very good, but of course her opinion don't amount to a d — when it comes to the great American peooplee."[56]

Faithful friends like Jack LaGorce, John Levi, and Father Barry still visited. Father Barry brought Carl *The Testi-*

mony of Christ. Carl told him he would join the church and read religious books if Barry would pray that he could have a liver like Galloway's. "I can't pray the Lord to give you a new liver," Father Barry answered. "He gave you a splendid one when you started out in life... you are the one that ruined it. But I can pray for you and I pray for your soul."[57]

Carl sought Father Barry's friendship; spending his healthy days with him whenever possible. Carl knew the end was near and Father Barry's presence provided him the tranquility and peacefulness he needed for his new journey ahead.

Carl and Father Barry enjoyed going to boxing matches and movies; both wept while watching the film *Boys' Town.* According to Jane, the next day Carl called and told the priest that he thought that his Key Largo Club might fail, and if it did, he intended to turn it over to St. Patrick's Church for a boys' school.[58]

He and Father Barry cooperated on another project. Helen Rich, in a column entitled "An Echo of Yesteryear — Carl Fisher" in the *Miami Herald,* wrote about its origin.

> Years ago Carl Fisher stopped on a hot dusty road in Cuba to watch some nearly nude Negro boys tugging at the rope of a huge church bell. It was the hour of the Angelus... .and Carl was so impressed with the beauty of the scene and with the chiming melody that ran through the countryside, that he decided at once that his Miami Beach must also have bells. He immediately planned for some... the best that he could find....[59]

After his return to Miami Beach, Carl ordered a set of bells from the Deagan Brothers in Chicago for the Community Church on Lincoln Road, for which he had donated the land years earlier. The church, however, never built a bell tower, and the bells were never installed.

On July 12, 1930, Carl wrote to Father Barry, telling him that he had paid $2,250 down on the bells. "I would like to donate these to the church if you can dig up the balance, and I will help you to dig it up from some of the Catholics this winter."[60]

On July 28, 1930 Father Barry replied to Carl's letter.

Beggars are choosers in this case. Let me say that constantly you embarrass me with your kindness and generosity. Will you accept a wee prayer to show my gratitude?

I was going to write you a detailed account of my financial status but why should you submit to that? At present I have not the place ready for the Carillon but I assure you that I shall attend to it with reasonable speed. You know we have built under the greatest difficulty and stress a church, a rectory, a convent. Now we are building school, since 1927, and for each we have had to contract a debt. Your thought and mine is to have a campanile on the property which will grace the Beach and which will be pleasing to all — the only and proper place for the Carillon.

Now I know the Deagan people and if you will refer them to me I think you will be relieved of further worry about the whole matter.

I regret that so far I have been unable to take a holiday. I fear that I must remain here to see that my school is built and ready in time.

Take good care of yourself. Be assured of my affection and my prayers. To Mrs. Fisher say the same.[61]

A letter from Carl to Father Barry indicated that he was determined to obtain the bells. "I will steal it out of my sock," he wrote the priest on August 2, 1930, "and then if you really get in a hell of a hole, I will dig up another thousand, but I think we should have those bells."[62]

With hard financial times upon them, neither was able to raise the money and the project was dropped.

When Jane visited Carl in the spring of 1939, he was well aware that he had little time left. "I won't be seeing you again, Jane,"[63] she said he told her.

But when he felt well enough, Carl went to his office. On April 11, he wrote to E. S. Dallenbach at the Indianapolis Speedway.

Please send tickets for two good grand stand seats to Mr. C. W. Laidle, c/o Sears, Roebuck & Company, Biscayne Boulevard at 13th Street, Miami, Florida, and if necessary charge them to me.[64]

No words by this author can better describe the bond

which existed between individuals than their own handwritten words. On July 7, 1939, Carl received an invitation from Thomas Pancoast to a luncheon at the Pancoast Hotel on July 13 to celebrate the 19th anniversary of the Miami Beach Chamber of Commerce. "I would feel honored to have you as my guest,"[65] Pancoast wrote.

Carl replied on July 10, thanking Pancoast but declining the invitation.

> You fellows at these luncheon parties live too high for me. I am on a diet, mostly of pretzels and bird seed, and some of these I have to take with a high pressure gun; so, I couldn't possibly enjoy the luncheon and I know you wouldn't have any fun out of me — but, just the same, you all have my best wishes.[66]

Carl added a P. S. "If you are going to sneak in any young lobster (which I know is out of season), save me a piece and I will get it at the office later in the afternoon."[67]

In the interim, Carl changed his mind and decided to attend. The day after the luncheon, Thomas Pancoast wrote Carl a letter of appreciation for his coming to the luncheon.

> Of all the people who attended the Birthday luncheon yesterday at the Pancoast Hotel, I felt more honored by having you present than anyone else. I know as a rule you shy away from functions of this kind and that is why I feel so deeply appreciative of your presence.
>
> I hope you did not mind the little joke we played on you, for I know everyone present enjoyed it, and that you did not feel any bad affects [sic] from the celebration.
>
> Please accept my heartfelt appreciation, and with best wishes and kindest personal regards, I am[68]

Carl never saw the letter. On July 15, the day it arrived, he was rushed to St. Francis Hospital with a gastric hemorrhage and passed away that afternoon at 4:52 p.m. Fred Humpage, Dan Mahoney, Frank Katzentine, and Dr. Vorhis were at his side.[69]

Jane was at Sobre Mundo, her estate in the Catskills, when a newspaper reporter called her to say that Carl Fisher was dying and asked to see her. But Carl died before she was able to leave for Florida.

Margaret arrived an hour after Carl's death.

Father Barry was in Europe. In an interview with Jane Fisher published in the *Miami Beach Daily Sun* on March 22, 1964, Father Barry recalled:

> I loved Carl Fisher with no ulterior motive. He was one of the finest men I ever met. The biggest regret of my life is that I was away from Miami Beach when he died. I had been assured by the doctors that he was in no immediate danger and would probably go through the summer all right. So off I went to Europe, not expecting the sad news that was cabled me soon after I landed.[70]

Flags flew at half mast in Miami Beach to honor Carl. In his open casket at the W. H. Combs Funeral Home, Carl presented a more formal appearance than he had appeared in life, dressed in a tuxedo with a rose in his lapel and wearing his familiar horn-rimmed glasses.[71]

He was taken to the Collins Memorial Library for the service four days after his death. Services were held in front of the library, where oleander bushes and tall palms formed a natural amphitheater. The pall bearers included Barney Oldfield, William Vanderbilt, and Gar Wood.

Jack LaGorce delivered the eulogy:

> Carl Graham Fisher was but human and therefore not perfect — which made him more beloved by those who understood him. Starting from the bottom, with only his innate qualities of integrity, industry, sincerity, love of country and the unquenchable urge to build and contribute as best he knew how something to make the world a happier and better place to live, our friend's accomplishments should be an inspiration to American youth. I know he has been, and always will be to me.[72]

When Carl died, Miami was returning to its former prosperity. Even at his funeral, one newspaper reported, a construction machine could be heard pounding out a staccato beat, as though it were playing taps for the funeral.[73]

Carl's estate amounted to $52,198, according to the *Miami Herald* of March 16, 1940.

In August, Margaret wrote to my grandfather, Amos, about Carl's final resting place.

Your letter of Aug. 7 has been forwarded to me here. You asked where Carl was buried..... we tucked him away in a crypt at Woodlawn Memorial Park, out on the Tamiami Trail, just west of Miami (between Miami and Coral Gables) I had never been there before; and did not know they had such a beautiful place. All marble crypts.... everything very pretty. Before I left Miami Beach; there was a plan being talked about to have him finally rest in a private mausoleum in a park across from our old Bay Front home, the city having dedicated it to him at a special meeting of the City Council held on Monday after his death. Nothing will likely be done about this plan until later on...possibly within a year. I went by plane to Miami — my first, and, I hope, my last plane ride... arriving there about an hour after Carl had passed on. Everything had been done for him that was possible: and his doctor told me it was one of the most peaceful passings he had ever seen.[74]

Carl was cremated and the urn containing his ashes remained in Miami until January of 1943. There were talks between Margaret and the city of Miami Beach as to where Carl should be buried and who would be responsible for the cost involved. No agreement was reached and the urn was later moved to his mausoleum at Crown Hill Cemetery in Indianapolis and placed with the rest of his family on January 12, 1943.

Ironically, Carl had given up his place in his mausoleum in 1918 to Captain Robert Hammond, a British Royal Flying Corps war hero, who died in his plane at the Speedway. Captain Hammond had been invited to make a publicity flight on September 22, 1918, for the Liberty Loan-War Bond celebration being held at the Speedway and was to be met by Lt. Roy Pickett of the U.S. Air Corps. "Flying about 600 feet high and preparing to land, the plane nose dived into a tailspin and plunged to the ground."[75]

Captain Hammond was given a full military funeral, his casket draped with both British and American flags. Since Hammond's relatives were living abroad, Carl wrote to the superintendent of the Crown Hill Cemetery on September 25, 1918: "This will give you permission to open the Fisher Mausoleum and allow Flanner and Buchanan, as undertakers, to place the body of Captain Robert Hammond in upper compartment unoccupied, for an indefinite period."[76]

No one ever came forward to claim the body of Captain Robert Hammond and today he remains in Carl's spot.

On April 10, 1941, Miami Beach citizens dedicated the only memorial in America that commemorates the accomplishments of Carl Graham Fisher. The cenotaph features a bronze bust of Carl, wearing his floppy hat and smiling. The inscription reads: "Carl Graham Fisher — he carved a great city out of a jungle."

There was, in a sense, another memorial already in place. Carl had never been able to raise enough money for the bell tower to house the carillon bells, and Father Barry had promised that one day he would build the tower.

In the summer of 1938, Father Barry visited Carl one day when he was very ill. According to columnist Helen Rich,

One afternoon, just to make him feel better, Mgr. Barry brought him a drawing of the Campanile he planned to build to house the bells, and discovered that those bells had meant more to

Memorial to Carl Fisher at Alton Road and 50th street. (HASF)

Carl Fisher than anyone had ever realized...and if he was to hear them, it would be necessary to work fast. The Campanile was started and as it progressed Carl Fisher progressed with it, so that he was among the many hundreds who attended the dedication last night. Nobody saw him because he stayed in his car... and so nobody knew that Carl Fisher... that man of great vision... sat with tears streaming down his rugged cheeks when at last he heard the Angelus ring out over his own Miami Beach.[77]

Afterword

Margaret Fisher purchased Carl Fisher's 20 acre estate house in the late forties from the Montauk Beach Company after they had previously allowed the military to use it as headquarters during World War II. Margaret remarried and moved to Miami in 1956. Carl Fisher's house has remained, especially the first and second stories, relatively unchanged. This has been attributed to the quality of construction used and to the care it has been given over the years.

The Montauk Manor, a National Landmark, still maintains its characteristic charm as described in this historical brochure:

> The Manor continued to thrive in the thirties and forties attracting presidents and foreign dignitaries, movie stars and corporate executives. The community also turned to the Manor for help. In 1938 a hurricane flooded out downtown Montauk. The villagers came up to the Manor for safe refuge. In 1991 during Hurricane Bob, 4000 members of the community again took their shelter in the Montauk Manor. The Montauk Manor is so well constructed that when the Army Corps of engineers looked into demolishing it in 1941, they determined that it was virtually indestructible and would take so much dynamite it would take down the hill upon which it stands. The foundation walls alone are 4 feet thick. Another plan was developed for the Manor in 1982. A plan that would restore it to grandeur and designate it as a significant nationally historic landmark. The process required 25 million dollars in renovation and reconstruction as the Manor was converted into the condominium complex and full service resort that it is today."[78]

Jane Fisher continued to live in Miami Beach where she wrote articles entitled "I Remember When" for the local newspapers. While on a visit to New York she died of a heart attack on December 6, 1968. She was 74. At the time of her death Jane lived in a small gabled house at 3747 Sheridan Avenue in Miami Beach with her two loyal companions, "Pizza," an Italian greyhound, and "Puddy Cat," a gray cat.

The *Miami Herald* recounted numerous stories about Jane after her passing.

> When an old friend from the affluent past gave her a $7,000 gold Cadillac last spring, Jane saved up to buy the license plate and quipped: "Perhaps I'll drive it down to the Welfare Office." Jane, a gifted hostess, spoke fluent French, was highly-competitive in backgammon, and enjoyed entertaining with small dinners. "I can cook chicken a hundred different ways" she would say, "but if you want champagne, you'll have to bring it yourself."[79]

I had the opportunity to meet Jane in December of 1963 and can recall, not only our conversations, but how impressed I was with her presence.

Jane continued to correspond with my mother and me until the last few months when she was unable to type. The handwritten letters showed the result of her arthritis and revealed her disappointments that "time had all but forgotten Carl"; the same message she gave me previously many years earlier.

Although frail, Jane still managed, in her letters, to relive her vivacious spirit and appreciation for life. On December 11, 1965, she wrote to my mother:

> This is the most glorious day...bright sunshine with just a little coolness in the air which is like wine.
>
> I had such a nice experience last week... I spoke before a group of 4th, 5th and 6th graders in their auditorium...there were about 150 boys and girls. I told them stories about [when] Carl and I came to Florida and the shipwreck and then about the elephant and they all loved it.
>
> I have been getting 'Fan' mail ever since. One little girl said, 'I wish you were my teacher.' Another little boy wrote, 'Did you

know I think you are very pretty?' ...They begin young these days, don't they? They all crowded round me and asked for my autograph... I felt like a movie queen."[80]

Shortly before her death, Jane Fisher posed with a portrait done of her 40 years ago in the salad days. (J.F.F.A.)

CARL G. FISHER, MIAMI BEACH DEVELOPER, STOOD ON THE CORNER OF LINCOLN ROAD and Washington Avenue 25 years ago watching the jungle of mangrove trees being chopped down and said, "Gentlemen, Lincoln Road will become one of the most beautiful shopping streets in the world." When the last vacant lot of Lincoln Road was sold in 1937 the price paid was at the rate of $700 a foot; construction now is under way at Lincoln Road and Washington on a site purchased at the rate of $5,000 a front foot. The above Miami Beach News Bureau picture shows Lincoln Road looking west from the spot where Fisher made his prediction. In 1937 Lincoln Road store sales amounted to $9,000,000; this year, $30,000,000, with an estimated $35,000,000 for next year. (Published date unknown)(J.F.F.A.)

Notes

Chapter 1

1. Jane Fisher, *Fabulous Hoosier* (NY: Robert M. McBride and Co., 1947), p. 38.

2. Howard H. Peckham, *Indiana: A History* (NY: W. W. Norton & Co., Inc., 1978), p. 104.

3. Polly Redford, *Billion-Dollar Sandbar* (NY: E. P. Dutton and Co., Inc., 1970), p. 45.

4. Fisher, p. 37.

5. *Ibid.*

6. Redford, p. 45.

7. History of Decatur County, Indiana (B. F. Bowen and Co., n.d.)

8. Carl Fisher, Letter to John Hertz, April 21, 1933, p. 4.

9. Henry H. Bennett, *County of Ross* (Selwyn A. Brant, 1902)

10. *Ibid.*

11. *Ibid.*

12. Fisher, p. 38.

13. Redford, p. 46.

14. *Think on These Things* by J. Krishnamurti (NY: Harper & Row, 1964), p. 112:

    "You may have all the academic degrees in the world, but if you don't know yourself you are a most stupid person. To know oneself is the very purpose of all education. Without self-knowledge, merely to gather facts or take notes so that you can pass examinations is a stupid way of existence. You may be able to quote the *Bhagavad Gita,* the *Upanishads,* the *Koran,* and the *Bible,* but unless you know yourself you are like a parrot repeating words. Whereas, the moment you begin to know yourself, however little, there is already set going an extraordinary process of creativeness."

15. Redford p. 47.

16. Robert Green Ingersoll, *American Authors 1600-1900*, Stanley J. Kunitz and Howard Haycraft, ed. (NY: H. W. Wilson Co., 1938), p. 402.

17. Robert Green Ingersoll, *Dictionary of American Biography,* Dumas Malone, ed., Vol. IX (NY: Charles Scribner's Sons, 1932), p. 470.

18. Orvin Larson, "Robert Green Ingersoll," *Encyclopaedia Americana,* 1994, XV:173.

19. Redford, p. 47.

20. Fisher, p. 37.

21. Carl Fisher, Letter to W. T. Anderson, February 12, 1930.

22. Carl Fisher, Memo to A. W. Howe, July 10, 1930.

23. Fred Wellman, "Commodore Carl G. Fisher: A Biographical Sketch," n.d.

24. *Our Century 1900-1910* (Belmont, California: David B. Lake Publisher, 1989)

25. Barney Oldfield, Letter to Carl Fisher, December 20, 1938.

26. Charles Edgar Nash, *The Magic of Miami Beach* (Philadelphia: David McKay Co., 1938), p. 94.

27. Redford, p. 47.

28. James Allison, undated memo, Collection of Jerry Fisher.

29. Nash, p. 96.

30. Al Bloemker, *500 Miles To Go* (NY: Coward-McCann © 1961), p. 19.

31. *Ibid.*

32 Redford, p. 47.

Chapter 2

1. Polly Redford, *Billion-Dollar Sandbar* (NY: E. P. Dutton and Co., Inc., 1970), p. 48.

2. Al Bloemker, 500 *Miles To Go* (NY: Coward McCann © 1961), p. 18.

3. Jane Fisher, *Fabulous Hoosier* (NY: Robert M. McBride and Co., 1947), p. 217.

4. *Ibid.*, p. 45.

5. John Bartiow Martin, Indiana: *An Interpretation:* (NY: Alfred A. Knopf, 1947), pp. 77-78.

6. *Ibid.*, p. 90.

7. *Ibid.*, p. 92

8. *Ibid.*

9. *Ibid.*, p. 99.

10. Fisher, p. 42.

11. *Ibid.*

12. *Ibid.*

13. *Ibid.*, p. 43.

14. *Ibid.*, p. 45.

15. Carl Fisher, letter to Barney Oldfield, December 20, 1938.

16. Fisher, p. 44.

17. *Ibid.*

18. "Carl G. Fisher Dead at Beach," *Miami Herald,* July 16, 1939, p. 11.

Chapter 3

1. Al Bloemker, *500 Miles To Go* (NY: Coward-McCann, Inc. © 1961), p. 19,

2. John Bartlow Martin, *Indiana: An Interpretation* (NY: Alfred A. Knopf, 1947), p. 117

3. Jane Fisher, *Fabulous Hoosier* (NY: Robert M. McBride and Co. © 1947), p. 50.

4. Bloemker, p. 36.

5. Fisher, p. 50.

6. Will Rogers, *Will Rogers' Weekly Articles, Volume 11*, James Smallwood, ed. (Stillwater: Oklahoma State University Press, 1980), p. 93.

7. Polly Redford, *Billion-Dollar Sandbar* (NY: E. F. Dutton and Co., Inc., 1970), p. 54.

8. Fisher, p. 76,

9. Alastair Gordon, "Fisher's Montauk Legacy Getting a New Look." *The New York Times*, December 23, 1984.

10. Fisher, p. 53.

11. *Ibid.*, p. 59.

12. "Business Before Pleasure." *Indianapolis Star,* July 16, 1939.

13. Fisher, p. 47.

14. *Ibid.*, p. 53,

15. *Our Century, 1900-1910* (Belmont, California: David B. Lake, Publishers © 1989).

16. Fisher, pp. 30-31.

17. Bloemker, p. 20.

18. *Ibid.*, p. 2 1.

19. *Ibid.*, p. 20.

20. *The Columbian.* January, 1906.

21. Newspaper clipping, n.d. Collection of Jerry Fisher.

22. William Herschell, "Motor Speedway: Carl Fisher's First Step In Amazing Career of Making Dreams Come True." *Indianapolis News,* July 17, 1939.

23. Fisher, p. 49.

24. Sir Malcolm Campbell's *Book of Famous Motorists,* Published by Floyd Clymer, 1937 & 1944, p. 61.

25. Bloemker, p. 25.

26. *Ibid.*, p. 26.

27. *Ibid.*, p. 27.

28. *Ibid.*

29. *Ibid.*, p. 31.

30. Herschell.

31. Fisher, p. 48.

32. Fred Wellman, "Commodore Carl G. Fisher: A Biographical Sketch." n.d.

33. Redford, p. 82.

Chapter 4

1. Jane Fisher, *Fabulous Hoosier* (NY: Robert M. McBride and Co. © 1947), p. 55.

2. Al Bloemker, 500 *Miles To Go* (NY: Coward-McCann, Inc. © 1961), p. 23.

3. *Ibid.*, p. 24.

4. Fisher, p. 56.

5. Shav Glick, "Fisher Turned the Indy into the 500," *Los Angeles Times*, May 24,1991

6. Bloemker, p. 24.

7. Fisher, p. 57.

8. *Ibid.*, p. 58.

9 *Ibid.*

10. Pat Heidenreich, "The Track Founders," *The Prest-O-Lite Story.* n.d. Speedway Public Library Collection, Speedway, Indiana.

11. James Allison memo, Collection of Jerry Fisher.

12. *Ibid.*

13. Allison.

14. Bloemker, pp. 32-33

15. David S. Lake Publishers, *Our Century 1910-1920*

16. Fisher, pp. 74-75.

17. *Ibid.*, p. 75.

18. *Ibid.*

19. *Ibid.*, p. 59.

20. *Ibid.*

21. "Early Auto Industry Inspired Development of Prest-O-Lite. Newspaper article (stamped February 27, 1946). Collection of Marion County Public Library, Indianapolis, Indiana.

22. Judy Keene, "The 500's Four Founders," *Indianapolis Magazine*, May, 1978, p. 68.

23. Will Rogers, *Will Rogers' Weekly Articles*, Volume II, James Smallwood, ed. (Stillwater: Oklahoma State University Press, 1980), p. 93.

24. Carl S. Fisher, "Fifteen Thousand Feet Above Dixieland," *Indianapolis Sunday Star*, June 20, 1909.

25. Polly Redford, *Billion-Dollar Sandbar* (NY: E. F. Dutton and Co., Inc., 1970), p. 56.

26. "Balloon and Auto Sail Through Sky," *Indianapolis Star*, October 31, 1908, p. 1.

27. *Ibid.*

28. *Ibid.*

29. William Stoner Doyle, "Carl Fisher: Builder of Miami Beach," *Coronet*, April, 1949.

30. Jane Fisher, p. 51.

Chapter 5

1. John Bartlow Martin, *Indiana: An Interpretation* (NY: Alfred A. Knopf, 1947), p. 118.

2. Al Bloemker, *500 Miles To Go* (NY: Coward-McCann © 1961), p. 27.

3. *Ibid.*

4. *Ibid.*, p. 28.

5. Jane Fisher, *Fabulous Hoosier* (NY: Robert M. McBride and Co. © 1947), p. 47.

6. Carl G. Fisher, Letter to Ray C. Thompson, May, 1937.

7. Martin, p. 115.

8. Wallace S. Huffman, "Indiana Autos: Indiana's Place in Auto History," *Indiana History Bulletin* 53, No. 3, March, 1976, 35-51, as footnoted by Howard H. Peckham in *Indiana: A Bicentennial History* (NY: W. W. Norton and Co., Inc. © 1978), p. 113.

9. Bloemker, p. 29.

10. *Ibid.*, p. 30.

11. *Ibid.*, pp. 31-32.

12. *Ibid.*, p. 33.

13. *Ibid.*

14. *Ibid.*, pp. 34-35.

15. *Ibid.*, p. 35.

16. L. Spencer Riggs, "Brooklands," May, 1983, p. 1.

17. Bloemker, p. 14.

18. *Ibid.*

19. Martin, pp. 71-72.

20. Bloemker, pp. 14-15.

21. *Ibid.*, p. 39.

22. *Ibid.*

23. *Ibid.*, p. 40.

24. *Ibid.*, p. 41.

25. *Ibid.*, p. 42.

26. *Ibid.*, p. 43.

27. *Ibid.*

28. *Ibid.*, p. 45.

29. *Ibid.*, p. 46.

30. *Ibid.*

31. Fisher, p. 10.

32. *Ibid.*, p. 30.

33. Bloemker, p. 49.
34. *Ibid.*, p. 51,
35. *Ibid.*, pp. 52-53.
36. *Ibid.*, p. 55.
37. *Ibid.*, *p.* 57.
38. "Carl Fisher: Legend in Automobiles and Real Estate," *Indianapolis Star,* July 14, 1966.
39. Bloemker, p. 61.
40. *Ibid,* p. 62.
41. *Ibid.*, p. 65.
42. *Ibid.*, pp. 65-66.
43. *Ibid.*, p. 67.
44. *Ibid.*, p. 68.
45. *Ibid.*, p. 69.
46. *Ibid.*
47. *Ibid.*, p. 71.
48. *Ibid.*, p. 72.
49. *Ibid.*, p. 73.
50. *Ibid.*, p. 76.
51. *Ibid.*, p. 77.
52. *Ibid.*, p. 79.
53. *Ibid.*, p. 80.
54. Copyright © 1991 by Rich Taylor. From *Indy: 75 Years of Racing's Greatest Spectacle* by Rich Taylor. Reprinted by permission of St. Martin's Press, Incorporated.
55. Bloemker, p. 88.
56. *Ibid.*, p. 96.
57. *Ibid.*, p. 98.
58. Eddie Rickenbacker, as quoted by Joseph Floyd Clymer, *Indianapolis Race History* (Los Angeles: n.p., 1946) *p.* 2., as cited in Peckham, p. 181.
59. Peckham, p. 181.
60. *Ibid.*, p. 182.
61. *Ibid.*

L. Spencer Riggs, author of the unpublished book *Half the Flag was Black* said:

> After his defeat of heavyweight boxing champion, Jim Jeffries, on July 4, 1910, the black prizefighter, Jack John–son, bragged that he was the greatest athlete in the world, and could beat the champion of any sport at his own game.
>
> To Barney Oldfield and his manager, the legendary huckster of racing, Bill Pickens, it looked like the perfect opportunity. They could make a fast buck, while evening a score of sorts. Barney was a close friend of Jeffries.
>
> 'I'd be happy to beat Mr. Oldfield at his own game as easy as I beat Mr. Jeffries in the ring,' Johnson was quoted in the press. Johnson offered a wager of $5,000 to back up his claim.
>
> The AAA, the major league of auto racing in those days, threatened to banish Oldfield from their events if he proceeded with the match race against Johnson.
>
> Paying little heed to the AAA, Pickens rented the Sheepshead Bay mile horse track in New York, scheduling the match race for October 25, 1910. The race was a complete farce, with Oldfield making short work of Johnson. The few spectators who did attend felt cheated. They booed as Barney was carried out of the track on the shoulders of his crew.
>
> The AAA promptly slapped Oldfield with a twelve month suspension. This not only relegated Oldfield to appearing in exhibition runs and "hippo–dromed" (fixed) races with smaller purses, it took him out of the big league when he was smack in his prime. He even missed the inaugural Indianapolis 500 in 1911.
>
> Oldfield was reinstated in April, 1912 but Indianapolis Motor Speedway president, Carl G. Fisher, refused his entry. 'Maybe the AAA can forget all the rules he broke, but I can't,' Fisher bristled. 'Barney knows the rules and he broke them anyway.' Since Fisher and Oldfield had been friends since their bicycle racing days, this gives some indication of Fisher's sense of fair play and moralistic sportsmanship. A champion, in Fisher's book, never flaunted the rules. As a matter of fact, while the AAA

barred Oldfield from the Indianapolis Motor Speedway's
grounds in 1911, Jack Johnson
was Fisher's preliminary guest at
the track! Fisher did not accept
Oldfield's entry for the Memorial
Day classic until 1914.

Chapter 6

1. John Bartlow Martin, *Indiana:
An interpretation.* NY: Alfred A.
Knopf, 1947, p. 120.
2. Jane Fisher, *Fabulous Hoosier.*
NY: Robert M. McBride and Co.,
1947, p. 14.
3. Martin, p. 118.
4. Polly Redford, *Billion-Dollar
Sandbar.* NY: E. P. Dutton and Co.,
Inc., 1970, p. 52.
5. *Ibid.*
6. Fisher, p. 4.
7. *Ibid.*, p. 3.
8. *Ibid.*, pp. 3-4.
9. *Ibid.*, p. 4.
10. *Ibid.*, p. 5.
11. *Ibid.*, p. 7,
12. *Ibid.*, p. 8.
13. *Ibid.*
14. *Ibid.*, p. 11.
15. *Ibid.*
16. *Ibid.*
17. *Ibid.*, pp. 11-12.
18. *Ibid.*, p. 12.
19. *Ibid.*
20. *Indianapolis News,* October 23,
1909.
21. Fisher, *p.* 13.
22. *Ibid.*
23. *Ibid.*, p. 14.
24. *Ibid.*, pp. 15-16.
25. Martin, p. 120.
26. *Ibid.*
27. *Indianapolis Star,* October 6,
1912.
28. Martin, p. 120.
29. Redford, p. 59.
30. *Ibid.*
31. Fisher, p. 15.
32. *Ibid.*, p. 1.
33. *Ibid.*, p. 17.
34. *Ibid.*, p. 18.
35. *Ibid.*, p. 17.
36. *Ibid.*, p. 20.

37 Redford, p. 60.
38. Howard Kleinberg, *Miami Beach*
(Miami: Centennial Press, 1994),
p. 219 (footnote).
39. Fisher, p. 21.
40. *Ibid.*
41. *Ibid.*, p. 28.
42. *Ibid.*, p. 32.
43. *Ibid.*, p. 28.
44. *Ibid.*, p. 32.
45. *Ibid.*, p. 33.
46. Betty Blythe, "First Photographic
Glimpse of Carl G. Fisher's Home,"
February 2, 1913.
47. J. Patrick Mercier, "Giants in
Indiana Industry, Auto Racing, and
Land Development, Carl G. Fisher,
James A. Allison, And Frank H.
Wheeler, The Men and Their Mansions." History Honors Project,
Marian College, Spring 1975, p. 35.
48. Jane Fisher, p. 34.
49. *Ibid..* p, 35,
50. *Ibid.*
51. *Ibid.*
52. *Ibid.*, pp. 69-70.
53. *Ibid.*, p. 70.
54. Redford, pp. 52-53.

Chapter 7

1. Jane Fisher, *Fabulous Hoosier*
(NY: Robert M. McBride and Co. ©
1947), p. 77.
2. Fisher's Salary To Go to Roads,"
Indianapolis Star, October 24,
1912.
3. *Ibid.*
4. *Ibid.*
5. *Ibid.*
6. *Ibid.*
7. *Ibid.*
8. Lincoln Highway Association,
The Lincoln Highway (NY: Dodd,
Mead, and Company, 1935), p. 56.
9. *Ibid.*, p. 6.
10. *Ibid.*
11. *Our Century, 1900-1910* (Belmont, California: David S. Lake
Publishers © 1989).
12. "Fisher's Salary To Go to Roads."
13. *Ibid.*
14. *Ibid.*
15. *Ibid.*

16. *Ibid.*

17. Jane Fisher, p. 70.

18. Lincoln Highway Association, pp. 4-5.

19. Jane Fisher, p. 78.

20. Anne Jardim, *The First Henry Ford: A Study in Personality and Business Leadership* (Cambridge, Massachusetts: The Colonial Press © 1970), p. 63.

21. Lincoln Highway Association, p. 14.

22. Joe McCarthy, "The Lincoln Highway," *American Heritage,* June, 1974, p. 33.

23. Carl G. Fisher, Letter to Henry Ford, September 6, 1912. Ann Arbor. Michigan, University of Michigan Library.

24. Carl G. Fisher and James Allison, Invitation. Ann Arbor, Michigan, University of Michigan Library.

25. Lincoln Highway Association, p. 10.

26. *Ibid.,* p. 1.

27. *Ibid.,* p. 14.

28. Jane Fisher, p. 81.

29. Lincoln Highway Association, p. 12.

30. *Ibid.,* p. 12.

31. *Ibid.,* p. 13.

32. "HOS" (identity unknown), Letter to Henry Ford, September 10. 1912. Ann Arbor, Michigan, University of Michigan Library.

33. James Couzens, Letter to Carl G. Fisher, September 18, 1912. Ann Arbor, Michigan, University of Michigan Library.

34. Carl G. Fisher, Letter to President William H. Taft, September 24, 1912. Ann Arbor, Michigan, University of Michigan Library.

35. Lincoln Highway Association, pp. 14-15.

36. *Ibid.,* p. 15.

37. Carl G. Fisher, *Ocean-to-Ocean Highway Bulletin,* Number 1, September 19, 1912. Ann Arbor, Michigan, University of Michigan Library.

38. Lincoln Highway Association, p. 16.

39. *Ibid.*

40. Jardim, p. 28.

41. *Ibid.,* p. 62.

42. *Ibid.,* p. 63.

43. *Ibid.,* p. 93.

44. *Ibid.*

45. James Couzens, Letter to Carl G. Fisher, October 25, 1912. Ann Arbor, Michigan, University of-Michigan Library.

46. Carl G. Fisher, Letter to Henry Ford, November 29, 1912. Ann Arbor, Michigan, University of Michigan Library.

47. Carl G. Fisher, Letter to Henry Ford, February 7, 1913. Ann Arbor, MIchigan, University of Michigan Library.

48. Jardim, pp. 51-52.

49. *Ibid.,* p. 65.

50. E.G. Liebold, *Reminiscences,* p. 2450, as quoted in Jardim, pp. 227-228.

51. Jardim, p. 228.

52. David L. Lewis, "The Gentle Businessman," *Michigan History Magazine,* pp. 22,23

53. Lincoln Highway Association, p. 86.

54. *Ibid.,* p. 208.

55. Carl G. Fisher, Letter to Edsel Ford, September 5, 1922. Ann Arbor, Michigan, University of Michigan Library.

56. Edsel Ford, Letter to Carl G. Fisher, October 2, 1922. Ann Arbor, Michigan, University of Michigan Library.

57. David L. Lewis, *The Public Image of Henry Ford,* pp. 365-367

58. Lincoln Highway Association, p. 97.

59. *Ibid.,* p. 19

60. *Ibid.*

61. *Ibid.,* p. 20

62. *Ibid.*

63. *Ibid.,* p. 18.

64. *Ibid.*

65. *Ibid.,* p. 23.

66. *Ibid.*

67. Carl G. Fisher, Letter to Leslie

T. McCleary, quoted in *The Lincoln Highway* by The Lincoln Highway Association, p. 24.

68. Leslie T. McCleary, Letter to Carl G. Fisher, April 11, 1913. Ann Arbor, Michigan, University of Michigan Library.

69. Arthur Pardington, Letter to Carl G. Fisher, October, 1912, quoted in *The Lincoln Highway* by the Lincoln Highway Association, p. 22.

70. Henry Joy, Letter to Arthur Pardington, quoted in *The Lincoln Highway* by the Lincoln Highway Association, p. 25.

71. Lincoln Highway Association, p. 25.

72. *Ibid.*, p. 26.

73. *Ibid.*, pp. 27-28,

Chapter 8

1. Lincoln Highway Association, *The Lincoln Highway* (NY: Dodd, Mead, and Company, 1935), pp. 29-30.

2. Jane Fisher, *Fabulous Hoosier* (NY: Robert M. McBride and Co. © 1947), p. 82.

3. Lincoln Highway Association, p. 6.

4. Joe McCarthy, "The Lincoln Highway," *American Heritage*, June, 1974, pp. 35-36.

5. Lincoln Highway Association, p. 6.

6. *Ibid.*, p. 7.

7. *Ibid.*, p. 8.

8. *Ibid.*, p. 7.

9. McCarthy, p. 35.

10. Lincoln Highway Association, p. 34.

11. *Ibid.*

12. *Ibid.*

13. *Ibid.*, p. 35.

14. *Ibid.*, pp. 32 -33.

15. *Ibid.*, p. 33.

16. *Ibid.*, pp. 33-34.

17. *Ibid.*, p. 30.

18. Fisher, p. 84.

19. Lincoln Highway Association, p. 31.

20. *Ibid.*

21. *Ibid.*

22. *Ibid.*, p. 36.

23. *Ibid.*

24. Fisher, p. 55.

25. Lincoln Highway Association, p. 37.

26. *Ibid.*, p. 39.

27. *Ibid.*

28. *Ibid.*, p. 38.

29 *Ibid.*, p. 37.

30. *Ibid.*, p. 38.

31. *Ibid.*, p. 39.

32. *Ibid.*, p. 40.

33. *Ibid.*

34. Fisher, p. 86

35. *Ibid.*, p. 88.

36. Lincoln Highway Association, p. 40.

37. Fisher, p. 88.

38. *Ibid.*, p. 86,

39. Lincoln Highway Association, p. 42.

40. *Ibid.*

41. Fisher, p. 88

Chapter 9

1. Carl Fisher, Letter to Mrs. K. Grab, July 21, 1913. University of Michigan Library.

2. Lincoln Highway Association, *The Lincoln Highway* (NY: Dodd, Mead and Company, 1935), pp. 45-46.

3. *Ibid.*, *p.* 46.

4. *Ibid.*, p. 47.

5. Drake Hokanson, *The Lincoln Highway: Main Street across America* (Iowa City: University of Iowa Press © 1988), p. 12.

6. Lincoln Highway Association, p. 47.

7. *Ibid.*, p. 48.

8. *Ibid.*

9. Colonel Sidney D. Waldon, quoted in the *Lincoln Highway Association*, pp. 49 -51.

10. Lincoln Highway Association, p. 51.

11. *Ibid.*

12. *Ibid.*, p- 52.

13. *Ibid.*, p. 56.

14. *Ibid.*, p. 57.

15. *Ibid.*, p. 55.

16. *Ibid.*, pp. 58-59.

17. *Ibid.*, p. 60.

411

18. *Ibid.*, p. 61.
19. *Proclamation of Route of the Lincoln Highway.* Lincoln Highway Association, pp. 61-64.
20. Lincoln Highway Association, p. 66.
21. *Ibid.*, p. 65.
22. *Ibid.*, p. 68.
23. *Ibid* , p. 106.
24. *Ibid.*, pp. 68-69.
25. Rev. Frank G. Brainard, quoted in Hokanson, p. 14.
26. Lincoln Highway Association, p. 69.
27. *Ibid.*, p. 70.
28. *Ibid.*, p. 107.
29. *Ibid.*, p. 74.
30. *Ibid.*, p. 70.
31. *Ibid.*, p. 74.
32. *Ibid.*
33. *Ibid.*, p. 73.
34. *Ibid.*, p. 75.
35. *Ibid.*, p. 77.
36. *Ibid.*, p. 80.
37. *Ibid.*, p. 83.
38. *Ibid.*, *p.* 81.
39. *Ibid.*, pp. 78-79.
40. *Ibid.*, p. 79.
41. Hokanson, p. 18.
42. Lincoln Highway Association, pp. 125-126.
43. *Ibid.*, p. 253.
44. *Ibid.*
45. *Ibid.*, p. 133.
46. *Ibid.*, p. 127
47. *Ibid.*, p. 141.
48. *Ibid.*, p. 211.
49. *Ibid.*, p. 213.
50. *Ibid.*, *p.* 161.
51. *Ibid.*, p. 163.
52. *Ibid.*, p. 177.
53. *Ibid.*, *p.* 182.
54. *Ibid.*, p. 193.
55. *Ibid.*, p. 149.

Chapter 10

1. Lincoln Highway Association, *The Lincoln Highway* (NY: Dodd, Mead and Co., 1935), p. 45.
2. Drake Hokanson, *The Lincoln Highway: Main Street across America* (Iowa City : University of Iowa Press © 1988), p. 77.
3. Lincoln Highway Association, p. 233.
4. Carl Fisher, as quoted by the Lincoln Highway Association, p. 233.
5. Hokanson, p. 77.
6. Bob Zimmerman, *The First Army Truck Train* (Dayton, Ohio: Packard Truck Organization Newsletter, 1994).
7. Lincoln Highway Association, p. 256.
8. Hokanson, p. 13.
9. Lincoln Highway Association, pp. 110-111.
10. *Ibid.*, p. 109.
11. *Ibid.*, p. 111.
12. *Ibid.*, pp. 111-112
13. *Ibid.*, p. 84
14. *Ibid.*, p. 197.
15. Hokanson, p. 91.
16. Henry Joy, as quoted by the Lincoln Highway Association, p. 269.
17. Hokanson, p. 82.
18. *Ibid.*, pp. 91-92.
19. James L. Handley, *New York Times,* June 16, 1912, as quoted in Hokanson, p. 22.
20. Hokanson, p. 87.
21. Frederic Van De Water, as quoted in Hokanson, p. 87.
22. Lincoln Highway Association, p. 198.
23. *Ibid.*
24. *Ibid.*, p. 202.
25. *Ibid.*, p. 204.
26. *Ibid.*, p. 208.
27. *Ibid.*, p. 203.
28. *Ibid.*, pp. 208 -209.
29. Seely, Bruce E., *Building the American Highway System* (Philadelphia, Temple University Press, 1987), p. 79
30. *New York Times* editorial quoted by the Lincoln Highway Association, p. 218.
31. Henry Joy, Letter to Gael Hoag, as quoted by the Lincoln Highway Association, p. 229.
32. Lincoln Highway Association, p. 218.
33. *Ibid.*, p. 216,
34. Gael Hoag, *Lincoln Highway Forum,* as quoted by the Lincoln Highway Association, p. 217.

35. Lincoln Highway Association, p. 219.
36. *Ibid.*, p. 220.
37. *Ibid.*, p. 251.
38. *Ibid.* p. 90.
39. Henry Joy, Letter to Arthur Pardington, as quoted by the Lincoln Highway Association, pp. 87-88.
40. Lincoln Highway Association, p. 273,
41. *Ibid.*, p. 90.
42. *Ibid.*, p. 113.
43. *Ibid.*, p. 93.
44. *Ibid.*, p. 119.
45. Hokanson, p. 112.
46. Lincoln Highway Association, p. 116.
47. *Ibid.*, pp. 247-248.
48. *Ibid.*, pp. 147-148.
49. Charles Edgar Nash, *The Magic of Miami Beach* (Washington Square: David McKay Co. © 1938), p. 112.
50. Hokanson, pp. 112-113.
51. *Ibid.*, p. 135
52. *Ibid.*, p. 136.
53. The Lincoln Highway Association, National Headquarters, P. O. Box 308, Franklin Grove, Illinois 61031 (815) 456-3030

Chapter 11

1. Jane Fisher, *Fabulous Hoosier* (NY: Robert M. McBride and Co. © 1947), p. 93.
2. Howard Kleinberg, *Miami,: The Way We* Were.(Tampa: Surfside Publishing © 1989), p. 22.
3. *Ibid.*, p. 8.
4. *Ibid.*
5. Hernando d'Escalante Fontaneda, *Memoir of Don d'Escalante Fontaneda Respecting Florida*, excerpt reprinted in Kleinberg, p. 9.
6. Charles Edgar Nash, *The Magic of Miami Beach* (Philadelphia: Washington Square Press, 1935), p. 53.
7. Kleinberg, p. 14.
8. Kleinberg, p. 14.
9. *Ibid.*, p. 59.
10. Julia Tuttle to James E. Ingraham, quoted in Kleinberg, p. 31.
11. Nash, p. 78.
12. *Ibid.*, p. 81.
13. Polly Redford, *Billion-Dollar Sandbar* (NY: E.P. Dutton and Co., Inc., 1970), p. 31.
14. Nash, p. 78,
15. *Ibid.*, p. 81.
16. Mary Barr Munroe, "Pioneer Women of Dade," *The Miami Metropolis*, July 3, 1909. Reprinted in Kleinberg, p. 65.
17. Captain Charles J. Rose, quoted in ""Miami Only Indian Camping Site When Captain Arrived," *Miami Daily News*, August 13, 1933. Reprinted in Kleinberg, p. 93.
18. 'The Story of a Pioneer," quoted in Kleinberg, p. 31.
19. *Ibid.*
20. "Miami Incorporated: *Miami Metropolis*, July 31, 1896. Reprinted in Kleinberg, p. 36.
21. Editorial, *Miami Metropolis*, July 31, 1896, as quoted in Kleinberg, p. 36.
22. Nash, p. 83.
23. Redford, p. 38.
24. *Ibid.*, p. 61.
25. Fisher, p. 94.
26. Redford, p. 65.
27. Nash, p. 99.
28. Redford, p. 65.

Chapter 12

1. Nash, p. 66.
2. Howard Kleinberg, *Miami Beach* (Miami: Centennial Press © 1994), p. 21.
3. Avery Smith, quoted in "Miami Beach History Related by Pioneer," *Miami Herald*, November 25, 1926. Reprinted in Kleinberg's *Miami Beach*, p. 21.
4. Kleinberg, *Miami Beach*, p. 22.
5. Nash, pp. 7-8.
6. *Ibid.*, p. 8.
7 Kleinberg, *Miami Beach*, pp. 4-5
8. *Ibid.*, p. 6.
9. Nash, p. 67.
10. Kleinberg, *Miami Beach*, p. 7.
11. Nash, p. 69.

12. *Ibid.*, p. 74.
13. *Ibid.*
14. *Ibid.*, p. 70.
15. *Ibid.*
16. *Ibid.*, p. 71.
17. *Ibid.*
18. *Ibid.*, p. 72.
19. *Ibid.*
20. *Ibid.*, p. 73.
21. Redford, p. 26.
22. Nash. *p.* 86.
23. Redford, p. 33.
24. Kleinberg, *Miami Beach. p.* 19.
25. Nash, p. 85.
26. *Ibid.*, p. 86.
27. *Ibid.*
28. *Ibid.*
29. *Ibid.*, p. 87.
30. Kleinberg, *Miami Beach*, p. 20.
31. Nash, p. 88.
32. *Ibid.*, p. 89.
33. *Ibid.*, p. 89.
34. *Ibid.*
35. Kleinberg, *Miami Beach*, p. 25.
36. Nash, p. 92.
37. Nash, p. 91.
38. *Ibid.*
39. *Ibid.*, pp. 92-93.
40. *Ibid.*, p. 115.
41. Kleinberg, *Miami Beach*, p. 28.

Chapter 13

1. Jane Fisher, as quoted in Redford, p. 44.
2. Redford, p. 65.
3. Thomas Pancoast, as quoted in Redford, p. 65.
4. Nash, p. 102.
5. Redford, p. 69.
6. *Ibid.*
7. *J. N.* Lummus, *The Miracle of Miami Beach* (Miami: The Miami Post Publishing Co © 1944), p. 13.
8. *Ibid.*, p. 29.
9. *Ibid.*
10. *Ibid.*, p. 27.
11. *Ibid.*, p. 29.
12. *Ibid.*, p. 32.
13. *Ibid.*, p. 31.
14. *Miami Metropolis,* January 10, 1913, as quoted in *Miami* Beach by Howard Kleinberg, p. 32.
15. Kleinberg, *Miami Beach*, p. 32.

16. Lummus, pp. 32-33.
17. *Ibid.*, p. 31.
18. *Ibid.*, p. 34.
19. *Ibid.*
20. *Ibid.*, p. 37
21. *Ibid.*
22. Kleinberg, *Miami Beach*, p. 31.
23. *Ibid.*, p. 33.
24. Nash, p. 101.
25. Kleinberg, *Miami Beach*, p. 33.
26. *Ibid.*, p. 40.

Chapter 14

1. Fisher, p. 97.
2. *Ibid.*, p. 98.
3. Redford, p. 70.
4. Fisher, p. 102.
5. James Allison, as quoted in Fisher, p. 104.
6. Nash, p. 142.
7. *Ibid.*
8. *Ibid.*, p. 120.
9. Fisher, p. 100.
10. *Ibid.*, p. 130.
11. *Ibid.*, p. 131.
12. *Ibid.*, p. 132.
13. Redford, p. 61.
14. Lummus, p. 44.
15. *Ibid.*, p. 45.
16. Nash, p. 108.
17. *Ibid.*
18. Redford, p. 71.
19. Fisher, p. 102.
20. *Ibid.*
21. Kleinberg, *Miami Beach*, p. 42.
22. Redford, p. 72.
23. *Ibid.*
24. Fisher, p. 103.
25. *Ibid.*
26. *Ibid.*, p. 105.
27. Redford, p. 71.
28. Carl Fisher, as quoted in Jane Fisher's *Fabulous Hoosier*, p. 130.
29. Nash, p. 110.
30. *Ibid.*, p. 109.
31. Redford, p. 72.
32. Lummus, p. 47.
33. Nash, p. 110.
34. Fisher, p. 132.
35. Lummus, p. 47.
36. Nash, p. 110.
37. Fisher, p. 133.

Chapter 15

1. *Miami Herald,* December 10, 1913, quoted in Redford, p. 80.
2. Redford, p. 81.
3. *Ibid., p.* 80.
4. Kleinberg, *Miami Beach,* p. 47.
5. Lummus, p. 49.
6. *Ibid.,* p. 50.
7. *Ibid.*
8. *Ibid.,* p. 51.
9. *Ibid.,* p. 55.
10. Redford, p. 83.
11. Russell Pancoast, quoted in Kleinberg's *Miami Beach,* p. 46
12. Kleinberg, *Miami Beach,* p. 46.
13. Fisher, p. 107.
14. *Ibid.*
15. *Ibid.,* p. 108.
16. *Ibid.,* p. 110.
17. *Ibid., p.* 111.
18. *Ibid.,* p. 109.
19. *Ibid.,* p. 111.

Chapter 16

1. Redford, p. 91.
2. Howard Laurence Preston, *Dirt Roads to Dixie* (Knoxville: Univ. of Tennessee Press © 1991), p. 36.
3. *Ibid.,* p. 12.
4. *Ibid.,* p. 18.
5. *Ibid.,* p. 19.
6. *Ibid.,* p. 21.
7. *Ibid.,* p. 25.
8. *Ibid.,. p.* 22.
9. *Ibid.*
10. *Ibid.,* p. 19.
11. *Ibid.,* p. 71.
12. *Ibid.,* p. 24.
13. *Ibid.,* p. 12.
14. *Ibid.*
15. *Ibid.,* p. 27.
16. *Ibid.,* p. 28.
17. *Ibid.,* p. 29.
18. *Ibid.,* p. 17.
19. *Ibid.,* p. 96.
20. *Ibid.,* p. 48.
21. *Ibid.,* p. 97.
22. *Ibid.,* p. 100.
23. *Ibid.,* p. 96.
24. *Manufacturers Record,* September 25, 1913, as quoted by Preston, p. 50.
25. *Ibid.,* p. 53.
26. *Ibid.,* p. 54.
27. Ray Boomhower, 'The Hoosier Barnum," *Traces,* published by the Indiana Historical Society, Spring, 1994, p. 27.
28. *Indianapolis News* as quoted in Redford, p. 92.
29. Preston, p. 55.
30. *Ibid.,* pp. 57-58.
31. Kleinberg, *Miami Beach,* p. 47.
32. *Ibid.*
33. Redford, p. 81.
34. *Ibid.*
35. *Ibid.,* p. 90.
36. *Ibid.,* p. 88.
37. Lummus, p. 66.
38. *Ibid.,* p. 67.
39. Jane Fisher, p. 180.
40. James Whitcomb Riley, as quoted in Redford, p. 89.
41. Jane Fisher, p. 127.
42. *Ibid.,* p. 128.
43. *Ibid.*
44. *Ibid.*
45. *Ibid.,* p. 178.
46. *Ibid.,* p. 137.
47. Lummus, p. 78.
48. Redford, p. 98.
49. Lummus, p. 83.
50. Redford, p. 98.
51. "170 [thousand] Cash Price Paid Today For Miami Beach Town Property," *Miami Daily News,* April 13, 1916, as reprinted in Lummus, p. 79.
52. Lummus, p. 80.
53. Kleinberg, p. 50.
54. *Ibid.,* p. 53.
55. Redford, p. 103.
56. *Ibid.,* p. 102.
57. *Ibid.*
58. *Ibid.,* p. 103.
59. *Ibid.,* p. 106.
60. Carl Fisher, as quoted in the *Miami Herald* in Redford, *p.* 104.

Chapter 17

1. Carl G. Fisher, "A Proposal for National Defense." Indianapolis: July 1, 1915, pp. 3-4. Carl Fisher Collection, The Historical Association of Southern Florida. (Hereafter referred to as CF: HASF)

2. *Ibid.*, p. 5.
3. *Ibid.*
4. *Ibid.*
5. *Ibid.*
6. *Ibid.*, p, 8.
7. Carl G. Fisher, Letter to George Bumbaugh, March 29, 1917. CF: HASF.
8. Carl G, Fisher, Letter to George Bumbaugh, April 9, 1917. CF: HASF
9. Redford, p. 110.
10. *Ibid.*, pp. 110-111.
11. Redford, p. 111.
12. Bloemker, p. 139,
13. *Ibid.*
14. Jane Fisher, p. 114.
15. Carl Fisher to Ralph DaPalma, July 22,1919. CF: HASF
16. *Indianapolis Star,* August 6, 1919
17. *Indianapolis News,* August 20, 1919
18. Jane Fisher, p. 112.
19. Redford, p. 111.
20. *Ibid.*, p. 113.
21. Kleinberg, p. 55.
22. Jane Fisher, p. 170,
23. *Ibid.*, p. 171.
24. *Ibid.*,
25. Carl G. Fisher, Letter to Thomas Pancoast, as quoted in Redford, p. 114.
26. Jane Fisher, p. 169.
27. *Ibid.*
28. *Ibid.*, p. 173.
29. *Ibid.*, p. 176.
30. Redford, p. 116.
31. *Ibid.*, p. 115.
32. *Ibid.*, p. 116.
33. *Ibid.*, p. 124.
34. *Ibid.*, p. 115.
35. Jane Fisher, p. 157.
36. Redford, pp. 125-126.
37. Kleinberg, *Miami Beach*, p. 60.
38. Redford, p. 170.
39. Kleinberg, p. 61.
40. *Ibid.*, p. 60.

Chapter 18

1. Carl G. Fisher, Letter to Senator Warren G. Harding, December 6, 1920. CF: HASF.
2. Redford, p. 131.
3. William M. Miller, Letter to Carl G. Fisher, January 4, 1921. CF: HASF.
4. *Ibid.*
5. Carl G. Fisher, Telegram to Warren G. Harding, January 8, 1921. CF: HASF.
6. Carl G. Fisher, Telegram to William M. Miller, January 6, 1921. CF: HASF.
7. Carl G. Fisher, Letter to William M. Miller, January 7, 1921. CF: HASF.
8. William M. Miller, Telegram to Carl G. Fisher, January 5, 1921. CF: HASF.
9. John Oliver LaGorce, Letter to Carl G. Fisher, January 11, 1921. CF: HASF.
10. William M. Miller, Letter to Carl G. Fisher, January 12, 1921. CF: HASF.
11. Warren G. Harding, Letter to Carl G. Fisher, January 12, 1921. CF: HASF.
12. Carl G. Fisher, Letter to John Oliver LaGorce, January 14, 1921. CF: HASF.
13. John Oliver LaGorce, Letter to Carl G. Fisher, January 21, 1921. CF: HASF.
14. Ann Rossiter, Letter to Carl G. Fisher, January 11, 1921. CF: HASF.
15. Kleinberg, *Miami Beach*, p. 62.
16. Warren G. Harding, *Miami Metropolis,* January 31, 1921, as quoted in Kleinberg, *Miami Beach,* p. 62.
17. John Oliver LaGorce, Letter to Carl G. Fisher, February 1, 1921. CF: HASF.
18. David Jameson, Letter to A. G. Batchelder, January 31, 1921. CF: HASF
19. A. G. Batchelder, Letter to Carl G. Fisher, February 4, 1921. CF: HASF.
20. George B. Christian, Jr., Letter to Carl G. Fisher, August 24, 1921. CF: HASF.
21. George B. Christian, Jr., Letter

to Carl G. Fisher, October 21, 1921. CF: HASF.

Chapter 19

1. Carl G. Fisher, Letter to Ida G. Fisher, January 13, 1919. CF: HASF.
2. Carl G. Fisher, Letter to Ida G. Fisher, February 10, 1919. CF: HASF.
3. Carl G. Fisher, Letter to Ida G. Fisher, March 24, 1919. CF: HASF.
4. Carl G. Fisher, Letter to Ida G. Fisher, March 26, 1919. CF: HASF.
S. Carl G. Fisher, Letter to Ida G. Fisher, April 2, 1919. CF: HASF.
6. Carl G. Fisher, Letter to Albert H. Fisher, April 25, 1918. CF: HASF.
7. Carl G. Fisher, Letter to Albert H. Fisher, May 20, 1918. CF: HASF.
8. Carl G, Fisher, Letter to Albert H. Fisher, February 7, 1919. CF: HASF.
9. H. A. DuBois, Letter to Carl G. Fisher, March 17, 1919. CF: HASF.
10. Carl G. Fisher, Letter to H. A. DuBois, March 22, 1919. CF: HASF.
11. Carl G. Fisher, Letter to Albert H. Fisher, March 22, 1919. CF: HASF.
12. Carl G. Fisher, Letter to Albert H. Fisher, December 26, 1919. CF: HASF.
13. Jane Fisher, p. 186.
14. *Ibid.*, p. 189.
15. "Campus Heritage Dates to Early 1900s," *The Magnet.* Indianapolis: Marian College
16. Carl G. Fisher, Letter to Frank Shutts, July 5, 1921. CF: HASF.
17. Redford, p. 139.
18. Carl G, Fisher, Letter quoted in Redford, p. 139.
19. Carl Fisher as quoted in *Fabulous Hoosier* by Jane Fisher, p. 188.
20. Jane Fisher, p, 190.
21. Carl Fisher as quoted in *Fabulous Hoosier* by Jane Fisher, p. 189.
22. Jane Fisher, p. 190.
23. Carl Fisher, Letter to Edward C. Romfh, October 14, 1921. CF: HASF.
24. Edward C. Romfh, Letter to Carl Fisher, October 18, 1921. CF: HASF.
25. Frank Shutts, Telegram to Carl G. Fisher, October 14, 1921. CF: HASF.
26. Julius Fleischmann, Letter to Carl G. Fisher, October 21, 1921. CF: HASF.
27. Jane Fisher, p. 190.
28. *Ibid.*
29. Carl Fisher, as quoted in *Fabulous Hoosier* by Jane Fisher, p. 191.
30. Carl Fisher, Telegram to Amos Fisher, November 9, 1909. CF: HASF.
31. Obituary notice. CF: HASF.
32. Carl G. Fisher, Letter to Superintendent of Crown Hill Cemetery, November 10, 1921. CF: HASF.
33. Jane Fisher, p. 191.
34. *Ibid.*, p. 188.
35. *Ibid.*
36. Jane Fisher, p. 192.
37. Redford, p. 140.

Chapter 20

1. Preston, p. 58.
2. *Ibid.*
3. *Ibid.*
4. *Ibid.*, p. 60.
5. *Ibid.*, p. 61.
6. Michael M. Allison, Letter to Carl G. Fisher, April 16, 1919. CF: HASF.
7. Carl G. Fisher. Letter to Michael M. Allison, April 25, 1919. April 25, 1919. CF: HASF.
8. Carl G. Fisher, Letter to A. F. Sanford, April 30, 1919. CF: HASF.
9. Carl G. Fisher, Letter to Michael M. Allison, May 9,1919. CF: HASF.
10. Carl G. Fisher, Letter to W. T. Anderson, May 12, 1919. CF: HASF.
11. W. T. Anderson, Letter to Carl G. Fisher, May 24, 1919. CF: HASF.
12. Carl G. Fisher, Letter to A. G.

Batchelder, May 26, 1919. CF: HASF.

13. *Ibid.*

14. *Ibid.*

15. Carl G. Fisher, Letter to Michael M. Allison, July 22, 1919. CF: HASF.

16. *Ibid.*

17. Carl G. Fisher, Letter to W. T. Anderson, September 4, 1919. CF: HASF.

18. Carl G. Fisher, Letter to W. T. Anderson, January 26, 1920. CF: HASF.

19. *Ibid.*

20. Carl G. Fisher, Letter to Michael M. Allison, August 6, 1920. CF: HASF.

21. Michael M. Allison, Letter to Carl G. Fisher, August 9,1920. CF: HASF.

22. Carl G, Fisher, Letter to Michael M. Allison, January 20, 1921. CF: HASF.

23. Michael M. Allison, Letter to Carl G. Fisher, June 9, 1921. CF: HASF.

24. Carl G. Fisher, Letter to W. G. Gilbreath, September 17, 1921. CF: HASF.

25. *Ibid.*

26. Carl G. Fisher, Letter to Michael M. Allison, November 17, 1921. CF: HASF.

27. Michael M. Allison, Letter to Carl G. Fisher, December 1, 1921. CF: HASF.

28. Carl G. Fisher, Letter to Michael M. Allison, December 7, 1921. CF: HASF.

29. Carl G. Fisher, Letter to Michael M. Allison, December 11, 1924. CF: HASF

Chapter 21

1. Redford, p. 141.

2. *Ibid.*

3. *Ibid.*, p. 112.

4. *Ibid.*, p. 141.

5. Jane Fisher, p. 148.

6. *Ibid.*

7. *Ibid.*

8. *Ibid.*

9. *Ibid.*

10. Kleinberg, *Miami Beach*, p. 121.

11. *Ibid.*, p. 101.

12. *Ibid.*, p. 123.

13. Jane Fisher, p. 147.

14. *Ibid.*

15. *Ibid.*, p. 146.

16. Carl G. Fisher, *Business*, as quoted in Redford, p. 115.

17. Redford, p. 115.

18. Redford, p. 186.

19. Carl G. Fisher, Telegram to Reinald Werrenrath, February 18, 1928. CF: HASF.

20. Edgar A. Guest, Letter to Carl G. Fisher, March 8, 1928. CF: HASF.

21. Carl G. Fisher, Letter to Edgar A. Guest, March 12, 1928. CF: HASF.

22. Gene Tunney, Letter to Carl G. Fisher, March 14, 1928. CF: HASF.

23. Carl G. Fisher, Letter to Thomas Meighan, March 1, 1928. CF: HASF.

24. Carl G. Fisher, Letter to Tex Rickard, March 8, 1928. CF: HASF.

25. Grantland Rice, Letter to Carl G. Fisher, March 1, 1928. CF: HASF.

26. John Golden, Letter to Carl G. Fisher and John O. LaGorce, March 5, 1928. CF: HASF.

27. Walter Trumbull, Letter to Carl G. Fisher, March 24, 1928. CF: HASF.

28. Redford, pp. 185-187.

29. Ed Ballard, Letter to Carl G. Fisher, in Kleinberg, *Miami Beach*, p. 79.

30. Carl G. Fisher, Letter to Ed Ballard, February 7, 1921, as quoted in Kleinberg, *Miami Beach*, p. 79.

31. Carl G. Fisher, Letter to John O. LaGorce, February 7, 1921, as quoted in Kleinberg, *Miami Beach*, p. 79.

32. Redford, p. 141.

33. *Ibid.*, p. 142.

34. Carl G. Fisher, Letter to John O. LaGorce, as quoted in Redford, pp. 133-134.

35. Jane Fisher, p. 151.
36. Nash, p. 121.
37. Kleinberg, *Miami Beach*, p. 80.
38. Carl G. Fisher, as quoted in Kleinberg, *Miami Beach, p.* 80.
39. Nash, p. 121.
40. Kleinberg, *Miami Beach*, p. 80.
41. Redford, p. 142.
42. *Ibid.*, p. 143.

Chapter 22

1. Kleinberg, p. 81.
2. Redford, p. 127.
3. Carl Fisher, Letter to Thomas Pancoast, May 11, 1920, as quoted in Kleinberg, p. 81.
4. Nash, pp. 122-123.
5. *Ibid.*, p. 123.
6. Redford, p. 176.
7. Nash, p. 123.
8. Jane Fisher, pp. 146-147.
9. *Ibid.*, p. 137.
10. Redford, p. 127.
11. Pete Chase, as quoted in Redford, p. 146.
12. Redford, p. 135.
13. Jane Fisher, p. 165.
14. *Ibid.*, pp. 165-166.
15. *Ibid.*, p. 162.
16. *Ibid.*, p. 160.
17. *Ibid.*, p. 153.
18. *Ibid.*
19. Redford, p. 134.
20. Kleinberg, *Miami Beach*, p. 93.
21. Redford, p. 135.
22. Kleinberg, *Miami Beach, p.* 93.
23. Redford, p. 154.
24. *Ibid.*
25. Kenneth Ballinger, *Miami Millions*, as quoted in Kleinberg, *Miami Beach*, p. 93.
26. Jane Fisher, pp. 162-163.
27. "The World's Here," *Miami Beach Register*, January 16, 1924, as quoted in Kleinberg, *Miami Beach*, p. 94.
28. Kleinberg, p. 89.
29. Jane Fisher, pp. 179-180.
30. *Ibid.*, p. 167.
31. Rogers, pp. 93-94.
32. Nash, p. 136.
33. Carl G. Fisher, Letter to M. J. Carney, June 21, 1920. CF: HASF.

34. Carl G. Fisher, Letter to Judge A. Frank Katzentine, December 31, 1931. CF: HASF
35. Carl G. Fisher, Letter to Thomas Pancoast, February 25, 1919. CF: HASF
36. Kleinberg, *Miami Beach*, p. 73.
37. *Ibid.*
38. Carl G. Fisher, Letter to Thomas Pancoast, September 28, 1920, as quoted in Kleinberg, *Miami Beach*, p. 74.
39. Redford, pp. 207-208.
40. John O. LaGorce, Letter to Gilbert Grosvenor, as quoted in Kleinberg, *Miami Beach*, p. 71.
41. Kleinberg, *Miami Beach*, p. 74.
42. Carl G. Fisher, Letter to Lyman Kendall, May 11, 1921, as quoted in Kleinberg, *Miami Beach.* pp. 74-75.
43. Kleinberg, *Miami Beach*, p. 75.
44. Carl G. Fisher, Letter to Eugene Stahl, October 6, 1921, as quoted in Kleinberg, *Miami Beach*, p. 75.
45. "$116,000 Is Paid by Hertz for House," *Miami Herald*, date unknown. CF: HASF.
46. Harry Klein, Letter to Carl G. Fisher, date unknown, as quoted by Ann Armbruster in *The Life and Times of Miami Beach* (NY: Alfred A. Knopf, 1995), p. 77.
47. Carl G. Fisher, Letter to Harry Klein, March 19, 1927. CF: HASF.
48. Carl G. Fisher, Letter to Mr. Rigaud, January 13, 1923. CF: HASF.
49. Julius Fleischmann, Note to Carl G. Fisher, May 2, 1924. CF: HASF.
50. Julius Fleischmann, Letter to Carl G. Fisher, February 3, 1925. CF: HASF.
51. Gettie Fleischmann, Letter to Carl G. Fisher, February 19, 1925. CF: HASF.
52. Carl G. Fisher, Letter to Captain H. C. C. Tippett, February 18, 1924. CF: HASF.
53. Carl G. Fisher, Letter to Glenn Adams, January 29, 1927. CF: HASF.

54. Robert H. Tyndall to Glenn Adams, January 7, 1930. CF: HASF.
55. Kleinberg, *Miami Beach*, p. 137.
56. Oral history interview with Mitchell Wolfson for Temple Israel by Marcia Kanner, November 24, 1970, as quoted in Kleinberg, *Miami Beach*, p. 137.
57. Redford, pp. 139-139.
58. *Ibid.*, p. 138.

Chapter 23

1. Kleinberg, *Miami Beach*, p. 103.
2. *Ibid.*, p. 82.
3. Carl G. Fisher, Letter to Thomas Pancoast, as quoted in Redford, p. 123.
4. Redford, p. 123.
5. Carl G. Fisher, Letter to Harold Talbott, Jr., as quoted in Redford, p. 139.
6. Carl G. Fisher, Letter to Antonio Giraudier, Jr., March 25, 1920. CF: HASF.
7. Redford, p. 140.
8. Preston, p. 116.
9. *Ibid.*, p. 125.
10. *Ibid.*, p. 113.
11. *Ibid.*, p. 116.
12. *Ibid.*, p. 118.
13. *Ibid.*
14. *Ibid.*
15. *Ibid.*, p. 119.
16. Redford, p. 151.
17. *Ibid.*
18. *Ibid.*, p. 150.
19. Jane Fisher, p. 204.
20. Redford, p. 152.
21. Jane Fisher, p. 204.
22. Carl G. Fisher, Letter to James Cox, July 29, 1925, as quoted in Redford, p. 153.
23. Redford, p. 154.
24. Kleinberg, *Miami Beach*, p. 104,
25. *Ibid.*, p. 105.
26. Redford, p. 145.
27. Isidor Cohen, as quoted in Kleinberg, *Miami Beach*, p. 96.
28. Kleinberg, *Miami Beach*, p. II 8.
29. Redford, p. 163.
30. Lummus, p. 103.
31. Redford, p. 163.
32. Kleinberg, *Miami Beach*, p, 98.
33. Carl G. Fisher, as quoted in Redford, p. 159.
34. Redford, p. 159.
35. Walter Bailey, Advertisement. CF: HASF.
36. *Ibid.*
37. Redford, p. 160,
38. Albert R. Holden, *A Pictorial History of Montauk* (Montauk: Holden's Publications © 1983), p. 22.
39. *Ibid.*, p. 23.
40. *Ibid.*, p. 8.
41. *Ibid.*, p. 23.
42. *Ibid.*
43. *Ibid.*, pp. 26-27.
44. *Ibid.*, p. 41.
45. *East Hampton Star*, September 18, 1925. CF: HASF.
46. Redford, p. 161.
47. *Ibid.*, p. 160
48. *Ibid.*
49. *East Hampton Star*, October 2, 1925. CF: HASF.
50. George F. Lyndon, *Eagle*, as reprinted in the *East Hampton Star*, October 2,1925. CF: HASF.
51. *Ibid.*
52. *Ibid.*
53. *Ibid.*
54. Jane Fisher, p. 214.
55. *Ibid.*, pp. 214-215.
56. *Ibid.*, p. 215.
57. *East Hampton Star*, September 25, 1925. CF: HASF.
58. *East Hampton Star*, December 4, 1925. CF: HASF.
59. *Ibid.*
60. Redford, p. 155.

Chapter 24

1. Carl G. Fisher, Letter to Mazie Rattay, May 20, 1922. CF: HASF.
2. Carl G. Fisher, Letter to George L. Denny, December 2, 1922. CF: HASF.
3. George L. Denny, Telegram to Carl G. Fisher, December 6, 1922. CF: HASF.
4. Carl G. Fisher to George L. Denny, December 9, 1922. CF: HASF.
5. Carl G. Fisher to George L

Denny, December 14, 1922. CF: HASF.

6. Jane Fisher, pp. 194-195.

7. Carl G. Fisher, Letter to Mazie Rattay, February 22, 1923. CF: HASF.

8. Carl G. Fisher, Letter to Mazie Rattay, August 6, 1923. CF: HASF.

9. Mazie Rattay, Letter to Carl G. Fisher, August 21, 1923. CF: HASF.

10. Carl G. Fisher, Letter to Mazie Rattay, August 23, 1923. CF: HASF.

11. Mazie Rattay, Letter to Carl G. Fisher, August 27, 1923. CF: HASF.

12. Mazie Rattay, Letter to Carl G. Fisher, December 3, 1924. CF: HASF.

13. Carl G. Fisher, Letter to Mazie Rattay, December 10, 1924. CF: HASF.

14. Jane Fisher, p. 154.

15. *Ibid.*

16. *Ibid.*, pp. 154-155.

17. *Ibid.*, p. 155.

18. *Ibid.*, p. 172.

19. *Ibid.*, p. 173.

20. *Ibid.*

21. *Ibid.*, p. 182.

22. *Ibid.*

23. *Ibid.*, p. 183.

24. *Ibid.*

25. *Ibid.*

26. *Ibid.*, p. 195.

27. *Ibid.*, p. 198.

28. *Ibid.*

29. *Ibid.*, p. 199.

30. *Ibid.*

31. Kleinberg, *Miami Beach*, p. 88.

32. Cloyd Hewes, as quoted in Redford, p. 121.

33. Jane Fisher, p. 192.

34. Carl G. Fisher, Letter to James Allison, April 28, 1921. CF: HASF.

35. Jane Fisher, pp. 192-193.

36. Helen Muir, *Miami U.S.A.*, as quoted in Redford, p. 121.

37. Jane Fisher, p. 193.

38. Redford, p. 121.

39. *Ibid.*

40. Jane Fisher, p. 193.

41. *Ibid.*, p. 184.

42. *Ibid.*

43. *Ibid.*

44. *Ibid.*

45. *Ibid.*

46. *Ibid.*, p. 208.

47. *Ibid.*, pp. 241-242.

48. Carl G. Fisher, Letter to Mrs. E. J. Kyle, Oct. 21, 1925. CF: HASF.

49. Jane Fisher, pp. 206-207,

50. Carl G. Fisher, Letter to Jane Fisher, as quoted in Jane Fisher, pp. 208-209.

51. Jane Fisher, p. 210.

52. *Ibid.*

53. *Ibid.*, p. 186.

54. Kleinberg, *Miami Beach*, p. 38.

55. Jane Fisher, p. 211.

56. *Ibid.*, p. 212.

57. *Ibid.*, p. 221.

58. *Ibid.*

59. *Ibid.* pp. 186-187.

60. *Ibid.*, p. 222.

61. *Ibid.*

62. *Ibid.*, p. 223,

63. *Ibid.*, p. 224.

64. *Ibid.*

65. *Ibid.*, p. 226.

66. *Ibid.*, p. 227.

67. *Ibid.*

68. *Ibid.*

69. Frank Shutts, Letter to Carl G. Fisher, February 24, 1926. CF: HASF.

70. Carl G. Fisher, Note on letter to him from Frank Shutts, February 24, 1926. CF: HASF.

71. Jane Fisher, p. 229.

72. *Ibid.*, p. 230

Chapter 25

1. "Carl Fisher Inspects Construction Work at Montauk Beach This Week; First Visit Since Purchase of Land," *East Hampton Star*, May 21, 1926. East Hampton Library.

2. Carl G. Fisher, as quoted in "Carl Fisher Inspects Construction Work at Montauk Beach This Week; First Visit Since Purchase of Land."

3. "Carl Fisher Inspects Construction Work at Montauk Beach This Week; First Visit Since Purchase of Land."

4. "Huge Dredge Arrives at Fort Pond; Construction Work in Full Swing," *Fast Hampton Star*, June 8, 1926. East Hampton Library.

5. Redford, p. 179.

6. *Ibid.*, p. 180.

7. Jane Fisher, p. 216.

8. Redford, p. 181.

9. Kleinberg. p. 106.

10. *Ibid.*

11. Marjory Stoneman Douglas, as quoted in Redford, pp. 168-169.

12. Redford, p. 169.

13. *Ibid.*

14. *Miami Daily News*, September 18, 1926, in Lummus, p. 104.

15. "Carl Fisher and Guests Rush from Montauk to Miami After Hurricane," *East Hampton Star*, September 24, 1926. East Hampton Library.

16. *Ibid.*

17. Redford, p. 171.

18. Kleinberg, p. 108.

19. Redford, p. 173.

20. Leo F. Reardon, as quoted in Kleinberg, p. 108.

21. Redford, p. 174.

22. Kleinberg, p. 106.

23. Al Powell, "Fulford-Miami Speedway," *The History of the American Speedway*, ed. by Allan E. Brown (Marr, Michigan: Slideways Publications, n.d.), p. 34.

24. *Ibid.*

25. *Ibid.*, p. 36.

26. *Ibid.*

27. C. W. Chase, Letter to owners of Miami Beach property, September 24, 1926, as quoted in the *East Hampton Star*, October 1, 1926. East Hampton Library.

28. Carl G. Fisher, Letter to John LaGorce, October 8, 1926, as quoted in Kleinberg, p. 108.

29. Carl G. Fisher, Letter to Jane Fisher, in Jane Fisher, p. 235.

30. Redford, p. 177.

31. *Ibid.*, p. 179,

32. Bloemker, p. 163.

33. *Ibid.*

34. *Ibid.*, p. 170.

35. Carl G. Fisher, Letter to E. V. Rickenbacker, July 12, 1927. CF: HASF.

36. T. E. Myers, Letter to James Allison, December 7, 1927. CF: HASF.

37. T. E. Myers, Letter to Carl G. Fisher, June 10, 1929. CF: HASF.

38. Carl G. Fisher, Letter to T. E. Myers, June 12, 1929. CF: HASF.

39. T. E. Myers, Letter to Carl G. Fisher, June 15, 1929. CF: HASF.

40. T. E. Myers, Letter to Carl G. Fisher, March 8, 1930. CF: HASF.

41 Redford, p. 179.

42. Carl G. Fisher, Letter to investor, March 27, 1927, as quoted in Redford, p. 180.

43. Jane Fisher, p. 237.

44. *Ibid.*, p. 238.

45. Carl G. Fisher, as quoted in Jane Fisher, p. 238.

46. Carl G. Fisher, as quoted in Jane Fisher, p. 241.

47. Redford, p. 182.

48. *Ibid.*

Chapter 26

1. Ralph Hausrath, "Carl G. Fisher and Montauk," *Long Island Forum*, November 1981, p. 255.

2. "Montauk Beach" brochure, published 1932.

3. Carl G. Fisher, Letter to C. W. Barron, April 22, 1927. CF: HASF.

4. Carl G. Fisher, Letter to Charles G. Dawes, July 12, 1927. CF: HASF.

5. Robert E. Byrd, Letter to Carl G. Fisher, February 11, 1928. CF: HASF.

6. Hausrath, p. 255.

7. *Ibid.*

8. *Ibid.*

9. *Ibid.*, pp. 254-155.

10. *Ibid.*, p. 255.

11. *Ibid.*, p. 226.

12. *Ibid.*, p. 255.

13. Carl G. Fisher, Letter to Parke G. Haynes, September 27, 1927, CF: HASF.

14. Redford, p. 196.

15. Jane Fisher, p. 196.

16. Redford, p. 198.

17. Jane Fisher, p. 225.

18. Redford, p. 178.

19. Kleinberg, p. 123.

20. *Ibid.*, pp. 112-113.

21. Redford, p. 193.

22. *Ibid.*

23. Robert J. Schoenberg, *Mr. Capone* (NY: William Morrow and Co., Inc. © 1992), p. 30.

24. *Ibid.*, pp. 35-36.

25. *Ibid.*, p. 202.

26. *Ibid.*, pp. 234-235.

27. *Fearon's Our Century 1910-1920* (Belmont, California: David S. Lake Publishers © 1989).

28. *Ibid.*

29. George L. Denny, Memorandum to Carl G. Fisher, May 7, 1921. CF: HASF.

30. Carl G. Fisher, Letter to James Allison, April 28, 1921. CF: HASF,

31. Carl G. Fisher, Letter to Cecil G. Fowler, May 7, 1920. CF: HASF.

32. Cecil G. Fowler, Letter to Carl G. Fisher, April 16, 1923. CF: HASF.

33. Carl G. Fisher, Letter to Herbert Duckwell, November 6, 1923. CF: HASF,

34. Robert L. Bacon, Letter to Carl G. Fisher, November 2. 1926. CF: HASF.

35. Carl G Fisher, Letter to Robert L. Bacon, November 5, 1926. CF: HASF.

36. Joseph T. Deal, Letter to Carl G. Fisher, January 17, 1927. CF: HASF.

37. Carl G. Fisher, Letter to Joseph T. Deal, January 31, 1927. CF: HASF.

38. Carl G. Fisher, Letter to William Anderson, December 13, 1926. CF: HASF.

39. Carl G. Fisher, Letter to George LeBoutillier, April 18, 1927. CF: HASF.

40. Carl G. Fisher, Letter to Albert C. Champion, July 13, 1927. CF: HASF.

41. Albert C. Champion, Letter to Carl G. Fisher, July 22, 1927. CF: HASF.

42. Carl G. Fisher, Telegram to Albert C. Champion, July 26, 1927. CF: HASF.

43. Albert C. Champion, Letter to Carl G. Fisher, July 29, 1927. CF: HASF.

44. Albert C. Champion, Letter to Carl G. Fisher, April 7, 1927. CF: HASF.

45. Carl G. Fisher, Letter to Parke G. Haynes, September 27, 1927. CF: HASF.

46. Montauk Manor tour guide information sheet.

47. Carl G. Fisher, Letter to A. G. Bums, January 9, 1928. CF: HASF.

48. Carl G. Fisher, Letter to Charles E. Bethell, February 4, 1928. CF: HASF.

49. C. F. Chapman, Letter to Carl G. Fisher, March 24, 1928. CF: HASF.

50. *Ibid.*

51. *Ibid.*

52. *Ibid.*

53. Redford, p. 194.

54. Carl G. Fisher, Letter to C. F. Chapman, March 27, 1928. CF: HASF.

55. W. H. Stayton, Letter to Carl G. Fisher, February 16, 1928. CF: HASF.

56. Carl G. Fisher, Letter to W. H. Stayton, February 20, 1928. CF: HASF.

Chapter 27

1. Art Pancoast, as quoted in Redford, pp. 118-119.

2. John Collins' grandson, as quoted in Redford, p. 116.

3. Carl G. Fisher, Letter to Parke G. Haynes, September 27, 1927. CF: HASF.

4. *Ibid.*

5. E. H. Adkins, Telegram to Carl G. Fisher, August 3, 1928. CF: HASF.

6. Carl G. Fisher, Letter to James Allison, January 2, 1920. CF: HASF.

7. James Allison, Letter to Earl Kiser, April 11, 1925. CF: HASF.

8. Kleinberg, *Miami Beach*, p. 111.

9. Rev. William Barry, Letter to Carl G. Fisher, August 19, 1927. CF: HASF.

10. Carl G Fisher, Letter to Rev. William Barry, August 24, 1927. CF: HASF.

11. Rev. William Barry, Letter to Carl G. Fisher, September 14, 1927. CF: HASF.

12. Carl G. Fisher, Memo to W. A. Kohihepp, September 27, 1927. CF: HASF.

13. Kleinberg, *Miami Beach*, p. 111.

14. Carl G. Fisher, Letter to Rev. William Barry, February 11, 1928, CF: HASF.

15. Rev. William Barry to Carl G. Fisher, January 29, 1929. CF: HASF.

16. Carl G. Fisher, Letter to Rev. William Barry, January 29, 1929. CF: HASF.

17. Kleinberg, *Miami Beach*, p. 110.

18. Carl G. Fisher, Letter to Rev. William Barry. January 22, 1930. CF: HASF.

19. Carl G. Fisher, Letter to George LeBoutillier, March 16, 1929. CF: HASF.

20. George LeBoutillier, Letter to Carl G. Fisher, March 9, 1929. CF: HASF.

21. *Ibid.*

22. *Ibid.*

23. Carl G. Fisher, Letter to George LeBoutillier, March 16, 1929. CF: HASF.

24. *Ibid.*

25. Kleinberg, *Miami Beach*, p. 91.

26. Bloemker, p. 59.

27. *Ibid.*, p, 163.

28. Carl G. Fisher, Letter to Harvey Firestone, September 22, 1921. CF: HASF.

29. W. D. Hines, Letter to Carl G. Fisher, October 19, 1922.

30. Carl G. Fisher, Day letter to Henry Ford, March 13, 1926. CF: HASF.

31. "Edsel Ford Arrives for Four-Week Stay, *Miami Herald*, 1930: exact date unknown. CF: HASF.

32. William K. Vanderbilt, Letter to Carl G. Fisher, December 27,1927. CF: HASF.

33. Secretary of Carl Fisher, Letter to William K. Vanderbilt, January 9, 1928. CF: HASF.

34. Carl G. Fisher, Letter to William K. Vanderbilt, March 12, 1928. CF: HASF.

35. William K. Vanderbilt, Letter to Carl G. Fisher, November 7, 1928. CF: HASF.

36. Jane Fisher, p. 219.

37. *Ibid.*, pp. 219-220.

38. *Ibid.*, p. 220.

39. Carl G. Fisher, telegram to Charles Thompson, August 29, 1928. CF: HASF.

40. Thomas Pancoast, Letter to Carl G. Fisher, July 12, 1929. CF: HASF.

41. Carl G. Fisher, Letter to Thomas Pancoast, July 16, 1928. CF: HASF.

42. Hausrath, December, 1981, p. 256.

43. *East Hampton Star*, October 18, 1929, as quoted in Hausrath, December, 1981, p. 256.

44 Charles Krom, Letter to Carl G. Fisher, November 18, 1929, as quoted in Kleinberg, *Miami Beach*. p. 125.

45. Carl G. Fisher, as quoted in Kleinberg, *Miami Beach*, p. 125.

46. Carl G. Fisher, Letter to Clem Keyes, March 21, 1930, as quoted in Kleinberg, *Miami Beach*, p. 125.

47. Kleinberg, *Miami Beach*, p. 125.

48. Carl G. Fisher, Letter to William T. Anderson, February 12, 1930. CF: HASF.

49. Carl G. Fisher, Letter to Major George E. Brown, May 9, 1930. CF: HASF.

50. Carl G, Fisher, Memorandum to A. W. Howe, April 19, 1930. CF: HASF.

51. Carl G. Fisher, Memorandum to A. W. Howe, July 10, 1930. CF: HASF.

52. Carl G. Fisher, Memorandum to

A. W. Howe, July 31, 1930. CF: HASF.

53. Carl G. Fisher, Memorandum to A. W. Howe, August 12, 1930. CF: HASF.

54. Carl G. Fisher, Memorandum to A. W. Howe, August 29, 1930. CF: HASF.

55. Carl G. Fisher, Memorandum to A. W. Howe, November 26, 1930. CF: HASF.

56. Carl G. Fisher, Letter to Rube Goldberg. December 24, 1930. CF: HASF.

57. Doyle E. Carlton, Telegram to Florida county sheriffs, March 19, 1930, as quoted in Schoenberg, p. 252.

58. Schoenberg, p. 262.

59. *Miami Daily News* editorial, as quoted in Schoenberg, p. 261.

60. *Miami Daily News* editorial, as quoted in Schoenberg, p. 261.

61. *Miami Daily News*, as quoted in Redford, p. 194.

62. Dan Mahoney, Letter to Carl G. Fisher, March 20, 1930. CF: HASF.

63. Board of Governors, Miami Beach Chamber of Commerce, Telegram to Doyle E. Carlton, March 27, 1930. CF: HASF.

64. Doyle E. Carlton, Letter to Carl G. Fisher, March 26, 1930. CF: HASF.

65. James A. Cox, Telegram to Carl G. Fisher, April 12, 1930. CF: HASF.

66. Schoenberg, p. 254.

67. Vincent C. Giblin and J. Fritz Gordon, Telegram to Doyle E. Carlton, as quoted in Schoenberg, p. 254.

68. Schoenberg, pp. 254-255.

69. *Ibid.*, p. 264.

70. *Ibid.*, p. 265.

71. *Ibid.*, p. 266.

72. Helen Muir, *Miami U.S.A* (NY: Henry Holt and Co., 1953), p. 183.

73. *Ibid.*

74. James Cox, Letter to Carl G. Fisher, May 7, 1930. CF: HASF.

75. Schoenberg, p. 268.

76. Carl G. Fisher, Letter to Victor Ehrhart, May 13, 1930. CF: HASF.

77. *Indianapolis Star,* May 17, 1930.

78. Schoenberg, p. 269.

79. Carl G. Fisher, as quoted in Schoenberg, p. 269.

80. Schoenberg, p. 269.

81. Victor Ehrhart, Letter to Carl G. Fisher, May 21, 1930. CF: HASF.

82. Schoenberg, p. 270.

83. *Ibid.*, p. 271.

84. *Ibid.*

85. Carl G. Fisher, Letter to Michael J. Glenn, May 27, 1930. CF: HASF.

86. Michael J. Glenn, Letter to Carl G. Fisher, May 29, 1930. CF: HASF.

87. Carl G. Fisher, Letter to John Levi, May 31, 1930. CF: HASF.

88. John Levi, Letter to Carl G. Fisher, June 6, 1930. CF: HASF.

89. Dan Mahoney, Letter to Carl G. Fisher, May 29, 1930. CF: HASF.

90. Michael J. Glenn, Letter to Carl G. Fisher, June 6, 1930. CF: HASF.

91. *Ibid.*

92. Kleinberg, *Miami Beach*, p. 116.

93. *Ibid.*

94. *Ibid.*

95. Edward Robinson, as quoted in Schoenberg, p. 272.

96. Schoenberg, p. 272.

97. Judge Paul D. Barns, as quoted in Schoenberg, p. 272.

98 James Cox, as, quoted in Schoenberg, p. 354.

Chapter 28

1. Hausrath, *Long Island Forum,* December, 1981, pp. 256-257.

2. *Ibid.*, p. 257.

3. *Ibid.*, pp. 257-258.

4. *Ibid.*, p. 257.

5. *Ibid.*, p. 258.

6. *Ibid.*

7. Carl G. Fisher, Letter to Fred A. Britten, February 19, 1932. CF: HASF.

8. Hausrath, December, 1981, p. 258.

9. Carl G. Fisher, Letter to Victor Erhart, April 30, 1932. CF: HASF.

10. Hausrath, December 1981, p. 259.

11. Carl G. Fisher, Letter to J. G. Vincent, August 3, 1928. CF: HASF.

12. Frank A. Seiberling, Letter to Carl G. Fisher, September 10, 1928. CF: HASF.

13. *Ibid.*

14. *Ibid.*

15. Carl G. Fisher, Letter to Frank A. Seiberling, September 12, 1928. CF: HASF.

16. Carl G. Fisher, Letter to R. A. Havey, September 2, 1928. CF: HASF.

17. R. A. Havey, Letter to Carl G. Fisher, September II, 1928. CF: HASF.

18. Carl G. Fisher, Letter to Walter O. Briggs, September 28, 1928. CF: HASF.

19. Carl G. Fisher, Letter to Roy Chapin, May 28, 1930. CF: HASF

20. *Ibid.*

21. Carl G. Fisher, Letter to Roy Chapin, December 24, 1930. CF: HASF.

22. Carl G. Fisher, Letter to Jess C. Andrews,

23. Carl G. Fisher, Letter to Margaret Fisher, September 27, 1930. CF: HASF.

24. *Ibid.*

25. *Ibid.*

26. Carl G. Fisher, Letter to Margaret Fisher, October 22, 1920. CF: HASF.

27. Carl G. Fisher, Letter to Margaret Fisher, November 3, 1930. CF: HASF,

28. *Ibid.*

29. Amos Fisher, Letter to Carl G. Fisher, March 11, 1924. CF: HASF.

30. John Fisher, Letter to Carl G. Fisher, June 6, 1930. CF: HASF.

31. Carl G. Fisher, Letter to John Fisher, June 16, 1930. CF: HASF.

32. John Fisher, Letter to Carl G. Fisher, August 9, 1930. CF: HASF.

33. John Fisher, Letter to Carl G. Fisher, September 12, 1930. CF: HASF.

34. Carl G. Fisher, Letter to Amos Fisher, April 30, 1930. CF: HASF.

35. Amos Fisher, Letter to Carl G. Fisher, August 13, 1930. CF: HASF.

36. Carl G. Fisher, Letter to Amos Fisher, August 30, 1930. CF: HASF.

37. Carl G. Fisher, Letter to Amos Fisher, December 27, 1932. CF: HASF.

38. Carl G. Fisher, Memo to Paul Kunschik, May 9, 1933. CF: HASF.

39. Amos Fisher, Letter to Carl G, Fisher, November 13, 1930. CF: HASF.

40. John Fisher, Letter to Carl G. Fisher, April 21, 1930. CF: HASF.

41. Amos Fisher, Letter to Carl G. Fisher, July 6, 1930. CF: HASF.

42. Newspaper clipping, undated. Jerry Fisher's family album.

43. Carl G. Fisher, Letter to Mrs. Keyes Winter, March 14, 1930. CF: HASF.

44. Redford, p. 109.

45. Jane Fisher, p. 254.

46. *Ibid.*, p. 217.

47. Carl G. Fisher, Letter to A. H. Godard, November 16, 1917. CF: HASF.

48. Ann Rossiter, Letter to A. H. Godard, May 31, 1918. CF: HASF.

49. Carl G. Fisher, Letter to Frank D. Stalnaker, October 1, 1920. CF: HASF.

50. John Bankett, Letter to Carl G. Fisher, May 31, 1927. CF: HASF.

51. Karlena Galloway, Letter to Carl G. Fisher, April 13, 1926. CF: HASF.

52. Carl G. Fisher, Letter to Karlena Galloway, May 28, 1926. CF: HASF.

53. Karlena Galloway, Letter to Carl G. Fisher, June 8, 1926. CF: HASF.

54. Jane Fisher, p. 248.

Chapter 29

1. Harwood Koppel, Letter to A. A. Rossiter, June 27, 1910. CF: HASF.

2. Fred Wellman, Letter to Harwood Koppel, July 3, 1919. CF: HASF.

3. George Derby, Letter to Carl G.

Fisher, October 19, 1933. CF: HASF.

4. John Dickson, Letter to Margaret Fisher, April 9, 1940. CF: HASF.

5. MEC (Carl G. Fisher's secretary), Letter to Betty Carter, August 6, 1925. CF: HASF.

6. Betty Carter, Letter to Carl G. Fisher, August 20, 1925. CF: HASF.

7. William G. Alexander, M.D., Letter to Carl G. Fisher, October 26, 1925. CF: HASF.

8. Carl G. Fisher, Letter to William G. Alexander, M.D., October 30, 1925. CF: HASF.

9. Carl G. Fisher, Letter to R. F. Garland, February 18, 1932. CF: HASF.

10. Mrs. J. W. Young, Letter to Carl G. Fisher, May 6, 1936. CF: HASF.

11. Carl G. Fisher, Letter to Mrs. J. W. Young, May 13, 1936. CF: HASF.

12. Mrs. J. W. Young, Letter to Fred Humpage, August 30, l938. CF: HASF.

13. Carl G. Fisher, Letter to Mrs. J. W. Young, September 20, l938 CF: HASF.

14. Carl G. Fisher, Letter to Charles E. Sorensen, December 15, 1932. CF: HASF.

15. Carl G. Fisher, Letter to Clem Keyes, April 17. 1933. CF: HASF.

16. *Ibid.*

17. Carl G. Fisher, Letter to J. N. Lummus, Jr., April 10, 1933. CF: HASF.

18. Carl G. Fisher, Letter to A. N. Fisher, March 27, 1933. CF: HASF.

19. Carl G. Fisher, Memorandum to Fred Humpage, March 27, 193:3. CF: HASF.

20. A. E. Stark, Letter to Carl Fisher, March, 1934, CF: HASF.

21. Carl G. Fisher, Letter to A. E. Stark, March, 1934. CF: HASF.

22. Redford, p. 190.

23. *Ibid.*

24. Carl G. Fisher, Letter to Claude Mercer, October 5, 1934. CF: HASF.

25. Redford, p. 191.

26. Carl G. Fisher, Letter to Margaret Fisher, August 3, 1935. CF: HASF.

27. *Ibid.*

28. Jane Fisher, p. 250.

29. Carl G. Fisher, Letter to William Galloway, November 12, 1920. CF: HASF.

30. Carl G. Fisher, Letter to William Galloway, November 27, 1923 CF: HASF.

31. William Galloway, Letter to Carl G. Fisher, December 7, 1923. CF: HASF.

32. Mr. and Mrs. William Galloway, Invitation to Carl Fisher. CF: HASF.

33. Carl G. Fisher, Letter of recommendation for William Galloway, May 22, 1933. CF: HASF.

34. Art (last name unknown), Letter to Carl G. Fisher, December 4, 1935. CF: HASF.

35. Jane Fisher, p. 251.

36. Carl G. Fisher, Letter to Jane Fisher, June 3, 1935. CF: HASF.

37. Carl G. Fisher, Letter to Margaret Fisher, June 9, 1936, CF: HASF.

38. Carl G. Fisher, Letter to Margaret Fisher, September 23, 1936. CF: HASF.

39. *Ibid.*

40. Carl G. Fisher, Letter to Margaret Fisher, September 15, 1937. CF: HASF.

41. *Ibid.*

42. C. W. Chase, Jr., Advertisement, CF: HASF.

43. Carl G. Fisher, Letter to Dr. E. B. Maxwell, January 7, 1938. CF: HASF.

44. Jane Fisher, Letter to Carl G. Fisher, June 28, 1938. CF: HASF.

45. *Ibid.*

46. Carl G. Fisher, Letter to Jane Fisher, July 8, 1938. CF: HASF.

47. Carl G. Fisher, Letter to Dr. Frank B. Vorhis, August 11, 1938. CF: HASF.

48. *Ibid.*

49. Fred Humpage, Letter to Margaret Fisher, August 18, 1938. CF: HASF.

50. Carl G. Fisher, Letter to La-Fayette Page, November 7, 1938. CF: HASF.

51. Irv Page, Letter to LaFayette Page, November 11, 1938. CF: HASF.

52. Redford, p. 189.

53. Carl G. Fisher, Letter to Barney Oldfield, November 7, 1938. CF: HASF.

54. Carl G. Fisher, Letter to Barney Oldfield, December 13. 1938. CF: HASF.

55. Carl G. Fisher, Letter to Barney Oldfield, April 25, 1939. CF: HASF.

56. *Ibid.*

57. Jane Fisher, p. 256.

58. *Ibid.,* p. 253.

59. Helen Rich, "Echoes of Yester-year - Carl Fisher," *Miami Herald.*

60. Carl G. Fisher, Letter to Rev. William Barry, July 12, 1930. CF HASF.

61. Rev. William Barry, Letter to Carl G. Fisher, July 28, 1930. CF HASF.

62. Carl G. Fisher, Letter to Rev. William Barry, August 2, 1930. CF: HASF.

63. Jane Fisher, p. 260.

64. Carl G. Fisher, Letter to E. S. Dallenbach, April 11, 1939. CF: HASF.

65. Thomas Pancoast, Letter to Carl G. Fisher, July 7, 1939. CF: HASF.

66. Carl G. Fisher, Letter to Thomas Pancoast, July 10, 1939. CF: HASF.

67. *Ibid.*

68. Thomas Pancoast, Letter to Carl G. Fisher, July 14, 1939. CF: HASF.

69. "Carl G. Fisher Died in City He Made Rise From Swamps," *Miami Herald,* July 16, 1939.

70. Rev. William Barry, as quoted in the *Miami Beach Daily Sun,* March 22, 1964.

71. Kleinberg, p. 135.

72. John LaGorce, Eulogy for Carl Fisher, *Indianapolis Star,* July 19, 1939.

73. *Ibid.*

74. Margaret Fisher, Letter to Amos Fisher, August 17, 1939. Fisher Family Album. Amos Fisher, the author's grandfather, died August 25, 1940, at the age of 78.

75. *Indianapolis Star,* September 23, 1918,

76. Carl G. Fisher, Letter to Superintendent of Crown Hill Cemetery, Indianapolis

77. Rich.

Afterword

78. Montauk Manor historical files

79. *Miami Herald,* Dec. 7, 1968

80. J. Fisher family file, Dec. 11, 1965

Bibliography

Collections

University of Michigan Library, Ann Arbor, Michigan

Historical Association of Southern Florida, Miami, Florida. Carl Fisher Collection.

East Hampton Library, East Hampton, Long Island, New York.

Marion County Public Library, Indianapolis, Indiana: "Early Auto Industry Inspired Development of Prest-O-Lite," (newspaper article, date unknown, stamped February 27, 1946).

Speedway Public Library, Speedway, Indiana

Heidenreich, "The Track Founders," *The Prest-O-Lite Story.*

Books

Armbruster, Ann, *The Life and Times of Miami Beach.* New York: Alfred A. Knopf © 1995.

Bennett, Henry H. *County of Ross.* Selwyn A. Brant © 1902.

Bloemker, Al. *500 Miles To Go.* New York: Coward-McCann © 1961.

Brown, Allen E., ed. *The History of the American Speedway.* Marne, Michigan: Slideways Publications © 1984.

Fisher, Jane. *Fabulous Hoosier.* New York: Robert M. McBride and Co. © 1947.

History of Decatur County, Indiana. B. F. Bowen and Co.

Hokanson, Drake. *The Lincoln Highway: Main Street across America.* Iowa City: University of Iowa Press © 1988.

Holden, Albert R., A Pictorial History of Montauk. Montauk: Holden's Publications © 1983.

Jardim, Anne. *The First Henry Ford: A Study in Personality and Business Leadership.* Cambridge: The Colonial Press © 1970.

Kleinberg, Howard. *Miami Beach: A History.* Miami: Centennial Press © 1994.

Kleinberg, Howard. *Miami: The Way We Were.* Tampa, Florida: Surfside Publishing © 1989.

David L. Lewis, *"The Public Image of Henry Ford."*

Lincoln Highway Association. *The Lincoln Highway.* New York: Dodd, Mead, and Company © 1935.

Lummus, J.N. *The Miracle of Miami Beach.* Miami: The Miami Post Publishing Co. © 1944.

Martin, John Bartlow. *Indiana: An Interpretation*. New York: Alfred A. Knopf © 1947.

Muir, Helen. *Miami, U,S,A*, Coconut Grove, Florida: Hurricane House © 1953.

Nash, Charles Edgar. *The Magic of Miami Beach*. Philadelphia: David McKay © 1938.

Our Century, 1900-1910, and *Our Century, 1910-1920*. Belmont, California: David B. Lake Publishers © 1989.

Peckham, Howard H. *Indiana: A Bicentennial History*. New York: W. W. Norton and Co., Inc. © 1978.

Powell, Al, "Fulford — Miami Speedway," *The History of the American Speedway*, ed. by Allen E. Brown. Marr, Michigan: Slideways Publications.

Preston, Howard L. *Dirt Roads to Dixie*. Knoxville: University of Tennessee Press © 1991.

Redford, Polly. *Billion-Dollar Sandbar*. New York: E. P. Dutton and Co., Inc. © 1970.

Rogers, Will. *Will Rogers' Weekly Articles*, Vol. II, James Smallwood, ed. Stillwater: Oklahoma University Press © 1980.

Schoenberg, Robert. *Mr. Capone*. New York: William Morrow and Company, Inc. © 1992.

Taylor, Rich. *Indy: 75 Years of Racing's Greatest Spectacles*. New York: St. Martin's Press © 1991.

Reference Books

"Ingersoll, Robert Green," *American Authors 1600-1900*, Stanley J. Kunitz and Howard Haycraft, ed. (New York: H.W. Wilson and Co. © 1938) "Ingersoll, Robert Green," *Dictionary of American* Biography, Dumas Malone, ed. Vol. IX. (New York: Charles Scribner's Sons © 1932)

"Ingersoll, Robert Green," *Encyclopedia Americana* © 1994. Vol. XV.

Newspaper Articles

"Balloon and Auto Sail Through Sky," *Indianapolis Star*, October 31, 1908.

Blythe, Betty, "First Photographic Glimpse of Carl S. Fisher's Home, *Indianapolis Sunday Star*, February 2, 1913.

"Business Before Pleasure," *Indianapolis Star*, July 16, 1939.

"Carl Fisher and Guests Rush from Montauk to Miami After Hurricane," *East Hampton Star*, September 24, 1926.

"Carl Fisher: Legend in Automobiles and Real Estate," *Indianapolis Star*, July 14, 1966.

"Carl Fisher Inspects Construction Work at Montauk Beach This Week; First Visit Since Purchase of Land," *East Hampton Star, May 21, 1926*.

"Carl G. Fisher Dead at Beach," *Miami Herald*, July 16, 1939.

"Carl G. Fisher, Miami Beach Developer, Stood on the Corner of Lincoln Road and Washington Avenue." *Miami Beach News Bureau*.

"Carl G. Fisher Died in City He Made Rise From Swamps," *Miami Herald*, July 16, 1939.

C. W. Chase, letter to owners of Miami Beach property, *East Hampton Star*, October 1, 1926.

"Edsel Ford Arrives for Four-Week Stay," *Miami Herald*, 1930.

"Far from the Racket, Scarface Al Capone." *International News*

"Fifteen Thousand Feet Above Dixieland," *Indianapolis Sunday Star,* June 20, 1909.

"Fisher's Salary To Go to Roads," *Indianapolis Star,* October 24, 1912.

Fisher/Watts wedding announcement, *Indianapolis News,* October 23, 1909.

Glick, Shav, "Carl Fisher Turned the Folly into the 500," *Los Angeles Times,* May 24, 1991.

Gordon, Alastair, "Fisher's Montauk Legacy Getting a New Look," *The New York Times,* December 23, 1984.

Herschell, William, "Motor Speedway: Carl Fisher's First Step in Amazing Career of Making Dreams Come True,:" *Indianapolis News,* July 17, 1939.

"Huge Dredge Arrives At Fort Pond; Construction Work in Full Swing," *East Hampton Star,* June 8, 1926.

"$116,000 Is Paid by Hertz for House," *Miami Herald,* 1927.

Rich, Helen, "Echoes of Yesteryear — Carl Fisher,:"

"Singer Asks Half-Million," *Indianapolis Star,* October 6, 1912.

Magazine Articles

Boomhower, Ray, "The Hoosier Barnum," *Traces,* the Indiana Historical Society, Spring, 1994.

"Campus Heritage Dates to Early 1900s," *The Magnet,* Marian College, Indianapolis.

The Columbian, January, 1906.

Doyle, William Stoner, " Carl Fisher: Builder of Miami Beach," *Coronet,,* April, 1949.

Fisher, Carl, *Ocean-to-Ocean Highway Bulletin* Number 1, September 19, 1912.

Hausrath, Ralph, "Carl G. Fisher and Montauk," *Long Island Forum,* November 1981, and December 1981.

Keene, July, "The 500's Four Founders," *Indianapolis Magazine,* May, 1978.

David L. Lewis, Michigan History Magazine, *"The Gentle Businessman"*

McCarthy, Joe, "The Lincoln Highway," *American Heritage,* June, 1974.

Riggs, L. Spencer, "Brooklands," May, 1983.

Zimmerman, Bob, "The First Army Truck Train," *Packard Truck Organization Newsletter,* 1994.

Unpublished Manuscript

Mercier, J. Patrick, "Giants in Indiana Industry, Auto Racing, and Land Development, Carl G. Fisher, James A. Allison, and Frank H. Wheeler, The Men and Their Mansions," History Honors Project, Marion College, Spring, 1975.

Additional Sources

"Along the Montauk Shore" Frederick P. Schmitt — *East Hampton Star* (reprint) 1962.

Beyer, George. *Pennsylvania's Roads in the Twentieth Century.* Harrisburg, Pa.: Pennsylvania Historical Commission, 1971.

Bement, Austin F., and Hoag, Gael S. *Achievement in the Lincoln Highway.* Detroit: Lincoln Highway Association, 1921.

Belasco, Warren. *Americans on the*

Road. Cambridge: MIT Press, 1981.

Hokanson, Drake. "To Cross America, Early Americans Took a Long Detour," *Smithsonian.* August, 1985.

Hulbert, Archer Butler. *Historic Highways of America.* NY: A.M.S. Press, 1971.

Jenkins, James T., Jr. *The Story of Roads.* Washington, D.C.: American Road Builders' Association, 1967.

Jordan, Philip D. *The National Road.* NY: Bobbs-Merrill, 1948.

Lincoln Highway Association. *Complete Official Road Guide of the Lincoln Highway.* Detroit, 1915. 1916 (reprint) 1918, 1920, 1921, 1924 (reprint).

"Montauk Beach: A Distinguished Summer Colony on the Slender Tip of Long Island, N.Y." — Montauk Development Corp., 1932.

"Montauk: Yesterday, Today and Tomorrow" — *On The Sound,* May 1974.

"Montauk 1960: A Long Look at the Point's Past, Present and Future" — *East Hampton Star,* May 26, 1960.

Montauk Almanac: Fishing Guide and General Information, Vol. I to VIII, Holden's Publications.

Partridge, Bellamy. *Fill 'Er Up.* NY: McGraw-Hill, 1952.

Post, Edwin. *Truly Emily Post.* NY: Funk and Wagnalls, 1961.

Post, Emily. *By Motor to the Golden Gate.* NY: D. Appleton and Co., 1917.

Rae, John N. *The Road and The Car in American Life.* Cambridge: M.I.T. Press, 1971.

Ramsey, Alice. *Veil, Duster and the Iron.* Castle Press, 1961.

Round, Thornton. *The Good of It All.* Lakeside Printing Co., 1957.

Seely, Bruce E. *Building the American Highway System.* Philadelphia: Temple University Press, 1987.

Schank, William H. *Indian Trails to Superhighways.* York: Buchart-Horn, 1967.

Stewart, George R. *U.S. 40: Cross Section of the United States of America.* Boston: Houghton-Mifflin, 1953.

The Story of Second House, Montauk, Jeanette Edwards Rattray, 1969.

Three Centuries in East Hampton, Long Island, N.Y., Jeanette Edwards Rattray, East Hampton Star Press, 1937.

Trustee Records, East Hampton — Montauk, Town of East Hampton, April, 1925.

Van de Water, Frederic F. *The Family Flivers to Frisco.* NY: D. Appleton and Co., 1927.

Vale, Thomas R. and Geraldine R. *U. S. 40 Today.* Madison: University of Wisconsin Press, 1983.

Wixom, Charles. *Pictorial History of Road Building. Washington, D.C.:* American Road Builders' Association, 1975.

Index

Other Available
Titles from Lost Coast Press

HISTORY & PHILOSOPHY

Olompali: In the Beginning
June Ericson Gardner
A brief history of the Coast Miwoks in Northern California.
Paperback • 64 pages • 6" x 9" • ISBN: 1-882897-02-1 • $7.50

The Spiritual Gyre: The Recurring Phases of Western History
Richard Sellin
A cyclical view of history for the new millennium.
Paper • 208 pages • 5½" x 8½" • ISBN: 1-882897-19-6 • $14.00

MEMOIRS & TRAVEL

Belo Horizonte: Around the World in 80 Years
Richard Abbott
High finance and hijinx on the high seas.
Paper • 248 pages • 5½" x 8½" • ISBN: 1-882897-01-3 • $14.95

Tonderai: Studying Abroad in Zimbabwe
Perrin Elkind
"A remarkable first book about a young woman's immersion in a foreign culture."
— Kim Chernin, author of *My Life as a Boy*
Paper • 208 pages • 6" x 9" • ISBN: 1-882897-20-X • $16.95

To Live in Paradise
Renee Roosevelt Denis
A delightful travel memoir.
Recommended by *National Geographic Traveler*
Paper • 352 pages • 5½" x 8½" • ISBN: 1-882897-07-2 • $15.95

Out of Darkness—Ramela's Story
Ramela Martin
Memoirs of a survivor of the Armenian Holocaust.
Casebound • 152 pp • 6" x 9" • ISBN: 1-882897-12-9 • $16.95

FICTION

God's Mafia
Alfred Fortino
An ethical and intelligent courtroom drama.
Paper • 240 pages • 6" x 9" • ISBN: 1-882897-09-9 • $23.95

Sepharad: The Embezzled Land
Salamon Eskinazi
A historical novel that follows a family of Sephardic Jews.
Paper • 610 pages • 5½" x 8½" • ISBN: 1-882897-17-X • $29.95

Time and the Maiden
Matthew R. Piepenburg
A tender love story spanning 70 years and two world wars.
Paper • 248 pages, 5½" x 8½" • ISBN: 1-882897-15-3 • $15.95

Malmond
Ivan Laszlo
Intrigue and sexual politics in a parallel universe.
Paper • 208 pages • 5½" x 8½" • ISBN: 1-882897-00-5 • $12.95

The Kid from Custer
Richard Clason
A young cowboy searches for the man who killed his father.
Paper • 208 pages • 5½" x 8½" • ISBN: 1-882897-05-6 • $12.95

Zalacain the Adventurer
Pio Baroja
Translated from the Spanish by James P. Diendl
A comic novel of the Carlist wars by a 19th Century Spanish
novelist, beautifully translated by an American scholar.
Paper • 192 pages, 5½" x 8½" • ISBN: 1-882897-13-7 • $16.95

BUSINESS & FINANCE

Money & You—A Woman's Financial Guide
Holly Nicholson
How to protect your assets and provide for your future.
Casebound • 160 pp • 6" x 9" • ISBN: 1-882897-14-5 • $24.95

EDUCATION

Drama in the Classroom:
Creative Activities for Teachers, Parents and Friends
Polly Erion
Fun and games in an educational setting for children from Kindergarten to 8th Grade.
Paper • 192 pages • 8½" x 11" • ISBN: 1-882897-04-8 • $24.95

Barbara and Fred—Grownups Now
Living Fully with Developmental Disabilities
Lotte Moise
An activist mother teaches her daughter and the nation how to overcome life's barriers.
Paper • 212 pages, 5½" x 8½" • ISBN: 1-882897-08-0 • $16.95

Dear Substitute Teacher
Margaret Sigel
Restoring discipline and responsibility in the classroom.
Paper • 80 pages • 5½" x 8½" • ISBN: 1-882897-10-2 • $9.95

On Wings Like Eagles
Lamar Dodson
Instilling moral precepts in elementary school children.
Paper • 160 pages • 5½"x 8½" • ISBN: 1-882897-16-1 • $12.95

ANIMAL WELFARE

Greyhound Tales: Stories of Rescue, Compassion and Love
edited by Nora Star
How abused racing dogs are saved and raised.
Paper • 128 pages • 5½" x 8½" • ISBN: 1-882897-18-8 • $15.95